Fundamentals of the Creation

Fundamentals of the Creation

Joseph Alonso

ISBN 9798227672971

Translation of: *Fundamentos de la Creación*
25

Dedicated to
all believers

Contents

Prologue

There is broad consensus on the affirmation that humanity is on the road to progress. Advancements have been characterized by an erosion of superstition and its replacement by religious beliefs and scientific knowledge. Due to the observation of natural phenomena, both within ourselves and in our surroundings, we humans have shared different experiences to discover later an underlying order. Consequently, our ignorance, both individual and collective, has been progressively diminished, and our shared knowledge and beliefs have increased.

Over the centuries, bodies of belief and knowledge have been grouped and systematized in admirable religious compendiums. Many of them are full of valuable information and useful precepts for individual well-being and social progress. The most important beliefs deal with their own source, particularly those of the four great religions coming from the Fertile Crescent. All of them remit in the last instance to God the origins of their beliefs and knowledge. Nonetheless, given the inability of the majority to act as a means of divine expression, such truths would have been revealed to intermediaries aligned with his provisions.

Science from the fourth century BC up until the Middle Ages limited itself to knowledge of the material, formal, efficient, and final causes of the natural phenomena proposed by Aristotle (the fourth century BC). The next step was taken in the early modern ages (the fifteenth through the eighteenth centuries AD), when the emphasis on experimental science as practiced nowadays was introduced. After the first five centuries, one of the most important achievements of the scientific method has been the recognition of its own limitations—in particular, its inability to predict the outcome of the processes involving the elementary particles (any physical object whose structure is unknown) of which everything would be made. In fact, the proliferation of interpretations of quantum mechanics is due, above all, to the absence of significant advancements in its predictive capability. Even so, the different standpoints have been useful in the comprehension of a problem, the solution to which shall involve new and radical proposals. It is precisely within these limitations of science where it is possible to fit the beliefs in free will inherent in some creatures and the consent of the Creator for the realization of everything. More so, both beliefs hold the key to precisely comprehending all the cosmic potential of the human and to discovering its roots in the performance of divinity.

Given the concept of a revealed God as developed by theology (the study of God and his relationship with his Creation), a dead end has been reached in search of its universal acceptance. Humanity is still divided between two large groups, one made up of those who believe in the existence of God and the other of those who believe in his nonexistence. Even among believers in God's existence, there are noticeable doctrinal differences, some of them insurmountable as far as their content and meaning. It is due to these discrepancies, frequently the cause of bloody actions, that this book was written, with the intention of contributing to the achievement of peace between all believers.

As for humans, it is imperative for them to redouble their efforts in finding common ground between the beliefs of the religious and atheists (those who believe in the nonexistence of God) concerning the origins of and their relationships with the transcendent. The knowledge achieved due to this effort shall allow a better understanding of the factors that condition human nature and its cosmic context. The greatest benefit of all these endeavors should be concretized in the opening of new roads to surmount the present state. It is not difficult to imagine how useless it would be to appeal to old schemes already abandoned due to the insignificance of their evident results. Something more drastic is required to reduce the distance between religious and scientific ends, given the impact on the spiritual progress of humanity.

Scientific knowledge and secular ethics have certainly demonstrated their potential to further the social progress of humanity. Hence they have constrained a religiosity that is vain and incapable of motivating the once faithful, especially the young, who ignore it the most. In fact, the coarse Manichaeanism to which a significant part of the religious discourse has been reduced only motivates blind fanaticism or encourages the greatest indifference. In a similar vein, scientific progress only oriented to the personal or collective material benefit is not enough to open a course for the enormous potential locked within human interiority.

The problem is more serious since we are not alone; there are other beings with well-defined objectives intervening in the heart of matter. Some of these entities are devoted to the service of God, while others are dedicated to reaching their own goals. Therefore, it is indispensable to be aware of the roles of each one in this tangle called matter, with aims to identify patterns of conduct from which to derive objective progress. Religious truths will only have meaning when they deal with what we are made of and, based on that knowledge, show the way forward. Scientific knowledge, on its side, will only develop all its potential to serve humanity when it recognizes the power of that which transcends it.

In order to bridge the divide between religion and science, this book proposes a new exegesis of the Sacred Scriptures taking into consideration the basic tenets of quantum mechanics. The first lesson to be learnt from this approach is that human nature is rooted in the relationship between God and his Creation, which then expresses itself at the most fundamental levels of physics—in field generation and particle-wave duality. Therefore, from an ontological perspective, human nature first exteriorization is a physical issue rather than a biological one. However, the chief objective here is to uncover how the physics of human nature develops into the "entheogenic potential" of biochemical systems capable of eliciting the divine within. In general, the lay reader will be pleasantly surprised by the methodological simplicity and by the possibility of drawing up his own conclusions.

Part I

The Religious Truth

Chapter 1

Introductory Remarks

The possibility of objective knowledge rationalization opened the doors to superior beliefs about the origin and existence of a sacred and immutable order. The immediate consequence was the emergence of the "religious man" (*homo religiosus*), of whom M. Eliade (the twentieth century AD) has so successfully written about. Even though the histories of religion, philosophy, and science are very exciting, these matters are not intended to be dealt with here—basically, due to the existence of monumental works in which almost all that is necessary to say has been said. Rather, the standpoint of this work will be of practical order and oriented to the convergence of scientific and religious knowledge. The idea, thus, is to identify the presence and physical nature of human existence beyond its biological expression, emphasizing its cosmic context and the patterns of conduct conducive to its individual and collective improvements.

In order to reach the maximum number of readers, the method to be followed here shall be heuristic, and the language will be moderately rigorous. Nevertheless, in order to organize concepts and assure the convergence of religious and scientific knowledge, it might be of great help to utilize the "mathematical representation theory," albeit in a rudimentary way. The said tool shall be of great use when systematizing the "correspondence between structures and forms." The theme is a complex one and requires a good measure of intellectual audacity, which shall certainly be rejected by the most conservative. Nevertheless, there is hope that the majority will give the author the benefit of doubt until the end.

Throughout this book, the emphasis will be on discovering the common good of all variants of human thought, in spite of the criticism about syncretism by the purists. The greatest incentive to look for convergence between religious and scientific knowledge resides in the vastness of both. A good portion of religious heritage is susceptible to scientific valuation, and the truths of science have a numinous (as conceived by R. Otto [the nineteenth to the twentieth centuries AD]) character. The benefits shall be for both religion and science since each one possesses knowledge that proponents of the other need and would value.

The objective to pursue a synthesis of both truths is the emergence of a *unique knowledge* oriented toward a *new thought*. The initiative to undertake a project whose objective is the unification of knowledge is in no way a novel one. In the long history of civilization, there have been plenty of social organization models ruled by *unique knowledge*. Perhaps the most notorious is ancient Egypt, which began around 3300 BC and ended with the pharaoh Ptolemy XV (the first century BC).

The levels of knowledge reached in ancient Egypt were unparalleled, as testified by the two migrations of Israel to that empire and that of Jesus of

Nazareth during his upbringing. The Bible tells that Abram (the nineteenth to the eighteenth centuries BC) (God had not changed his name yet) started his first trip because, according to the book of Genesis, there was a famine in his homeland, and so he went to Egypt to live there. When Abram arrived, the pyramids were at least five centuries old. Hence, his visit was not precisely aimed at the teaching of arts and crafts or any other form of knowledge. At a second opportunity, it was Jacob (the eighteenth to the seventeenth centuries BC) who took his people to Egypt following an invitation by the pharaoh to his son Joseph (the seventeenth century BC). And God told Israel not to fear going down into Egypt since he would make a great nation out of her. Isaiah proclaimed about the ancient peoples that Israel should be third after Egypt and Assyria, as God refers to Egypt as "my people," to Assyria as "the work of my hands," and to Israel as "my inheritance."

Regarding Jesus, Matthew (the first century AD) says that an angel of the Lord appeared to Joseph (the first century BC to the first century AD) and ordered him to take the child and his mother, Mary (the first century BC to the first century AD), and flee into Egypt until further notice. When returning, Jesus led a discreet life in Nazareth, but at twelve he got out of sight of his parents. This happened after Easter in Jerusalem, and he was later found among the doctors in the temple. According to Luke (the first century AD), everyone admired his intelligence and his responses.

Nowadays, most of our civilization obtains knowledge from three sources. One of them is religion, which preserves knowledge attributed to God in the last instance. Another is the individual or collective heart of hearts, contributing on an intersubjective common ground. Finally, social organizations and their professional and academic structures focus on systematizing objective knowledge. Great religions have traditionally employed philosophies in order to respond to secular criticism and to try to justify their doctrines and beliefs. The results of those initiatives have been doubtful at best. The rhetoric has proven more useful in getting out of trouble, since the criticisms to religious doctrines have neither been precise nor substantial.

On the other hand, the usefulness of the scientific method in order to support the theological constructs is practically ignored. Even in today's Islam, after a favorable valuation of objective knowledge by the prophet Muhammad (the sixth to the seventh centuries AD), surah The Cow of the Koran clearly states: "Indeed, in the creation of the heavens and earth, and in the alternation of the night and the day…and in the changes in winds and clouds made submissive between heaven and earth, there are ayat addressed to people who use reason" (*ayat* are verses of the Koran). In fact, "objective reality," as a divine realization, should be considered the most sacred of scriptures, and in relation to its truths there can be no discrepancies but errors.

Efforts on behalf of knowledge unification have not been absent from modernity but have been marked by jealousy and mistrust. This matter touches on powerful interests in religious and secular camps, where territories have been demarcated with the intent of avoiding the sour arguments of the past. In this sense is the relatively recent case of the Jesuit theologian and anthropologist T. de Chardin (the nineteenth to the twentieth centuries AD). His seclusion demonstrates the zeal with which power groups of Catholicism guard dogmatic content as their own. The French thinker emphasized the necessary convergence of science and religion in order to reach the evolutionary goal he named "omega point." His ideas were a little far from the Catholic thinking of the midtwentieth century AD, hence the tepid reception given by his colleagues. Even so, the idea of the spiritual potential of matter deserves a reevaluation in light of scientific progress. The reader is advised to read carefully the "Hymn to Matter," by T. de Chardin (available in different media), for its pertinence with the themes being developed in this book. Regarding the theologian's practice of silencing those who proclaim the truth, Luke reports what Jesus said: "if these keep silent, the stones will cry out."

This work has been divided into two parts. The first and more extensive one is aimed at postulating the nature of the human and its cosmic context, all on the basis of a new exegetical perspective based on an interpretation of the scriptures made compatible with scientific knowledge. Therefore, this interpretation shall be called "natural exegesis." The second part is oriented toward the establishment of correspondences between the formulations of natural exegesis and the objects studied by physics. The aforementioned correspondences shall allow contextualizing the appearance of the human in matter as well as the influence of other creatures present in it. This contextualizing should be conducive to an awareness of the importance of human behavior, aiming to reorient it toward its improvement.

With regard to the *Fundamentals of the Creation*, it shall not always be possible to ask, "Why?" since human knowledge has its limits. This is not only true in the religious scope but also in science. Once the resources of thinking allowed by religious doctrines have been exhausted, the following answer is reached through every path followed: "This is what the Creator has provided." On the scientific side, the final answer to any search is as blunt: "This is how they behave."

The references to the Holy Scriptures here have been obtained from several sources and have been translated and paraphrased in order to ease their reading and interpretation. When referring to the Supreme Being, the terms *God, Lord, Creator*, and *divinity* among others have been used to make the reading less monotonous. With the purpose of specifying the meanings of some terms pertaining to the knowledge of some disciplines, an immediate explanation shall be offered within parenthesis. Measurement units like grams (g), meters (m), and seconds (s) as well as multiples and submultiples and their compositions are used and shall be written verbatim. Also, the frequently used grapheme & should be read as "in conjunction with." With regard to dates, the Gregorian calendar has been adopted for the Romance and Anglo-Saxon language versions of this book. In light of the uncertainty around the historicity of some biblical and ancient characters, the dates related to them only seek to generate a hypothetical historic context.

Chapter 2

Specifying Fundamentals

The time has come to enter fully into the matter, which implies defining a scope so as not to get lost in the vastness of human religiosity. For this reason, it is convenient to circumscribe to four great religions, Judaism, Zoroastrianism, Christianity, and Islam, whose influence in the course of history through their faithful is indisputable. In relation to the proposed religious context and aside from the obvious links of Christianity with Judaism, the Koran in surah The Cow confirms the revelation given "to Abraham and Ishmael, to Isaac, to Jacob and his descendants and in what it was given to Moses, to Jesus and to the prophets," without distinction or qualifications. The prophet Muhammad groups followers of such revelations under the name "people of the Book." He also recommends in surah The Spider tempering discussions with this group and bringing them to a successful conclusion. The inclusion of some followers of Zoroaster (the fifteenth to the ninth centuries BC) or magi among the people of the Book is based on another Koranic declaration, presented in surah The Pilgrimage.

The "people of the Book" designation will be changed here to "people with the Book" to include the Muslims in that group. The new denomination can then be specified based on the temporal ordinal and cardinal essence (power of a number without reference to an order) of its four great religions according to the following scheme:

- First religion and religion one, Judaism. Its maximum human exponent is Abraham. Its holy book is the Hebrew Bible. Its doctrinal feature is one God.

- Second religion and religion two, Zoroastrianism. Its maximum human exponent is Zoroaster. His holy book is the Zend-Avesta. His doctrinal trait is dualism.

- Third religion and religion three, Christianity. Its maximum human exponent is Jesus. Its holy book is the Christian Bible. Its doctrinal feature is the dogma of the Holy Trinity.

- Fourth religion and religion four, Islam. Its maximum human exponent is Muhammad. Its holy book is the Koran. Its doctrinal characteristic is to consider itself as the prophetic seal of the four revelations.

The four religions are distinct and independent ways of approaching the human individual and collective behavior before God. In addition to being organized in a great quaternary scheme, each of the four has its own quaternary symbolism and formulations. Much of what follows will be devoted to delving into their schemes, contents, and meanings.

Chapter 3

Bases for Quaternary Representations

In this chapter, we face the challenge of representing religious architecture, opening the road to its full compatibility with scientific knowledge. The problem is complex for several reasons; the first one is related to the difficulties inherent to the subject, and the second to the language. To overcome the inherent difficulties, each relevant topic will be addressed by means of a comparative approach, from the points of view offered by various sources. As for the language, it would not be entirely practical to stick exclusively to a literary presentation, especially nowadays when there is a strong inclination toward visual means. But the graphic illustrations, in turn, are not exempt from limitations, especially when presenting the objects of an essentially multidimensional Creation on the two available dimensions of the media of expression. There is also the possibility of resorting to formal mathematical representations, but unfortunately the use of such language would distance this effort from many readers. The most convenient would be to opt for a combined use of written language and graphics, to establish correspondences between religious concepts and natural objects whose structures show similarities. The search for isomorphisms (correspondences between structures) between the components of a religious concept and the objects of study of the sciences constitutes the essence of the present exercise of natural exegesis.

The initial requirement is to discover a natural object, where four independent ways of acting are linked together, as is the case with the great religions. A brief search immediately points to carbon atoms (C, from the Latin *carbo*) and silicon (Si, from the Latin *silex*) for their similarities with the requirements to relate the components of the aforementioned quaternary structure. These two chemical elements are part of group 14 (carbon family) of the periodic table, along with others that are not relevant to mention. The selection of both elements is also due to their chemical behaviors and their eminent figuration in the biological and social development of humanity. Carbon plays a fundamental role as a structural element in key substances of biology and construction materials such as limestone. Silicon is relevant for its dominant presence in the earth's crust and in construction materials such as sand and granite.

As with all elements, the chemical activity of carbon and silicon depends on the configuration of the probability of occurrence of some elementary particles called electrons. These objects have a decisive figuration in the valence or incomplete outer subshell of the atoms. In the case of carbon and silicon, the incomplete subshell has four electrons, and another four are required for its completion. The way to complete it is to bond carbon with chemical radicals (a group of elements with their incomplete electronic configuration) that provide the four missing electrons. The probabilities of spatial occurrences of the electrons in the valence shell, as well as in the other shells, are called orbitals. In both chemical elements, said orbitals are of the s-type (s comes from the abbreviation for *sharp* in spectroscopic notation) with spherical symmetry and of the p-type (p comes from *principal*) like directed lobes, as indicated by the dark clouds in figure 3.1, below.

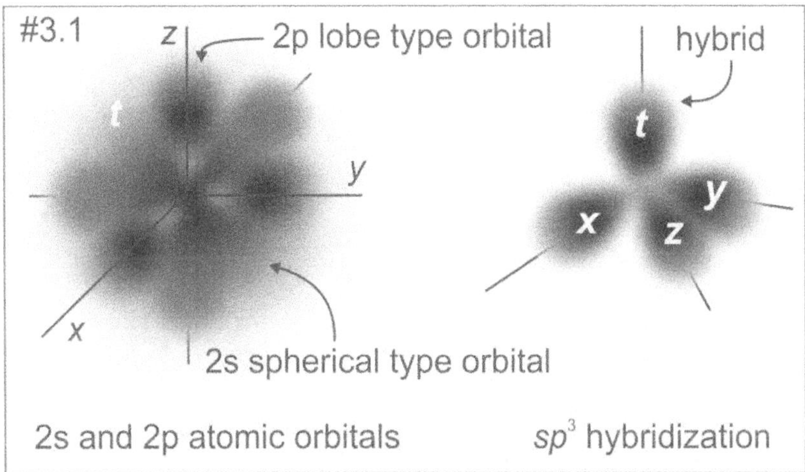

The figure on the left shows a Cartesian representation of the incomplete outer subshell of carbon and silicon in their fundamental states. In the technical literature, the Cartesian bases of representation (named after their proponent, the French philosopher R. Descartes [the sixteenth to the seventeenth centuries AD]) are constituted by the triad: x, long; y, wide; and z, high. Dark clouds describe, as has been said, the orbitals that are the probabilities for the occurrence of the four electrons in the chemical valence subshell. The fundamental states illustrated on the left have two electrons in the spherical s orbital labeled t (transverse) and two in the lobular p orbitals in the x, y, or z direction.

When both elements are linked to four chemical radicals, the orbitals are reconfigured by combining the spherical character of s and the directional of p. Reconfigurations of orbitals are called hybridizations, such as sp^3, as illustrated on the right. In sp^3 hybridization, the four orbitals are directed from the center (barycenter) of a tetrahedral configuration toward their four vertices. In both representations, it has been indicated with a t the orbital that would represent a direction transverse to the triad x, y, and z, abbreviated xyz (even though in fact the four are transverse to each other). The tetrahedral model will be the preferred one for the quaternary representations in what follows.

The tetrahedral shape allows it to represent on its four axes of symmetry and in equivalent conditions the great religions. It would be a situation similar to that of carbon when it is linked to four chemical radicals, each with its own behavior. In the same way, we will proceed with numerous archetypal formulations that constitute the *Fundamentals of the Creation*. Of course, it would have been very easy from the beginning to plot the four religions on a tetrahedron and have that be it. However, here something more is pursued, since the intention is to naturalize religious approaches as far as possible. Figure 3.2 schematically illustrates the isomorphism between both representations.

In addition to the chemical elements mentioned, there are several natural manifestations clearly committed to directing human attention toward quaternary representations. Most of the time, there is a temptation to catalog them as coincidences, which in principle would be reasonable as long as they were not too many. Such is the case with the four rocky planets, the four phases of the moon, the need to add a day in the calendar every four years, and the four seasons in temperate climates, just to mention a few. Figure 3.3 illustrates the quaternary representations of the phenomena brought up.

It would then be necessary to ask some rigorous questions: Why are the rocky planets four and not five or any other number? Why are the speeds of translation and rotation of the moon such that its hidden and visible faces are always the same? Why do rotations of the earth on its axis synchronize with its translation around the sun so that about a quarter of a day each year needs to be added? Why is the axis of rotation of the earth tilted enough to give rise to four stations? Why all those peculiarities in some questions whose observations have been vital for the survival of the primitive humans?

Not all religious or natural representations must be quaternary. In the Creation, there are archetypes of form whose components admit exact representation on bases of different rank. For the time being, the ternary, binary and even unitary bases will be of interest, which may be composed to form quaternary bases or of lower rank. For example, a unitary basis can be composed with a ternary one to form a certain type of quaternary basis, which will be called the odd 1-3 type. Religions lend themselves to this type of representation. Thus, Zoroastrianism, of Indo-Aryan origin, could be represented on a unitary basis, and the three Abrahamic religions of Semitic origin, Judaism, Christianity, and Islam on a ternary basis. In the same way, quaternary bases could be built, grouping two binary bases or according to other possible combinations.

Some ternary formulas have an intrinsic order, which should extend to their representation. Such is the case with the spatial triad xyz due to certain existing degrees of freedom, whose origin and importance will be discussed at the time. According to that intrinsic order xyz, it is not the same as yxz; in fact, they are contrary in a certain sense. In order to distinguish one from the other, a convention called the right-hand rule, illustrated in figure 3.4, is usually employed.

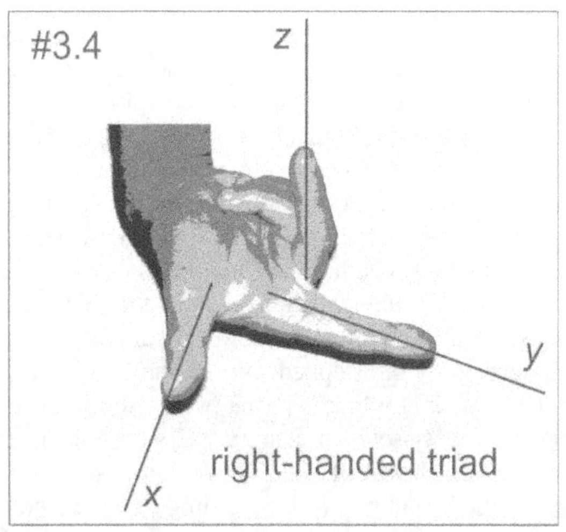

The issue is relevant because its image in a mirror cannot be superimposed on itself; it is not the same object. That concept, however, should not be extended to the manifold $txyz$, since on t the same formulations have not been developed. For this reason, all the illustrations should resort to aligning the direction where it has been represented t as if it were parallel to a hypothetical mirror. Figure 3.5 illustrates how to isolate the direction t of the other three, whose mirror images cannot be superimposed.

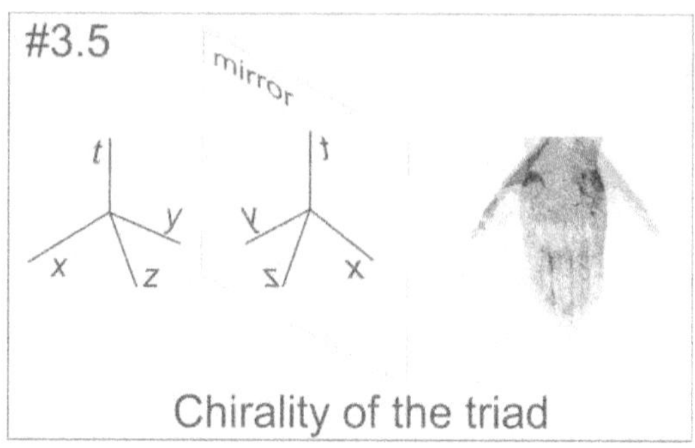

Chirality of the triad

It is said that both specular configurations are "chiral" (a term introduced by the Irish physicist W. Thomson [the nineteenth to the twentieth centuries AD], which comes from *keir*, the word for hand in Greek), given the impossibility of superimposing them as happens with the hands of anyone. In the framework of a natural exegesis, these details are of the utmost importance due to the chirality of the carbonaceous substances in living beings—a feature they share with the representations of some archetypes of creation. For example, among sugars, D-glucose is metabolized by living beings, while its specular image, or L-glucose, is not, being just a laboratory curiosity. The same happens with amino acids and other more complex molecules (chemical compounds of two atoms or more).

The use of quaternary bases in the representation of religious formulations and their cosmic implications reached a monumental scale in ancient Egypt. From the twenty-seventh to the thirteenth centuries BC, the pyramids constituted the maximum expression of the *unique knowledge* of Egyptian civilization. Since the beginning of the twentieth century AD, there has been a broad consensus about the funerary functions of the pyramids. It is also argued that their colossal dimensions would be a demonstration of the importance of the subject of death and of the forms of existence after it for the Egyptians. The trapezoidal funerary monument of the first dynasties, known as a mastaba, is considered to be the precursor of pyramidal construction. Such an assumption is supported by the stepped form of the first large pyramid, built at Saqqara (west of Memphis) by Imhotep (the twenty-seventh century BC) for the pharaoh Djoser (the twenty-seventh century BC) at the beginning of the Third Dynasty. However, the thesis of the Norwegian historian of religions W. Kristensen (the twentieth century AD), according to which the theme of eternal life was the true source of inspiration, is more accurate. In this context, the pyramids would represent the Egyptian radiant island or Benben (island of Aztlan in the Aztec creation myth) emerging from the primordial waters.

With the rhomboidal pyramid of the pharaoh Snefru (the twenty-seventh to the twenty-sixth centuries BC), a simpler and more powerful plastic language began. The equilateral pyramids built by his successors, the three most outstanding pharaohs of the Fourth dynasty, Khufu (the twenty-sixth century BC), Khafre (the twenty-sixth century BC) and Menkaure (the twenty-sixth to the twenty-fifth centuries BC), represent this type of construction in its maximum perfection. Until the Eighteenth Dynasty, it dominated the pyramidal form to represent the radiant island with its four couples. These forms were then raised to become the pyramidion with which the obelisks (*tehen*, in the sacred language of ancient Egypt, means "protection") were crowned. As plastic expressions of divine power, the obelisks reached their maximum splendor from the reign of Hatshepsut (the fifteenth century BC), daughter of Thutmose I (the sixteenth to the fifteenth centuries BC).

According to studies by the Egyptologist of the Netherlands A. de Buck (the twentieth century AD), the radiant island symbolizes the life of the divinities spontaneously born of primordial waters. In the aforementioned emergence, there are four representable couples on the quaternary morphology of the pyramids. The buildings express symbolically in a monumental plastic language, the theology of the four original couples present in the Ogdoad (the souls of Thoth) of Hermopolis and in the ennead of Heliopolis. It is presumed that all doctrinal variants around the theme of the four couples had their origin during the predynastic period (before the thirtieth century BC).

The geometrical language of the pyramids complements the hieroglyphic texts in the expression of the theological formulations of ancient Egypt. Much has been the speculation about the geometrical properties of the pyramids, sometimes with very little depth and other times ignoring questions of context. Despite the doubts, it would not seem prudent to adopt a skeptical position such as that of the Romanian prince M. Ghyka (the nineteenth to the twentieth centuries AD). According to the illustrious thinker, the architects of the great pyramids were probably not aware of the geometrical properties discovered in them. In the pyramids, the most obvious should be observed in order to discover all their great secrets, and that is precisely what is going to be tried here. Beginning with elementary observations, it is possible to affirm that mortals can only observe from the ground two or three of the four oblique edges of the pyramids, while only the divinity in his heights can observe them all simultaneously. Figure 3.6 shows an example of a quaternary representation of the pyramids.

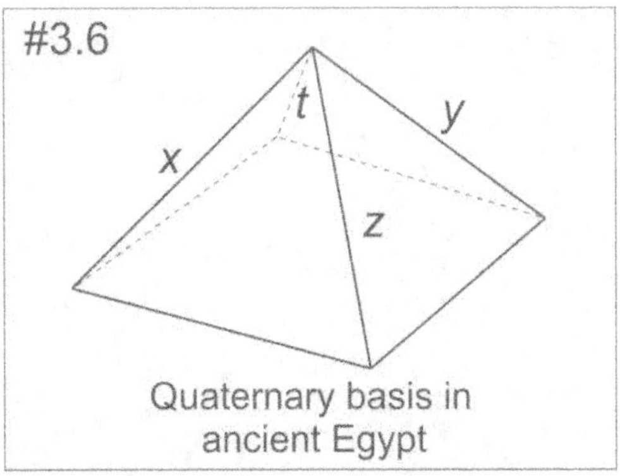

Quaternary basis in
ancient Egypt

In the schematic illustration of the aerial view of the pyramid, the four independent directions, the direction t and the triad xyz have been represented on their oblique edges.

Chapter 4

Bases for Quaternary Representations of the 1-3 Type

There are numerous religious truths with an exact representation on quaternary bases composed by a unitary basis and a ternary one, both independent but relatable. As mentioned, the representation basis so divided shall be referred to as an odd quaternary of the 1-3 type. These bases shall be fundamental in the observations of nature and in the interpretation of texts and artistic representations of religious inspiration. Starting with ancient Egypt and centering on the observation of its pyramids from a distance, some notable situations can be observed. One of these emerges when pyramids are observed from the prolongation of the diagonals of their square base. From these positions, it is possible to observe three of the oblique edges, two at each side, of equal size and symmetrical with respect to a central one of an apparent lesser length. Also, from these four equivalent positions, there is always one hidden edge, on which to represent that which transcends the representations on the three visible ones. In these cases, the pyramid offers four bases of representation of the 1-3 type, one transcendent hidden (beyond in every sense) (the Thuban star) and three visible and immanent (present and active) (the three stars of the Orion Belt), as shown in figure 4.1.

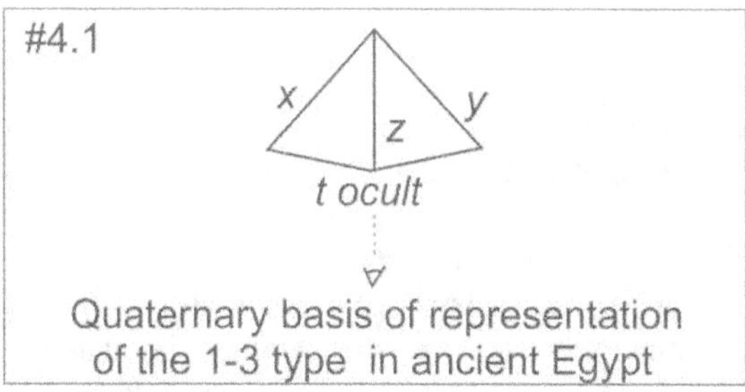

Quaternary basis of representation
of the 1-3 type in ancient Egypt

In this illustration, the spatial triad is represented on the visible edges of a pyramid, while the transverse direction t remains hidden. It is also possible to represent geographical and historical aspects as well as religious truths of ancient Egypt on those quaternary bases. Such is the case of the four influential metropolises of that empire (less Akhenaten); one of them, Heliopolis, is located in the Nile River delta. In the city of Heliopolis resided the cult of the sun god, under the name Atom, plus an Ogdoad integrated by four originating couples. The other three metropolises, Memphis, Hermopolis, and Thebes, were established more to the south in the course of the Nile River. It is believed that the ancient city of Memphis was founded by Menes (the thirty-second century BC), and its Greek name intends to reproduce the Egyptian term *Men-nefer*, city of the pyramid. In the Memphite theology, the god Ptah represents the ineffability of the transcendent, as evidenced by the frequent invocation, "Ptah...the occult, of whom no one knows his being." Hermopolis, (in

Egyptian, *Hnmw*, the eighth city), whose Greek name, "city of Hermes," refers to the cult rendered there to the god Thoth (Hermes in Greek mythology, the god of wisdom and agent of revelation), centered its theology on the creative power of Amun. According to the theologians of Hermopolis, the creative act of Amun is framed within the eight powers of the Ogdoad expressed by means of four couples. Before its demise, Thebes had an enviable cultural level for any city in ancient times. There, the god Ra was worshiped in the person of Amun-Ra, the occult and the supreme Creator. Amun also belonged to the fourth couple in the Ogdoad of Hermopolis. Figure 4.2 illustrates the cities of ancient Egypt over a geographic basis of the 1-3 type.

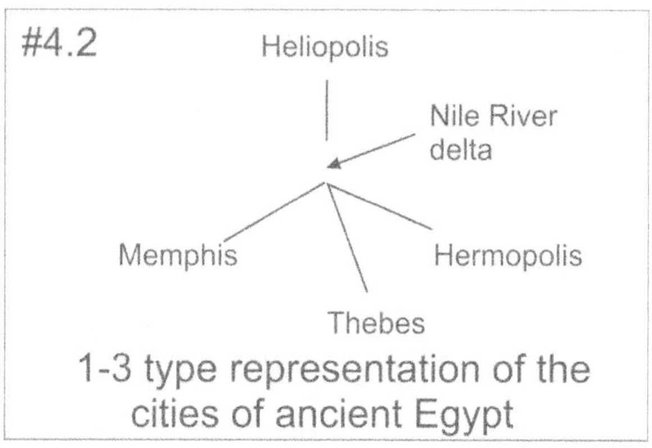

When representing ancient Egyptian cities on a quaternary basis of the 1-3 type, the geographical accident of the River Nile branching into its delta has been intentionally highlighted. Such demarcations frequently occur in religious symbolisms to underscore the independence of the formulations represented over one of the components in relation to the other three.

Another important feature of the pyramids is related to their building materials. The most used stone was limestone, a sedimentary rock formed on the sea bottom by the accumulation of shells and skeletons or of fossilized organisms. In other words, the building stone of the pyramids emerged from the waters like the radiant island, with signs of life. The main chemical component of limestone is calcium carbonate ($CaCO_3$) (Ca, calcium, from *lime* in Latin), as it is also of calcite and marble. Chemically, calcium carbonate is a salt of carbonic acid (H_2CO_3) in which its two hydrogen atoms (H, hydrogen, from the Greek *hydros*) have been replaced by one of calcium.

The common group for all the carbonates is the one called ion (a chemical element or group of these with an electrical charge) carbonate (CO_3^{2-}). This ion is formed by a central carbon atom bonded to three oxygen atoms (O, oxygen, from the Greek *acid*) located in the vertex of an equilateral triangle. While carbon requires four electrons to complete its outer shell, each oxygen requires only two because it has six of the eight necessary. Once carbon shares four electrons with three oxygen atoms, these have two nonshared remaining and will require two more for completion.

When dissolved in water, the carbonate ion takes the two electrons of its ionic counterpart, which it needs for its own completion, hence its double negative charges. Also in the carbonate ion, each of its three oxygen atoms compete for the fourth carbon electron in surplus since each oxygen takes one of the other three. This dispute of the three oxygen atoms for the fourth carbon electron generates a type of bonding termed resonant. With one oxygen doubly bonded to carbon, the equivalence of the three does not allow one to know which will be the next oxygen disputing the electron in order to establish its own resonant bonding. It is an indeterminate fact, not an uncertain one, since it will not be known until it happens. Therefore, it is feasible to represent the bonds of the carbonate ion in limestone on a quaternary basis of the 1-3 type, as shown in figure 4.3.

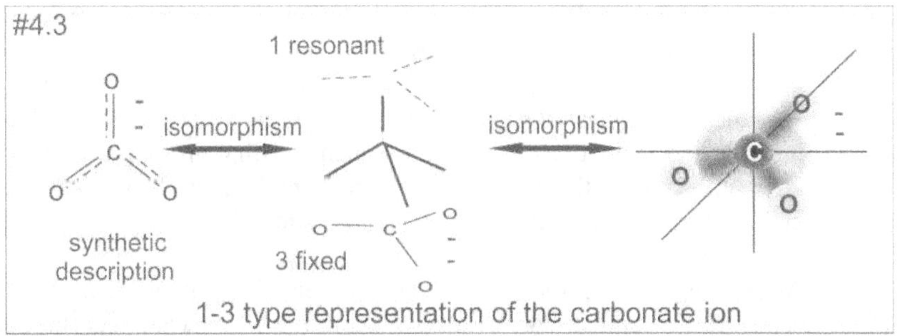

The illustration indicates the three fixed bonds with a solid line, while the resonant bonding is shown as a dashed line or as an annular gray cloud between the carbon and the three oxygen atoms. Even though molecular orbitals are complex to draw and characterize, it is possible to simplify the matter for an illustration in perspective as shown to the right. The two minus signs indicate the permanent presence of two electrons in the oxygen taken from its ionic counterpart.

The wise architects used limestone in the pyramidal body and granite in some parts of its interior, both composed with carbon and silicon. Granite is an igneous granular rock whose volumetric composition is approximately one-quarter quartz (silicon dioxide SiO_2) and three-quarters other silicon compounds. Quartz is accompanied by different aluminum silicates like feldspar, micas, and amphiboles, whose approximate proportion includes 72 percent of silicon dioxide (SiO_2), 14 percent of aluminum oxide (Al_2O_3, Al, aluminum from *alum*) plus other compounds. Since silicon adopts an sp^3 tetrahedral hybridization in the aforementioned compounds, its chemical and crystallographic structures offer analogies to the previously discussed carbon. Nevertheless, the complexity introduced by the ample variety of silicates and aluminum silicates in granitic rocks suggests leaving a deeper investigation to the reader.

The importance of the quaternary bases when representing divine manifestations in the Hebrew religion is deposed by prophet Ezekiel in his vision of the "chariot of the glory of God". The object in question appears in the middle of a fire, where four living beings with four faces and four wings could be recognized. The Bible also offers plenty of symbologies related to divinity where quaternary representations of the 1-3 type fit. It is convenient to clarify that, nevertheless, an exegesis on the Hebrew Bible gives as a result the strictly monotheistic (the belief in the sole God) character of Judaism. This affirmation shall adjust with the scriptural plural expressions about God, like the reference to the Canaanite God or "God the Father" (*El'Eb*), "the Eternal God" (*El Olam*), "the Most High God" (*El Elyon*), and "God Almighty" (*El Shadday*). The Hebrew Bible references related to the divinity-associated manifestations that are representable on odd 1-3 type bases are few but key. One of them, in the book of Genesis, tells how Abraham the patriarch refers to God in the singular, before an evidently ternary presence:

And the Lord appeared unto him in the valley of Mamre...He lifted up his eyes and looked, and he saw three men standing in front of him and after he had seen them, he ran to meet them from the tent door, and bowed himself toward the ground. And he said: "O Lord..."

As for the interpretations of these representations, they have almost always been confusing and ambiguous ever since the first hermeneutical (the set of rules for text interpretation) attempts of ancient Hebrew thinkers like Philo of Alexandria (the first century BC to the first century AD). In his voluminous works, the Alexandrian thinker tried to shed light on the question by indicating that patriarch Abraham addresses them not as three people but as one person.

The God portrayed in the Bible is undoubtedly a personal God (*person*, from the Etruscan cult to Phersu, also a character or behavioral modality), whose way of being is revealed to theists (those who believe in a Creator God compromised with the upholding of his Creation) in his many and decisive actions. In one of his important interventions, referred to in the book of Leviticus, God establishes a ternary patriarchy initiated by Abraham, followed by Isaac (the nineteenth to the seventeenth centuries BC) and culminating with Jacob. This institution was sealed by a covenant with each of them: "Then will I remember my covenant with Jacob and also my covenant with Isaac and also my covenant with Abraham and I will remember the land." The three patriarchs and their consorts were buried in the cave of Machpelah (the double cave) acquired by Abraham at the death of Sarah (the nineteenth to the eighteenth centuries BC) for a value of 400 shekels (weight unit of measurement in Mesopotamia and Canaan; equivalent to some 11.4 g of silver [Ag, from the Latin *argentum*]).

The basic question is whether with the triple patriarchy God reveals something of himself committed to his Creation. Many, even among the cabalists (a current in the Hebrew mystique), have seen a positive answer to this question in the vision of the prophet Isaiah with the Lord sitting on his throne:

> Above the throne stood the seraphim, each one had six wings, with two they covered their faces, with two they covered their feet, and with two they did fly. And one cried unto another, and said: "Holy, Holy, Holy is the Lord of hosts! The whole earth is full of His glory!"

According to this passage, the triple sanctity of the Lord would be proclaimed by his creatures, the seraphim with three pairs of wings. Nevertheless, the mention of his hosts raises doubts as to whether the triple sanctity would refer only to the manifestations of the Lord with them. In fact, the three men received by patriarch Abraham at Mamre had the mission of destroying Sodom and Gomorrah, both confederated in a pentapolis submitted to idolatry.

Without a doubt, the clearest ternary expression related to divinity appears in the book of Exodus, when God describes himself to Moses (the thirteenth century BC) as "Grace," "Mercy," and "Love." The Hebrew mystique interpreted this triplicity as an unequivocal reference to some kind of triple manifestation of the divinity in the midst of his Creation. As the Bible asseverates in Genesis 1:1, "In the beginning God created the heaven and the earth," and just as simply as that, it is proposed the representation of heaven on a unitary basis and the earth on a ternary basis. Such representation is feasible because the earth is planet number three from the sun. Figure 4.4 shows some quaternary representations over bases of the 1-3 type present in the Hebrew Bible.

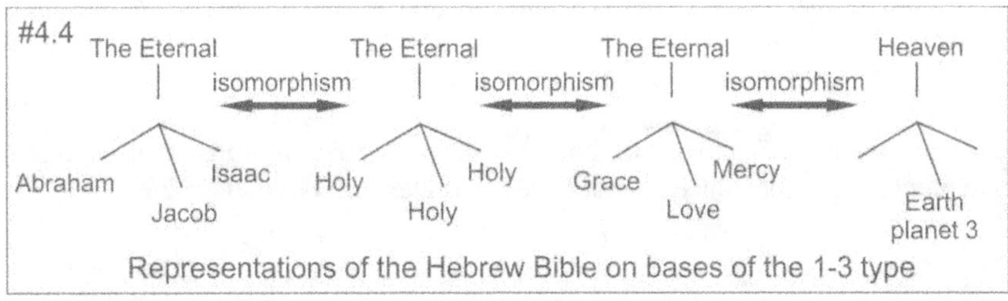

Representations of the Hebrew Bible on bases of the 1-3 type

In Christian religious literature, there is also no shortage of quaternary representations on bases of 1-3 types, a foreseeable issue being this religion, the number three—so much so that the best reference is the quaternary structure of the Gospels. Regrettably, in the long history of the evangelical exegesis, the interest for an analysis of their structure as a whole has been late. It was not until the end of the eighteenth century AD that the first attempts appeared. Until then, there was only knowledge of the observations made by Papias of

Hierapolis (the first to the second centuries AD) and Augustine of Hippo (the fourth to the fifth centuries AD), who presumed that the Gospel of Matthew antedated the ones of Mark (the first century AD) and Luke. But the aforementioned antique synoptic relationship that gave chronological priority to the Gospel of Matthew was solved in favor of that of Mark.

The German critic J. Griesbach (the eighteenth to the nineteenth centuries AD) was the first in grouping the Gospels of Matthew, Mark, and Luke under the synoptic denomination in order to distinguish them from the Gospel of John (the first century AD). Maybe the clearest example of the triple synoptic relationship is in the question posed by Jesus, which is reported in these three Gospels, "Who do you say that I am?"—a key question absent in the Gospel of John. The 330 common verses in the synoptic Gospels, half by Mark and approximately a third by Matthew and Luke, are known as the triple tradition. The Gospel of John is isolated from the synoptic tradition, and it gravitates toward a dense load of spiritual and theological symbolism. The synoptics follow a four-phase chronology; to wit, the preparation of Jesus, the ministry in Galilee, the coming to Jerusalem and his passion, and the period comprising his Resurrection to his Ascension. The earthly life of Jesus passes through phases one, two, and three, while phase four is devoted to Jesus's Resurrection.

The Christian biblical canon was definitely established at the Synod of Hippo (AD 393) with the inclusion of the Apocalypse of John. Thereupon, from the fifth century AD, began the artistic representations of the four evangelists under the tetramorph denomination. The artists took inspiration from the beasts beside God in his throne as described in the Apocalypse of John after the prophet Ezekiel:

> And the first living creature was like a lion, and the second living creature, like a calf, and the third living creature had a face as a man, and the fourth living creature was like a flying eagle…day and night they did not take a rest from saying: "Holy, Holy, Holy is the Lord, the Almighty, which was, is and is to come."

Figure 4.5 shows the correspondence of tetramorphs with evangelic architecture and the concepts associated with the Trinitarian doctrine.

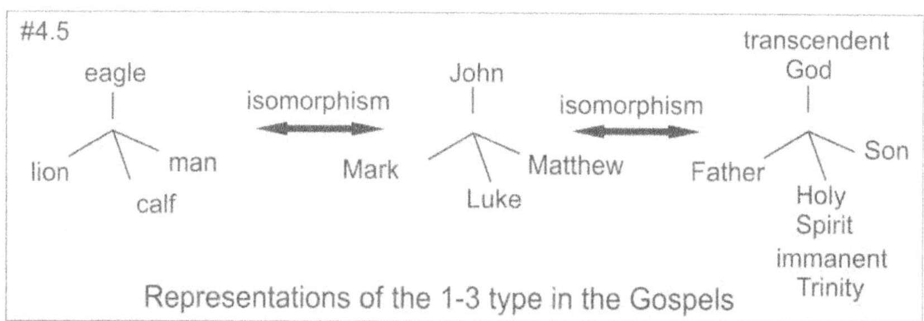

The most relevant doctrinal proposal in the Gospels deals with God, whose transcendental unity comes as testimony from the Hebrew people's religious heritage, to which Jesus, his disciples, and first followers belonged. Nevertheless, in spite of his monotheistic origins, Jesus surprises us all when, according to Matthew, he sends them to baptize their converts "in the name of the Father and of the Son and of the Holy Spirit." The passage where Matthew introduces this formula was the subject of discrete consideration in the first days of the church. As time passed, the matter acquired major significance, and the discussions heated up until becoming a scandal. Due to the importance of the Trinitarian doctrine for religion three and religious architecture in general, a succinct recount of its evolution is offered as follows.

Regrettably, the discussions were not always limited to disagreements, verbal reprimands, or excommunications, since occasionally, cruel and unjust penalties were enforced. An example is that of Maximus the Confessor (the sixth to the seventh centuries AD), who, after two trials against him, was sentenced during the papacy of Vitalian (the seventh century AD). The punishment included mutilation of his tongue and right hand for opposing the "Monothelite" doctrine (Monothelitism, two natures in Jesus, the divine and the human, and only one divine will) and professing the "Dyothelite" (two affirmations, human will and divine will)—issues that may well have been solved in previous councils. The theologian died in exile because of endured mistreatments, to later be restored by the Third Council of Constantinople (AD 680) and then canonized.

Most of the Trinitarian controversies that arose during the first centuries of Christianity were centered on the identification of Jesus with the second person of the Holy Trinity. That great step, taken in the midst of the development of the Trinitarian doctrine, raised the question of his nature in that he could be human, divine, or both. The first one after Matthew in being vocal about the triple divine manifestation was Theophilus of Antioch (the second century AD). The bishop from Antioch employed for the first time the term *trias* in his work *Apology to Autolycus* (*Apologia ad Autolycum*), addressed to a pagan by the name of Autolycus and written by the turn of the second century. The term *trias* was introduced in a metaphysical context (speculative knowledge of what is out of reach from the senses) in order to properly denominate the three divine aspects: God, verb, and wisdom (Father, Son, and the Holy Spirit). The intention was to insert them into the scheme of comprehension of "being" as pertaining to the Greek train of thought in which Theophilus had grown up.

In the west, Tertullian (the second to the third centuries AD) coined the term *trinitas* but kept in sight the unity in divinity, "*Trinitas unius Divinitatis, Pater et Filius et Spiritus Sanctus.*" It was also Tertullian who was the first one to adopt the concept of a person at the time of referring to any of the three aspects. Also, in his work *Against Praxeas* (*Adversus Praxean*), the writer introduced the formula of one substance in the three persons, since the unity of the Trinity so disposes. Those three do not have differences in state, degree, substance, authority, or species. Thus, even though Tertullian did not solve all the questions, it is pertinent to recognize his coherent treatment of an issue whose solution defied the passing of time.

Among those who contributed to worsening the problems instead of solving them was Theodotus of Byzantium (the second century AD), the first and most notorious of the excommunicated and father of one form of Adoptionism. According to this heresy, Jesus (the Son) was a man adopted by God in baptism. Theodotus even went as far as negating the divinity of Jesus, with the sole purpose of escaping Rome from one of the many persecutions against him. Other adoptionist tenets held that the adoption takes place at the moment of resurrection. Adoptionism was derived from the Trinitarian heresy of Monarchianism, in which the interdependence among all the three persons of Trinity was negated, leaning toward a radical Hebraic monotheism.

Another heresy with notable influence over numerous church thinkers of those days, such as Justin (the second century AD), Irenaeus (the second to the third centuries AD), Tertullian, Origen Adamantius (the second to the third centuries AD), and Novatian (the second to the third centuries AD), was Subordinationism. This doctrine considered the Son inferior to the Father, who, in turn, was erected into a supreme God. The Christian gnosis (Gnosticism, an effort in knowing, based on transcending reason toward intuition) of Origen centered its efforts on distinguishing among the three persons, granting supremacy upon the Father. Consequently, there was an oversight related to unity and hierarchical equality, leaving the road open for followers to adopt diverse positions. The theology of Origen also presented the Son as the Logos (a term introduced by Heraclitus of Ephesus [the sixth to the fifth centuries BC] in order to name the reason that makes Creation intelligible), who gives sense, reveals, and does the Creation from beginning to end, as proclaimed in the book of the Apocalypse: "I am the alpha and the omega, the first and the last, the beginning and the end." In fact, when referring to the Son in *On the First Principles* (*De principiis*), Origen used the formula that there was no moment in which he did not exist, but he proceeds from the Father. Many accuse Origen of causing one of the major doctrinal crises in the church, provoking face-offs like no others since then. The subordinationistic orientation of Origen was radicalized to the extreme of relegating the Son as any other element of the Creation, reserving only to the Father the divine qualification.

Arius (the third to the fourth centuries AD) was the one who better incarnated these early conflictive positions. Born in what is today Libya, Arius was the most inquisitive of the disciples of Lucian of Antioch (the third to the fourth centuries AD). At forty, he took part in the sectarian schism of Meletius (the third to the fourth centuries AD) from which he retracted later. He was then ordained as a deacon and assigned to the church of Baucalis in Alexandria. During his numerous trips to the west, Arius preached the most extreme adoptionistic and subordinationistic formulas, emphatically negating that the divinity of the Son was comparable to that of the Father. The formula Arius proposed considered that even when the Son was previous to any creation, there was a moment in which he did not exist. He also thought that God was not the Father since the beginning because there was a time in which he was alone. The Son did not exist always due to the fact that all the things were made from nothing, including the verb of God. Such was the turmoil caused by Arius with his ardent polemics, particularly with Alexander of Alexandria (the third to the fourth centuries AD), that the emperor Constantine I (the third to the fourth centuries AD) had to intervene. Due to prior experiences with Donatism (only those who were impeccable could practice priesthood) and its repercussions in the Mediterranean, the emperor sent them a letter with his friend Hosius of Corduba (the third to the fourth centuries AD), severely repressing the two of them. The failure of Hosius made the emperor call up the first Greek ecumenical council, held in May AD 325. The event took place in Nicaea, close to the imperial residence of Nicomedia, today Izmit in Turkey. The emperor started the council making a welcoming speech in Latin and was followed by Eusebius of Nicomedia (the third to the fourth centuries AD), who read the Arian formula, which was rejected by the assembly. The council was then adjourned by Constantine with banquets and generous gifts to the attendants, for his twenty-fifth anniversary as emperor since his proclamation at the age of eighteen.

The Council of Nicaea introduced the term *consubstantial* to refer to the sole essence of the Father and Son. The Son is true God from true God, begotten, not created, of the same substance as the Father, leaving for later times issues related to the third person, the Holy Spirit. Those who did not subscribe to the faith of Nicaea were Arius, Secundus of Ptolemais (the third to the fourth centuries AD) and Theonas of Marmarica (the third to the fourth centuries AD), who were excommunicated on the spot and exiled to Illyricum in the Balkans. Three months later, Eusebius of Nicomedia joined them, exiled for three years until his restoration by the emperor. The meetings at Nicaea were directed by the influential Athanasius (the third to the fourth centuries AD), who was appointed bishop of Alexandria three years later. The theology of Athanasius considered the Son as the highest realization of the Father as an expression of himself. The Father eternally generates the Son, his sole expression, interpreted by us as the wisdom and power of God. The Holy Spirit is given by the Son, as is everything else, so the verb of God (the Son) is a divine instrument of his own substance. But in Nicaea the controversies did not come to an end, since numerous resentments and opposing positions persisted because of cruel persecution. The dissents forced the calling up of a new council in Tyre (AD 335), with the support of Constantine, where eastern bishops condemned Athanasius.

Even though the faith of Nicaea signified a victory against Arianism, it left much to be desired concerning the treatment given to the Holy Spirit, eliciting posterior considerations. The first one who raised the Holy Spirit to divine status was Athanasius himself, who opened the question about a Trinitarian context. The Alexandrian theologian gave no quarter to those whom he called Pneumatomachists (adversaries of the Spirit), like Macedonius (the third to the fourth centuries AD), for considering the Holy Spirit just another creature of the Creation. In the Trinitarian context, Athanasius portrays the Holy Spirit as what is given by the Son originally pertaining to the Father (circumincession). After clarifications from Athanasius, important refinements followed, mainly by the so-called Cappadocian Fathers.

During the fourth century, the three Cappadocian Fathers Basil, the bishop of Caesarea (the fourth century AD), Gregory Nazianzus (the fourth century AD), and Gregory of Nyssa (the fourth century AD), amply acknowledged for their spirituality, made decisive contributions to the Trinitarian doctrine. The Cappadocians introduced the term *hypostasis* (Greek for sediment from a liquid, that solid or consistent part that a liquid may give) to refer to the individual and incommunicable nature that the three persons of the Holy Trinity maintain in their intra-divine exchange. Basil also adopted the formula of Athanasius, elevating the Holy Spirit to the rank of aspect of divinity. Gregory Nazianzus differentiated the Son from the Holy Spirit, postulating that the first is begotten by the Father while the second one proceeds from the Father. Gregory of Nyssa distinguished the three persons in their actions more than by origin. He placed the Father as the source of power (the Almighty) and identified the Son with the power of the Father (the force itself) and the Holy Spirit as the power of the Son expressed in the existing ones (the action). The Cappadocian Fathers contributed to clarifying the hierarchical equality and the relationship among the three aspects attributed to God in the midst of Christian doctrine. Nevertheless, it is also owed to them much of the eastern speculation by which the Father was considered superior to all others (Monarchianism) due to his genetic role.

In AD 381 after his victory over the Goths, the emperor Theodosius I (the fourth century AD) promulgated an edict in Thessaloniki forcing the adoption of the Roman and Alexandrian Nicene creed. After his entrance to Constantinople, he pressed for the resignation of the Arian Demophilus (the fourth century AD) to order Gregory Nazianzus as patriarch and immediately called up a council at the imperial palace. This council was attended by Gregory Nazianzus and Gregory of Nyssa, considered the most relevant among others. The difficulties in finding a formula to the satisfaction of all derived into the construction of a creed based in quotes from the New Testament about the Holy Spirit. In Constantinople, the two Gregorys imposed the doctrine of Basil, exposed in his work *On the Holy Spirit* (*De Spiritu Sancto*) and finalized in AD 375. In it, the baptismal faith was reaffirmed, giving recognition to the divine rank of the third person. To the formula of the Cappadocians, one "substance" (the first substance, from the Greek ousia, that thing that contains its own determination and hence, pertains to the sole thing), three hypostases were also imposed, affirming that the Holy Spirit and the Son proceed in the last instance from the Father. The doctrine was interpreted distinctly by the Greeks and Latins. The Greeks thought that the Holy Spirit proceeds from the Father through the Son. On the other hand, the Latin ideas were that the Holy Spirit proceeds from the Father and the Son. The Latin doctrine was named *filioque*, which originated new controversies until being declared as an article of faith by the Roman Church at the Fourth Lateran Council (AD 1215).

It was not until Augustine of Hippo that the substantiation and consolidation of the Trinitarian doctrine came, placing it at the center of the philosophical thought of the Latin Church. Aurelius Augustine was born in Thagaste in Numidia (today Souk Ahras, in northeastern Algeria) in AD 354 to a pagan father and Christian mother (Monica), who decisively influenced his orientation. Augustine's life was an example of the continuous search for the truth; in his youth he was a passionate man in search of earthly pleasures as well as his studies. He achieved a high cultural level, thanks to which he taught rhetoric in Carthage, Rome, and Milan. He started his philosophical studies reading *Hortensius*, from Cicero (the second to the first centuries BC), which increased his passion for knowledge. Later, he adhered to the Manichaean heresy (a religious and philosophical doctrine founded by Manes [the third century AD] centered on the conflict between good and evil), becoming an anti-Christian fanatic. Weary and disappointed with Manichaeanism, he left for Rome to convert to skepticism (the tendency of thought that affirms nothing) but without making a dent in his quest for knowledge. Later in Milan, after a reencounter with Christianity practiced by his mother, he pronounced himself in favor of the Neoplatonism of Plotinus (the third century AD) and Porphyry (the third to the fourth centuries AD). Finally, in AD 387, he was baptized by Ambrose of Milan (the fourth century AD), and in AD 391, he was ordered as a priest by Bishop Valerius of Hippo (the fourth century AD), whom he succeeded.

After long periods of meditation, Augustine outlined in his treatise *On the Trinity* (*De Trinitate*) (AD 399 – 420), his broad vision of Latin thought about the triple manifestation of God. It is an extensive work that was destined to exert great influence on the Christian faith. The one God is the Father, the Son, and the Holy Spirit, not three different individuals but one and only one. Besides, it substitutes the concept of a person for a relationship. According to Augustine, there are three relationships that reinforce the community and its unitary nature. In summary, the three relationships are different in the unity of one substance. It also focuses separately on the problem of the Trinity from the economic point of view (economy, the eternally provided by God for the salvation of humanity and realized through time) as from the perspective of its immanence within man. In this way, Augustine suggests searching for the Trinity also inside ourselves, as if it were a reflection of God, who made us by saying, "Let us make a man in our image and in our likeness," as the book of Genesis asserts.

Subsequently, considerations of the dogma of the Holy Trinity since the beginning of the late Middle Ages were divided into two tendencies, the personalistic mysticism and the intellectualist. The first one was introduced by prominent mystics such as Bernard of Clairvaux, from Burgundy (the eleventh to the twelfth centuries AD), and Giovanni di Fidanza, from Tuscany (Bonaventure) (the thirteenth century AD). While the second one was promoted by two Italians, Anselm of Canterbury (the eleventh to the twelfth centuries AD), from Aosta, and Thomas Aquinas (the thirteenth century AD), from Roccasecca. According to the personalists, the three persons of the Holy Trinity reside one inside the other, interpenetrating one another without deriving it in fusion or mixture but in conjugation. The dynamic impulse of the three is unique and the same since the three persons are their God. On the other hand, the approach of the intellectualists was somewhat contrary and similar to that of Augustine, in that God is one and he expresses himself in three different ways.

Throughout the centuries, the dogma of the Holy Trinity evoked passionate answers from thinkers and mystics of all tendencies. From the reform side, John Calvin (the sixteenth century AD) adopted the Trinitarian dogma, emphasizing unity in the essence where the three persons shall be understood. Other reformers such as Lelio (the sixteenth century AD) and Fausto Sozzini (the sixteenth to the seventeenth centuries AD) were openly anti-Trinitarian. They both had to flee from their place of birth in Siena, Italy, to northern Europe because of the radicalism of their doctrines. Fausto settled into Poland, linking himself to the Polish Brethren (*Fratres Poloni*), who were as anti-Trinitarian (or even more) as he. At the beginning of the seventeenth century AD, after the death of Fausto, the most important aspects of his doctrine were collected in the Racovian Catechism. His thoughts synthesized the highlights of the anti-Trinitarian positions of M. Servet (the sixteenth century AD), from Spain, and the humanist V. Gentile (the sixteenth century AD), from Italy. The first one was burned alive atop a pile of its own books, and the other one was beheaded because of his ideas.

Among the fathers of science J. Kepler (the sixteenth to the seventeenth centuries AD) was an ardent advocate of heliocentrism and of the Trinitarian doctrine seeing in the sphere an image of Holy Trinity, taking God the Father for the center, the Son for the outer surface and the Holy Spirit for the intermediate space. But the Socinian influence was decisive in the most recalcitrant anti-Trinitarian environments in the Netherlands and England among the likes of figures such as I. Newton (the seventeenth to the eighteenth centuries AD). The outstanding English physicist recorded his anti-Trinitarian beliefs in numerous theological writings.

Formal speculation on the Trinitarian dogma continued in the Catholic Church, in complete disconnection with the chores and feelings of its faithful followers. As the German theologian J. Moltmann (the twentieth to the twenty-first centuries AD) correctly pointed out, whether God is triune or one does not seem to matter much, either in faith or in ethics. The generalized indifference to endless polemics about the dogma of the Holy Trinity has led to a crisis that continues to this day. Far from converging toward a coherent proposal, the discussions continue to expose starkly dramatic disagreements among theologians after nearly two millennia of discussion. On the one hand, the German theologian K. Rahner (the twentieth century AD) reformulated the dogma with his famous phrase, "the economic Trinity is the immanent Trinity, and vice versa." The Neapolitan theologian B. Forte (the twentieth to the twenty-first centuries AD) disagrees, arguing that the economic Trinity is the narrative of the history of God in our own history, and the immanent Trinity is simply God to himself.

In short terms, the history of the dogma of the Holy Trinity is definitely unusual and surprising. It seems incredible that a single passage in one of the four Gospels could have become such a distinctive and controversial feature of an entire religion. Even more surprising is the fact that the issue turned with the passage of time into a mere statement ignored and devoid of meaning to the faithful. Despite the outcome, it is up to the Christians to accommodate, in a single representation, the transcendent God of the Old Testament with the Holy Trinity as conceptualized and debated by their theologians.

The discussions about the Trinitarian dogma were not confined only to the bosom of the church. On the contrary, the scandals reverberated strongly within the confines of the ancient world, generating all kinds of apprehensions. In fact, the prophet **Muhammad** recorded his emphatically antitritheist position in the **ayat of suwar The Cow, The Women, and The Food**, just to mention some of them. In those suwar, he emphasized the unicity of God and warned against exaggerations in saying God is three or by placing him third in a trio.

The geometry of the "cubic" sanctuary, or Kaaba, in whose eastern corner the Black Stone of Abraham is located, should be interpreted following the antitritheist warnings of the Koran. The Kaaba as a whole offers an extraordinary plastic representation of the quaternary formulism of religion four, on a 1-3 type odd basis. The construction of this sanctuary is attributed to patriarch Abraham and his son Ishmael (**the nineteenth to the eighteenth centuries BC**), and it welcomed the **cults** of divinities of the most diverse nature throughout its long history. At the moment of being adopted by the prophet Muhammad, the Kaaba housed the **cult** of 360 idols headed by Hubal, the highest deity of the ancient Nabataean tribe. The central ceremony of the **cult** of the Nabataean god consisted of praising him while circumambulating around the Kaaba (in a sense indicated by the four fingers of the right hand when the thumb points upward), sometimes naked, other times spraying the blood of sacrificed animals. The elders of the tribes gave the prophet Muhammad an aerolite called the Black Stone of Abraham, with the intention of his placing it in the sanctuary. The Prophet placed it wisely in a corner close to the east, which coincides with the entrance door to its interior, as shown in figure 4.6.

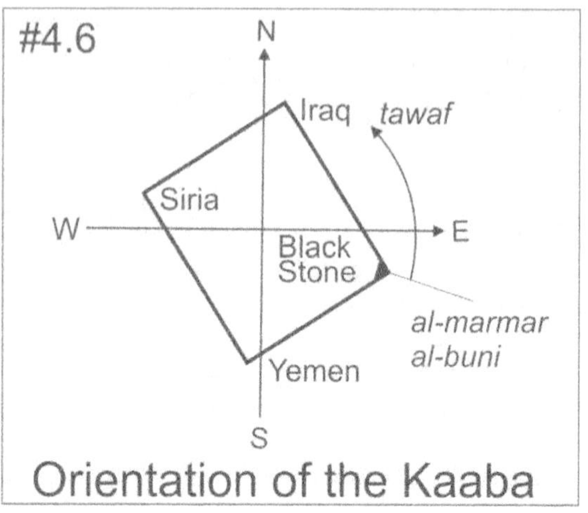

Orientation of the Kaaba

The figure shows the four cardinal points, the corner of the Black Stone of Abraham, and the marble strip (*al-marmar al-buni*). This mark indicates the beginning and end of the seven circumambulations around the Kaaba (*tawaf*), following the order of the corners of Iraq, Syria, and Yemen. In the context of a 1-3 type quaternary base, the Black Stone of Abraham represents the transcendent and therefore should figure on a unitary basis separate from the triad, whereas the other three corners (the Iraqi, the Syrian, and the Yemeni) could be considered allusive to a subordinate immanent triad. The correspondences between the square base of the Kaaba and the tetrahedral model selected for the quaternary representations are indicated in figure 4.7. The southern corner, also called the Yemeni, has been linked with an arrow to the corresponding component of the quaternary base.

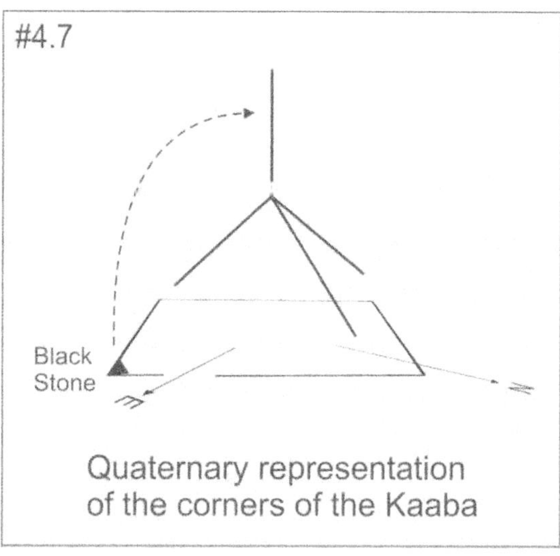

Quaternary representation of the corners of the Kaaba

Despite the antitritheist warnings of the prophet Muhammad, some thinkers and mystics of Islam have cautiously hinted at their Trinitarian inclinations. A clear example of the discretion with which the subject is treated in Islam is offered by the Murcian **Ibn Arabi** (the twelfth to the thirteenth centuries AD) in *The Bezels of Wisdom (Fusus al-Hikam)*, where he states that singularity has a triple composition since it comes from the three.

The present chapter has been focused on showing the potential usefulness of the 1-3 type quaternary bases for the representation and organization of some religious concepts. The topic discussed here will be expanded opportunely in order to address other approaches aimed at contextualizing the divine unicity with the multiplicity observed in his Creation.

Chapter 5

Bases for Quaternary Representations of the 2-2 Type

Quaternary bases can also be configured by the composition of two binary bases, which is in turn a binary expression of the 2-2 type. As the unicity belongs exclusively to God, the first act of creation begins with the number two. Not in vain, the first verse of the Bible dedicated to the beginning of creation starts with the letter ב (bet, the second letter of the Hebrew alphabet, whose numeric value is two). Likewise, the figuration of the waters in the prelude of all creations is a constant in the most documented cosmogonies of antiquity. Such preeminence leads one to think that God created the waters in the first place to impose on them an odd partition of the 1-3 type.

The best way to understand the hydric connotation given to the binary medium, from which the cosmos would have arisen, goes through an exploration of the nature of chemical water. The previous statement presumes that the phenomenology of water is, to a great extent, an exteriorization of the binary archetypes of Creation. At the comfort temperature for humans, water is in its liquid state, and unlike any solid, it takes the form of the vessel where it is contained. Under the mentioned conditions, chemical water lacks the most elementary capacities to define its own shape. It is an indispensable substance in the emergence and maintenance of life, as the inhabitants of any desert on the face of the earth well know. However, its role is largely limited to acting as a medium for the transport and dissociation of other substances. Physicochemically, water is considered a dielectric (electrical insulator) that maintains in dissociation the ions of acids, bases, and their salts, as it does even in the processes of biological life.

Chemically speaking, common water is a compound with binary traits, as its H_2O molecular formula indicates—one oxygen atom bonded to two of hydrogen. As previously mentioned, oxygen has an incomplete outer electronic subshell with an orbital configuration similar to that of carbon. However, the element has six electrons in this subshell instead of four, and therefore only two are required to complete it. This duality is the cause of the key role of oxygen, making chemical water to figure among natural models representable on binary bases. One of the ways in which oxygen obtains the two missing electrons is by sharing its own with those of the incomplete outer shell of two hydrogen atoms. Each of these atoms of hydrogen has one electron available and requires another one for its own completion.

In the atom of oxygen, two orbitals are saturated with two electrons each, while the remaining two have one each, and that is where the two atoms of hydrogen provide theirs. As with carbon and silicon, the incomplete outer subshell of oxygen can be configured under sp^3 type hybridization. Unfortunately, not everything is so simple, because although there is a consensus that oxygen sp^3 hybridization is the preferred condition, in certain cases the question may be different. Evidence suggests that water oxygen can also adopt sp^2 plus p hybridization. Under this configuration, only two p orbitals share the spherical character of the s orbital, while a third p orbital does not hybridize. Both forms maintain the binary trait of the hydrogen bonds, enabling the establishment of correspondences with representations on binary bases, as will be done with the primordial waters. Figure 5.1 presents schematically to the left and in the center the hybridizations of oxygen orbitals, while on the right there is a representation of two independent directions in conjunction with the archetype of the primordial waters of the Creation.

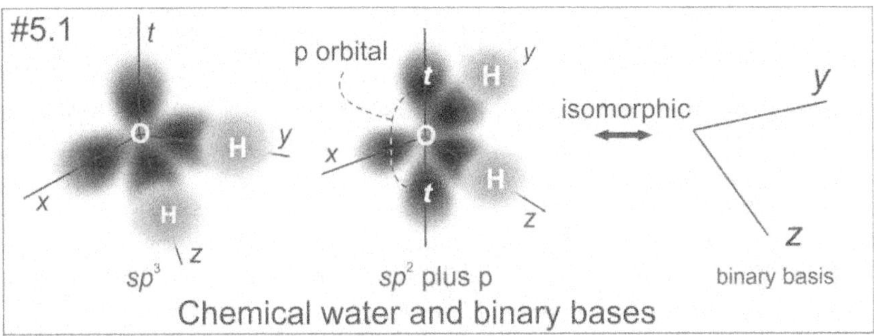

Chemical water and binary bases

In the figure, two quaternary representations have been made to coincide with a tetrahedral shape and a trigonal bipyramid. One of the representations corresponds to the directions of the spatial triad xyz plus t, and the other to the oxygen orbitals.

Due to the imbrication of odd and even formulations, chemical water is not purely binary. In fact, even when there are two varieties, called para-water and ortho-water, both occur in proportions of one to three as in a quaternary basis of the 1-3 type. This is because para-water and ortho-water are part of a scheme called singlet-triplet. Such a situation is produced by a parallel or antiparallel combination of the magnetic moments of the nuclei of both hydrogen atoms (called protons). Due to the electrical charge (in this case positive [+]) of the protons, their intrinsic turns generate antiparallel magnetic moments if they are opposite or parallel if they rotate in the same direction. Figure 5.2 attempts to facilitate understanding of this phenomenon.

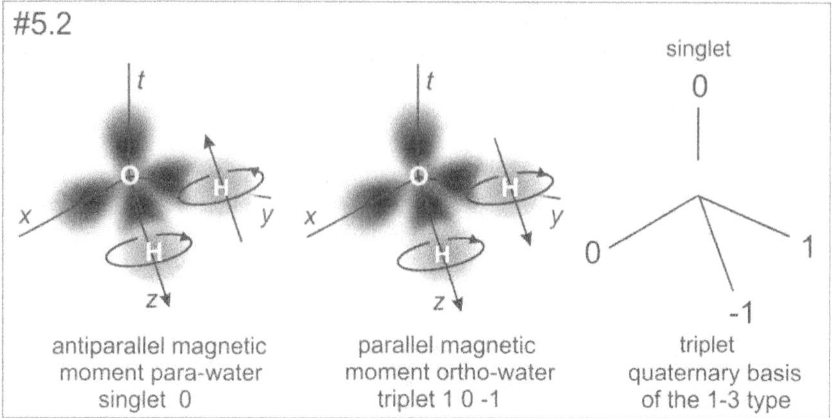

The figure shows the two magnetic configurations mentioned, leaving the interested reader to investigate other possible configurations, as well as the symmetric and antisymmetric compositions of the basis states. The contrast in the pair of 1 and -1, to the right of the figure, reflects an essential feature of the waters, while the 0 refers to their absence.

The thinkers of antiquity saw a manifestation of chaos in the liquid state of water because of its inability to define its own shape at a temperature comfortable for humans. They did not know, however, that in spite of its fluidity, water conserves aspects of the molecular organization of its solid state, a feature that other liquids do not exhibit. In fact, the electrostatic attractions between the oxygen atoms of one molecule and the protons of another give rise to the so-called hydrogen bond, with enough force to join them. Hence, liquid water exhibits locally cells with arrangements similar to those of its solid state.

The archetypal primordial waters are an essential element in the Egyptian cosmogony and in its doctrine concerning eternal life. The aqueous medium from which the radiant island emerges has its representation in the pyramids when its triangular faces are observed from the front. From this observation point, it is possible to see only two oblique and equal edges (Sirius and Kochab stars), as is shown in figure 5.3.

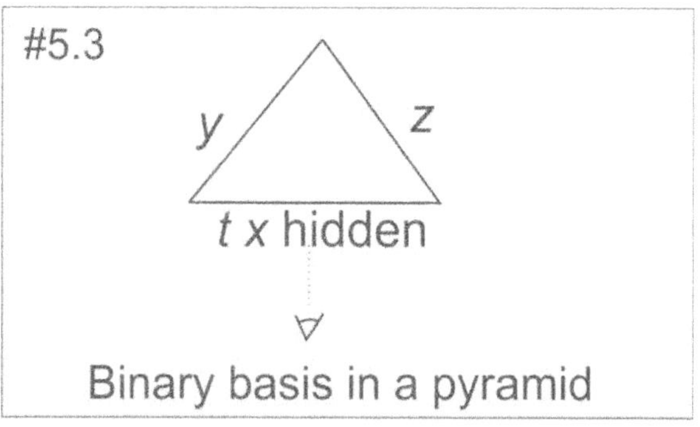

Dehydration, as a means for water extraction, played an extraordinary role in the Egyptian funerary ritual of mummification, associated with the consecution of life after death. In those processes, carbonates were used as an extraction medium. These salts appeared on the rims of lagoons formed during the flooding of the Nile, after the evaporation of water caused by the effect of the heat from the sun. The carbonates symbolized then what was left behind by the disappearance or retreat of the waters, as was the case with limestone. The most abundant carbonate on the banks of these lagoons is sodium carbonate (Na_2CO_3), sodium (Na, from the Latin *natrium*) being best known for its presence in common salt. That carbonate was collected and then calcined in ovens and used to cover the mortal remains of the upper class in order to extract the two-thirds of water present in their bodies. The drying process left only one-third remaining, formed by all those compounds other than water. That one-third remnant was the essence of oddness, which would be waiting for new waters, the clean waters of resurrection, elementally represented by those poured from the sky every year to green the desert.

In the Bible, it is not necessary to search much to find references to primordial waters. In fact, they appear in the text of Genesis preceding all creation, because "the earth was waste and in chaos, and the Spirit of God was hovering over the surface of the waters." The enthronement of the Creator on the chaos of the primordial waters is a fundamental fact, impossible to ignore in any exegetical attempt due to its repeated mentions, among which are those of the Psalmist when he states that "the voice of God is over the waters. The God of glory thunders. God is over many waters and is enthroned over the Flood," which establishes the importance granted by the Bible to the primordial waters as binary bases in the context of every new creation—as it happens, for example, in relation to the episode of the Universal Flood.

In religion two, Zoroastrianism, it is hard to miss the binary type tetramorphisms that Zend-Avesta in Yasna LVII presents, as the prophet Ezekiel did in terms of a chariot. The tetramorphic essence of Sraosha (the messenger of Ahura Mazda and incarnation of his word) is expressed in the figure of a quadriga with four horsemen and by the tenor of his countenance: "white and bright, beautiful and powerful," which is 2-2. In the Gospels, the waters have a contextual and introductory character to the action of God, as in the recount by John of the wedding at Cana. In that event, and at the request of his mother, Jesus transforms into wine the water contained in six stone vessels. The same can be said of the water baptism by John, a prelude to the baptism of spirit and fire of Jesus. According to **surah Hud** of the Koran, waters are present in every creative act: "And He is Who has created the heavens and the earth in six days and His throne is always on the waters, to manifest which of you does best."

In relation to the importance of distinguishing between the basis of 1-3 and 2-2 types, said Akiva ben Joseph (the first to the second centuries AD), when the marble stones are reached, do not say "water"! Water! Readers should remember that marble is mostly calcium carbonate, and its carbonate ion has been associated with natural representations of the 1-3 type. According to its representation within a quaternary basis, it is possible to distinguish two types of binary bases or waters. On the one hand, there are those in which the unitary basis of the 1-3 type formulation participates. On the other are the binary bases inscribed within the earth or lower triad. Figure 5.4 illustrates separately the two types of binary bases represented on a quaternary basis.

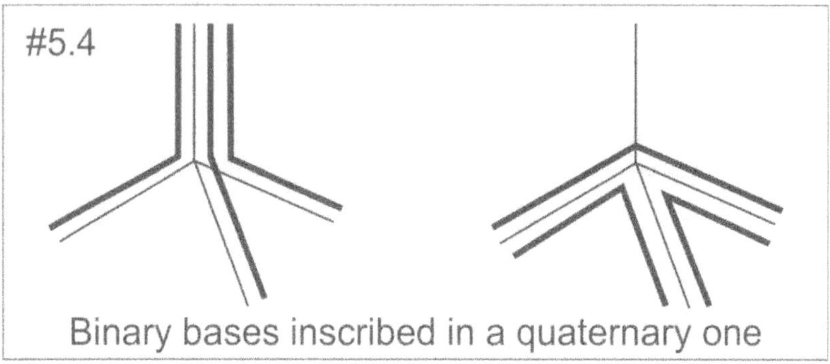

Binary bases inscribed in a quaternary one

In total, six binary bases are shown in two groups of three, not only to facilitate visualization but also due to significant differences in the roles of each one. In fact, the Bible dedicates two verses just at the beginning of the book of Genesis with the intention of establishing differences between them: "God said: 'Let there be an expanse between the waters separating one from the other'… And God called the expanse heaven." Figure 5.5 illustrates some representative cases of the expanse between the waters.

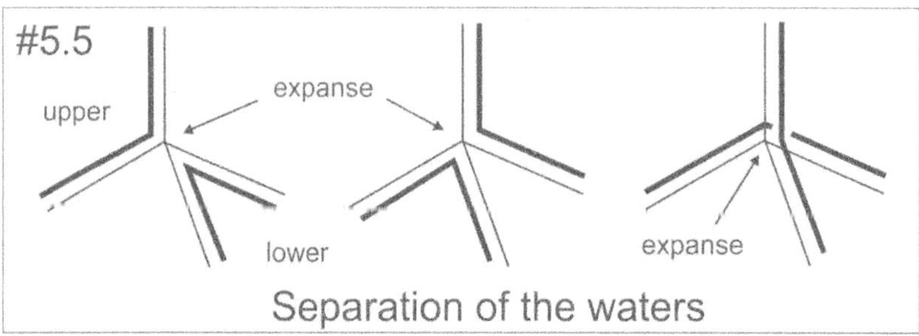

Separation of the waters

Disciples from Akiva, especially Simeon ben Azzai (the second century AD) and Simeon ben Zoma (the second century AD) argued that the voice of the Holy One became the angel over the waters, who gathered them in one place, barely leaving a span between the upper and lower ones.

The Koran also makes distinctions between the waters in **surah The Cave**, when Moses says to his servant: "I will not rest until I get to where the two rivers meet, otherwise I will continue to do so for years." But above all, surah The Discrimination illuminates us, distinguishing them by their salinity, which had its origin in an important event to be discussed later: "And it is He Who has made the two seas flow freely, one sweet and drinkable, the other salty and bitter. And between them he has placed an insurmountable barrier." Fresh waters discharged from the sky that then flow downward in torrents and rivers on the earth symbolize the "upper ones." Meanwhile, the brackish waters gathered in the seas have been associated with the "lower ones," which are inscribed in the triad.

In ancient Egypt, the stars Thuban and Alnitak (belonging to the Orion belt and often associated with the god Osiris) were stellar representations of upper or masculine waters. The alignment of the north and south shafts beginning at the upper, or king's, chamber in the Khufu pyramid suggests this. These symbolic shafts representing the upper or masculine waters are open to the sky, allowing exchanges between their two components and the Most High God beyond the empyreal vault. Later, a pair of obelisks located at the entrance to the great temples represented these waters.

The shafts running from the queen's or lower chamber—north and south—align with the stars Kochab and Sirius (associated with the goddess Isis), representing the feminine waters. Since both components of the feminine waters oppose one another, their interaction is mutual and confined to the earth. The absence of interaction between the lower or feminine waters and the Most High God was the reason to place blocking stones at the end of these shafts.

Chapter 6

Composite Bases

The first verse of Genesis 1 gives an account of the creation of heaven and the earth as separate domains and thereby lays the groundwork for certain considerations of great relevance. In fact, according to Holy Scriptures, the Creator formulated different types of creatures, some whose development is circumscribed to heaven and others to the earth. For this reason, these creatures find it impossible to represent the totality of a quaternary cosmos. The inability of creatures to project on the first representations on their bases, and to act from these in cosmic domains that transcend them, gives rise to important incomplete representations. In addition to the separation existing in odd formulations of the 1-3 type, it is important to consider the expanse between the upper and lower waters, expressed in the 2-2 type, whose effects are comparable.

Given the separation between heaven and the earth, the ternary creatures circumscribed to the last can only represent on their bases one of the two components of the upper waters. In their separate representations, both components are usually considered masculine. Based on the above, R. Levi (the third century AD) thought that the upper waters were masculine and the lower feminine and that the lower should receive the upper ones as messengers of God. Levi's sentence is not an isolated event because the masculinity of the upper waters is also addressed by cabalist authors and appears in prayers of the Hebrew liturgy. The rule for the upper waters is that they consist of 2 components of different kinds pursuing the same goals.

According to previous considerations, it is advisable to introduce additional unitary bases and to contemplate different types of compositions. Figure 6.1 illustrates some of those remarkable compositions between unitary, binary, and ternary bases, together with odd ones of the 1-3 type and even ones of the 2-2 type already raised.

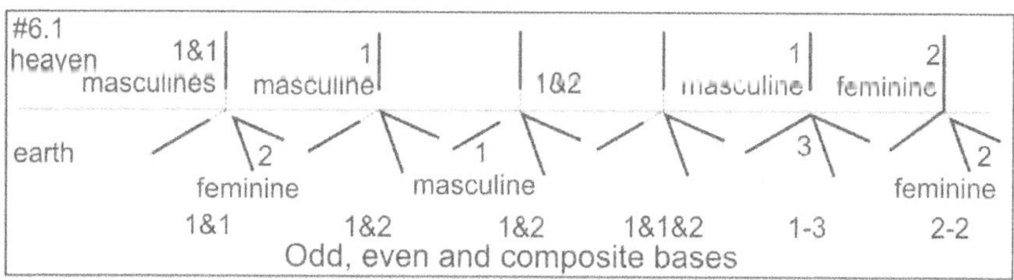

The composite bases would be of 1&1, 1&2, and 1&1&2 types, which will be of great help in representing in a coherent whole the concepts and religious truths of the most diverse origins. These schemes will facilitate comparative analyses and will uncover relations of isomorphism, or similarities, which would otherwise go unnoticed.

Beyond the archetypal level, no object structured in the cosmos is purely odd or even. This important feature is due to the imbricated participation of both types of formulations in the formation of the creatures. Hence the Koranic exclamation in surah The Daybreak, "By the daybreak!…And the even and the odd!"

Chapter 7

The Protoelements

According to the bases of representation considered so far, some formulations contemplated in the originating provisions of the Creation and therefore of perpetual character will be postulated. That is, they govern the creatures and none can modify or dispense with them. In ancient times, there must have been a common knowledge body for all civilizations (perennial philosophy), where the referred formulations played a preeminent role in the articulation of human understanding. Unfortunately, this knowledge has been largely forgotten or abandoned, as has happened with the so-called constituting elements of everything. The most ancient written reference to the elements appears in the *Enuma elish* (the thirteenth to the twelfth centuries BC), where earth, water, god-fire, and wind or air star in a cosmogony born of the chaos of primordial waters.

The elements also appear in the Hebrew Bible, whose oldest book was probably written around the seventh century BC—for example, the waters under the sky and the dry, with which air (sky) and water and earth (dry) are mentioned. The Bible also talks about the creation of luminaries in the sky, a greater luminary for the day and a smaller one for the night. The heat, infused by the sun during the day and by the oil lamps in the nights, would allow one to presume an allusion to fire.

The Koran mentions four constituent elements: air (wind), water, earth (component of clay), and fire. The formation of humans from clay is affirmed in suwar The Cattle and Sad. For its part, surah The Discrimination establishes water as a formative element. Surah Sad also clearly specifies the creation of the jinn from protoelement fire. In the Koranic revelation, the word *air* does not appear as an element, but there are eighteen mentions of the wind, whose relationship would be subject to discussion. Opinions among Islamic exegetes and people of high religious significance about the doctrine of the elements have not been uniform. It is known, for example, that the sixth imam of the Shia (a fraction of followers of Ali ibn Abi Talib [the seventh century AD], cousin and son-in-law of the prophet Muhammad), Jafar ibn Muhammad al-Sadiq (the eighth century AD), based on his knowledge of alchemy, ridiculed the doctrine of the elements, while others adopted it without reservation. The religions of the People with the Book do not support a number of elements greater than four, except in Zoroastrianism, where the number could be extended to six.

The doctrine, according to which everything that exists in the cosmos is constituted by a small group of elements, seems to come from a common origin. In ancient times, this doctrine was part of the cultures of the Far East, India, Mesopotamia, the Near East, and Greece. However, the classic doctrine of the four elements (whose denomination is attributed to Plato [the fifth to the fourth centuries BC]) had its origin in the cosmogonies of the pre-Socratic philosophers. Thus Thales (the seventh to the sixth centuries BC) proposed water as the fundamental and originating element, Anaximenes (the sixth century BC) proposed air, Heraclitus proposed fire, and Xenophanes (the sixth to the fifth centuries BC) proposed water and earth. Finally, it was Empedocles (the fifth century BC) who formulated the doctrine of the four elements best known at present. According to the Agrigentian thinker, the four roots (the name given by him to the elements) were at the origin of everything: fire, air, water, and earth. By virtue of love and conflict, the roots were united and separated to constitute all the known substances. The four roots were simple, perpetual, and unalterable, but their participation in the substances was given in varying proportions. In relation to the elements, Plato went even further by attributing forms of geometric solids to them. Thus, the atom of fire would have a tetrahedral shape, air's would be an octahedron, water's an icosahedrons, and earth's a cube.

The origin of atomism as a theory to describe the constitution of matter and to explain its behavior has its roots in the Far East. In India, for example, the origin of the Jain atomism (from the Sanskrit *jina*, "victorious") is lost in the past of this ancient religion (the eighth century BC). The Greek atomism was suggested by Anaximander (the sixth century BC) (homoeomeries) centuries later and turned into doctrine by both Leucippus (the fifth to the fourth centuries BC), founder of the school of Abdera, and by his disciple Democritus (the fifth to the fourth BC). At the same time, in India, atomism was considered by the oldest orthodox philosophical current of Hinduism, founded by Kashyapa Kanada (the sixth to the second centuries BC) (who eats atoms) and called the Vaisheshika *darsana* (point of view on individuality). Atomism has also formed a substantial part of the philosophical doctrine of Buddhism since the fourth century BC. According to Buddhist thinkers, there were four types of atoms, with properties that allow them to act in the bosom of matter in a characteristic way. Later, during the seventh century AD, a novel approach was consolidated according to which atoms are essentially point-like objects made of pure energy.

Among the People with the Book, some Islamic thinkers were the first to introduce atomism into their theological systems, while medieval Europe was immersed in the Dark Ages (a period that mediates mainly between the fall of the Roman empires of the West [the fifth century AD] and of the East [the fifteenth century AD]). It has not been possible to specify a common origin to all the atomistic currents of Islamic thought. However, its popularity has been known since the ninth century AD, when it was adopted by the Muʿtazilite (the separated ones) thinkers until the Abbasid decline, for which they were blamed. The greatest exponent of the late and clandestine Muʿtazila and then afterward its detractor was al-Ashʿari (the ninth to the tenth centuries AD), a native of Basra (Iraq) and founder of a renowned school of Islamic thinkers. The full insertion of atomism in the school of al-Ashʿari is due to Abu Bakr al-Baqillani (the tenth to the eleventh centuries AD). The outstanding jurist of the Maliki school (one of the four schools of lawyers of Islam) and "master" (sheikh) of the sunna (norm of conduct) made atomism the cornerstone of his theology.

Followers of al-Ash'ari thought that once the indivisibility of matter was accepted, its dependence on a transcendental agent to whom it owed its determination ("how, where, and when it is") was unequivocally established. If, on the contrary, matter could be divided without any limits, it would enclose in itself its own determination. They also argued that the formation of anything based on the grouping of a certain number of atoms, as well as their changes, depended on something external to them, called accidents. The most common accidents are position, rest, movement, color, heat, and duration. **If the atoms could not explain themselves, they could neither explain the origin of their accidents.** God is who realizes the atoms of matter as well as their accidents that dynamize and particularize the Creation. He holds them for the duration of each instant and creates them each time, at the beginning of each instant. In this way, God creates the cosmos again at every change and makes it last. The God of the school of al-Ash'ari plays the main role, as creator and supporter of the cosmos. Therefore, God would not be simply responsible for the start-up at the beginning of the cosmos, as the doctors of the Mu'tazilite school said. Critics of the doctrine of al-Ash'ari adopted by the kalam (interpretation of the word of God) ended up working in its favor because they could not offer better answers to those issues.

The translation into Latin of the works of the Islamic thinker Ibn Sina (the tenth to the eleventh centuries BC) by several scholars, among them the archdeacon of Toledo D. Gundissalinus (the twelfth century AD), contributed decisively to the Aristotelian renaissance in medieval Europe. As a result of that resurgence, all other aspects of Greek thought were eclipsed for a long time. Against atomism was the postulate of Aristotle stating that every material object could potentially be divided in principle into as many parts as might be wanted, **but in practice** only to a certain extent. Also, the need for a vacuum among atoms would conceptually violate the continuity of matter. And so the Aristotelian predominance and its criticism of atomist doctrines made them go unnoticed until the seventeenth century AD, when they were retaken by P. Gassendi (the sixteenth to the seventeenth centuries AD) and Descartes.

At the end of the Enlightenment, the French scientist A. de Lavoisier (the eighteenth century AD) published in his *Elementary Treatise of Chemistry* (*Traité élémentaire de chimie*) a list of elements chemically indivisible. These included oxygen, nitrogen (N, *nitro*, "to generate" in Greek), hydrogen, phosphorus (P, *phosphoros*, "carrier of light" in Greek), mercury (Hg, *hydrargyros*, "water and silver" in Greek), zinc (Zn, Zink, "tooth" in German), and sulfur (S, from the Latin *sulfur*), as well as light and heat, whose objectivity, at that time, could not be put into doubt. However, twenty-two elements already discovered at that time were absent from the list, such as copper (Cu, from the Latin word *cuprum*, for its Cypriot origin), known and used for more than one hundred centuries. Nevertheless, the notion of chemical indivisibility of elements and frequent additions to the list of Lavoisier relegated the doctrine of Empedocles to the sphere of alchemy.

Subsequent pages will demonstrate that it is neither possible nor convenient to carry out the natural exegesis of the Holy Scriptures, in complete disregard of the doctrine of the four elements. In fact, there are fundamental concepts in the Scriptures whose understanding becomes very difficult for not having an adequate formulation of it. They will be called "protoelements" in order to avoid confusion with the chemical elements of the periodic table and due to their role as archetypal precursors of the creatures existing in the cosmos. Ironically, the odd and even bases of representation inspired by carbon and silicon will restore the doctrine of the protoelements to its rightful place. Like the four roots of Empedocles, the protoelements will be considered perpetual since their formulations are part of the originating provisions of the Creation.

Chapter 8

The Protoelement Air

Any created object that can be represented on an independent unitary basis in heaven (outside the triad) will be considered to be constituted exclusively by the protoelement air. In addition to its uniqueness, it is characterized by its own identity, coming from its origin, which unfolds in all its developments. Its name was taken from that which, being invisible, determines the earthly forms, on the surface of the waters and on the flames of fire. The air is in heaven, above all things, and houses a higher reality constituting a model of everything below. Its cardinality is equal to one, and therefore it can be considered masculine. Sexual connotations of oddness and evenness were commonly accepted in antiquity, since, as Philo summarized, in the existing ones, the odd number is the male, and the even is the female. Figure 8.1 shows the protoelement air on a unit basis outside the triad.

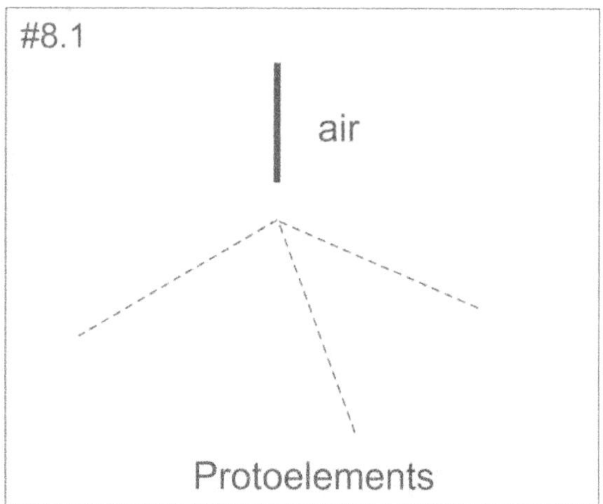

The protoelement air will be associated with the verb *to determine,* and its importance will be better understood in the chapter dedicated to the formulations of the spirit and the human archetype.

Chapter 9

The Protoelement Earth

Every created object whose exact representation can only be given on unitary bases in the triad will be considered to be constituted exclusively by the protoelement earth. In the next chapters, the use of the word *earth* will be restricted when referring to the domains coinciding with the triad in order to avoid confusion with the protoelement defined here. In addition to its unicity, it is characterized by its own identity, coming from its origin, which extends to all its developments. The name *earth* is inspired by its form of participation in created objects of a composite nature, rather than in any connotation of telluric character. The protoelement earth will be considered a representative par excellence of the male sex in the triad, just as the air is in heaven. It was created in the image and likeness of the performance of the divinity on its Creation and of the protoelement air on the binary creatures that both share. The book of Genesis reveals that God said, "Let us make a man in our image and in our likeness…" Figure 9.1 illustrates the three possibilities of unitary representation of the protoelement earth in the triad.

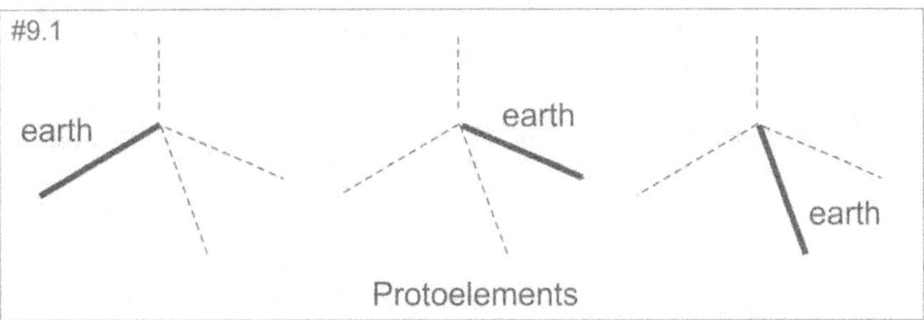

The cardinal number of the protoelement earth is one. Its associated verb is *to direct*, and together with the air, it can form a semblance of the upper waters, playing a fundamental role in the formulation of the human archetype.

The main antagonist characters made of protoelement earth in the Sacred Scriptures are the Earthly Adam and Jesus, both associated with their heavenly counterparts, the Heavenly Adam and Christ, who belong to the immanent aspect of God.

Chapter 10

The Protoelement Water

Every created object will be considered to be constituted exclusively by the protoelement water when its representation can only be given exactly and jointly on the two independent components of a binary basis. Both components of water share the same identity, coming from their unique origin, and are deployed in their multiple developments. Additionally, each of the components of water is conditioned by a pair of binary attributes, which will be called "chiaroscuro contrast," for a lack of a better name (remember the pair 1 −1 in chemical water triplets). With each of the two components of the water conditioned by a binary attribute, its permutations thereof must be taken into account. Consequently, it can be said that the protoelement water oscillates between two states.

In previous chapters, water was considered in a broad quaternary context, making reference also to an expanse between them, which would divide them into upper and lower. In what follows, the term *water* will be reserved to denominate the lower ones; for example, the waters in the triad in any of the three versions. When it becomes necessary to address the issue of the upper waters or any other waters, the relevant clarifications will be made.

The protoelement water will be considered a representative of the feminine nature par excellence in all its aspects and participation forms. Figure 10.1 illustrates the three possibilities of representing the waters in the triad.

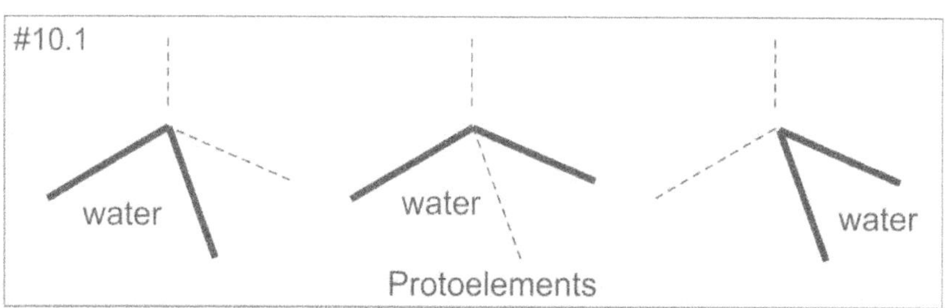

The cardinal number of the protoelement water is two. Its verbs are *to transcribe* and *to compose*, both operating on a pair of objects. The first one acts ordinally and the second cardinally. Like the protoelements air and earth, water acquires its greatest significance in the formulation of the human archetype.

Religion two, or Zoroastrianism, emphasizes the dualistic features of traditional religious themes, in close connection with the definition given to the protoelement water. Yasna XXX in the Zend-Avesta describes them as two spirits of the same kind with opposing endeavors. The feminine character of waters will be one of the pillars of the ongoing natural exegesis, in full harmony with the Zend-Avesta, which even worships them in Yasna XXXVIII.

Chapter 11

The Protoelement Fire

Every created object will be considered to be constituted exclusively by the protoelement fire when its exact representation can only occur concomitantly on the three independent components of a triad. The three components of fire have a unique identity coming from their origin, which is displayed in all its developments. Additionally, each of them is conditioned by one of three distinctive attributes endowed with an intrinsic order. For convenience, each ternary attribute will be named using the denominations of the primary colors blue, green, and red, even when there are no phenomenological reasons to do so. Any of the three components can be infused with one of the three attributes, which is why their three cyclic permutations should be taken into consideration. No sex is attributed to it, but its odd nature allows it to operate in a similar way to the protoelements air and earth—an issue that will merit quite detailed considerations later. Figure 11.1 illustrates the representation of the protoelement fire on a triad.

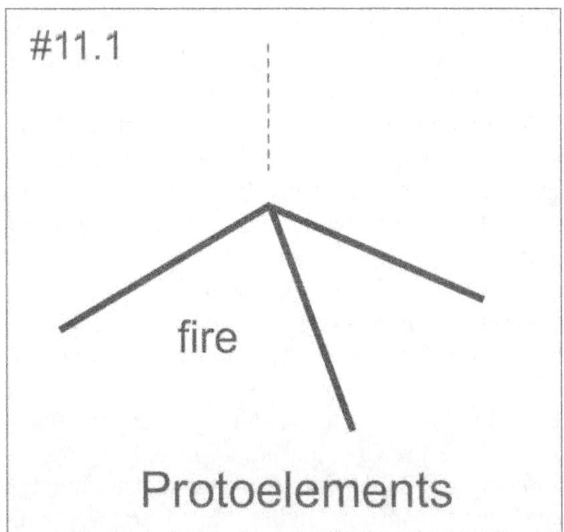

The protoelement fire's cardinal number is three and participates in the concomitant conjugation of the verbs *to direct*, *to transcribe*, and *to compose*.

Chapter 12

The Creation of Spirit

The term *Spirit* is one of the most severe cases of homonymy in the field of religious themes. Ambiguities in this sense pose problems, some almost insoluble, in trying to harmonize the various beliefs about its true meaning. Henceforth the term *Spirit* (first letter capitalized) will be reserved to refer to a creature constituted exclusively by the protoelement air, to whom the Bible situates in Genesis 1:2 as "hovering over the waters" (of the triad). The imposition of the formula Spirit (air) and fire on the primordial waters of the Creation is present in the four great religions, both in their Holy Scriptures and in traditions. It even figures preeminently in religion two, or Zoroastrianism. In fact, Yasna XLVII describes the righteousness of Spirit (air) and fire as a vehicle for the action of the divinity, in the chaotic context of the waters formed by the "confronted."

The becoming of creation has been of such nature that the triad *xyz* was the epicenter of important changes in its own course. For its part, the Spirit in heaven maintains its attachment to the initial conditions established by the Creator. In the Bible, the term *Ruach HaKodesh*, whose translation would be "Holy Spirit," appears a few times, one of them for example in the Psalms in a petition to God: "Do not keep me away from Your presence and do not take away from me Your Holy Spirit." Another appears in the book of Isaiah: "they themselves provoked wrath by afflicting their Holy Spirit, Who became their enemy...Where is He Who placed His Holy Spirit in their midst?" The term *Ruach* is interpreted as the breath of God, or wind, more frequently and will be easier to identify with the Spirit made of air. The Spirit appears in the Bible, sometimes as an impulse from God, sometimes with personal traits, and sometimes even as a personification of the divine.

In post-biblical Hebrew literature to this day, *Ruach* has been confined to the prophetic realm, almost always as a power whose purpose is to enable man to speak in the name of God and to perfect his ethical behavior. In a natural exegesis, where the Creation is considered a prophetic manifestation, *Ruach* would then be a faithful vehicle for God in determining the course of his Creation. Under the figure of divine breath, *Ruach* will be considered masculine. However, when *Ruach* (air) intervenes with the Man (earth), also masculine, both would form an object with feminine semblance, like upper waters. Being a word of feminine gender in the Hebrew language, *Ruach* should be understood as the breath of God in something, particularly in regards to Man.

In the Christian Bible, there are clear references to the Holy Spirit as the instrument of God in determining his Creation. In this sense, it is asked without question in the book of Wisdom: "Who can know the will of God if He does not grant wisdom and does not send His Holy Spirit from on high?" In the Gospels, God also works through the Holy Spirit and does it frequently. The most notorious intervention of the Holy Spirit is fecundating the Virgin Mary to give birth to Jesus, as Matthew explains, because of "Mary, mother of Jesus, being engaged to be married to Joseph. But before they lived together, she was found to be pregnant through the Holy Spirit." Luke adds the same: "The Holy Spirit will come upon Mary and the power of the Most High will cover her, so that the child that is born will be Holy and will be called Son of God." In the episode of the fertilization of Mary, the masculinity of the Holy Spirit is undeniable, and Jesus himself through John also implies it when he makes him to couple with water:

> ...there was an important man among the Pharisees named Nicodemus. He approached Jesus at night... and asked him: "How is it possible for a man to be born again when he is old?..." Jesus answered by saying: "I truly tell you that if the birth of a man does not come from the water and the Spirit, it is not possible for him to enter the kingdom of God. That which is born of the flesh is flesh and that which is born of the Spirit is spirit...The wind goes where it pleases, its sound comes to your ears, but you are unable to say where it comes from and where it is going, so it is with everyone born from the Spirit."

As previously noted, the Catholic Church incorporated the Holy Spirit proceeding from the Father and the Son into the formula of the dogma of the Holy Trinity. In this context, the Holy Spirit determines the endless succession of the always new in history or, if it is preferred, over time. In the Christian tradition, the doctrinal variants that attribute to the Holy Spirit a feminine nature have not been absent, especially in the early Judeo-Christian sources and in the Syriac ones that employed Aramaic and Syriac languages, both of which inherited the word *Ruach* from Hebrew. Based on this background, it would not seem strange that some Gnostic or Syriac Christianity considered the Holy Spirit a mother. The strange thing is that even the Father was described with breasts to breastfeed his creatures. The *Odes of Solomon*, written in the Syriac language at the beginning of the second century AD, is perhaps the greatest exponent of feminist doctrines in early Christianity. It describes the Holy Spirit uncovering her breast and mixing the milk from both breasts of the Father to offer its preparation to the world.

All tendencies aimed at an effeminate divinity or his immanent presence did not enjoy long life within the nascent church. Since women in representation of cosmic femininity were kept under observation by a growing number of influential figures, such as Tertullian, Origen, and Jerome (the fourth to the fifth centuries AD). The somewhat misogynistic attitude of some church fathers may have been due, in part, to the content of the first letter of the apostle Paul to Timothy, in which he said: "Let the woman not be allowed to teach, or dominate her husband, for she must remain in silence. For Adam was formed first, then Eve. And Adam was not deceived, but Eve was deceived and sinned." The last assertion certainly would not refer to those archetypal waters faithful to God, who manifests himself over and through them.

In the Koranic text, the Spirit of God is mentioned under two denominations: *Ruh al-Qudus*, whose translation would be "the Holy Spirit" and *Ruh-Allah*, or "the Spirit of God." In surah The Food, the Holy Spirit appears as a support given by God to Jesus and Mary when he mentions the favor dispensed to both by strengthening them. The Koranic quotations to the Spirit are enlightening; for example, surah The Dispute indicates that God has decreed faith in the hearts and gives them support with his Spirit. Clearly, according to the Koran, the Spirit is the instrument through which God determines the state of things in his Creation. Even though the Spirit of God has been the subject of intense exegetical debates, there has not been unanimity regarding the knowledge we can have of him. Like Jesus before Nicodemus, the prophet Muhammad also points out the limits to knowledge about the Spirit. This is what surah The Night Journey tells when it suggests answering to those who seek to inquire about the Spirit that "the questions of the Spirit are matters reserved to the Lord and only little knowledge has been given."

Precautions in approaching the subject of the Holy Spirit in Islam have not prevented some from identifying it with the archangel Gabriel, the source of Muhammad's prophetic inspirations. In support of this presumption, surah The Cow asks: "Who can declare himself an enemy of Gabriel for surely he descended revelation to your heart by command of God?" Similarly, surah The Bee describes the Spirit as an instrument in the service of revelation: "Say: The Holy Spirit has revealed it from your Lord with truth, with the purpose of identifying those who believe and as a guide and good news for those who submit."

Undoubtedly the subject can lend itself to endless discussions, especially when making emphasis in the details. The important thing is to retain the idea of a divine expression, whose realization according to the originating provisions determines from heaven the course of creation. Among the many things that humans can do, only those determined by the Spirit are realized. If so, God and his Spirit would then be extremely close to creatures, as clearly states surah Qaf of the Koran: "And certainly We have created man and We know what his mind suggests. For We are closer to him than his own jugular vein."

Chapter 13

The Creation of Iblis

Before considering the creation of Iblis in exclusively igneous terms, it is necessary to bear in mind the relevance of fire in ancient thought—particularly in reference to the context imposed by the other protoelements and their natural representations. Apart from its domestic and liturgical uses, physical fire was always feared as a manifestation of supernatural power. In fact, planet three, or Earth, has terrorized its inhabitants throughout the centuries for its frequent and sometimes catastrophic manifestations of igneous character. In the planetary context, the fire is confined or enclosed in the subsoil, while on the surface the earth and water dominate and above all is the air. This disposition is allusive to the protoelements and influenced decisively the formation of ancient myths and can be felt in the liturgies and the discourses of today's religions.

The Mediterranean basin, the cradle of western civilization and of its great religions, has always lived under the threat of igneous episodes of colossal proportions; the explosion of Santorini in the seventeenth century BC, which shook empires, and the mortifying eruptions of Mount Vesuvius are just two examples. One of those Mediterranean volcanoes feared by neighboring towns was Mount Etna, located on the island of Sicily, also known for its three capes. According to Roman mythology, Mount Etna is located on the forge of Vulcan, god of fire and consort of Venus (goddess of love, beauty, and fertility). The three Greek people who arrived on this island were the Elymians, the Sicels, and the Sicani, who called it Trinacria because of the triple geographic feature of the capes. Geology and history have been united so that one of the great symbols of the igneous activity in the Mediterranean was associated with a ternary morphology manifesting over the waters. According to Gaius Plinius II (the first century AD), the three Greek people adopted the triskelion as the emblem of the island, in recognition of its morphological features. After being used as a symbol of the island for centuries, the Sicilian parliament incorporated the so-called Sicilian triskelion into the flag of Sicily in February 2000. This symbol gathers some myths of antiquity in a three-legged triskelion. Figure 13.1 shows an illustration of the ternary symbol of the island of Sicily.

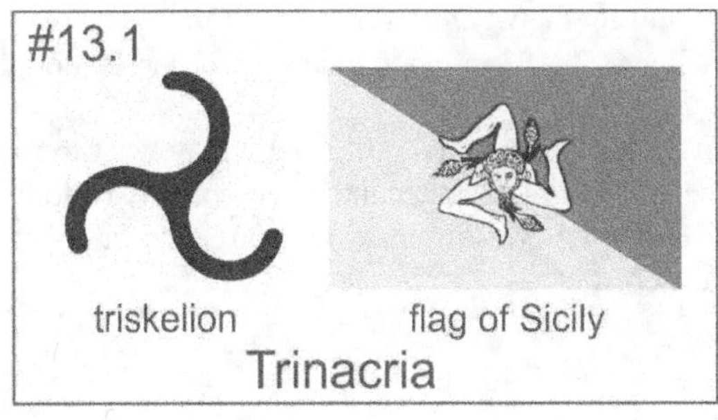

The associations of the igneous to the divine are not absent in the Bible. Even in Exodus III, God manifests himself to Moses through a burning bush. This episode stands out with the formula "God of Abraham, God of Isaac and God of Jacob." Notice there the immediate connection between the fire, the numbering of the chapter, and the triple reference to the patriarchate—particularly in relation to a man, whose name means "drawn out of the waters," as the book of Exodus explains. In total there are three appearances of the aforementioned formula in chapter 3 of Exodus and once more in chapter 4. In this way, the igneous formula, with its three aspects, appears as embedded in the four components of a 1-3 type odd basis.

Explicit references to the ternary aspects of fire are as rare in the Gospels as in the Bible. Only two evangelists, Matthew and Luke, mention the baptism of fire, in their third chapters, on the occasion of the baptism of Jesus with water by John the Baptist (the first century BC to the first century AD). In both stories, baptism with water is presented as a step previous to baptism in the Holy Spirit and fire. Also, the preeminence of the second over the first one is clearly stated. There is also a contextual relationship, since Matthew and Luke will soon be associated with water and femininity in the structural exegesis of the four Gospels.

Mentions of fire in the Koranic revelation are mostly related to suffering for opposing the will of the Creator. On rare occasions, it allows a glimpse of the ternary character of fire, as it happens in **surah** Those Sent Forth, where fire is described as a formation of three columns of smoke. The Koran also recognizes the igneous manifestation of God before Moses in **surah The Ant**, when a voice blesses the one who is in search of fire. The nature of the protoelement fire is a complex issue, with many references but little information, which is why it is advisable to treat the subject with caution. Apart from the difficulties, the Koran establishes in **surah Sad** that this protoelement is the substance from which the jinn are made, including Iblis, their maximum representative. God makes Iblis a coparticipant with the protoelement air of the essence of oddness by forming him with the protoelement fire.

The Islamic tradition (hadith, traditions and sayings of the prophet Muhammad) places the throne of Iblis on the waters, as it corresponds to an imposition of oddness over evenness. As the imam Muslim ibn al-Hajjaj (the ninth century AD) states, "Jabir reports that the messenger of **Allah** said that Iblis places his throne on water." In any case, Iblis is often described as the angel destined to fall by the weight of his own pride to become Satan, who also assumes the challenge of tempting humans in order to derail the course of creation.

The advocates of perennial philosophy may want to recall at this point the ancient Aztec god of fire (Xiuhtecuhtli) permanently residing in the midst of three stones—like in today's traditional Mexican home fires—framed within the four corners of the cosmos.

Chapter 14

The Formation of the Human Being

The human being to which the title of this chapter refers should not be confused with the biological human body, for in a person's physical nature and becoming, other creatures intervene besides God. The human being to consider from this point is the archetypal formulation of the 1&2 type or masculine&feminine, as it would be in the case of the composition of the masculine unitary protoelements air (Spirit) or earth (Man) with the lower waters of the triad (Woman), which represents the nature of the feminine (the words *Man* and *Woman* will have their first letters capitalized when referring to archetypes to differentiate them from their common usage). The composition of earth and water in the constitution of the human being is called "the flesh" in the neotestamentary literature. Regarding the fidelity toward God of human formulation, Jesus recommends through Matthew, "Watch and pray so as not to fall into temptation. For the spirit may be willing, but the flesh is weak." The reader will surely remember the basis of quaternary representation 1&1&2, where it is possible to represent together two formulations of the human being: the heavenly one, air&water; and the earthly one, earth&water. Being both formulations of ternary nature, each one of them lacks the capacity to represent in its totality an essentially quaternary cosmos. For this reason, everything pertaining to the entire cosmos, with exact representation on the ternary basis of the earthly human being, will be called "universe."

The conception of the human in terms of a couple with one odd masculine component (the Man) and one even feminine component (the Woman) goes back to the origins of civilization. In ancient Egypt, the same formulations prevailed, as can be seen in the ogdoads already mentioned—for example, those constituted by four male gods and their respective consorts. Given the possibility of representing each male power in an independent direction and its consort over two, it is useful to use the views of three pyramidal edges as seen from the ground to locate the four couples. In these views, the masculine components should be placed on the vertical edges in the middle, and the feminine ones on the two oblique edges at each side. In total it is possible to represent four couples, one for each prolongation of the diagonals of the basis. Such representations occupied a preeminent place in the Egyptian cosmogonies from the establishment of the first city-states of the lower and upper Nile.

In a scheme devised by the theologians of Hermopolis, for example, the creative act of Amun is framed in a total of eight primordial powers. Nun and Naunet form the couple of primordial water. Huh and Hauhet govern the primordial vastness. Kuk and Kauket are masters of the primordial darkness, and Amun and Amunet form the couple possessing the hidden power of the Spirit over the waters and the air. Figure 14.1 illustrates the pyramidal representation of the Hermopolitan Ogdoad.

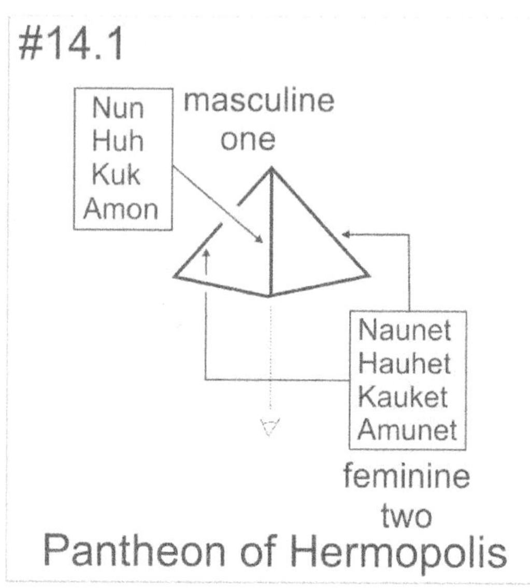

The city of Heliopolis, located in the delta of the Nile River, was the political capital of Egypt in prehistoric times. Later, Heliopolis became a religious and cultural center of great importance until the culmination of its long life in the first century BC, when it was gradually abandoned. In that city, from the twenty-seventh century BC approximately, resided the cult to the personification of the sun god under the name of Atom. According to Heliopolitan theology, Atom created himself from primordial water, called in this case Nun. The texts of the pyramids give glory to Atom and also to Khepri for engendering themselves and reigning over the radiant island. The Heliopolitan pantheon is constituted by an ennead, with Atom plus an Ogdoad of four gods, Shu, Geb, Osiris, and Seth, and their consorts, Tefnut, Nut, Isis, and Nephthys.

The Egyptians knew firsthand the reduction in weight of living beings when they died and dehydrated completely in the desert. The heat coming from the sun and delivered by the sands, plus the mechanism of water exchange with the dry air, constituted a natural version of the process of mummification. As it has been mentioned, the Egyptians used calcined sodium carbonate with the purpose of removing the water from its natural occurrence in living beings more quickly and to a large extent. It would not have been very difficult to notice a reduction in weight, tending to be about two-thirds of the total. In fact, in one-year-old infants, the proportion of water is almost exactly two-thirds, 66 percent, while in nonobese adults, the percentage drops to 60 percent, reasonably close to two-thirds, the same proportion of water in formula 1&2.

In the Hebrew Bible, the human formulation 1&2 has its roots in the relationship between God and his Creation, where the unicity of God is represented by the letter א (alef, the first letter of the Hebrew alphabet, whose numerical value is one) and accompanied by the waters, as suggested in the narrative of Genesis 1:1, which begins with the letter ב (bet). The book of Genesis tells how Man or the masculine component of the couple was created first from the dust of the earth, from which steam rose, whereas his consort was created later—hence her ordinal specification will be equal to second.

There are also numerous associations among water, Woman, and the binary basis in the book of Genesis of the Bible. An example is when patriarch Abraham sends one of his servants with a gift of commitment to Rebecca (the nineteenth to the seventeenth centuries BC), the future wife of his son Isaac:

> She was an extremely elegant woman, one of the most beautiful virgins and unknown to men. She descended to the spring and filled her pitchers with water…And the servant ran to meet her and said: "Give me some water from your pitchers." And she replied: "Drink my lord." Then, after the camels drank, the servant took a gold ring of 0.5 shekels of weight and two bracelets of 10 shekels of gold…

In the story, Rebecca provides water to the envoy and his camels before receiving the gifts. Water jugs and gifts to the fiancée of the second patriarch of the Hebrew people offer unequivocal references to a binary nature. The small ring symbolizes the "virtual cavity" of the Woman, with which she receives her husband within her bosom and the two bracelets (twenty times heavier), do reflect her binary condition. Another example appears in Leviticus, exposing a ratio of one to two in the periods of purification after the birth of a male or a female: "A woman, if she gives birth to a male, will remain unclean for seven days…and she must purify herself for thirty-three days…But if she gives birth to a female, she will remain unclean for two weeks…and she will purify herself for sixty-six days." In the absence of apparent biological reasons for such precepts, they would fit in an interpretation based on the formula 1&2 for the double measure in Women.

The Bible is not too explicit when it comes to precisely defining the nature of the human being. However, in an unexpected way, the book of Exodus introduces its formula in a cosmic context, in reference to the question of Moses on what should be his response to the people when they ask the name of God: "The Lord answered him: 'tell them: "I am who I am, sends me"'" The name of God in Exodus 3, "I am Who I am" or "I will be Who I will be" (in Hebrew *eh'ye asher eh'ye*) derived, with the passage of time, into the IHVH tetragram. The word *IHVH*, stripped of its vowels, has been unpronounceable since the destruction of the Second Temple (called by some the third) by Titus of Rome (the first century AD) in the year AD 70. It is presumed that the tetragram comes from the third-person conjugation of the verb *to be*, in Hebrew *HIH*. In any case, IHVH is representable on a quaternary basis, especially on those where both formulations of the human being, the heavenly and the earthly ones, converge. Figure 14.2 gives a quaternary representation of the name of God on a composite basis of the 1&1&2 type.

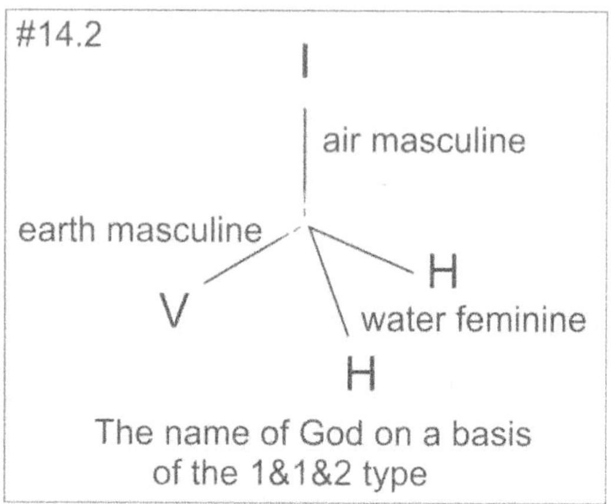

Apart from the quaternary representation shown in the figure, the wise cabalists permuted the letters in order to know the full name of God. The four letters *IHVH* give rise to twenty-four permutations ($24 = 4! = 4 \times 3 \times 2 \times 1$), where the two *H*s are considered different components in the same pair (chiaroscuro contrast). Cabalistic literature also affirms that the structure of the cosmos, in addition to its quaternary trait, is also triplicate, a question that was previously raised in relation to quaternary representations embedded by fire. Cabalists of Provence associated the content in Hebrew of Numbers 6:24–26, where it is written, "God bless you and keep you," "Make you shine His face in grace," and "Give you His approval and peace" with the name formed by the twelve letters *IHVH, IHVH, IHVH*. This provision was interpreted as an indication that the divine denominations consist of three groups of four permutable ones. They also thought that the groups and their names were similar to one another and that each one when permuted in twenty-four ways yielded a total of seventy-two. A figure present in Exodus 14:19–21 says, "…the angel was ahead…he then went behind and it came between the armies of Egypt and Israel…and the hand of Moses stretched out," which consists of seventy-two ($72 = 3 \times 24$) letters in the Hebrew language.

In the Bible, the couples formed by the three patriarchs and their consorts, Abraham and Sarah, Isaac and Rebecca, and Jacob and Rachel (the eighteenth to the seventeenth centuries BC) were all sterile. God had to come to the three Women, Sarah, Rebecca, and Rachel, in order to fertilize them to achieve patriarchal descent. In other words, the Bible explicitly states that the earthly human being (Man) is sterile and requires the intervention of the Spirit made of air for its determination. The masculine component of the earthly human being (Man) only directs possibilities and corresponds to the Spirit of the heavenly human being the respective determinations.

In the Gospels, there are no clear references to the dual nature of Women. There are only two quotes from Matthew and Mark, where Jesus speaks of the marriage union as "one flesh" that should not be separated. Humans are described as being formulated by the union of two parts and free to contravene the Creator's provisions when acting together. In the neotestamentary literature and in the Hebrew Bible, the ternary character of the human being is not only a cardinal one but also flows naturally from an ordinal provision. As indicated by Paul in his already mentioned first letter to Timothy, the masculine comes first and the feminine second.

It was mentioned in previous lines the presence of a metamessage in the quaternary structure of the Gospels. In this sense, recent analyses have focused on the matter of some shared material in two of the synoptics, Matthew and Luke, which is known as tradition Q (*Q*, *quelle*, "source" in German). While it is true that the three synoptic Gospels contain "common material," those of tradition Q (Matthew Luke) (water) have a greater proportion. In this way it is possible to discern two traditions, that of Mark and the Q tradition of the source, of the sayings. Thus the synoptics offer a representation of the earthly human being, with Mark as the protoelement earth, while Matthew and Luke represent water. Having made the previous observations, it is now worth pointing out the dialogue carried out between the Gospel texts and their own structure. The issue is put in evidence by the fact that Matthew and Luke are the only ones to mention the birth of Jesus of a virgin Woman. If the theological Gospel of John, representing the Spirit, is added to the synoptics, a configuration representable on a basis 1&1&2 is achieved. In this formulation, the sterile couple earth&water, formed by Mark&(Matthew Luke) and personified by Joseph&Mary, is present together with the agent for fertilization. Figure 14.3 illustrates the four fertilizations of couples, three patriarchal in religion one and one regarding Mary in religion three.

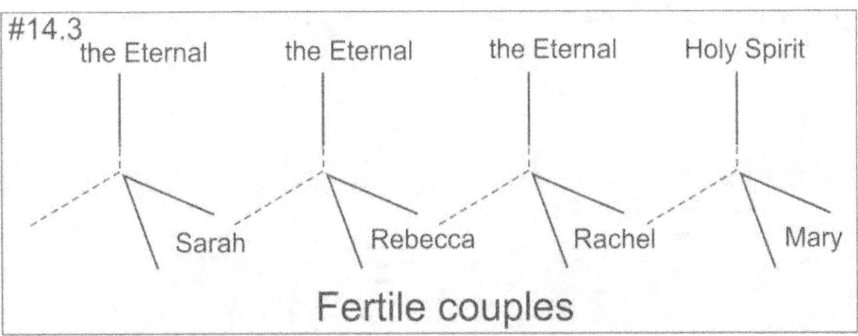

There are many mentions of the creation of Man in the Koran; in fact, there are so many that any superficial reading could be somewhat confusing. By focusing attention on the components used by God in that creation, the issue could be settled in many cases by interpreting the word *man* as "an earthly human being." For example, suwar The Rock,   The

Discrimination, The Romans, The Adoration, and The Believers mention the elements used in the formation of the human being. Among these elements are dust from the earth, moist earth in the form of clay, mud, and water.

As far as the creation of Women is concerned, **suwar The Women** and The Elevated Places endorse the thesis of the book of Genesis, according to which the Woman was created in second place. Interestingly, according to **surah The Cow**, when comparatively assessing Man and Woman, two Women are required to replace one Man: "And call two men to testify, but if there are no two men, then one man and two women…so if one is wrong the other will correct it." Similarly, **surah The Allies** reports a double retribution to Women: "Oh, women of the Prophet, whoever of you is guilty…the punishment will be doubled…And whoever of you is obedient…will be given a double reward."

The holy book of Islam is quite generous with the Virgin Mary, mother of Jesus of Nazareth, to the point of dedicating surah XIX ("Mary") to her. In its verses, it refers to her fertilization on the part of the Spirit of God:

> And mention Mary in the Book, when she moved away to a place in the east. So she covered herself with a veil. Then We sent her Our Spirit as a well-formed man and He appeared to her. She said: "I take refuge from you in the Beneficent, if you are one of those who guard against the devil." He replied: "I am only the carrier of a message from your Lord to give you a pure boy." She asked: "How can I have a child if no mortal has touched me, because I am chaste?" He answered: "It will be so. Your Lord says: 'It is easy for Me and We will make him an example and proof of Our Mercy.'"

One of the most exalted representations of the human formula in Islam is found in the dense symbolism hidden within the Kaaba. Inside, there are three columns holding the roof of the sanctuary, separated into two groups by a small altar. The column on the left when entering would represent divinity, while the two columns on the right symbolize his Creation as a consort. The interior layout of the Kaaba has been illustrated schematically in figure 14.4 for the benefit of readers.

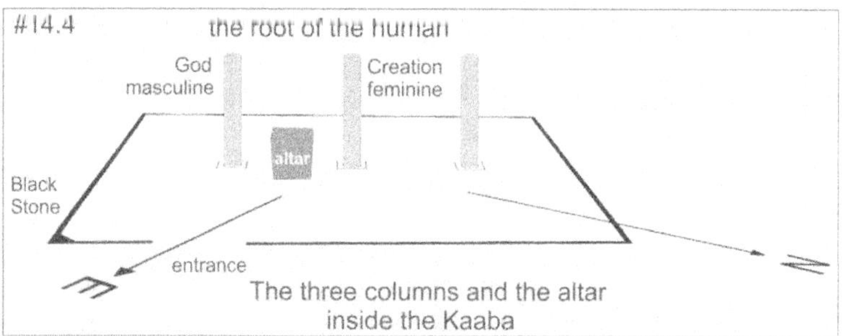

The quaternary archetype will only be completed when heavenly and earthly human beings agree on their ultimate goal. The failure to fulfill the quaternary symbolism in the design of the 9/11 attacks would imply that the Holy Spirit (*Ruh al-Qudus*) did not endorse a lesser jihad based on terror at that time. Figure 14.5 shows the four components involved.

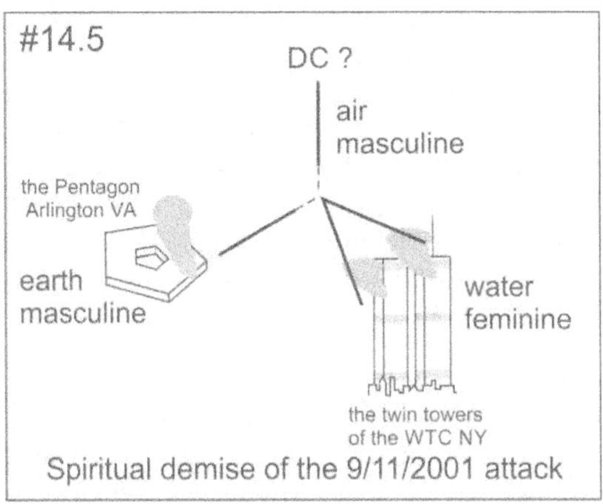

Also, there was a flaw in the airlines configuration running in parallel. The fact is that the pair of opposing (competing) airlines destined to hit the WTC correctly represented the lower or feminine waters in the triad, but those aiming at the Pentagon and DC (the upper waters or masculine ones) should have concurred instead of opposing each other.

The primacy of the masculine over the feminine was a constant in the ancient culture, and its extension to the biological and social level should be eliminated—just as feminist movements try to do, because the imbrications of all the odd and even archetypes in human biology would not justify it. One of the best examples of these imbrications is in the word אב —father in the Hebrew language—whose gematria is 2+1, similar to 1&2, our synthetic formula for the human being. This chapter has been a bit more extensive due to the importance to humans of their own archetypal formulation, because from their first representations they derive both their ability to perceive the universe and to act freely on it.

Chapter 15

The Sacerdotal Institution

Within the framework of the present natural exegesis, the sacerdotal institution is equal in importance to that of the human being, with which the union between masculine and feminine is consecrated. In the case of the sacerdotal institution, air and earth, or Spirit and Man, are composed in a joint performance at the service of the designs of God. In fact, priesthood establishes the necessary link to ensure coherence between the heavenly human being and his earthly counterpart. In the Holy Scriptures, it is posited as an interrelation whose purpose is to lead the Creation to its God. The four great religions of the People with the Book consider the priesthood a matter exclusive to the masculine, both in heaven and on earth.

In ancient Egypt, the sacerdotal institution reached a relevance rarely seen. Essentially, the pharaoh represented the divine in his unique and masculine figuration, just as his body did for the earthly counterpart of the former. There was, however, an exception to be brought up, as it helps to explain how the ancients viewed the joint realization of air and earth. The Theban theological movement would have justified the endowment of Queen Hatshepsut as high priest, giving prominence to the feminine semblance of the union of Spirit and Man (air and earth) (Thuban and Alnitak stars). Hatshepsut married her half-brother Thutmose II (the fifteenth century BC), who had a son from another union named Thutmose III (the fifteenth century BC). Because of the young age of the heir, Hatshepsut was first constituted as regent and later ascended to the throne.

Being in a leading position, Hatshepsut dedicated to Amun (the occult), the god of Thebes, two obelisks of pink granite covered with electrum (natural alloy of gold [Au, from the Latin *aurum*] and silver). One of those monuments still standing but stripped of its metallic ornament continues to witness the care taken by the sages of ancient Egypt in their plastic expressions of quaternary formulism. The obelisk of Hatshepsut, with its 29.6 m of height, was raised in the temple of Karnak (the name of the neighboring Arab village, al-Karnak). Fortunately for all, it still keeps an inscription at the base where the queen left testimony of her purpose: "From my palace I meditate on Who created me, my heart imposed on me to build for him 2 obelisks of electro…the 2 obelisks I have covered with electro and I dedicate them to Who created me, Amun…" In that period of the history of Egypt, the pharaohs in turn tried to show signs of greater devotion, beating their ancestors in the magnificence of their obelisks.

After the death of Hatshepsut, Tutmosis III finally ascended to the throne of Egypt and erased any trace of the queen except for the remaining obelisk. Even though it could have been knocked down, the pharaoh opted to keep it but surrounded it with a wall with the purpose of hiding the lower two-thirds of its total height (the proportion corresponding to water in the formulation 1&2)—all with the intention of expressing his rejection of the queen's pretensions in distorting the exclusively masculine character of the sacerdotal institution in ancient Egypt.

The Holy Scriptures are generous in references to the sacerdotal institution, and the Bible offers several models. On the one hand is the relationship of God with Abram and of him with Melchizedek (the nineteenth to the eighteenth centuries BC), the king of Salem and priest of the Most High God. Melchizedek received Abram, and:

> …he brought bread and wine and, after blessing him, said: "May the blessing of the Most High God, creator of heaven and earth, be upon Abram. And praise be to the Most High God, Who has delivered your enemies into your hand." And Abram gave him tithes of everything. And the king of Sodom said to Abram: "Give me the prisoners and keep the assets." But Abram answered the king of Sodom: "Raising my hands I made an oath to the Lord God Most High, creator of heaven and earth, that I will not take a thread or a shoe strap from you, so that you will not be able to say: I have made Abram rich."

In the aforementioned passage of Genesis appears the first reference to Jerusalem (citadel of Salim, the Syrian god of the setting sun), at that time a young city whose king was priest of the Most High (*El Elyon*), the God on high.

On the other hand, there is the relationship of God with Moses and Aaron (the thirteenth century BC), and of both among themselves, outlined in the book of Exodus and posed by the Lord in the following terms:

> Is not Aaron the Levite your brother? I know that he speaks well. And now he is on his way to meet you and he will be glad to see you. You shall speak to him and put words in his mouth. And I will be with your mouth and with his mouth and I will tell you what to do. He will speak for you to the people and will serve you as your mouth and you will be for him as God.

The quote extends the context of the sacerdotal institution to include God in the joint action of the Spirit and of the masculine component of the earthly human being (Man) for the cosmic realization.

In the Gospels, there are several references to the same scheme outlined by the book of Exodus. Perhaps the most eloquent is offered in the Transfiguration of Jesus on Mount Tabor, referred to by the three synoptics, Matthew, Mark, and Luke. In that episode:

> Jesus took Peter, James and John, his brother, to a high mountain. And he was transfigured before them. His face shone like the sun and his clothes became white as light. Moses and Elijah appeared talking to him… While he was still speaking, a luminous cloud covered them and

a voice from the cloud said: "This is my beloved son, in whom I am pleased, listen to him."

The narrative gives an account of the special relationship between God and Jesus and of Jesus with Peter (the first century AD), who answered the triple question, "Who do you say that I am?" Simon was designated by Jesus as the visible head of the sacerdotal institution in the Christian church for having answered:

"You are the Christ, the Son of the living God." Jesus then said to him: "Blessed are you, Simon, son of John, because that truth does not come from flesh or blood, but from my Father in heaven. And I tell you that you are Peter, and upon this rock I will build my Church and the gates of hell will not prevail against it. I will give you the keys of the kingdom of heaven and whatever you bind on earth will be bound in heaven and what you loose on earth will be loosed in heaven."

Figure 15.1 attempts to illustrate some relationships of the sacerdotal institution.

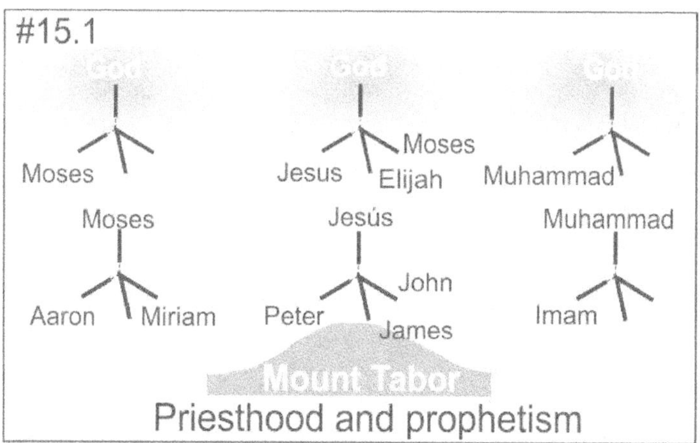

As John points out, the sacerdotal institution extends to Christian discipleship by subjection to God of all of his Creation. For Jesus proclaims himself as the vine and God the Father as the vinedresser when referring to the necessary dependence of the faithful or branches.

The Koran also raises the pooled character of the prophecy, the essence of the relationship between God and the prophets and with his representatives: "Our Lord! Raise up a Messenger among them to recite your verses and teach them the Book and Wisdom and purify them" (surah The Cow); "And We made them leaders who guided the people under Our command and We revealed to them how to do good, to keep the prayer and to give alms. And they only served Us." (surah The Prophets).

Chapter 16

Natural Representations

Up to this point, the quaternary bases have been used with the purpose of representing contextually some sidereal phenomena and also to relate in a coherent way certain religious concepts without apparent connection. Although the Holy Scriptures offer an inexhaustible reservoir in regard to quaternary formulations, it is also necessary to pay attention to nature—particularly when developing a natural exegesis whose main objective is to expose correspondences between the topics addressed by the Holy Scriptures and the objects of the study of science. Due to the exact representations of the archetypes of the Creation on quaternary bases, a wide range of possibilities in nature could be expected. For this reason, it is convenient to focus on some areas of interest, with a view to reinforce the heuristic value of the bases of representation explored up to now. An interesting area is the physiology of the human body, because its own observations are projected on the first representations on the underlying bases, and their actions are undertaken from them.

It will probably be useful to start with something simple, such as the physiology of vision in the three primary colors of a small portion of the electromagnetic spectrum. This spectrum is formed by a practically infinite number of frequencies, most of which escape the biological sense of sight. It is known that the eyes, more specifically the conical cells of the retina, have a normalized response to a ternary basis of three colors: blue, green, and red. In AD 1964, the Americans P. Brown (the twentieth century AD) and G. Wald (the twentieth century AD), at Harvard, and E. MacNichol (the twentieth to the twenty-first centuries AD) and W. Marks (the twentieth to the twenty-first centuries AD), at Johns Hopkins, demonstrated that each conical cell responds to one of three sectors of the spectrum. At the beginning of the 1980s, the American J. Nathans (the twentieth to the twenty-first centuries AD) discovered the genetic origin of the pigments responsible for the vision in three colors. The genes that produce the pigments responsible for the vision of red and green are found on the X chromosome. On the other hand, the pigment genes for the blue color are located on chromosome seven. In these terms, the perception of each of the three primary colors has a well-identified physical and sensory base. The correspondence is full since each color corresponds to a range of frequencies in the spectrum, and there is a cone type in the retina for each of them.

Coincidence in the time and space of light particles with frequencies associated with the three primary colors becomes a psychic impression in our brain corresponding to the white color. This color does not correspond to a sector of the electromagnetic spectrum since it does not have an associated frequency. There is no such thing as a single photon (particle or quantum of light) associated with the color white. In relation to the frequencies of the spectrum not covered by the human vision, there are practically infinite numbers of them. That is the case with frequencies below that of red and those above that of violet, all of them invisible to humans. In terms of a quaternary basis, it is possible to represent the visible colors on a triad, and the nonvisible frequencies on a separate but related unitary basis. Both would constitute a 1-3 type odd basis. Figure 16.1 illustrates the type of representation proposed.

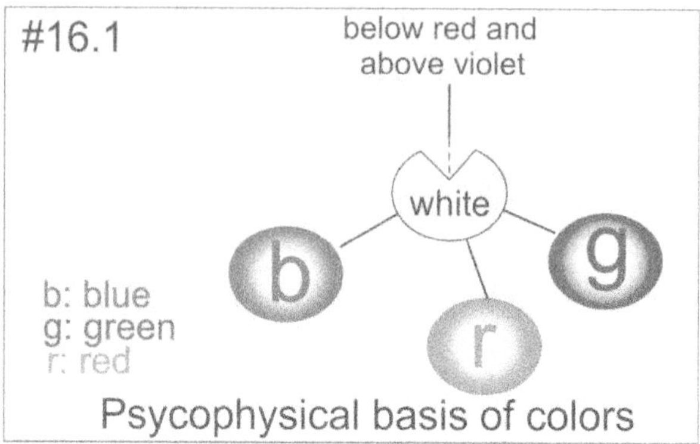

Human physiology is an inexhaustible source of configurations that can be represented on quaternary, ternary, binary, and unitary relatable bases. Relations of isomorphism between the representations on these bases and the archetypes of the Creation explored until now constitute the fundamental pillars of any exercise in natural exegesis. At the moment of interpreting the symbolic charge present in the physiology of the male and female human body, both will be considered as a whole. For this, it is enough to follow the formula of "one flesh" presented by Matthew and Mark, which bears a close parallel with the definition of the human being.

The biological separation of the sexes occurred in the Stenian period, about 1,200 million years ago, as attested by the first fossils of gametes and spores. Thus it cannot be considered a recent event, nor can it be argued that such separation anticipates the exteriorization of archetypes, which are characteristics of the sexual manifestations of the biological human body. It is up to the reader to decide if there was a plan or not.

From an organic point of view, the evidence points to a dimorphic human structure, particularly in relation to sex, where the formula 1&2 (earth&water or male&female) is expressed in several ways. An example of physiological representation of the 1&2 type in sexuality can be observed in the female reproductive organs. They consist of a virtual cavity to receive the male sexual organ, and two fallopian tubes for the migration of ovules coming from the ovaries. Figure 16.2 schematically illustrates the concept.

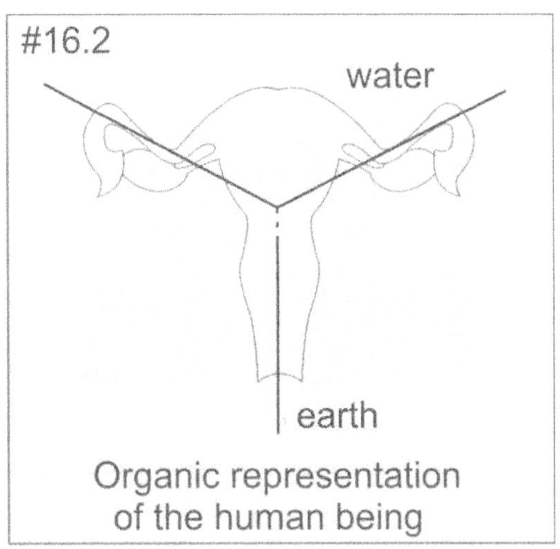

As usual, the protoelement water, associated with female sex, carries the notion of periodicity implicitly, in cycles or phases. Remember the permutation of the chiaroscuro contrast represented in the case of sex by the alternation of the ovaries in the ovulation of each menstrual cycle of twenty-eight days, almost exactly a lunar cycle. For men, there is no proper sexual cycle, and they remain fertile throughout their sexual lives until the climacteric stage is reached. The absence of periodicity, of phases or cycles associated with masculine sex, immediately brings to mind the mathematical concept of **divergence**. The biblical example par excellence of the masculine divergence is offered by Abram, who after leaving the house of his parents in Mesopotamia would never return to it. That nonreturn is conceptually the characteristic and contrasting feature of divergence, versus the recurrent character of rotational phenomenologies.

One of the most prospective areas in the search for natural representations of the formulation of human being is undoubtedly the biochemistry of sex. However, there are restrictions to addressing the issue deeply, as it is too broad and complex a study area. Sexual and reproductive activity in human biology begins with the gonadotropin-releasing hormone (GnRH), produced in the hypothalamus. The GnRH induces the production of the luteinizing hormone (LH) and the follicle-stimulating hormone (FSH) in the pituitary gland. The human chorionic gonadotropin hormone (hCG), which is also produced in the pituitary and by the fetus during pregnancy, completes the picture. Suffice it to note, however, that the fundamental hormones are four, and one of them, namely the GnRH, is determinant for the performance of the other three.

Fortunately, the mentioned hormones regulate others, not so complex, which are frequently cited by publications addressed to all audiences. However, even though they are practically of general interest, the chemical structures of these hormones could intimidate some readers. That is the reason why it is requested not to emphasize so much on the details of the illustrations and to stick to the simple observations that will be made. The first hormone to consider is testosterone, undoubtedly the best known among the governing hormones of male sexuality. It is mainly produced in the Leydig cells of the testicles, whose regulation is by the LH hormone. Its presence remains relatively constant, at levels dependent on the age.

If formula 1&2 of the human being has some predictive character, it would be expected that the corresponding female hormones would be of two categories at least, which happens to be the case. Among the female hormones are estrogen and progesterone. Of the three main estrogens, estradiol will be selected for its importance in the reproductive cycles, mainly due to the fact that estriol is a metabolite of estradiol and only reaches some relevance during pregnancy, while estrone becomes important during menopause. The same can be said of minor estrogens, whose omission detracts in no way from the following considerations. It would then be possible to represent testosterone, estradiol, and progesterone on a 1&2 basis, which will be left to the imagination of the reader. Both estradiol and progesterone intervene in successive and complementary phases of the women's menstrual cycle. This alternation would allow associating its binary nature with phases and cycles and to the permutations of the chiaroscuro contrast again.

Human formulations inscribed on the chemical structures of the sex hormones can be discovered by observing the functional groups in the four rings of their steroid structure. One of these groups is hydroxyl (–OH), and the other is a doubly bonded oxygen (=O). In testosterone, one of each is present, which could be interpreted as a representation of the sacerdotal institution. According to this interpretation, doubly bonded oxygen would represent the Spirit made of air and the hydroxyl group the component identified with the protoelement earth (Man). From a hydroxyl perspective, the testosterone&estradiol pair could be interpreted according to formula 1&2 as a natural representation of the earthly human being. Figure 16.3 shows on the left the aforementioned configuration corresponding to the earthly human being.

Representation of the human in sex hormones

However, the hormonal representation of the human formula is twofold, following the earthly and heavenly versions introduced earlier. Therefore, the testosterone&progesterone pair on the right of the figure shows a 1&2 formulation in terms of the three doubly bonded oxygen atoms representing the heavenly human being. For each female hormone, similar groups have different figurations, in what appears to be a reference to the binary attributes of the chiaroscuro contrast. The testosterone&estradiol pair, allusive to the earthly human being, is insufficient for a fertile reproductive cycle. In fact, estradiol activates ovulation, but the progesterone in the other pair, representing the heavenly human being, is responsible for establishing the conditions of the endometrium for fertility.

Another area of human body biology with a profuse symbolic language is genetics. In this area of science, figures such as the Englishman F. Crick (the twentieth to the twenty-first centuries AD) and the American J. Watson (the twentieth to the twenty-first centuries AD) have stood out, as have legions of talented scientists and organizations from many countries. Thanks to the contribution of all of them, it is possible to extend the scope of natural exegesis to that area of knowledge. The efforts have been focused on projects aimed at identifying and mapping physically, chemically, and functionally about twenty-five thousand genes present in the human genome. There have also been numerous attempts to decipher the genetic code in terms of the relationships between its nucleotide keys and the amino acids to which they are associated. Most of them have been made with the intention of discovering some encrypted content left there by superior intelligence as proof of its greatness.

The possibility of finding a written message in the genetic code is supported by the fact that only one-tenth of the human DNA (deoxyribonucleic acid) is genetically useful. Of the total of around six thousand million bases, the vast majority remain outside the synthesis of some sixty thousand proteins required in the regular functioning of the human body. Unfortunately, all attempts to find more than pure genetics in DNA have been unsuccessful so far. As far as the present work is concerned, there is not the slightest possibility of joining such a search. The only reason why the genetic issue has been touched here is to exemplify the use of the quaternary bases, particularly as basic tools to elucidate in the future the ways of expression of the archetypes of form in the biological chain of exteriorization/interiorization until/from the social and religious spheres.

The greatness and complexity of the DNA molecule motivated F. Crick to investigate if its origin could have been purely terrestrial and by chance. In fact, he spent a lot of time calculating the probability that life would arise on its own on planet Earth. His calculations indicated that the spontaneous emergence of life from a primordial soup was close to impossible, even from the one concocted by the Americans S. Miller (the twentieth to the twenty-first centuries AD) and H. Urey (the nineteenth to the twentieth centuries AD). The achieved results and his decided atheism induced him to propose the emergence of life on some other unknown planet with greater chances. Others before him had already suggested an extraterrestrial origin of life, such as the Greek thinker Anaxagoras (the sixth to the fifth centuries BC), who affirmed the presence of the seeds of everything everywhere. More recently the Swedish physicist S. Arrhenius (the nineteenth to the twentieth centuries AD) adopted the term *panspermia* from the German biologist H. Richter (the nineteenth century AD) to name his theory about the dissemination of life through outer space. According to the physicist, despite distances and emptiness, worlds exchange forces, matter, and even living seeds. In the midst of the Space Age, in AD 1973, F. Crick and L. Orgel (the twentieth to the twenty-first centuries AD) presented a controversial theory. The renowned researchers proposed that extraterrestrial beings of unknown origin carried out a "directed panspermia" on planet Earth. This theory was based on the universality of the genetic code and therefore on its infectious origin. In fact biological life might be seen as an infection of the Mineral Kingdom.

When it comes to dealing with the subject of genetic biochemistry, readers should be alerted about a greater degree of complexity in the next illustrations. Despite such complications, readers are advised not to get lost in the details and not to advance conclusions that are not relevant and just observe what is indicated by the text. The effort will be focused on identifying the possibilities of representing the DNA molecule and its constituents on quaternary bases, taking into account their chemical and biochemical functionalities. These considerations will also be extended to the messenger ribonucleic acid (mRNA), to the transfer ribonucleic acid (tRNA), and to the set of amino acids required for protein synthesis in the human body.

DNA is a complex molecule that is rolled and folded at several levels, until it adopts an external form called a chromosome. From different types of chromosomes, it is worth mentioning those that define the biological sex of man and woman, with the chromosome pair XY corresponding to the male sex and the pair XX to the female. The Y chromosome has about 50 million pairs of nucleotide bases, while the X chromosome has about 150 million pairs. The X chromosome follows a 1&2 formulation in the biological human couple according to the formula X&XX (X in the male and XX in the female). The Y chromosome could be considered a reference to protoelement air, figuring in a ratio of one to three with earth (50 to 150).

Extended, the DNA molecule has a helical structure where two similar strands are coupled, leaving space for an absent third. The grooves between the helical strands are of two types; there is a thin one of twelve angstroms (Å, an angstrom is 0.000 000 000 1 m) and another of twenty-two angstroms, where the missing helix could be located. The approximate ratio between the grooves is one to two. The two helices have been named after F. Crick and J. Watson and could be represented on the components of a binary base. The DNA molecule would therefore correspond to a representation of the protoelement water and could host a third component—for example, a representation of the protoelements air or earth. In such a way it could participate in both formulations of the human being. The helices are constituted by strands that act as a support for bases that are responsible for storing genetic information. The alternation of phosphate and the β-D-2'-deoxyribose linked on one side to the carbons 3' and 5' on the other give sense to the strands. It happens that both are antiparallel, according to the orientation of deoxyribose in each—that is, two modalities like chiaroscuro contrast. Figure 16.4 illustrates the antiparallelism of both DNA helices.

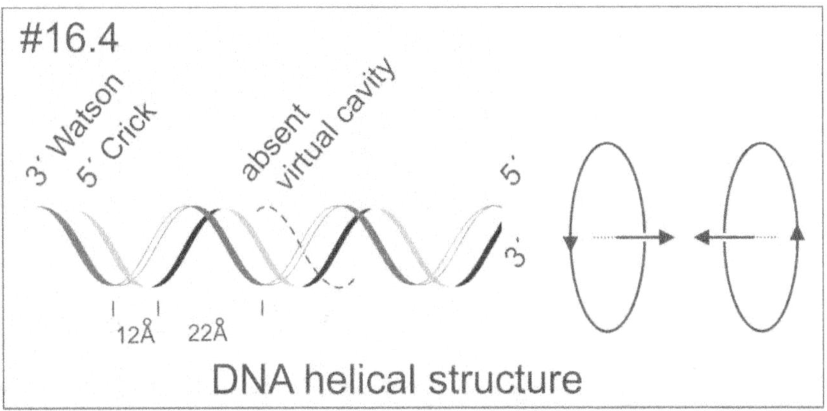

It could be argued that being both helices right and antiparallel, they would represent counterturns for a total equal to zero, an issue that happens to be a common feature of the waters. DNA can also adopt a left configuration in certain exceptional cases, which will not be discussed here, as the reader will be able to find meaning in the end. Nor will it be considered the interesting quaternary representations inscribed in phosphate and the β-D-2'-deoxyribose of the strands, in order to center the attention on the nucleotide bases of the genetic code.

One of the most remarkable features of the genetic machinery is the existence of two systems of four nucleotide bases. One of them stores the information in the molecule of DNA, while the other stores it in that of RNA. The base system of DNA consists of thymine (T) and three more bases, and the RNA system has uracil (U) instead and the same three bases, forming what we will call the twin tetrads. The structures of both systems will be considered succinctly, both chemically and biochemically, for the benefit of the reader. Thymine and uracil are similar molecules, whose differences can be represented on a 1-3 type odd basis, as shown in figure 16.5.

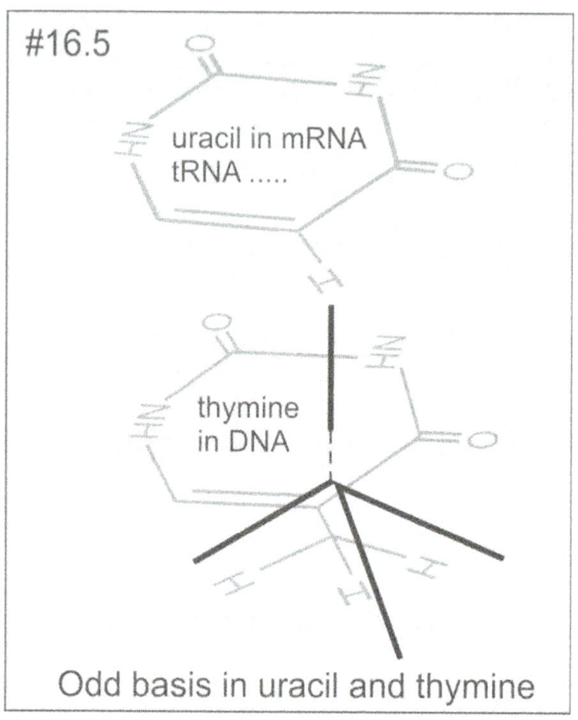

Where thymine has a methyl group ($-CH_3$) with three hydrogen atoms, uracil has only one (H). Incidentally, thymine with its ternary trait is present only in DNA, where the bases operate individually. By contrast, the uracil and its unitary hallmark appear in the RNA, where the bases operate in groups of three, called codons. The two nucleotide base systems would then be related, by means of cross representation of the 1-3 type. The RNA with uracil evolutionarily precedes DNA with thymine, and the step taken has been attributed to an increase in molecular stability. That stabilization was due to the substitution of one of the hydrogen atoms in the pyrimidine ring of uracil by the methyl group in thymine.

Chemically, the thymine and the three bases: adenine (A), guanine (G), and cytosine (C) can be represented on a quaternary basis of the 2-2 type, according to their structural similarities. Figure 16.6 below illustrates the case.

In this figure, it can be seen the four bases are grouped in two pairs according to the similarities in their chemical structures. The reader can observe one pair with one single ring, which is characteristic of the pyrimidines, and the other pair with two rings, the so-called purines. Each pair would represent one type of water—for example, the upper ones formed by thymine and cytosine, and the lower ones by the guanine and adenine.

The interpretation can go even further and can be conducted in different ways, of which an example is given below. Based on the chiaroscuro contrast of the waters, it is possible to identify with it the basic (N) and nonbasic (NH) nitrogen atoms inscribed in the rings (excluding the amino groups [–NH₂] outside the rings). Under the aforementioned interpretative scheme, there would be a representation of the lower waters in the cytosine, whereas in the thymine, there would be a representation of a semblance of the masculine upper waters (air&earth) (NH&NH), associable to the sacerdotal institution. A double 2-2 type formulation can be observed in the guanine, which is formed by the two pairs of basic (N) and nonbasic (NH) nitrogen atoms. In the case of adenine, a formulation of the 1&1&2 type is present, with a basic nitrogen atom (N) and a nonbasic (NH) one representing water and two additional basic nitrogens (N). The pair of basic nitrogen atoms (N) in adenine would represent another type of air and earth figuration. Both ways of representing the masculine waters will be interpreted later, when dramatic events that would reconfigure the Creation are considered. The amino groups ($-NH_2$) are present in three of the four bases—cytosine, guanine, and adenine—forming an igneous representation. Other interpretations incorporating double bonds and oxygen atoms are also possible but are left to the initiative of the reader.

While the chemical representation of nucleotide bases may be interesting from a systematic point of view, in practice the bases are genetically related in a different way. In the pairing of bases in the DNA molecule, the following biochemical pairs are established: thymine with adenine and cytosine with guanine, and vice versa in each pair (exchange thymine for uracil in the RNA). This pairing allows establishing another type of quaternary representations, as can be seen in figure 16.7.

#16.7

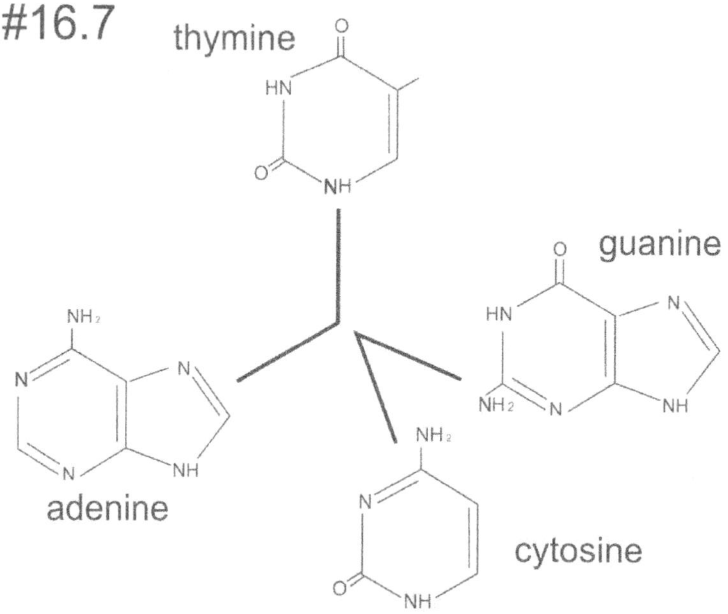

Biochemical representation of the nucleotide bases

The thymine adenine pair offers a confrontation between two ways of representing air and earth, with the water in between and whose interpretation is pending, as it has been indicated. In the guanine cytosine pair appear three different representations of the waters, corresponding to the totality of the lower waters.

The pairings of nucleotide bases in the DNA helices materialize by a link different to a chemical bond. Rather, it is the physical attraction of an electrostatic nature between the opposite charges of functional groups attached to the rings. The link in question is called a hydrogen bond, and as has already been said, it is fundamental in the macroscopic organization of chemical water and many molecules. The hydrogen bond is possible between molecules, where a proton (H) with its positive electrical charge can be attracted by a functional group with opposite or negative charge. In the bases of nucleotides, the opposite charges to that of the proton are present in the double-bonded oxygen atoms (=O) and the basic nitrogen atoms (N). Figure 16.8 shows hydrogen bonds in the ascending and descending helical strands of DNA, between thymine and adenine.

Double hydrogen bond
between adenine and thymine

The hydrogen bonds are illustrated by small diffuse clouds, distinguishing them from the solid traces indicating chemical bonds. The reader will observe a hydrogen bond of the type (O...H) and another one type (N...H), both are representable on a binary basis. In the pairing of cytosine and guanine, there is instead a hydrogen bond of the type (N...H) and two (O...H) bonds, which allows establishing a correspondence with the formulation of the human being. Figure 16.9 schematically shows the triple hydrogen bond in the guanine and cytosine pairing.

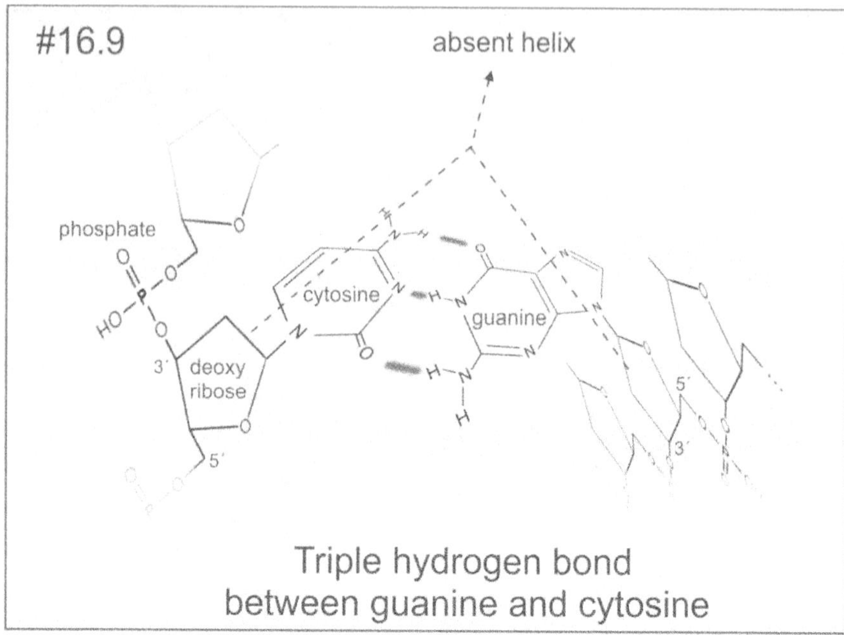

Triple hydrogen bond
between guanine and cytosine

The number of base pairs in human chromosomes ranges from about 40 million to approximately 240 million. The cumulative effect of hydrogen bonds then provides the necessary force to keep the two helices present in the DNA molecule firmly attached.

As anticipated, it is not very difficult to associate the double helix of the DNA molecule with the protoelement water in a macro context. However, that is not enough; it is necessary to place it in the context of the genetic machinery on a quaternary basis. It is known that the open space left by the absent helix allows the intervention of external agents in the processes of DNA duplication or transcription to produce mRNA. The process of deformation, separation, and transcription of DNA is carried out by a group of enzymes, such as topoisomerases, six families of helicase motors, and polymerases. At the moment of relating these enzymes with some protoelement, this would be air since it is responsible for the determination of all processes. However, the mentioned enzymes are not enough because ultimately they depend on other hormones, chemical agents, and even behavioral, environmental, and social factors to activate the aforementioned processes.

Given the fundamental characteristics, it is imperative to distinguish between the two types of processes: the duplication of DNA and the production of mRNA. Whereas both are indispensable and have invaluable symbolic implications, economic limitations require addressing only the role of mRNA in the initial phase of protein synthesis. In the mRNA, the uracil pairs with adenine, and the four letters of the genetic alphabet form words with only three of them. The whole process is structured around the following steps: In the first place is the double helix of DNA, in representation of the protoelement water, or mother. Then follows the fecundating determination of the process in charge of the RNA polymerase, and the product is the mRNA, or the advent of the son. Figure 16.10 illustrates schematically the mRNA transcription process, where the RNA polymerase untwists the double helix, enables transcription, and retwists.

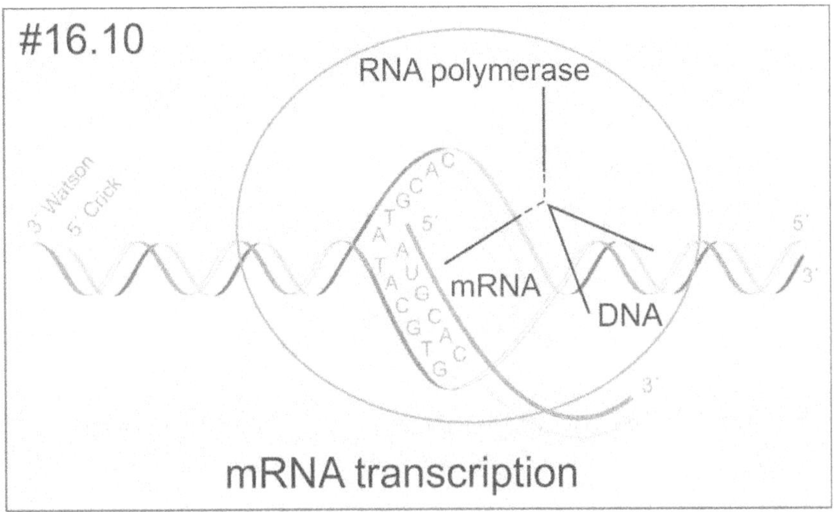

In eukaryotic cells such as those in the human body, mRNA is transcribed in the nucleus and then transferred to the cytoplasm, where protein synthesis occurs. For this, the mRNA is housed in the rRNA (ribosome RNA), where each group of three bases (genetic codon) of the sequence pairs with a variety of tRNA. Each tRNA containing the complementary bases enables protein synthesis at its other end. It is a case of variations with repetition of four bases of order three, and the total is calculated as 4^3 (4 × 4 × 4), which is 64. There are then 64 genetic codons formed by three bases taken from a set of four, and each of them is associated with one amino acid in tRNAs. The proteins to be synthesized are formed by linked amino acid chains, and the sequence thereof is encoded in the succession of codons of the mRNA. Figure 16.11 illustrates the process of translating the three base codons from the mRNA to amino acid, in the synthesis of a protein.

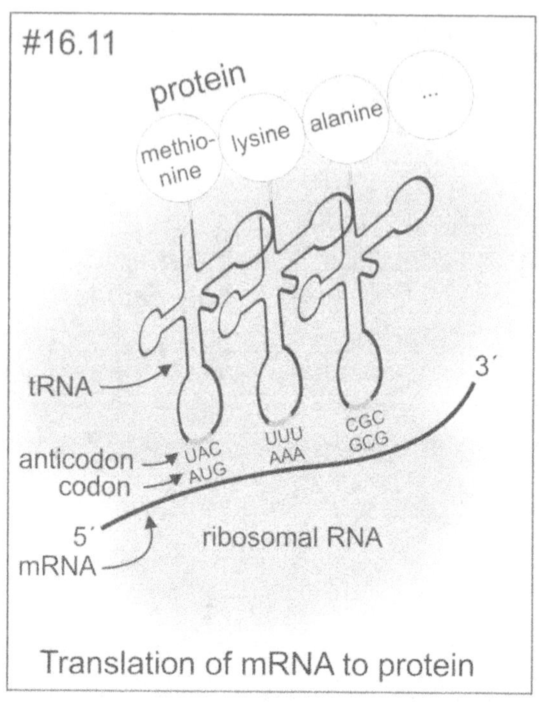

Translation of mRNA to protein

At this point, it is convenient to stop to mind the importance of this process in an effort to identify the archetypal exteriorization routes from their bases of representations. The occurrence of a genetic transcription mechanism operating with four bases, of which only three participate in the code of a codon, should be the subject of deep considerations. It could be considered a symbolic presentation of the role of ternary creatures within their quaternary cosmos, for purposes that transcend their own sphere of representation. The codon would be a stereoscopic window limited to three independent directions by which to observe and act partially upon a supra-stereoscopic cosmos—all this in order to penetrate into a realm not only represented by the synthesis of proteins but also by its exteriorization toward the performance of living beings, with humanity in its entirety acting as a limit in the first instance, including its expression in the social and religious spheres.

The sixty-four existing codons only generate twenty-one amino acids, almost exactly one-third, which points to the proportion of the masculine in the formulation of the human being. The other two-thirds of the total is redundant and produces nothing different, which is characteristic of the archetypal female component. In connection with the figures mentioned, it should be kept in mind that the Hebrew alphabet consists of twenty-one letters, excluding the first א (alef), which would represent the transcendent unicity of God.

In the window of the codon, three typical situations arise, corresponding to the three ways of being three that are observable in the Creation: the three bases of nucleotides are the same, one base of nucleotides differs from the other two equal to each other, and the three bases of nucleotides are different. The first of them corresponds to a representation of the protoelement fire, the three interdependent. The following way of being three can be associated with the formulation of the human being in all its manifestations, whereas the last mentioned represents the "triplicity" of protoelement earth, where the three are mutually independent like, for example, in the triad *xyz*.

Thus concludes this brief dissertation aimed at demonstrating the use of quaternary bases, with a view to representing concepts and natural realities eventually relevant to a natural exegesis of the Holy Scriptures. Readers will have noticed that in this chapter, examples of representations of objects studied by physics have not been offered. The main reason behind such a procedure is that much of the following effort will focus on discovering the descriptions of those objects in the Holy Scriptures.

Before leaving this chapter and for the benefit of the reader it is necessary to make some clarifications on the use of the terms *masculine* and *feminine*, *man* and *woman* all along this book. The terms *masculine* and *feminine* were chosen because they have sexual and gendered connotations and therefore can be used to describe both, albeit in an imperfect way. Archetypal protoelements were described previously in terms of their masculine (active) and feminine (passive) essence, even though they do not have sex or gender but they couple and have characteristic protobehaviors.

Some events, analyzed in the following chapters, fragmented part of the archetypal structure and opened the way for diversity, imbrication, and archetypal sodomy, which in turn blurred the sharp differences of their original essences. The derived complexities of biological individuals have also paved the way for many combinations, as happens, for example, for sexually defined genetics in the context of hormonal and physiological imbalances. Thinkers of antiquity also helped to make things worse when using terms like *masculine water*, meant to contrast pairs of components with concurring actions from the feminine ones, where they oppose one another.

Social power structures and performativity also influenced gender evolution, as *gender theory* post-structuralist authors like M. Foucault (the twentieth century AD) and J. Butler (the twentieth to the twenty-first centuries AD) demonstrated. However, judging by the ongoing critique, *gender theory* has a long way to go before it can deliver a conceptual framework satisfying the majority and minorities of individuals. *Gender theory*, as it stands today, makes a marginal contribution to the bridging of the divide between religion and science—the main goal of this work— and will not be dealt with in the following chapters. The reader should consider the terms *masculine* and *feminine* in this book to apply to every active and passive instance in the unfolding of Creation.

Chapter 17

From Unicity to Multiplicity

Arguing in favor of the concept of divine unicity and accommodating it with the prevailing multiplicity has not been an easy task. Particularly when the Holy Scriptures present God speaking in the plural, perhaps, according to some, in order to emphasize his majesty and magnificence (*pluralis majestatis*). To address the issue of the origin of multiplicity, some efforts in the mystical and philosophical spheres of the four major religions will be brought up. Some of the proposals evoke the tetractys of Pythagoras (the sixth to the fifth centuries BC) and their four numbers generating the decade (10 = 1 + 2 + 3 + 4). However, the decimal cosmogonies precede the Greek philosopher, and their origin is difficult to determine.

The first documented controversies on the subject within the Hebrew religion occurred shortly after the destruction of the temple of Herod the Great. As a result of that tragic event, the abandonment of the land given in inheritance to patriarch Abraham began. But not all was destruction in the first century AD because, along with social and political instability, an important effort was taking shape over time to consolidate the Hebrew religion. Paradoxically, the disappearance of the state helped strengthen this religion until it became the support of a new type of identity. Although the origins of this process go back to the reading of the Bible, its interpretation reflected the need to adapt it to the changing demands of time. This effort of adaptation led inevitably into controversies between the Pharisees (community of Hebrews) and the Sadducees (descendants of Zadok [the tenth century BC], High Priest of King Solomon [the tenth century BC]), both in the leadership of the state and in religious matters. That division was extended to scholars from the school of the pairs (Zugot). This school succeeded the scribes (Soferim) in the custody of religious orthodoxy. In it, each pair of masters occupied the first two positions of the council (Sanhedrin), that of patriarch (*nasi*) and that of his substitute (a*b bet din*). The last of the five pairs of scribes was made up of Hillel the Elder (the first century BC to the first century AD) and Shammai (the first century BC to the first century AD), whose doctrinal discrepancies were legendary.

During the siege of Jerusalem, one of the disciples of Hillel the Elder, named Johanan ben Zakkai (the first century AD), managed to escape. Once free, he obtained permission from the Roman authorities to establish a center for religious studies in Jamnia, today Yavne in Israel. There the Pharisaic tradition flourished again with absolute control of the council, giving rise to the rabbinic Judaism of the school of teachers (Tannaim). Thanks to that effort, the canon of the Hebrew Bible was definitively established, the religious calendar could be calculated annually, and the precepts and the religious rituals were regulated. The merits of the work of ben Zakkai made him honored with the title "our master" (rabban), an honor he shared with some descendants of Hillel the Elder, who followed him as head of the council.

Reflections on the Scriptures and oral traditions over the centuries were compiled by Tannaim and poured into a voluminous text called "study and repetition" (Mishnah). After the first efforts of Akiva and Ishmael (the first to the second centuries AD), the Mishnah could finally be edited by Yehudah ha-Nasi (the second to the third centuries AD) at the time of the revolt of Simeon Bar Kokhba (the second century AD). The Mishnah was complemented with a collection of comments and sayings called Gemara, whose origin and relationship with the first have not been fully elucidated. Both compendiums constitute a vast work called the "study" (Talmud), which served as a reference to Hebrew scholars well into the modern age. In its vastness, the Talmud includes three major themes: the interpretation of the Holy Scriptures (Midrash), the law and commandment of the Hebrew tradition (Halakhah), and the history of Israel (Aggadah). Until shortly after the death of Yehuda ha-Nasi, in the year AD 217, the school of Tannaim formed six generations of students. In parallel, this effort was disseminated to the academies of Tiberias, Sepphoris, and Caesarea in Judea and to those of Nehardea, Pumbedita, and Sura in Babylonia.

At the heart of the academy, not all interpretations of the Holy Scriptures were coincidental. The controversies were of the most varied nature, both on midrashic and halakhic themes; interesting above all were those centered on God. In this respect, two accurately delineated positions were considered irreconcilable judging by the content and intensity of the debates. Followers of Hillel the Elder affirmed the absolute transcendence of God, while those of his rival, Shammai, elaborated on his immanence. For the school of Hillel (Beit Hillel, the House of Hillel), God would have created a cosmos without intermediation, governed by a set of laws, and everything about its evolution could be eventually be rationalized. The human being would fully exercise his free will and be responsible for his actions in that same measure. According to the school of Shammai (Beit Shammai, the House of Shammai), God created an intermediary power, the Torah, with which he actualized his immanent presence in his Creation. Therefore nothing could ultimately be the object of reason, because in the end we would always stumble upon his inscrutable design. Human beings are free to choose but must have the consent of God to realize, both good and evil. The controversies contributed to maintaining the tension between those two ways of conceiving God, characteristic of the Hebrew Religion, search without rest for a point of equilibrium.

Zoroastrianism is, in essence, a fundamentally monotheistic religion whose god Ahura Mazda is unsurpassable and in the end will prevail. However, the cosmos goes through a period in which divine supremacy is disputed by an entity that distorts the meaning of his Creation, Angra Mainyu. The opposition of both powers stages a dualism whose preeminence constitutes the feature by which Zoroastrianism is known. Even in that dualistic context, there is room for a decimal progression, as can be seen in the Yasna XI of the Zend-Avesta, which is dedicated to the Haoma offering (Soma, a god and also a hallucinogenic Indo-Aryan drink). This text presents a development in which the one is deployed progressively to reach a decade.

On the Christian side, the incipient and unfinished Trinitarian approach of the first centuries was propitious for all sorts of ramblings by emanationists. One of the first to devise a scheme with a strong inclination toward emanationism was Basilides (the second century AD), the first gnostic of Egypt. According to the Alexandrian thinker, the unknowable God in his first and highest expression is Abrasax (or, according to some Latin translators, Abraxas), sovereign of the first heaven. In space-time succession, 365 angels with their respective heavens would come, in what is naturally expressed by the days of the year. The angel of the last heaven was, according to Basilides, the Hebrew God and creator of the world under his dominion, in terms exposed by the book of Genesis of the Bible.

For Ptolemy the Gnostic (the second century AD), instead the Creation would begin with the conception of the only begotten intellect in the bosom of the unknowable God. From the intellective process proceeds its exteriorization as a salvific expression, enabling the return to God of his entourage (pleroma). The only begotten from God the Father embodies in his interior the multiplicity of thirty eons, from the Logos to Sophia. The disorder, caused by Sophia when wanting to unite with the Father, would have degenerated into the formation of amorphous matter. The divine intellect, acting in a natural way, expels the disorder from the amorphous matter giving origin to the created universe—all this to act spiritually on multiple perfections in order to direct the return toward the Creator. The cross of the savior in the pleroma marks the most distant point and the beginning of the return to the source.

Apart from the gnosis of the emanationists, there were skirmishes between philosophers and theologians to sow the seeds of ones in the territory of others. The result of these maneuvers was a set of doctrinal variants, where thoughts as dissimilar as Neoplatonism and Christian theology seem to have been born for each other. An example of this coexistence occurs in the *Corpus Areopagiticum*, a work attributed to a Christian versed in Neoplatonism who would have lived between the fifth and sixth centuries AD. The theology of Pseudo-Dionysius the Areopagite refers to a first transcendent principle, immutable and separate from everything. A second principle emanates from the first, with the mission of returning to the original source. In synthesis, the divine activity is of a cyclical nature and is governed by unions and distinctions leading to multiplicity. God is the light illuminating other beings according to gradations of hierarchical types and whose union in love integrates them to the supreme unity. Despite its early influence, proposals made by emanationists were relegated to oblivion as the Christian dogma of the Holy Trinity came to dominate the scene.

One of the first and most remarkable attempts in Islam to explain the passage from the unicity of God to the multiplicity was by al-Farabi (the ninth to the tenth centuries AD). Latinized Alpharabius, the thinker of Turkish origin, born near Farab (Turkmenistan nowadays) was able to give a decisive turn to Islamic philosophy. Its influence attenuated the Aristotelian predominance incorporating without mentioning it, the Neoplatonic doctrine of emanations from a divinity from whom would proceed the existence of everything else. The one God in the Farabian scheme is the first cause of being; al-Farabi is distinguishing himself from Aristotle, who only recognized the existence of a first mover. Such a turn would have had its origin in the teachings of his Christian masters, who were versed in the thought of John Philoponus of Alexandria (the fifth to the sixth centuries AD). In his critique of Aristotle, the Alexandrian philosopher had proposed thinking in something other than movement to start the causal chain.

The one God of al-Farabi is an intellect in full action when he thinks of himself and by this thinking creates a new being, the first intellect. This new being already has two things to think about; the first is obviously to think in the one God and the other of himself. When he thinks of the one God, he creates a second intellect; whereas when he thinks of himself, he creates the first celestial sphere which is the first rotor of the orb. With successive repetitions of thinking in the being to which they owe their origin and in themselves, ten intellects and nine rotors, plus the sublunary sphere, are progressively generated. The tenth intellect or agent intellect concludes the progression, which gives being to the cosmos and makes it an intelligible object. The sublunary sphere where humans live is then generated when the agent intellect thinks of him. He identified the first sphere with the dark sky behind the visible fixed stars, the empyrean. His darkness represents our inability to understand two things: on the one hand, what he thinks of himself who is, what God thinks of himself; on the other hand, the same darkness would also represent the antecedent of the great event of the advent of the being. The decimal character of the Farabian philosophical approach is by no means original, since among the thinkers of antiquity, the cosmogonic proposals inspired by said number abounded.

Despite innovations introduced by the Farabian cosmogonic scheme, only a handful of followers are known. In fact, the fame of al-Farabi was due to his influence on Ibn Sina, another great name of the Islamic philosophy already mentioned. Known in the medieval west under the name of Avicenna, the Persian thinker came from an influential family that knew how to give him a conscientious education. His father, a fervent Ismaili (followers of Isma'il in the Shia) leaning toward the Fatimid cause (followers of the descendants of Fatimah [the seventh century AD] [daughter of the prophet Muhammad] and **Ali ibn Abi Talib**), came to occupy the position of governor in a village near Bukhara, cultural center of the Samanid dynasty. The ascendancy of the family in the Samanid government to some extent surprises, given the Sunni zeal of those rulers. The Samanids were descendants of a family of Zoroastrian priests with deep roots in the Persian culture, to which they also gave great impulse. So, from his childhood, Ibn Sina had the opportunity to get to know the Sunni and the Ismaili Islam as well as the jewels of ancient Persian tradition.

The Avicennian cosmogony is based on an intellectual process initiated by an eternally necessary being. The intellectual activity of this necessary and eternal being generates a chain of beings also of an intellectual nature but not necessary by themselves, owing their existence to the first. The chain of beings not necessary by themselves is then a chain of beings barely contingent. However, the created intellects are, in addition to contingents by themselves, also necessary because the necessary and eternal being gives them that condition, which they can transmit. It follows, then, that the long chain of beings hardly contingent on their own—that is, of all those who may not have existed—must necessarily have some beginning. Otherwise, it would never have come into existence. That principle, to which all owe their existence, cannot also be contingent but must necessarily exist.

The first intellect emanating from the eternally necessary being then has three things to think about, while that of al-Farabi had only two. The first archangelic intellect whose creation occurs when the one God thinks of himself acquires knowledge, first thinking about the being to whom he owes his origin. Second, he gains new knowledge when he thinks of himself as being necessary by virtue of his principle. Finally, he achieves a third form of knowledge when he thinks to be contingent. While performing the triple activity, it gives rise to a second archangelic intellect, to the angelic soul of the first celestial sphere, and to its material body or first celestial rotor. In this case, the first rotor corresponds to the black sky behind the fixed stars. From then on, the process follows as in the decimal scheme of the Farabian cosmogony until completing the nine spheres. With the descent in scale, the possibilities of continuing to generate new intellects run out. Thus the tenth archangelic intellect can only generate the multiplicity of human souls and the sublunary sphere of temporal contingent beings.

According to the Iranian thinker S. Nasr (the twentieth to the twenty-first centuries AD), Avicenna understood the different branches of scientific knowledge as an exercise of exegesis of the great text of the reality of the cosmos. He left a deep impression on the philosophical and scientific rebirth of medieval Europe. He was also widely recognized for his medical work, which enjoyed great popularity well into the seventeenth century AD. Even in present days, his medical texts continue to be used by Islamic practitioners in the Indian subcontinent. Emanationism in his philosophical thoughts and cosmogony represents a synthesis of Aristotelian-Neoplatonic style of great originality. It would be unfair, however, to simply catalog his philosophical work and ignore his remarkable efforts to assimilate them into the Koranic tradition, as well as his reflections of a mystical character. His works were translated into Latin by several translators, among them Gundissalinus, contributing decisively to the Aristotelian renaissance in medieval Europe and to the diffusion of his philosophical thoughts.

Criticism against the Avicennian thought was not long in coming; the most caustic of all came from the French theologian William of Auvergne (the twelfth to the thirteenth centuries AD). The bishop of Paris rejected the fact that God worked out of necessity, that the cosmos was coeternal with him—a creation in charge of intermediaries and above all the content of his "angelology" (study of the angels). However, like many theologians critical of Avicenna, Islamic and Christian, he appropriated in part the Avicennian philosophy of being—particularly in regard to the identification of the essence of God with his existence, which was an issue that important discussions focused on. Apart from criticism, Avicenna exercised a notable influence among the great theologians of medieval Christianity, such as Albert the Great (the twelfth to the thirteenth centuries AD) and his disciple Thomas Aquinas. The latter borrowed from Avicenna the distinction between evil and wrongdoing and two proofs about the existence of God. The first proof related to the efficient cause, and the second was based on the contingency of the beings. However, the Christian philosopher also rejected some ideas of Avicenna about God and his relationship with his Creation, especially the coeternity of both.

Among the thinkers born of the Aristotelian renaissance on the Iberian Peninsula, who were concerned with accommodating the divine unicity with observable multiplicity, the Hebrew Moses ben Maimon (the twelfth to the thirteenth centuries AD) stood out. The Sephardi came from a family with religious roots and had the opportunity to be educated in the rabbinic sciences by his own father, ben Joseph (the twelfth century AD). The difficulties arising from the Almohad conquest forced the family to pretend its conversion to Islam and later to flee from Cordova. After leaving Andalusia, the family group emigrated to Fez when the young ben Maimon was just over twenty years of age. There, in Fez, still under the Almohad rule, ben Maimon established a close relationship with the great Talmudist Judah ha-Cohen ibn Sosan (the twelfth century AD), who was to inspire him. Finally he went to Palestine and later to Egypt, where he settled definitively. The work for which he has been placed among the great thinkers of all time is his *Guide for the Perplexed* (*Dalalat al-Hairin*), later translated from Arabic into Hebrew with the title *Moreh Nevukhim*. In defense of the unicity of God, the Sephardi maintained that in God, one from every point of view, no multiplicity should be admitted, nor can it be added to his essence. He thought that the great diversity of divine attributes with which God is qualified in the Scriptures had to do with the abundance of his Acts and not with his essence. For ben Maimon, then, the origin of multiplicity in the Creation derives from the different ways of acting by only one God.

During the twelfth century AD, the mystical current of the cabalists flourished among the Hebrews of Provence, who focused their discussions on the great themes exposed by the Holy Scriptures. Among the most prominent topics of discussion were the "work of creation" (*Ma'aseh Bereshit*) and the "work of the chariot of the glory of God" (*Ma'aseh Merkabah*). They also studied in depth the symbolism of the Hebrew alphabet, its numerical values (whose study is known as gematria, from the Greek *grammar* [*grammateia*], or perhaps remotely *geometry*) and the cases of numerical synonymy (association of words based on their numerical value more than by their etymology). But perhaps the theme for which they are best known is the doctrine of the ten Sefirot of the *Book of Formation* (*Sepher Yetsirah*), which would date from the period between the third and sixth centuries AD. Regarding this doctrine, the cabalists extended beyond the numerical meaning associated with each Sefira, speculating fully on aspects related to their essences. In the context of a dense amalgam of symbols, the existence of the one God was considered to be residing in the entourage of the plenitude of his Sefirot. The doctrine of the Sefirot originally derived from the ten sayings of God as Creator in the book of Genesis: "And God said," (Genesis 1:3, 1:6, 1:9, 1:11, 1:14, 1:20, 1:24, 1:26, 1:29, and 2:18). Some of the eternities, or Sefirot, were identified with certain components of the work of the chariot of the glory of God (as described by Ezekiel) and with key elements in the narrative of the book of Genesis. Nonetheless, the cabalistic efforts showed a great deal of dispersion in their form of presentation, where elements of diverse origins coexisted. Many of these elements were foreign to Hebrew beliefs, which undermined their coherence with previous traditions.

In relation to the ten eternities, the eternities were usually divided into three and seven—three because according to the *Book of Brightness* (*Sepher HaBahir*), the holiness on high is three by three. Next to the letter א (alef), representing the separated unicity of the Creator, there would be the three praising the Lord with the "Holy, Holy, Holy," leaving then seven sayings. Cabalists of that time used to follow the order of the last seven Sefirot, according to the first book of the Chronicles: "Yours, O Lord, is the greatness and the power and the glory and the victory and the majesty. For all that is in heaven and on earth is yours. Yours is the kingdom, O Lord..." According to that order, and placing in parentheses the names with which they were later designated, we have greatness (*Chesed*), power (*Gevurah*), glory (*Tiferet*), victory (*Netzach*), majesty (*Hod*), all (*Yesod*), and kingdom (*Shekhinah*). The seven Sefirot emanated from an upper triad of *Kether* (crown), *Hokhmah* (wisdom), and *Binah* (intelligence), around the inaccessible reality of Ein-Sof, the cause of causes absolutely transcendent.

The environment in Narbonne at that time was certainly not amenable to continuing with the development of the Kabbalah. In fact, despite the decree of protection issued at the beginning of the thirteenth century AD, the Hebrew people were heading toward their expulsion. Thus, after more than seven centuries of continuous presence in Provence, the Hebrew people were finally banished in AD 1306. Among the most prominent scholars of Provence before that tragic end were Abraham ben Isaac of Narbonne (the twelfth century AD), his son Abraham ben David (the twelfth century AD), and his grandson, nicknamed Isaac the Blind (the twelfth to the thirteenth centuries AD). There is consensus in considering Isaac the Blind the most influential and in a strict sense perhaps also the first cabalist of Provence. The master contributed decisively to establishing the doctrine of the Sefirot, with the purpose of approaching the theme of the divine transcendence and the origin of multiplicity.

While the mystic schools of Provence began to decline, others were gathering pace in Catalonia, particularly in Girona. The political link between Catalonia and Provence until the crusade against the Cathars (Albigensians), at the beginning of the thirteenth century AD, favored exchanges of a cultural and religious nature among Hebrew communities. The first cabalists of Girona were influenced to a large extent by Isaac the Blind, Moses ben Nahaman (the twelfth to the thirteenth centuries AD) being perhaps the most renowned of them all. Nahaman and Isaac the Blind were in favor of restricting discussions on cabalistic issues to a small group of followers. On the contrary, Azriel of Girona (the twelfth to the thirteenth centuries AD), the youngest disciple, favored the disclosure of the discussions, as a result of which he received a severe reprimand from his masters.

Thanks to that opening, the topics of discussion among the cabalists at that time and with their rivals in the philosophical field are known. The discussions were mainly focused on clarifying the question of whether the emanating ones formed a unit with their source or if on the contrary they were independent of it. In the first case, the reality of divinity would close on itself in its transcendence, becoming inaccessible rationally and inexpressibly, although approachable to some extent by the contemplation of its symbols. In the second case, the emanating ones are immanent to the world and approachable by means of interpretation of the allegories present in the Holy Scriptures and the tradition. For Azriel, Ein-Sof is a term used to refer to the Creator in his transcendent absolute incomprehensibility, who could be described using a negative theology (which only affirms what it is not). On the other hand, the Sefirot are positive aspects of the creative activity of God, understood as emanations from his infinity to the finite.

Shortly after Azriel, emerged an enigmatic character of whom little is known apart from certain dubious anecdotes. Despite the mystery that surrounds him, no one doubts his influence on the new course followed by the Kabbalah from the fifteenth century AD. The character in question was Moses ben Shem Tov de Leon (the thirteenth to the fourteenth centuries AD), who in his youthful days was a passionate follower of ben Maimon and then a scholar of the Talmud. Finally, he became an influential cabalist author with the dissemination of his great work *The Book of Radiance* (*Sefer ha-Zohar*), which he attributed to Simeon ben Yohai (the second century AD). His influence extended even after the period that followed the expulsion of the Hebrew people from the Iberian Peninsula. The dreaded decree of expulsion was promulgated by Ferdinand V of Castile (Ferdinand II of Aragon) (the fifteenth to the sixteenth centuries AD) on March 31, AD 1492. Moses conceived the first exteriorization of the Creator in his absolute transcendental incomprehensibility, whom he called the Holy Elder, in terms of nine lights flaming from his disposition. Those nine sparkling and flashing lights emanate and radiate toward the confines of the Creation on all sides.

Within a few years of the consummation of the expulsion of the Hebrew people by the Catholic kings, new communities began to flourish east of the basin of the Mediterranean Sea. Obviously the Holy Land offered a special attraction under the tutelage of Sultan Suleiman I the Magnificent (the fifteenth to the sixteenth centuries AD), who at that time led the Ottoman Empire to its maximum power. The opportunity was particularly propitious for the resurgence of the Kabbalah in the Holy Land, especially in Safed, where mystics and aspirants were concentrated. In AD 1522, an outstanding young man named Moses ben Jacob Cordovero became established (the sixteenth century AD) in that city. Under the tutorship of masters of the stature of Joseph Karo (the fifteenth to the sixteenth centuries AD) and Solomon ha-Levi Alkabetz (the sixteenth century AD), Cordovero penetrated the secrets of religious literature and the Kabbalah. In relation to the Creator, Cordovero used to express himself in philosophical terms affirming that the Creator, Ein-Sof, is one and is not seconded. He is the cause of causes and prime mover. However, despite his inclinations toward emanationism, Cordovero worked hard to defend the unicity of the Creator. He affirmed that the first three Sefirot should be thought of as a unit since they are three aspects of a unit and that believers should think of the whole emanation as a unit as well.

Cordovero was not the most influential mystic from Safed, despite showing prodigious literary fecundity during his short life, as he died at forty-eight years of age. His work was soon forgotten after the arrival in northern Israel of another great figure, but one lacking comparable literary abilities, Isaac ben Solomon Luria Ashkenazi (the sixteenth century AD). Born in Jerusalem in AD 1534, Luria lived most of his short life in Egypt under the protection of the family of his mother. There he studied with Talmudists of the stature of Solomon ibn Abi Zimra (the fifteenth to the sixteenth centuries AD) and Bezalel Ashkenazi (the sixteenth century AD). Later he retired to the Island of Jazirat al-Rawda on the banks of the Nile River, where he devoted himself to the contemplation and study of the Zohar attributed to Moses de Leon. In AD 1569, he went to Safed with the purpose of joining the school of Cordovero, one year before the death of the master and three before his own, in AD 1572.

The Lurianic Kabbalah was known through a disciple of Cordovero, later the most fervent follower of Luria, the then alchemist Hayyim ben Joseph Vital (the sixteenth to the seventeenth centuries AD). The disciples of Luria continued to study under the tutorship of Vital the doctrine of the master, under oath not to disclose it. However, the brother of Vital was bribed to allow a copy of the original manuscript, which was used for its dissemination in Safed and subsequent introduction in Italy. Anyone would have thought that everything was said after the systematization of the Kabbalah undertaken by Cordovero, but that was not the case. According to Vital, Luria was able to give an unsuspected conceptual overturn to the Kabbalah, preserving the traditional elements as part of a new doctrine. Perhaps the most notorious feature of the new approach was to give a theist foundation to an essentially pantheistic doctrine (which holds that the universe is God).

Luria thought that the creative act was not purely effusive as proposed by the emanationists but was preceded by a "retraction" from the infinity originally occupied by God. In his retreat, the Creator was leaving behind a trace of light, *reshimu*, occupying his absence. This was possible because during the retraction; God would selectively abandon his unicity. In that "residue" left behind, there would be "reflections" of the infinite light of Ein-Sof, hence the fact that to some extent it can be considered that the Creation occurs in something of God. The process of retraction of God toward his interiority was called *tzimtzum*, and Luria made this concept the foundation of his doctrine. The concept of retraction was not original to Luria, for gnostic authors such as Basilides, masters of the midrashic period, and even cabalist authors had cherished similar ideas. But undoubtedly it was Luria who made the *tzimtzum* a central topic of discussion among the cabalists to this day. This concept is fully compatible and to a certain extent justifies all the religious traditions that place God after the empyrean and call him the Most High.

The reader might have appreciated the high degree of sophistication achieved by efforts to contextualize the unicity of God with the multiplicity present in his Creation. But the ideas developed by these systems were not considered suitable for the masses, so they were concealed by symbolisms, sometimes extravagant and presented by figures almost impenetrable. That is the reason why all those efforts were relegated to the margin, being of interest only to a scant number of mystics and scholars. The brief story offered up to now has had as its objective the planting in the mind of the reader some concerns about a key issue whose inherent difficulties would hardly be overcome someday. Perhaps the natural exegesis developed throughout this book evokes answers aimed at clarifying the mysterious relationship of God with his Creation.

Chapter 18

Enlarging the Context of the Bases of Representation

The quaternary bases used so far have been enough to organize and relate some religious concepts and to establish correspondences with certain natural structures. However, from a theistic point of view, those same bases are clearly insufficient to articulate the immanent action of the divinity in the realization of the Creation. To correct this deficiency, it would be sufficient to add an additional independent direction on which to implement the passage of things from possible to real. Regarding the realization of things, we could say that through the Anointed One—for thinkers of antiquity, the quintessence—God grants epistemic realism to possibilities—things exist even if not observed by humans. The direction in which they act will be labeled a. Only possibilities in compliance with the originating provisions are anointed; therefore, the realizing media represented in a is also responsible for ensuring the perpetuity of the full validity of these.

The notion of the directionally transversal presence of that in God committed to the realization of his Creation is not a novelty, as had already been suggested by S. Boethius (the fifth to the sixth centuries AD). The Roman philosopher affirmed that God sees everything from the tower of his Providence. From above, God sees everything at once, while those below on the ground can only see what is right in front of them. Thomas Aquinas would also subscribe to a similar thesis in his *Summa Theologica* (*Summa theologiae*). The theologian explained in his work that a man walking on a road cannot see all those in front or behind him but that a man on a hill can see at the same time all those who travel along, just as God does.

The four independent directions previously contemplated are enough to establish a domain to represent the formulations of some creatures with inherent "degrees of freedom" or "valences." Making use of their freedoms, said creatures direct and determine the course of creation, and out of love, God realizes "all those actions subject to the originating provisions." Without that condition there would only be God.

There are also domains "external or lateral" to the bodies formed in the five independent directions of the manifold $atxyz$, extended in an ancillary direction, which will be called i. These external or lateral domains are called "wings" in the Holy Scriptures because of the periodic character of certain "mechanistic abstractions" developed in them. Even if the a priori introduction of i at this moment looks preconceived, it will provisionally allow the completion of the six independent directions mentioned in various traditions. For example, the six directions and four qualities referred to by Cordovero, which were denominated in early cabalistic circles in terms of height, depth, east, west, north, and south. They are present also in numerous directional symbologies, associated with the four cardinal points (from Latin *cardo maximus*) plus zenith and nadir.

With the six proposed directions, the heavenly domains count from this point with three independent directions *a*, *i*, and *t*, whereas the domains of the earth will continue to be defined by the directions of the triad *x*, *y*, and *z*. There are then three contexts: the Creation, with six independent directions *a*, *i*, *t*, *x*, *y*, and *z*; the cosmos, with four *t*, *x*, *y*, and *z*; and the universe, with three *x*, *y*, and *z*. When adopting the electronic configuration of the carbon valence subshell to illustrate quaternary bases, the need to have two additional possibilities for *a* and *i* was implicit. Both directions would have their parallelism, with the two electrons in a spherical orbital of the complete inner shell of carbon. Electrons in the inner shell do not intervene directly in the four degrees of freedom or chemical valences of the element, but they are fundamental in their performance. For this reason, the cartesian and tetrahedral representations of the orbitals of the carbon valence shell will continue to be useful. Figure 18.1 graphically illustrates three ways to represent the six independent directions of the Creation.

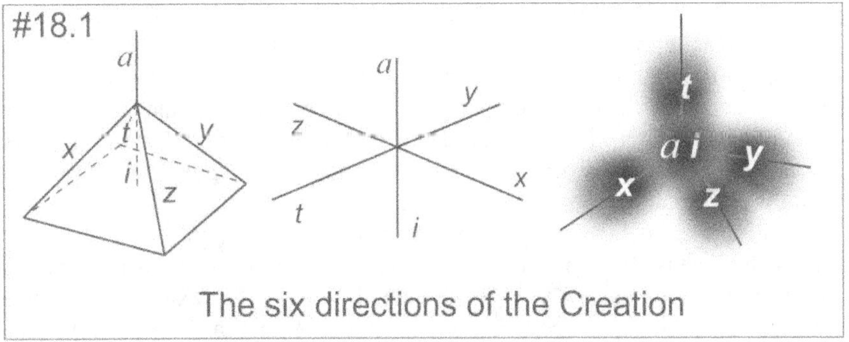

The six directions of the Creation

The first representation on the left is based on the Egyptian pyramidal shape, while the central representation is of the geographical cardinal type plus the zenith *a* and the nadir *i*. The representation on the right is based on the tetrahedral sp^3 hybridization of the elements of group 14 of the periodic table, such as carbon and silicon.

The fundamentally quaternary structure of the cosmos continues to be maintained, but it will have to be considered in the context generated by the fifteen definable planes in the hexadirectional manifold of the Creation. In this context, the ten formable planes with the five directions *a*, *t*, *x*, *y*, and *z* stand out and will be classified into three groups. The plane *at* will be called the most holy plane. The three planes of the triad *xyz*, as *xy*, *yz*, and *zx*, will be the earthly planes. Finally, there are the six planes *ax*, *ay*, *az*, *tx*, *ty*, and *tz*, called intermediates. Additionally, there are five ancillary planes, or wings, *ai*, *ti*, *xi*, *yi*, and *zi*.

The five directions *a*, *t*, *x*, *y*, and *z* also form ten independent right-handed triads according to the rule indicated in figure 3.4. These triads can be divided into two groups: the nine angelic triads: *atx*, *aty*, *atz*, *axy*, *ayz*, *azx*, *txy*, *tyz*, and *tzx*, and the lower or earthly triad *xyz*. It is possible to establish some correspondences between the nine angelic triads and the nine orders proposed *On the Celestial Hierarchy* by Pseudo-Dionysius, dully commented by Thomas Aquinas in his *Summa Theologica Part I Question 108*. The first three triads correspond to the cubic shrines, such as the holy of holies (*Kodesh HaKodashim*) of the Tabernacle and the temple built by King Solomon, the cubic framed Jerusalem, and the Kaaba. These shrines house the Seraphim, the Cherubim, and the Thrones, who rule the mechanics of prophecy. The Hebrew shrines had, according to the Sacred Scriptures, sculptured Cherubim inside. The remaining angelic triads house the Dominions, Virtues, Powers, Principalities, Archangels, and Angels. The earthly triad *xyz* is the realm of the earthly human being and fallen angels. The beings populating the nine triads outside of *xyz* are the angels seen by Jacob "ascending and descending" (Genesis 28:12) a stairway going from heaven to earth. The direction *i* does not form triads with the other five directions, hence the qualification of external or lateral given to the wings or planes formed with it.

One aspect of utmost importance relative to the hexadirectional context of the Creation is the distribution of the waters between the heavens and the earth. Up to now, only the upper and lower waters have been considered. The first have one of their two components in heaven *t* and the other on earth *xyz*. The second ones, or lower waters, have their two components on earth. The first ones were classified as fresh and old sages compared to the waters of rain and with those running down in torrents and rivers. The second ones, by contrast, were described as brackish and compared with the waters of seas and oceans. With the extension to six of the independent directions of the Creation, it is possible to introduce a new type of water. It is about the waters of the cloud, whose components are both in the manifold of heaven *ait*, and which the prophets, mystics, and visionaries compared to those steamy formations. If there is something characteristic in all the stories of the People with the Book, it is the frequent apparitions of the divinity in the bosom of a cloud and surrounded by winged beings. One of the first in Islam to give the cloud an originating character in the framework of his cosmogony was the Andalusian Ibn Masarra (the ninth to the tenth centuries AD). The ideas of the Islamic thinker are known through followers of the stature of Ibn Arabi, who placed the "sublime Calamus" *a* in that cloudy environment.

Relations between formulations in the cloud, with a semblance of waters like those constituted by *a* and *t*, as well as the upper ones formed by each with *x*, *y*, and *z*, deserve special attention. Those relations linked to the sacerdotal institution hitherto dealt with tangentially should be considered with a little more detail, given their importance to the ongoing natural exegesis. For the sake of convenience, they are repeated here and commented on with the Torah passage, where they are more clearly stated:

> Is not Aaron the Levite your brother? I know that he speaks well. And now he is on his way to meet you and he will be glad to see you. You

shall speak to him and put words in his mouth. And I will be with your mouth and with his mouth and I will tell you what to do. He will speak for you to the people and will serve you as your mouth and you will be for him as God.

The text leaves little doubt about the link between one of the Anointed Ones a and the Spirit t ("I will be with your mouth" [that of Moses, representing the Spirit]), as well as the relationship between the Anointed One and the earth in xyz ("and with his mouth" [that of Aaron, in representation of the priest and masculine component of the earthly human being or Man]), for the consummation of the priestly institution. Additionally, it is said, "and I will tell you what to do. He will speak for you to the people and will serve you as your mouth and you will be for him as God"— that is, t or a in connection with the possibilities within earth xyz. The Anointed One and the Holy Spirit lead the archetypal twin tetrads previously defined in terms of nucleotides, this time determining and realizing spatial events.

Once the definitive context of the Creation has been established, it would be advisable to "validate" the formulations of the protoelements and creatures, which can be represented on unitary, binary, and ternary bases, in the framework of the 1-3 odd quaternary bases of Spirit (air) and fire as well as in the even ones of the 2-2 type, corresponding to the primordial waters. Both base types are divided into heavenly and earthly domains, where the institutions addressed so far are inscribed. For example, the marriage of human couples 1&2 and the sacerdotal institution 1&1. The formulations are ratified again and again by their presence in the relative measurements of the most important objects and cult centers of the Hebrew people. As a sample, some of these measures will be offered below, leaving the reader with a more exhaustive review.

The measurements of the Ark of the Testimony in cubits, according to Exodus 25, are 1.5 high, 1.5 wide, and 2.5 long. These measurements can be decomposed by subtracting 0.5 cubits in the representation of a. They would then stand one high by two long for the heavenly human being and one wide by two long for the earthly human being. According to Exodus 26, 36, and 38, the Tabernacle housing the Ark had an atrium of one by fifty cubits wide and two by fifty long following the earthly human being formula. For its part, the holy place inside the atrium was one by ten cubits wide and two by ten long, representing the heavenly human being. The holy of holies was one by ten cubits wide, one by ten long, and one by ten high, symbolizing the sacerdotal institution to which it was reserved.

The temple built by King Solomon, according to 1 Kings 6 and 2 Chronicles 3, consisted of three areas: the porch, the holy place, and the holy of holies. The porch measurements were one by ten cubits long and two by ten wide, representing the earthly human being. The height of the porch was twelve by ten cubits, in representation of the twelve tribes of Israel, to be considered later. The holy place of the temple was one by twenty cubits wide and two by twenty long, representing the heavenly human being. The holy of holies was one by twenty cubits wide and one by twenty long, symbolizing the sacerdotal institution. The holy of holies also had a height of one by twenty cubits, which could refer to the presence of the Creator via one of the Anointed Ones in a together with the Spirit t and the priest (any possibility within xyz).

In Apocalypse 21:16, John describes the square and cubic framing of Jerusalem, which according to angelic measurements, has 12,000 stadia in length and is as wide and high as it is long.

The cubic shrines, such as the holy of holies, the cubic framed Jerusalem, and the Kaaba, allow the consideration of similar correspondences. These represent, in their three directions, height, width, and length, the Anointed One a, the Spirit t, and the priest (any possibility of protoelement earth in xyz). In the case of the Kaaba, there is an additional correspondence between the Black Stone of Abraham and the origin, where the three directions of the three triads cross—the presence of the transcendent God (Allah) is implicit there.

To the relief of everyone, additional independent directions will not be required in the future, and most formulations will continue to be represented on a quaternary basis.

Chapter 19

The Luminous Discourse

The best way to develop a new model of reality would be to take as a starting point, the first discursive statement from the Creator offered by the book of Genesis: "And God said: 'Let there be light' and there was light" (Genesis 1:3). Similarly, in subsequent verses, the description of all that is provided by God is preceded by the same expression: "And God said." The three words would reveal a decided intention to pose creation in the manner of discourse. In total, ten repetitions of the mentioned verb can be counted in verses devoted to creation, an emblematic figure, and the foundation of numerous decimal cosmogonies. In the next chapters, the importance of this figure will also be addressed in connection with the ten planes and ten triads formable in the manifold *atxyz*. In a similar way, the Gospel of John presents the act of God using a discursive figure when he expresses the following:

> In the beginning was the Verb, and the Verb was with God, and the Verb was God. This Verb was with God in the beginning. Through him all things came to existence, and without him nothing was made. Everything that came into existence in him is life and life is the light of men.

John then reaffirms the creative and luminous tenor of the divine verb, which will be interpreted here as a verb conjugation. No less explicit is surah The Cattle of the Koran when it refers to the creative discourse by saying, "And He is Who created the heavens and the earth in the truth and when He says: 'Be,' it is. His word is the truth…"

According to the previous quotations, everything becomes necessarily by divine intervention, and that would allow postulating the verb *to create* as an originating one. However, it is practically impossible for the human mind to further the natural exegesis of the Holy Scriptures, counting on only one verb. Nor would it be very useful to have an open and endless list. The ideal would be to project the verb *to create* over the six independent directions of the Creation, with a view of obtaining six verbs that reflect the actions taken on each of them. Since the rest of this book will be dedicated to justifying the choice of the six verbs, a proposal is offered a priori.

In the direction where *a* is represented, the verb *to create* is projected as *to realize*, whose conjugation consumes the transit from possible to real, incidentally ensuring the validity of the originating provisions. Upon direction *i* the projection of the verb *to create* becomes *to harmonize*, whose function is merely ancillary. With the representation of *t*, the verb *to create* is projected as *to determine*. For their part, the directions of the triad *xyz* concur indifferently with the projections *to direct*, *to transcribe*, and *to compose*. With the verb *to direct*, the possible courses are defined. With the verb *to transcribe*, transfers through the generation of "copies" are produced; and with the verb *to compose*, objects of the same tenor condense as a single one. Projecting the verb *to create* over the six independent directions of the Creation is equivalent in principle to assigning verbs to the protoelements already postulated. For this reason, when addressing the issue of the formulation of air, it was assigned to it the verb *to determine*. The protoelement earth was associated with the verb *to direct* and the protoelement water with the verbs *to transcribe* (ordinally) and *to compose* (cardinally), both related to pairs of objects. The protoelement fire conjugates the verbs *to direct, to transcribe*, and *to compose* concomitantly.

Creatures determine, direct, transcribe, and compose possibilities in creation, but they only construct empty vessels, which will only be filled when the Creator realizes them. According to Eliezer ben Zadok (the first to the second centuries AD), the life of those improperly using the vessels with which this world and the future are created will be torn from both. The verbs act from and on the luminous discourse, which is conceived as a geometric domain where they are conjugated.

The use of point-like formulations will be restricted for reasons that will become evident as the development of the model progresses. In fact, except at the origin, it will not be based on a geometry formed with points or geometric entities lacking parts according to the definition of Euclid (the fourth to the third centuries BC) nor with zero-dimensional objects according to more modern versions but rather with "elementary units," or monads, to which the circular form lends itself particularly well. As for its dimensions, its radius is established according to the smallest physical unit of measurement, the *Planck length* 1.6×10^{-35} m (0.000 000 000 000 000 000 000 000 000 000 000 016 m). Named after the German physicist M. Planck (the nineteenth to the twentieth centuries AD), the unit of length selected is denoted by the symbol ℓ_p. Its magnitude is so small that the thickness of a hair is approximately halfway between ℓ_p and the diameter of the entire known universe.

During the first six days of the Creation, the six verbs are conjugated as a single one, *to create*. Later, after the sixth day, when God finishes his solitary performance as Creator, new stages and instances are opened where the differentiation between the verbs will be possible. Heavenly and earthly human beings will freely determine, direct, transcribe, and compose possibilities, counting on the divinity for their realization. The Holy Scriptures are extraordinarily explicit in proclaiming the absolute freedom with which the odd creatures of the Creation can act, even expressly contravening some of the initial conditions established by the Creator; hence the amazing affirmation of the Bible offered by Isaiah: "I am the giver of light and the maker of darkness. I send blessings and I cause evil. I am the Lord, Who does all those things." That freedom of action, or free will as it will also be called, is associated with the verbs *to determine* and *to direct* in the cosmic domain. Both are features of creatures with odd formulations whose role as "cocreators," or conductors of creation, has been granted through the articulation of their geometric possibilities. Obviously, however, with regard to the freedom the Creator may grant, it will never be an absolute one. Particularly when granting it, God has also placed limits on his own. It would therefore be inappropriate to consider God as a simple automatic realizer.

To subordinate the realization of created things to divine intervention, imparts an Ash'arite character to the natural exegesis here developed, since both ways of thinking share the view of the absolute dependence of the Creation upon its Creator God. In tune with al-Ash'ari is the proposal that the actions of any creature via the verbs *to determine*, *to direct*, *to transcribe*, and *to compose* require their realization by God. However, the creatures assume their participation with full consent, and they are responsible for their actions. There are no realizations in the absence of divine intervention, and the creatures can only formulate possibilities according to their own attributions. Not in vain does Zend-Avesta in Yasna XLIV ask God, "Who from below sustains the earth and the clouds permanently?"

Chapter 20

The Role of Numbers

Much has been published about the history of numbers and mathematics in general. For this reason, the intention is not to repeat here what has been written and documented by others so well. However, it is convenient to bring to mind how the use of numbers has been closely linked to the possibilities of individuals and groups for their survival. Therefore, in general terms, it could be affirmed that mastering mathematics has also been indispensable to building empires and power structures. The use of numbers has allowed the administration of resources and the development of science and technology to the present. That is the reason why mathematics has been elevated to the rank of universal language. Success in the use of numbers for administrative, analytical, and predictive purposes rests on their affinity with natural phenomena.

The Holy Scriptures also reflect on the numerical content of the Creation, and the question acquires particular significance in the Hebrew Bible. The importance of numbers in the Bible lies in the fact that the letters of the Hebrew alphabet have each been assigned a numerical value. Thus, each word and each biblical verse also have an arithmetic reading, which sometimes has surprising results. However, the study of numerical relationships in the text of the Hebrew Bible, known as gematria, has had a variable importance throughout the centuries. In the oldest cabalistic circles it was already thought that God had created the cosmos by numbers, letters, and words, similar to a flash of light and with infinite reach. The question of numbers acquired significant relevance with the development of the Kabbalah, constituting an issue impossible to ignore in any natural exegesis.

All ancient civilizations developed their own mathematical systems, and in most cases they both had the same fate. Western mathematics had its origin in the confluence of the mathematics of ancient Greece and the Hindu-Arabic numeral system and spread in Europe during the tenth century AD by order of G. Aurillac (the tenth to the eleventh centuries AD), Pope Sylvester II. It was believed that decimal number systems had an anthropological origin based on the use of fingers. In fact, various civilizations of the past developed such systems, even when they were not positional like the Hindu-Arabic one.

The Greek mathematics used in Europe remained unchanged until the nineteenth century AD, when there was an explosion in the development of new mathematical systems in the West. Based on apparently self-evident axioms and on the use of logic to carry out deductive processes, Greek mathematics accumulated insoluble problems and inconsistencies. The quantity and seriousness of the problems disturbed the modern mathematical thinkers. During the nineteenth century AD, a critical culture about the state of mathematics arose for the first time, which led to the development of metamathematics. This discipline is concerned not with making deductions but with how they should be approached and carried out.

Modern mathematics is centered on an unrestricted attachment to the logic of the demonstrations of its propositions and does not care for the nature of its application or its results—so much so that B. Russell (the nineteenth to the twentieth centuries AD) described it as the science in which it is not known what is being talked about or if what is said is true. The process of self-criticism of mathematical procedures was hard and tedious, and the metamathematical proposals were scant. The efforts finally came to fruition when B. Russell and A. Whitehead (the nineteenth to the twentieth centuries AD) devised a supposedly coherent and error-free mathematical system. The intention was to be able to demonstrate, through logic and a reduced number of symbols and rules of expression and transformation, the veracity of all known propositions. This finite set of symbols and rules, perhaps with some additions, was considered to be sufficient so that the human being could demonstrate any mathematical proposition that could be raised in the future. However, it did not take much time until not only errors but also flagrant contradictions were discovered in that proposal. Doubts about the internal consistency of the mathematical systems burst again with force, opening the way to new episodes of confusion and perplexity.

In AD 1921, the Austrian philosopher L. Wittgenstein (the nineteenth to the twentieth centuries AD), who came from one of the wealthiest families in his milieu, demonstrated the extent of the misuse of logic, especially in connection with the use given in the proposal of the already mentioned British mathematicians. As the French mathematician H. Poincaré (the nineteenth to the twentieth centuries AD) had already pointed out, the logical propositions and the result of applying its deductive rules were for Wittgenstein nothing more than tautological series (useless repetitions of what is obviously true). Logic does not bring new knowledge, nor does it say anything other than what is already implicit in its starting axioms. It is simply a mechanistic procedure that when well applied allows for expressing any proposals in different ways and without ambiguities. Russell immediately answered, arguing that mathematical truths were not tautological but synthetic. However, he soon succumbed and then regretfully remarked that he had lost the certainty he had expected to find in mathematics.

The issue went through an unexpected turn in AD 1931 with the entry on the stage of K. Gödel (the twentieth century AD), a young Czech mathematician who was just twenty-five years of age. To the surprise of everyone, the young entrant showed that there are infinite arithmetic propositions that are not deductible through a closed set of rules. Remaining as a corollary, that arithmetic is incapable of proving that it is free of contradictions. The intentions of Russell, Whitehead, and other eminences, including D. Hilbert (the nineteenth to the twentieth centuries AD), to cover with their proposals the whole field of mathematical truths vanished forever.

To achieve his goal, Gödel relied on a paradox formulated by the French mathematician J. Richard (the nineteenth to the twentieth centuries AD). On that basis, the Czech mathematician devised a way to assign a number to each logical symbol, numerical variable, propositional variable, and predicate variable. The intention was to identify each mathematical expression with a unique Gödel number. The seven logical symbols used in his demonstration were associated with integers. The numerical variables could be associated with prime numbers greater than a given number—for example, ten. Propositional variables (those whose value can only be "true" or "false") could correspond to prime numbers also greater than ten but squared. Finally, the predicate variables of the type "less than" etc. would be linked to prime numbers greater than ten cubed. With these assignments, the mathematician was able to formulate a calculation method with the aim of identifying all mathematical expressions with a specific number in such a way as to make it possible to obtain the corresponding mathematical expression from these numbers in return.

Readers may notice that Gödel used prime numbers (only divisible exactly by themselves and by the unit) as a basis for representation. Thus, with the "arithmetization" of mathematics, Gödel was able to represent the properties of mathematical expressions within the calculus for the purpose of his conclusions. Also, Gödel, in Platonic terms and unlike Wittgenstein, thought that the objects of mathematics were real and that the task of the human being was not to invent them but to discover them.

The role of numbers in the Creation has been addressed timidly so far in this book. Only the first six natural numbers have been used to characterize the directional power of the Creation, its bases, and the formulations of the protoelements represented congruently over them. Regarding the belief of whether the numbers exist by themselves or in something, here will be chosen the second. In the following development of the natural exegesis, the arising of numbers in the articulation of the luminous discourse through its unfolding and without any limitation will be considered. The postulates on the articulation of the luminous discourse will be developed under the tutelage of the Holy Scriptures, always within the framework of an effort oriented toward the objective of achieving the maximum correspondence of its conclusions with the scientific knowledge available at present.

Chapter 21

The Keys of Genesis 1:1

The Holy Scriptures offer plenty of information to take the next step, but they do so in a nonexplicit way. The main reason is to protect humans, because the sudden knowledge of the whole truth would blind them and make them lose their reason individually and collectively. Ignorance and doubt protect humans from madness, and so the Lord warned Moses:

> "Show me your glory." He answered: "I will make My goodness pass before you and I will proclaim the name of the Lord before you. And I will be gracious to whom I will be gracious, and I will be merciful with whomever I please." And He added: "You cannot see My face. For no man who sees Me can be left alive." And He said: "There is a place close to Me where you can station on a rock. And when My glory passes, I will put you in a crevice in the rock and protect you with my hand. And then I will remove My hand and you will be able to see My back, but My face will not be seen."

The backside of God is beyond the dark sky of the empyreal vault, and his face precedes the source of all existing lights—in physics, the origin of all point particles.

The methodology to be used in what follows will be based on the evidence offered by the book of Genesis and will proceed alternately. First, the data of interest will be extracted from the text, and when the amount becomes significant, a model of the luminous discourse will be proposed. Some postulates to fill the gaps will also be introduced a priori to ensure the coherence of the proposals. From the next quotation from the Bible, the impossibility of downplaying the importance of numbers will become evident. And this quote cannot be other than that of its own commencement: "In the beginning God created the heaven and the earth." Undoubtedly, the first paragraph is the most read of any book, and as it is the most-read book, the reader will be wondering if there is something left to discover in the text. Literally, the verse is a simple statement of the necessary divine intervention to create the context in which all creatures are to unfold, including both formulations of the human being. When analyzing the text with a little more detail, a wording key can be discovered in terms of seven words in the Hebrew language using twenty-eight letters ($28 = 4 \times 7$) (like the Egyptian royal cubit with its seven palms and twenty-eight fingers).

Previously, heavenly domains were defined in terms of the three independent directions a, i, and t, and the earth was configured by the three directions x, y, and z. A question that can be considered is represented in the Hebrew language by the first three and last three words of the verse, where the central word figures as God. In fact, the plenitude symbolized by the number seven refers in the first instance to the six directions of the Creation and to his transcendent God represented in its origin. Apparently, this is all that could be said of the literal content quoted. However, it would be convenient to explore the resources offered by gematria, with the intention of analyzing each word and partial sums of words and their relations with the total sum.

Before undertaking the decomposition into factors of the indicated totals, it is worth remembering that the natural numbers are classified into three categories. Then we have the number one, the prime numbers, and the compound numbers. The number one is not included among the prime numbers in order to avoid recurrence in the decompositions of other numbers. The prime numbers are all those only divisible exactly by themselves and by the unit. Compound numbers have more than one exact divisor other than one and themselves. The letter א (alef) of the Hebrew alphabet has the numerical value of one, which is why it usually represents symbolically the unicity of the Creator, so much so that the first verse of Genesis about the Creation begins with the letter ב (bet), whose numerical value is two. Both א and ב represent the root of the human incarnation in the work of God according to the formula 1&2. Figure 21.1 shows the numerical values of each letter of the first verse, on the first line below the Hebrew text without vowel points. In the second line, the totals corresponding to each word are shown, and in the third the total of the verse.

Now it might be possible to understand the reasons why it is not easy to comment on the first verse of the Bible—not only because of the inherent difficulties of the subject but also because of the tenor of the controversies around its literal and numerical meaning. Outside the work of creation, which is discussed within cabalistic circles, there is very little existing referential material on the numerical content of the Bible. The absence of publications and academic studies also extends to the isopsephy (the study of the numerical value associated with letters, words, and phrases in the Greek language) of the Gospels written in the Greek language. While criticism of the few attempts to enter into the numerical mysteries of the Scriptures has been abundant, contributions stand out for their scantness. One of the secular studies of gematria and biblical isopsephy was realized at the beginning of the twentieth century AD by I. Panin (the nineteenth to the twentieth centuries AD), a Russian immigrant living in the United States. The free thinker published several works where he exposed his discoveries about certain numerical keys of the Bible, until then taken seriously only by the cabalists. It is not worth relating the avalanche of attacks from critics he had to withstand late in his life until his death in the middle of the Second World War. However, his merits must be recognized for calling attention to a subject largely ignored by western scholars very well versed indeed in the linguistic filigree of the Holy Scriptures. Some of the numerical aspects of the first verse of Genesis to which reference will be made inevitably coincide with his observations and of those of renowned cabalists. Unfortunately, apart from some exaggerations, Panin emphasized the study of numbers as such, without seeking a contextual meaning in a broader sense.

The word in the middle of the sentence of Genesis 1:1 and distinguished by the number one consists of two letters, the first and last of the Hebrew alphabet. This word yields a total of 401 (prime). It has a purely grammatical origin; neither does it has its own meaning, as do the other six, nor can it be translated. Also 401 is the only prime number in the totals of the words, which would confer to it a particular meaning. Subtracting א (alef), or 1, representing the Creator, from 401 is equivalent to stripping it of its distinctive feature to obtain 400 (compound), the value of the letter ת (tav). The value of the last letter of the Hebrew alphabet can be broken down into $4 \times 10 \times 10$ (four and ten compound). The three factors can be interpreted as a reference to a quadruple conditioning in the ten planes and ten triads, where all the geometrical bodies of the Creation are formed. For a second appreciation of the meaning of the two decades, it would be convenient to follow the cabalistic guide of the ten Sefirot. Based on this reference, a partition could be made into three (prime), *Kether, Hokhmah,* and *Binah,* and seven (prime), *Chesed, Gevurah,* Tiferet, *Netzach, Hod, Yesod,* and *Shekhinah.* The division into factors expressed in terms of commutated addends would allow the decomposition of 400 in the following manner: $4 \times (3 + 7) \times (7 + 3)$. Curiously, this division is related to the decomposition in factors of the total of verse 2,701 (compound) $(2,701 = 37 \times 73)$ into thirty-seven (37) and seventy-three (73), both prime numbers.

The figuration of the number seven in a verse as preeminent as Genesis 1:1 reflects its importance in the formulations of the Creation. Such a distinction can be taken as a prelude to its frequent occurrence in multiple instances. In fact, its figuration in different types of formulations could generate some confusion, especially when the septenary symbols appear embedded in each other. The question tends to get a little more complex because some formulations based on the number seven arise from the composition of two odd 1-3 formulas partially overlapping one over the other. In Genesis 1:1 for example, the case of two odd 1-3 formulations is presented. One of them is formed by the letter א and the words two, three, and four and the other by the letter ת and the words five, six, and seven. Under the suggested division, it would be possible to give a second interpretation to the verse, where two transcendents represented by *a* and *t* would relate independently with triad *xyz*, in clear allusion to the sacerdotal institution. It is a configuration analogous to that posed by the two nucleotide base systems, where uracil and thymine are related to the same three bases: adenine, guanine, and cytosine.

The amino group related protons (H) in key neurotransmitters and neuromodulators like tryptamine and N,N-dimethyltryptamine (DMT) —both with the same 3-indolyl group—could give rise to similar considerations, as figure 21.2 suggests.

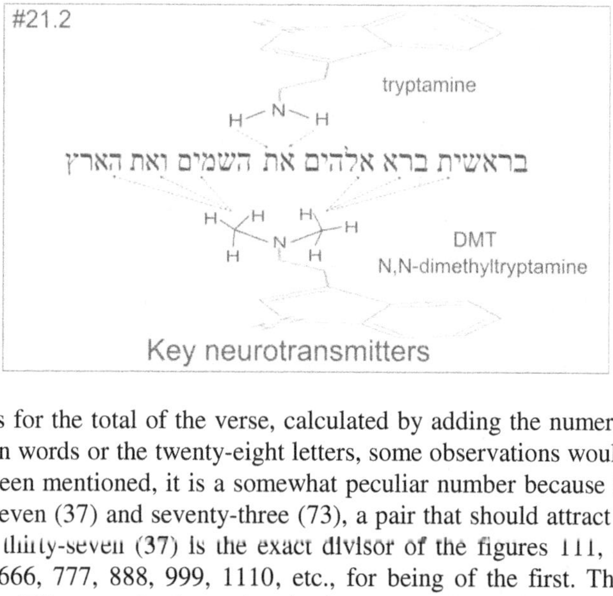

As for the total of the verse, calculated by adding the numerical value of the seven words or the twenty-eight letters, some observations would also fit. As it has been mentioned, it is a somewhat peculiar number because its factors are thirty-seven (37) and seventy-three (73), a pair that should attract attention. Curiously, thirty-seven (37) is the exact divisor of the figures 111, 222, 333, 444, 555, 666, 777, 888, 999, 1110, etc., for being of the first. The number thirty-seven (37) must also have singular importance because it is present as a factor not only in the total of the verse but also in twenty-two (22) partial sums of words—just the same number of letters with which the Hebrew alphabet is formed. It necessarily happens that when thirty-seven (37) appears as a factor in one word, it will also do so in the sum of the remaining six. When it is a factor of the total of any two words, it will also be of the total of the remaining five. Finally, if it is a factor of the total of any three words, it will also be of the remaining four. Figure 21.3 clearly shows the intention of Genesis 1:1, to underline the importance of the number thirty-seven (37).

#21.3	.earth the	and	heavens the		God	created	BEGINNING THE IN	TOTALS DIVISIBLE BY 37	
	הארץ	ואת	השמים	את	אלהים	ברא	בראשית		
	90 / 200 / 1 / 5	400 / 1 / 6	40 / 10 / 40 / 300 / 5	400 / 1	40 / 10 / 5 / 30 / 1	1 / 200 / 2	400 / 10 / 300 / 1 / 200 / 2		
7	296	407	395	401	86	203	913	2,701	1
1	296							296	
6		407	395	401	86	203	913	2,405	2X2
1		407						407	
6	296		395	401	86	203	913	2,294	
2	296	407						703	
5			395	401	86	203	913	1,998	
2			395		86			481	2X3
5	296	407		401		203	913	2,220	
2					86		913	999	
5	296	407	395	401		203		1,702	
3	296		395		86			777	
4		407		401		203	913	1,924	
3	296				86		913	1,295	
4		407	395	401		203		1,406	
3		407	395		86			888	
4	296			401		203	913	1,813	2X6
3		407			86		913	1,406	
4	296		395	401		203		1,295	
3			395	401		203		999	
4	296	407			86		913	1,702	
3				401		203	913	1,517	
4	296	407	395		86			1,184	

Totals of words in Genesis 1 : 1 divisible by 37

Also striking is the factorization of the partial totals written in the column on the right. The three groups recall the ideas of Philo of Alexandria about the number six. The Alexandrian thinker stated that the world was made in six days because created things require an arrangement, and numbers are relative to that arrangement. He also rated number six as the most productive, being composed of factors three and two, male and female.

The number seventy-three (73 = 1 + 36 + 36, for water) two digits like those of thirty-seven (37 = 1 + 36, for air or earth), and the three ones of one hundred nine (109 = 1 + 36 + 36 + 36, for fire) add to ten (10). Remarkably, the binary representation of seventy-three (73) is 1001001 a palindrome —having two half opposing one another (mirror images) as the two components of lower or feminine waters plus the source (1). The binary representation of thirty-seven is 100101, where 100 corresponds to earth and 01 to air, the so-called masculine waters. The number seventy-three is also a factor of 2,701 and of two partial totals of two words and the remaining five, giving an additional feminine connotation. Figure 21.4 below summarizes it.

#21.4

.earth the	and	heavens the		God	created	BEGINNING THE IN	TOTALS DIVISIBLE BY 73
90 200 1 5	400 1 6	40 10 40 300 5	400 1	40 10 5 30 1	1 200 2	400 10 300 1 200 2	
7 296 407	395	401	86	203	913		2,701 1
2			401			913	1,314
5 296 407	395		86	203			1,387 1X2

Totals of words in Genesis 1 : 1 divisible by 73

The number seventy-three (73) would mean an additional step in symbolism intended to describe the development of the first created object. However, its smaller figuration in the gematria of Genesis 1:1 confers, without doubt, a secondary role linked perhaps to its feminine trait.

To interpret the scope and meaning of the numbers thirty-seven (37) and seventy-three (73), it would be convenient to subtract the unit, which will be a common practice from now on with prime numbers. The results obtained from the subtraction are thirty-six (36) and seventy-two (72), respectively, figures both related by a factor equal to two (72 = 2 × 36). As the reader may have anticipated, the relationship immediately evokes the formulation of the human being, 1&2. The subtracted units would correspond to the unique source associated with each protoelement; thus, air or earth would each come from its own source, while the two components of the water would have their own result of the composition of two. Despite its secondary role, the number seventy-two is present in the main religious traditions—for example, in the divine denominations according to Hebrew mysticism, in the seventy-two disciples of Jesus, and in the seventy-two virgins of Islamic paradise.

The figure thirty-six (36) is of the utmost importance for Hebrew traditions, like in the symbolism of the thirty-six lights (excluding the Shamash) to celebrate the miracle of Chanukah. The decomposition of thirty-six into factors like 6 × 6 would suggest a multiplicative progression from a primordial hexagon during the six-day creation, as stated by the Koran in 6 + 1 suwar: "created … the heavens and the earth … in six days" (The Heights: 54, Jonah: 3, Hud: 7, The Criterion: 59, The Prostration: 4, Qaf: 38, and The Iron: 4).

In Zoroastrianism a divine heptad proceeding from Ahura Mazda is headed by Spenta Mainyu (the source to be substracted) and unfolds into six amesha spentas—referred by the seven Yasnas from XXXV to XLI (the Haptanghaiti). The Apocalypse of John mentions extensively the number seven and portrays God seated on his throne, and before him, seven lamps are blazing, which are the seven spirits of God. Surah *Al-Fatiha* opening the Koran has seven ayat, the first four dedicated to the names of God. Surah *Al-Nur* mentions seven times the word *light* (*nur*) and says explicitly: "Allah is the Light of the heavens and the earth."

Chapter 22

The Incarnation of the Luminous Discourse

According to Genesis 1:3–5, the luminous discourse is created as a radiant object and complemented by a mechanism of alternate phases: "And God said: 'Let there be light' and there was light. And God, looking at the light, saw that it was good, and He separated the light from darkness. And He called the light day and the darkness night. And there was evening, and there was morning, the first day." The quoted text constitutes the first biblical specification of the chiaroscuro contrast, which are the two distinctive attributes of both components of the protoelement water. The representation of the contrast in days and nights is due to the turn of planet Earth on its axis and to the projection of the solar light on its surface. Figure 22.1 illustrates the geographical representation of the cyclic and periodic nature of the chiaroscuro contrast during the Southern Hemisphere summer.

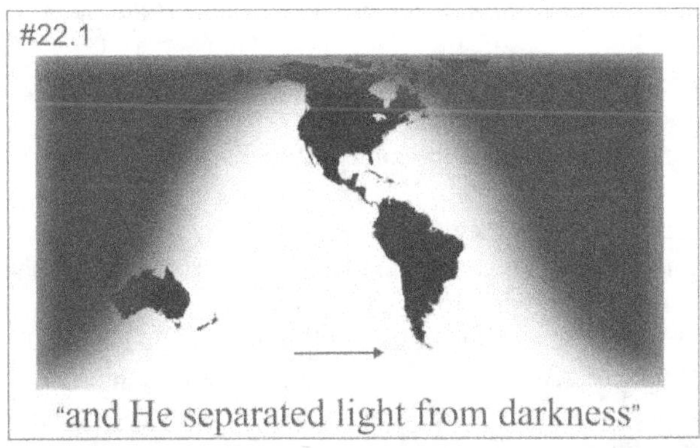

The radiant aspect of the luminous discourse will be associated with the masculine component of an ordinal formulation of human type 1&2, and it will be called the "divergent aspect of the light." On the other hand, the cyclical or periodic behavior that comes after will be considered feminine and called the "rotational aspect of light." So far, there have been mentioned two complementary versions of the human incarnation of the luminous discourse in the Torah. One of them is in Genesis 1:1, related to the pair of figures thirty-six (36) and seventy-two (72) plus their respective sources and referred to as a cardinal incarnation. The other one, in Genesis 1:3–5, just considered, is related to an ordinal incarnation. Both masculine and feminine natures are imbricated in such a way in the cardinal and ordinal incarnations of the luminous discourse that it will be almost impossible to consider them independently. Despite the difficulties, in the following chapters, an effort will be made to treat them separately as much as possible, with the intention of forming a coherent overall picture.

The first step to elucidate the structure of the luminous discourse is to expand the language through the incorporation of some mathematical concepts, with a view to a more expeditious development of the subject. The odd creatures associated with masculine archetypes and the even creatures associated with feminine ones are endowed with the ability to act. The only thing is that the formulation of the latter, unlike the former, contemplates compensation mechanisms, in view of which the results of their individual actions are null.

According to observations made in the scientific field, two phenomenologies that fit the feminine manifestations of the cardinal and ordinal incarnations of the human formulation stand out. Feminine expressions in cardinal incarnations correspond to the notion of rotation or turn commonly experienced by solid bodies in the triad xyz. The model to be developed will generalize these rotations and turns to all the planes and triads that are formable in the manifold $atxyz$ under certain restrictions. In the lateral planes or wings, a different type of rotation will be considered that escapes to the common experience and constitutes the essence of the feminine manifestations typical of ordinal incarnations. To address the last ones in the next chapters, it is convenient to introduce some concepts in the remainder of this. The details can be tedious for some, which is the reason why they can choose to skip them and go to the next chapter.

The model of the luminous discourse will be developed then in the manifold of five independent directions structured as "real fields" (in a mathematical sense). The developments in the wings or ancillary planes instead will be framed in "complex number field" structures (in a mathematical sense) since the direction i will be treated as an imaginary axis. In both cases numerical sequences are laid in their independent directions. The purpose of this is to represent quantitatively both the divergent radiation of the masculine component and the harmonic functionalities typical of feminine periodic phenomena in bodies and wings.

The Italian mathematicians G. Cardano (the sixteenth century AD) and R. Bombelli (the sixteenth century AD) discovered a peculiar type of number, imagined by Descartes and denoted by the Swiss L. Euler (the eighteenth century AD) with the letter i, for *imaginary*. Its mathematical definition coincides with the requirements necessary to represent some variants of the rotational aspect of light in close parallelism with some models developed by physics. At that time, i was simply the inconceivable square root of minus one ($\sqrt{-1}$), but today that vision has already been overcome. The perplexity of the thinkers of that time increased with the frequent appearances of i, until they learned to see it as something common.

Almost a century later, the Norwegian C. Wessel (the eighteenth to the nineteenth centuries AD) formulated the "complex plane" by placing an imaginary type direction i on a vertical perpendicular to a real horizontal one. Such representation assimilated multiplication tables that yield additively opposite results in each case, which allowed for harmonic compensation mechanisms typical of certain feminine manifestations. For example, for the real numbers in a, t, x, y, or z, when multiplying plus one (+1) by plus one (+1), the result is plus one (+1). Instead, by multiplying plus i (+i) by plus i (+i), the result is minus one (−1), which is conveniently the opposite additively. Also, when multiplying minus one (−1) by minus one (−1), the result is plus one (+1) for the real numbers. Whereas by multiplying minus i (−i) by minus i (−i), the result is minus one (−1), equally convenient and consistent. Now, when multiplying plus one (+1) by minus one (−1), or vice versa, the result is minus one (−1) for the real numbers. But by multiplying plus i (+i) by minus i (−i), or vice versa, the result is plus one (+1), as it should be, so that all the products in i are additively opposed to those obtained in a, t, x, y, and z. The combined multiplications of a real number by i, or vice versa, follow the prescription for the real numbers.

Chapter 23

The Masculine Character of the Luminous Discourse

The realization of the luminous discourse follows a set of perpetual originating provisions, departing from certain initial conditions established by the Creator. A set of degrees of freedom belongs to said conditions, subject to the discretion of "odd creatures." The ability of odd formulations to act obeys to the absence of internal contradictions in some of their formative aspects, thus making them able to exercise non-null actions. The postulation of the originating provisions and their initial conditions in geometric terms is essentially the only possible description of these. In one of Plato's Socratic dialogues, written about 385 BC, he reproached his student Gorgias, saying to him: "You forget that geometric equality reigns, all powerful, among the gods as well as among men." Understanding then that "gods" refers to the original archetypes of the Creation, this chapter will be dedicated to the development of the luminous discourse geometry, which will be called "zero conditionality."

It is a progressive geometric development based on a polygonal expansion in the fifteen (15) planes from its sources since the first day of creation. It can be conceived as a single attribute by component ($1 = 1 \times 1$), without a definite opposite and expressing itself as the model and foundation of all geometry. In its development in *atxyz*, it defines new possible locations of its own source located at its origin. Its radially divergent nature is expressed in the religious sphere, in the unwavering rectitude of patriarch Abraham and his advances always forward, without returning to his starting point. The liturgical expression of the divergent advance is the raising of the hands pointing to the empyrean, toward which the polygonal expansion is directed. For his righteousness, Abraham is the father of three religions: Judaism, Christianity, and Islam. Also, in religion two, of Zoroaster, "divine righteousness" (Asha) is praised frequently above all things, as in Yasna XXVIII of the Zend-Avesta.

The "points" in the vertices of polygonal expansion, usually called "eyes" in the Holy Scriptures, have already been defined in terms of domains for the conjugation of the verb *to create*. The only object strictly conceivable as a point in a mathematical or geometric sense is the source located at the origin of the expansion. All other conjugation domains of the verbs will have a radial extension of $1 \ \ell_p$. In these localities, the Creator and his creatures converge in the realization of the transcriptions of the sources. The polygonal exteriorization at the end of the first day is a hexagon with six possible occurrences of the verb *to create*, which will be defined from the points of a geometry inspired by the form of Genesis 1:1.

For its part, the source has, from the point of view of any performance, the highest significance. Therefore, and as a result of the comparisons of the case, it is established as a unit of measure with a value equal to one. The significance of the hexagon is the same as that of its source. However, the six domains of conjugation of the verb *to create* in its vertices divide equally among themselves the total significance, resulting in a "point significance" equal to one-sixth of that total. It is also possible to develop this model from a hexagram, which would introduce some differences in its expansion process—not be confused with the unicursal type or *hexagrammum mysticum*. A model starting from a hexagram has a particular appeal given the composition in Genesis 1:1 of two odd formulations of the 1-3 type. However, in order to simplify the model and its illustrations as much as possible, the hexagonal version shown on the left of figure 23.1 will be preferred. Both hexagon and hexagram are developed on the plane *xy*, leaving the reader the visualization on the other fourteen (14) planes of the manifold *aitxyz*.

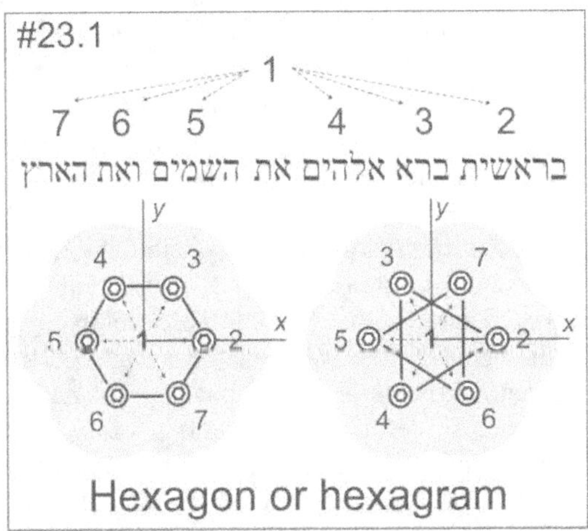

All polygonal expansions have their own identity, associated with the protoelemental archetype to which they belong. From day seven of the development, the possibility of starting a new process of polygonal expansion from newly generated domains is open. The transcription of the source to the domains generated after day six are always accompanied by the formation of a primordial hexagon in its immediate surroundings.

The hexagram has been used by diverse cultures from the most remote antiquity, in decorative figures or to express symbolically some beliefs. In fact, it was already present in the Holy Land when Joshua (the thirteenth to the twelfth centuries BC) entered. Archeology shows that its appearances in Hebrew culture over the centuries were not more profuse than in others. Its widespread use among the Hebrew people originated belatedly by a decree of Charles IV of Luxembourg (the fourteenth century AD), the king of Germany and Bohemia, crowned emperor in Rome in AD 1355. This decree sought to identify the only properties allowed in the Jewish quarter of Prague, through the use of a standard whose Hebrew origin could not be established—most likely the design was imposed, as is often the case in similar circumstances. From Prague it passed to Vienna, where it began to be seen in the middle of the seventeenth century AD and from there to Germany a century later. During his stay in the Balkans, the Hebrew philosopher F. Rosenzweig (the nineteenth to the twentieth centuries AD) adhered to the symbolism of the hexagram and used it as a source of inspiration in his *Star of Redemption* (*Der stern der erlösung*). Despite its popularity throughout Europe at the time, the hexagram was rejected by the most influential sectors of Hebrew orthodoxy.

Representing the primordial hexagon on the fifteen (15) planes allows, among other things, for the postulation of a radius (in a hexagon, the radius and the sides have the same length). For this it is convenient to go back to the smallest physical measurement available, the *Planck length*. The primordial hexagon would then have its radius and sides all equal to 1 ℓ_P in length. Additionally, the speed of light (approximately 300,000,000 m/s) is adopted as the luminous discourse transcription speed, which establishes the *Planck time* t_p as a unit for the measurements of time. The length adopted for the radius and sides of the primordial hexagon implies an overlap of neighboring domains of conjugation of verbs. As has been suggested, the source and its polygons are concomitant, and for this reason the first one will not be considered as an independent point-like object.

The next step in the divergent expansion of polygonal development consists of the generation of transcription domains of its source beyond the primordial hexagon. Thus, at the end of the second day of creation, the multiplication of the hexagon to the dodecagon (twelve [12] sides) takes place in all planes. In essence it is a model of expansion and polygonal propagation and therefore discrete, in terms of generations of centers of conjugation domains. All these domains will be separated from one another by distances of the order of 1 ℓ_P. The radial divergence of the model will be evident as it progresses and constitutes a distinctive feature of the masculine component of the luminous discourse, called to occupy the domain opened by divine retraction. Depending on how the polygonal progression is considered, the need to cancel out a certain rotational bias generated by it can be evidenced or maintained implicit. In view of the need to incorporate some rotational aspect into the model, for the representation of the feminine character of the luminous discourse, the explicit version is favored.

Because of the divergent nature of the masculine character of the discourse, the rotational features are inadmissible in their formation and must be annulled in the fifteen (15) planes of the Creation. Fortunately, there is a quick fix by considering two rotational attributes or accidents opposing each other for their mutual cancelation. An alternate solution is to contemplate two polygons rotating in opposite senses, but this will add complexity to the model, particularly after introducing other attributes. In both cases, the rotations are identified as a "second conditionality" of the luminous discourse given its periodic and feminine traits. Both rotations will be considered, from now on, as a set of two attributes inherent to all polygons. Figure 23.2 attempts to illustrate the creation of the light on day one and its divergent propagation to the dodecagon at the end of day two.

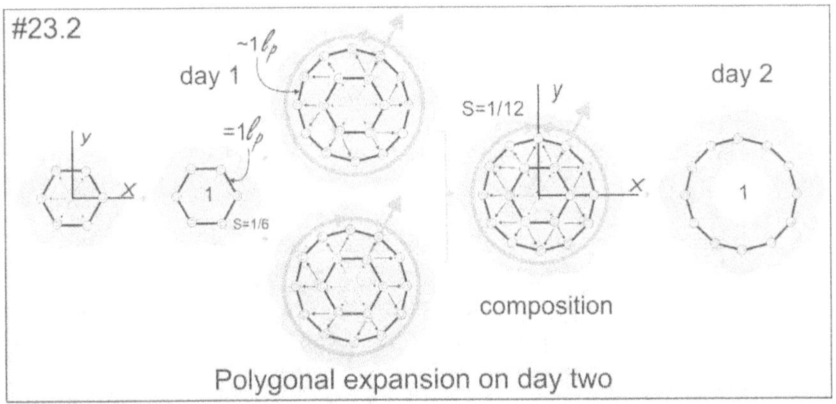

Polygonal expansion on day two

In this illustration, the propagation to dodecagon through a transcription pathway is shown graphically, highlighting the rotational attributes opposing one another. The gray circles in thick lines represent the rotational bias and on both have been indicated their opposite senses. There is also a straight gray arrow pointing outward at each one, indicating the divergent aspects of the expansion. For its part, the radius of the dodecagon has increased to 2 ℓ_P, while the length of its sides continues to be of the order of 1 ℓ_P. The total significance of the dodecagon is one, while that of its vertices is one-twelfth. By radially expanding the possibilities of transcription of the source in *atxyz*, the domains of conjugations are losing significance in the plane in terms of their possibilities of hosting it. However, the sum of the significances of all the vertices of each polygon will remain equal to one regardless of their order—that is, all polygons, including those furthest from the source, have the same significance of this.

The generation of the dodecagon (12 sides and vertices) on the second day is at the root of numerous symbologies—in some of them, the twelve are equivalent; others instead follow 1-3 formulations. Also, the multiples of twelve like twenty-four, thirty-six, and those originated from quaternary formulations play an important symbolic role and sometimes are almost impossible to distinguish due to their nested occurrences. For example, the city of Jerusalem, according to the book of Nehemiah, has twelve (12 = 2 × 6) doors (Neh. 3:1, 3:3, 3:6, 3:13, 3:14, 3:15, 3:26, 3:28, 3:29, 3:31, 8:16, and 12:39). Later the authors wisely referred to the expansion, saying that heavenly Jerusalem was only created because of the love of God for earthly Jerusalem, which would expand until it reached his throne.

The occurrence of the twelve (12) annual lunar cycles and their inductive power over the human mind ensured a preeminent place for this figure in ancient cultures. Since the time of ancient Mesopotamia (the twenty-fourth century BC), the number twelve (12) was present in the formulation of calendars and times of day and night. The question is related to the development of an arithmetic based on the twelve (12) phalanges of the four fingers (excluding the thumb). Subsequently, the division of the sky into twelve (12) sectors established the basis for the definition of the zodiac, whose most elaborate ancient plastic expression is the Egyptian zodiac of Dendera (the first century BC). Also in ancient Egypt, apart from its late use in the zodiac and in the measurement of time, the number twelve (12) possessed extraordinary importance. This is attested by the great pyramidal monuments and their subsequent evolution into large obelisks.

No less important is the figuration of the number twelve (12) in the modeling of human structures on a social and religious scale and in the formulation of some of their doctrinal content. In the ancient pagan world, where Greece has been among its greatest exponents, the amphictyony of twelve (12) cities or religious leagues was founded in the sixth century BC. Each of these groups was represented by two hieromnemon for a total of twenty-four (24). Their meetings took place at the temple of Demeter at Anthela or at the Oracle at Delphi.

The Semitic religions of the People with the Book have all reserved an outstanding place for "dodeca" formulations. For example, in the Torah, the tribes of Israel conformed by the descendants of Jacob are twelve (12), who together with the Eternal complete the number thirteen (13). On the Christian side, the apostles of Jesus were twelve (12) until moments before his death, and during the Last Supper, there were present thirteen (13), featuring Jesus as the source. In Islam the importance of the number twelve (12) is exposed by the Koran itself by dedicating surah 12 to Joseph, son of Jacob, and his eleven (11) brothers. The Shia recognizes twelve (12) imams as successors of the prophet, descendants of the lineage of Fatimah and **Ali ibn Abi Talib**. The twelfth imam of the Shia (al-Mahdi), hidden since the ninth century AD, would return with Christ to complete the redemptive work a few days before the Last Judgment. Along with the "dodeca" formulations of Islam, the source of revelation must be considered to reach the number thirteen (13).

However, not all twelve (12) usually have equal figuration. As for the twelve (12) tribes of Israel, because of mixtures, wars, migrations, and exiles, the number of profane tribes was reduced to two, those of Judah and Benjamin. Additionally, the tribe of Levi would complete three, but it was absorbed by others by virtue of its dedication to priesthood and is thus excluded from the list. Among the twelve (12) apostles of Jesus, there were also distinctions since his predilection for three of them, Simon Peter and the sons of Zebedee, James the Greater and John, is well known.

The propagation of the luminous discourse continues during the subsequent days of creation, until day six. At the end of that day, the primordial hexagon will have expanded to a triacontakaihexagon, a polygon with thirty-six (36) vertices and sides. Following the prescriptions previously applied to the dodecagon, there are two counterrotational attributes to be considered. The radius of the triacontakaihexagon increases to $6\,\ell_P$ and each side remains in the order of $1\,\ell_P$. The point significance of conjugation domains in each vertex has been reduced to one-thirty-sixth, while its total in the whole polygon is still one. Figure 23.3 illustrates the state of the luminous discourse on day six.

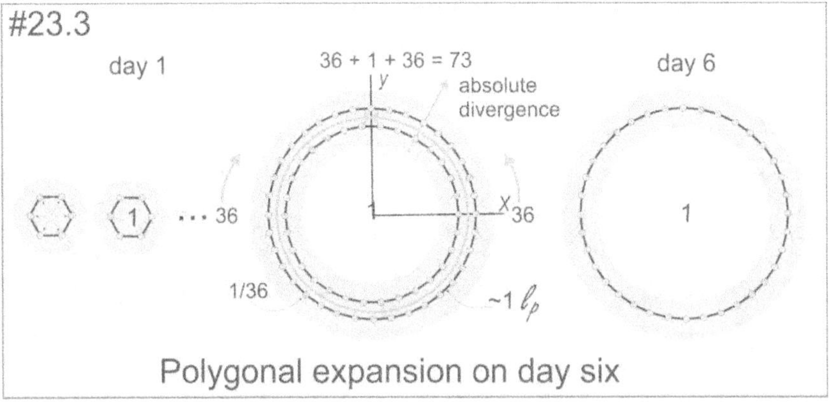

Polygonal expansion on day six

The number thirty-seven $(37 = 36 + 1)$ indicated in the figure is associated with the masculine character, with its thirty-six (36) domains or points of the resulting divergent development plus the source. Whereas the number seventy-three $(73 = 36 + 1 + 36)$ corresponds to its feminine counterpart, plus the source. At the end of day six, with the completion of the triacontakaihexagon, the development of the so-called hidden light (in the Hebrew *Ohr HaGanuz*), which Adam and Eve enjoyed in the Garden of Eden, culminates. In the four planes *at*, *xy*, *yz*, and *zx*, the corresponding number amounts to 144 $(144 = 4 \times 36)$, over which says the Apocalypse of John: "And he showed me the sacred city of Jerusalem, descending from the heavens from God...And measured the wall that surrounded it one hundred and forty-four cubits, the measure of a man and also of an angel."

During day seven, and unlike the previous ones (where a single polygon was generated every day), the first seven polygons are generated again in the manner of a series. The source then generates and maintains a new hexagon and the subsequent polygons so that at the end of the seventh day, seven polygons will be present. The formation of the tetracontakaidigon (forty-two $[42 = 6 \times 7]$ vertices and sides) at the end of day seven marks a milestone in the development of the luminous discourse as the development of the "manifested light" begins. The object created in that instance will be called "divergent quantum" for being the basic unit for modular creation and its autonomy in transcribing inside and outside its limits—the particle-like behavior in the *atxyz* manifold and ancillary planes. According to the book of Genesis, day six stands out for the culmination of the creative activity of God in solitaire, while in day seven the performance of the human being begins. In the ordinal couple, the feminine will have to appear as an indispensable carrier of the source between transcriptions. The issue will be treated with some degree of detail in the next chapter and has only been mentioned here in order to place the divergence in a context.

The propagation of the divergent series will continue on its own in the days following the sixth as long as the source does not decide its transcription. The terms are still the same as those already expressed, with the number of sides of the polygon in the light front increasing without boundaries. This is depicted in figure 23.4, where conjugation domains of the verbs have been omitted with the purpose of simplifying it.

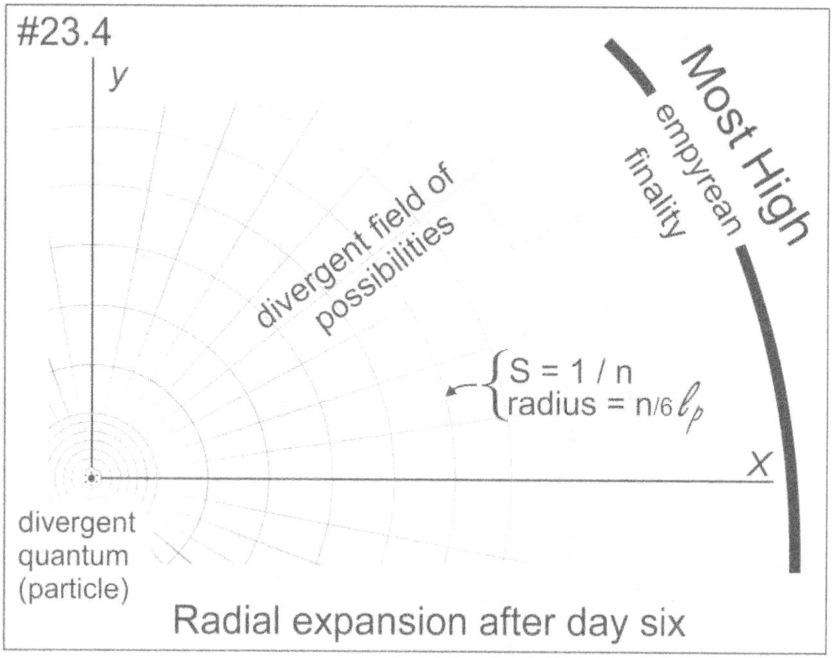

The illustration shows how after n/6 divergent **propagations, the polygon will have n vertices and sides, the radius** will have increased to n/6 ℓ_p. The size of the sides will remain at approximately 1 ℓ_p and the point significance at each vertex will be reduced to 1/n. In the limit, when n is infinitely large, the polygons will be practically circumferences, marking the transition from a finite hexagonal perfection to an infinite circumference.

God is at the beginning and at the end of the transit between two perfections, from the hexagonal to the circumference. This is suggested by the presence of the first and last letters of the Hebrew alphabet א (alef) and ת (tav) in word one of Genesis 1:1. This is also indicated in chapter 1 of the Apocalypse of John by the statement: "I am the alpha and the omega, says the Lord God, who is, who was and who is coming, the Almighty." It could be affirmed then that something of God "speaks to himself" through the creation of his luminous discourse. Following the Pesikta de-Rab Kahana (priska 20:7), **figure 23.5 shows schematically the luminous discourse in all its amplitude.**

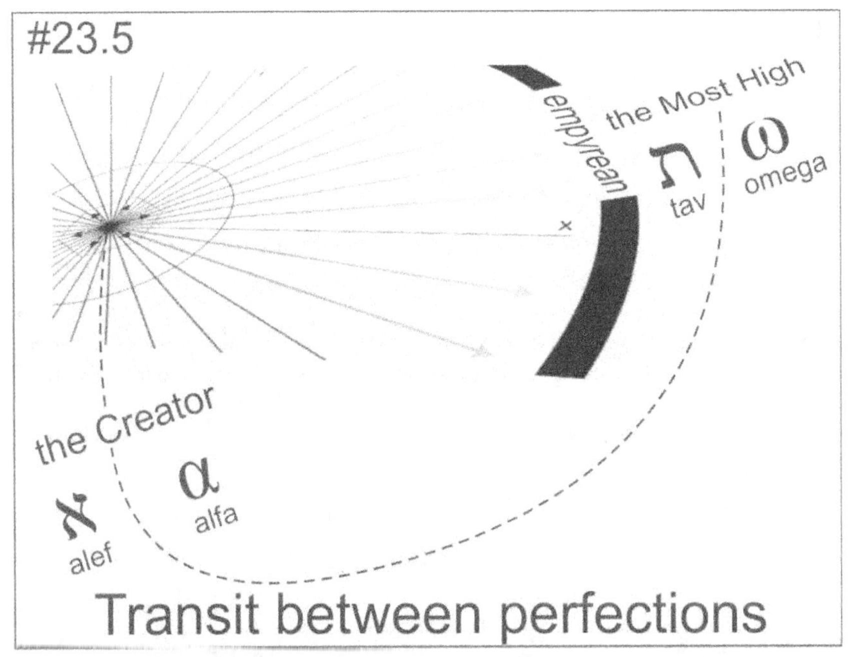

From a panoramic view, as the one shown in the previous figure, it could be inferred that there are only closed loop circulations in the whole constituted by God and his Creation. Such closure would imply some type of curvature inherent to the whole development. There would then be two types of circulation or rotation. On the one hand, there is the polygonal expansion of the divergent aspect of light in circulation via a closed loop, "passing through God extracosmically," identified with the masculine component of the discourse. On the other hand, the counterrotational feminine attributes would be closing in on themselves "intracosmically and without passing through God." Circulation via the divergence "passing through the divine infinity" and represented by the word one (א ת) is humanly observed in terms of a projection toward the vault of the empyrean. Affirmations of the previous paragraph would suggest in principle that God would have created only waters due to the feminine character of the closed loop circulation, even those "going through him."

Just as the opposed rotations in the planes were contemplated, the counterturns around the two directions with which they are defined will have to be considered in the manifold *atxyz*. However, the question is not so simple because there are limitations to formally addressing rotations and turns in said manifold with the mathematical tools used for three directions. Fortunately, the problem is surmountable because the model to be developed in this natural exegesis does not contemplate creatures whose domain of existence and performance is greater than three independent directions. Consequently, the ten (10) triads definable in the context *atxyz*, in addition to having an intrinsic order, could also be considered mutually independent. Each of these triads would house creatures confined to them whose rotations and turns do not transcend them. For example, an angelic creature of the triad *txy* does not have definite turns around *z* or *a*, only around its three directions. Despite its independence, all the entities in the ten (10) triads of the manifold *atxyz* are subordinated via the sources in their origins, where it resides the subjection of the Creation to its transcendent God. Just as on *a* and *t*, the realization and determination of the events in *xyz* is decided with the concurrence of the angels.

To continue with the topic of rotations and turns, it is necessary to consider their formal treatment, at least within the triads mentioned. In geometry, rotations and real turns are conveniently defined in terms of the product of two magnitudes with direction and a sense called vectors. In triads, for example, *xyz*, the results of said products, are usually represented on a third vector transverse to the plane of rotation. In addition to its direction, that vector will be given a sense by the right-hand rule, according to the illustration in figure 23.6.

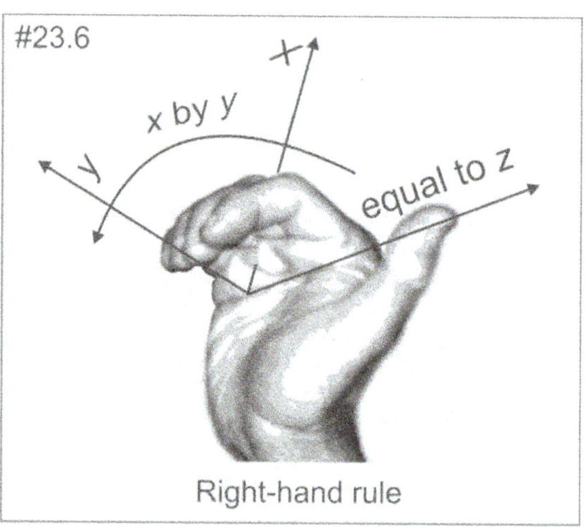

Right-hand rule

The right-hand rule stipulates that the four curved fingers enter first by *x* and then by *y* for the product of *x* by *y*, corresponding to the rotations indicated in the plane *xy*. The result is represented on a third direction transverse to said plane—in this case *z*, with its sense indicated by the thumb. The same rule applies to turns around *z* of the two planes *yz* and *zx* of the triad. If the fingers enter first by *x* and then by *y*, by reversing the senses in both directions concomitantly, as befits the water-type formulations, the same will continue to occur. Therefore, the result will be the same, an observation that confirms the null character of the performances of binary or feminine archetypes. Figure 23.7 tries to illustrate the above observation in a schematic way.

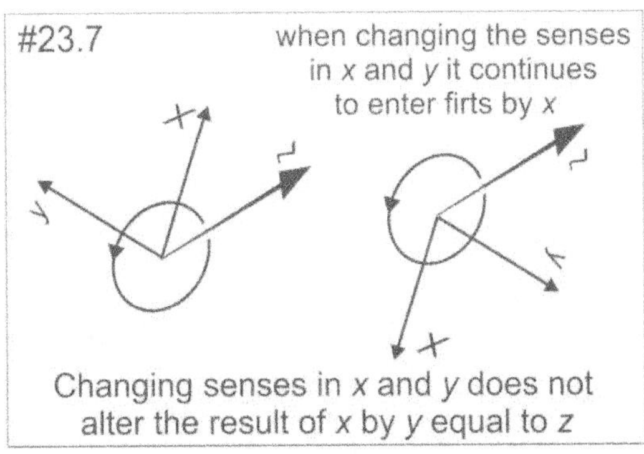

In short, a polygonal development in the plane xy belonging to a creature of the triad xyz will have its counterrotations around z and its counterturns around x and y. The same goes for the other two planes, yz and zx, in such a way that two groups might be formed. The first group could gather the attributes corresponding to right rotations and turns—for example, around z—while in the second, all the remaining opposite left rotations and turns will have to be grouped.

As for the masculine character in the ancillary planes or wings, they only have counterrotations confined to their own domain. They do not counterturn because they do not form triads, nor do they follow the rules previously introduced for the triads in *atxyz*. These planes also complete a second cardinal incarnation of the luminous discourse under the formula one plane and two pairs of wings. Figure 23.8 illustrates schematically the masculine character developments associated with the plane xy of the triad xyz, with their ancillary planes or wings formable with x and y. For the effect of the illustrations, it is considered that the wings are transparent in such a way that the pair of wings xi are seen from behind.

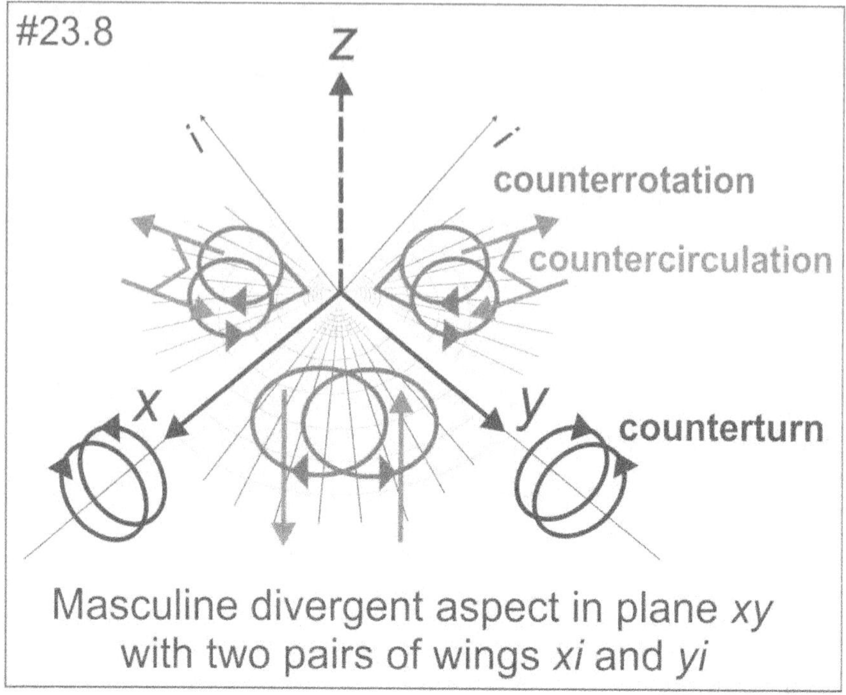

The figure shows the radial countercirculations aspiring to pass through God indicated by double straight arrows and counterrotations and counterturns around the axes by curved ones. All of them annulled each other in the initial conditions of the Creation in all planes, but not the divergent advance indicated by arrows in the axes, including i. The neutrality in the circulations "passing through God" is due to counterorientations, and these will be called the "first conditionality" of the luminous discourse. Said conditionality appears as a pair of additional attributes compounded with those of zeroth and second for a total of four ($4 = 1 \times 2 \times 2$) conditions.

Initial conditions contemplated degrees of freedom in the configuration of the orientations in the ten (10) planes of the manifold $atxyz$, corresponding to the masculine character. For this reason, the arrows with which they are represented in the figure appear unlinked, as if they were independent. The same goes for the counterrotations and counterturns indicated. In the ancillary planes, however, there were no degrees of freedom either in orientations or in rotations; hence there are linked in the figure by pairs like waters. Those conditions are maintained to perpetuity. According to previous considerations on orientation, earthly Jerusalem would then have twelve (12) doors of entry and exit.

The twenty-eight (28) letters of Genesis 1:1 would refer to the development of the hexagon plus the source or the seven polygons of the divergent quantum, both in a quadruple context. Based on the above, the quadruple trait should be interpreted in terms of the quaternary formulas already discussed (28 = 4 × 7)—in particular the odd ones of the 1-3 type. An interpretation based on an odd quadruplicity would contemplate the geometric unfolding of the hexagon or the quantum in four key planes, including the most holy *at* and the earthly ones *xy*, *yz*, and *zx*. These planes are fundamental to the development of the heavenly and earthly human being and of the sacerdotal institution. The reader should note that the quadruplicity just mentioned is subordinated to the four conditionalities referred to when considering the value of the letter ת (tav).

In relation to the contrast between divergence and rotations and turns, perhaps this is the moment to take into account the Farabian decimal cosmogony. In this scheme a new archangelic intellect is generated when it thinks of the being to which it owes its origin (divergence) and a rotor of the orb is produced when it thinks of itself (rotation). Each point or domain in the polygonal geometry houses the possibility of conjugating the verb *to create*. But its election as a destination for the transcription of the protoelemental source is a question of the exclusive competence of the last one. From an observational perspective, the affirmation of the previous paragraph would imply that the absolute freedom of the sources is synonymous with unpredictability. Nevertheless, a sufficiently high number of transcriptions would reveal the finiteness of the possibilities in the geometry of the luminous discourse.

The bases of the Cartesian type have been used here to represent the geometric relationships in the different domains of the luminous discourse due to their general acceptance. However, it should be kept in mind that the significance of the points of the geometry depends on the radius and the Cartesian coordinates play a secondary role in this. The significance of the points in the manifold *atxyz* depends on the divergent developments of the four-sphere in which their locations are defined. In the specific case of the triad *xyz*, the points are located on the surface of a two-sphere (a sphere in three dimensions) centered on the source. In relation to the aforementioned surface, their points have a significance equal to 1/n per 1/n ($1/n^2$). The quadratic formula of point significance in the sphere derives from the product of the significances on two mutually perpendicular circumferences. Both are necessary to form spheres and pinpoint locations around them. When the radius is doubled, the significance of each point or domain of conjugation on the surface of the sphere is reduced to one-fourth. The "law of the inverse of the square of the radius" is thus obtained, which refers in this case to the possibilities of each point in the sphere to accommodate an eventual transcription of its source. Each concentric sphere surrounding the source possesses in its entirety a significance equal to one, as it happens with circumferences far from the source in all planes. At the origin of a source, it is possible to visualize an infinite number of possible independent plane triads, and at the destination of its transcription, an infinite number of independent plane pairs passing through said origin. Figure 23.9 presents schematically the development of previous concepts.

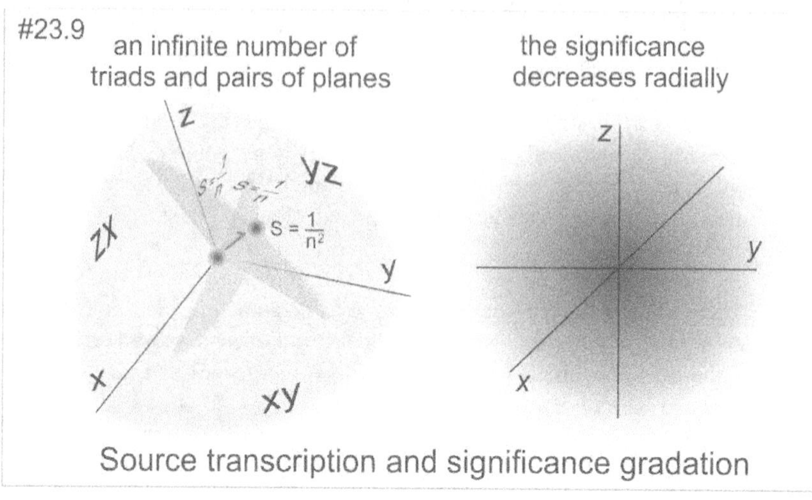

Source transcription and significance gradation

In the originating provisions, the masculine component of the earthly human being (Man) has been conferred the power to direct the transcriptions of the source to any point of the domain *xyz*—inasmuch as the heavenly human being determines them on the transverse direction *t* and God realizes them via *a*, with the concurrence of the angels. With the finality of the divergence toward the empyrean in mind, Augustine of Hippo stated in book 1 of his *Confessions* (*Confessiones*): "You are great, O Lord…because You have made us for Yourself." The third **ayah of surah The Iron** in the Koran summarizes all of the above, stating: "He is the First and the Last, the Most High and the Most Near, and He knows all things." The Most High is beyond the empyreal vault, the Most Near at the point source of every light.

Chapter 24

The Feminine Character of the Luminous Discourse

Before going into the subject of this chapter in depth, it is necessary to specify some differences between the two types of feminine expressions of the luminous discourse mentioned up to this point. The cardinal type is linked to the verb *to compose* and the ordinal ones associated with the verb *to transcribe*. The first ones have been developed so far in three contexts, while the second will be addressed next. The first two cardinal contexts, treated in the previous chapter, are related, on the one hand with countercirculations and on the other with counterrotations and counterturns. Both are similar in terms of annulment by pairing their opposed feminine nature. A third cardinal context was contemplated in relation to the duality of the pairs of wings for each plane of the ten (10) of the manifold *atxyz*. The discussion in this chapter will focus on the ordinal incarnation mechanism of the luminous discourse as well as in additional cardinal formulations.

According to the book of Genesis, the human couple was created on day six; therefore, their procreative role would begin from the seventh. The statement made by Paul in his first letter to Timothy is in line with Genesis 2:22 ("Adam was formed first, then Eve"), exposing also the ordinal character of the procreative act—a question that the Torah raises from its beginning when associating the divine unicity with the letter א (alef) and creation with ב (bet).

The ordinal incarnation of the luminous discourse is given when the source decides to transcribe to any polygon of the light generated from day seven. Even though the source has complete freedom to transcribe to any polygon generated from that day, the initial intention was that it should remain within the walls of Jerusalem (or the boundaries of the Garden of Eden). As already mentioned, these limits were demarcated by the triacontakaihexagon of thirty-six (36) vertices and sides. When transcribing the source, the original divergence, or father, the first day is followed by the mother, or rotational aspect of the ancillary planes. During the second day, the mother receives the source, transports it, and returns it to the third day as her son in the form of the primordial hexagon of hidden light. This scheme is closely linked to the frequent and no less enigmatic "on the third day" sentence, enunciated eloquently by Hosea: "He will revive us after two days. On the third day He will raise us up, so that we may live before His eyes. Then we shall know the Lord."

Just as divergence completes seven polygons on day seven, the feminine character or "rotational quantum" is expressed in seven cycles or rounds that same day—the spin-like and wave-like behaviors in the *atxyz* manifold and its ancillary planes respectively. From the point of view of the quadruplicities considered in the previous chapter, it is also possible to establish correspondences between the rounds and the twenty-eight (28) letters of

Genesis 1:1. In the case of the feminine, the correspondence is between the seven rounds of its two pairs of synchronized wings associated with each plane of the divergent quantum (4 = 2 × 2). Curiously enough, the figure related to each plane has biological representation in the menstrual cycle of women, with its twenty-eight (28) days (28 = 4 × 7 × 1). Also, the 280 days of biological pregnancy for women could be related to the total corresponding to the ten (10) planes of the manifold *atxyz* (280 = 4 × 7 × 10). Other interpretations regarding figure twenty-eight (28) are left to the initiative of the reader, in the context associated with the rotational aspect of the luminous discourse. Figure 24.1 illustrates the mediating role of the female character in the transcription of a source from day seven to the polygon generated that day—just outside the walls of Jerusalem (or the boundaries of the Garden of Eden).

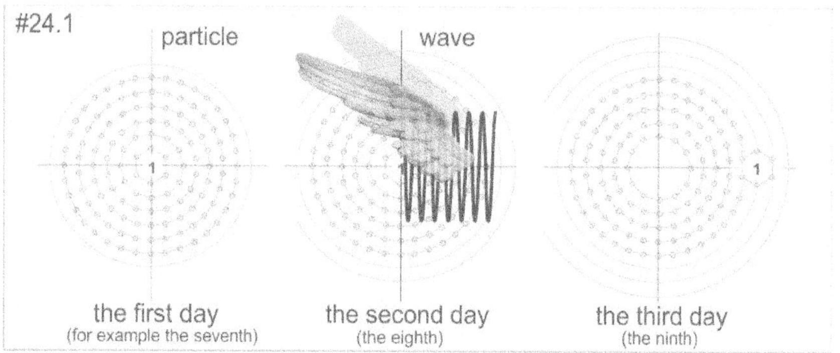

When the source is transcribed within the manifold *atxyz* by the mother or rotational aspect, the divergent progression in the ancillary planes stops while it rotates. Once the source is transcribed, the creation in six days follows and then the seventh day etc. For its part, the father diverges toward the empyrean without generating new polygons from its origin.

The present chapter will deal first with the mediating function of the feminine character or rotational aspect in the ordinal incarnation of the luminous discourse. Above all, in regard to its affectation of the significances at each point of the geometry. In the model to be developed, the cardinality of the figure seventy-three (73 = 36 + 1 + 36), representative up to now of the polygons in counterrotation in the feminine character, will be particularly relevant. In connection with the figure seventy-three (73) and the counterrotations, there is an imperfect sidereal representation in the biennial cycles of planet Earth around the sun, the maximum exponent of the luminous divergence. Each biennium consists of 730 days, a figure that can be related to the seventy-three (73) points of counterrotational polygonal developments, multiplied also in this case by the ten (10), according to the number of planes in the manifold *atxyz*.

For the sages of antiquity, the origins of the sidereal patterns were not due to randomness. The ancients thought that there was an inductive process deliberately orchestrated in order to bring to the attention of humans issues with a deeper meaning. Figure 24.2 shows schematically the partition of the biennium according to the terms indicated, together with a table of calendars from antiquity and related figures.

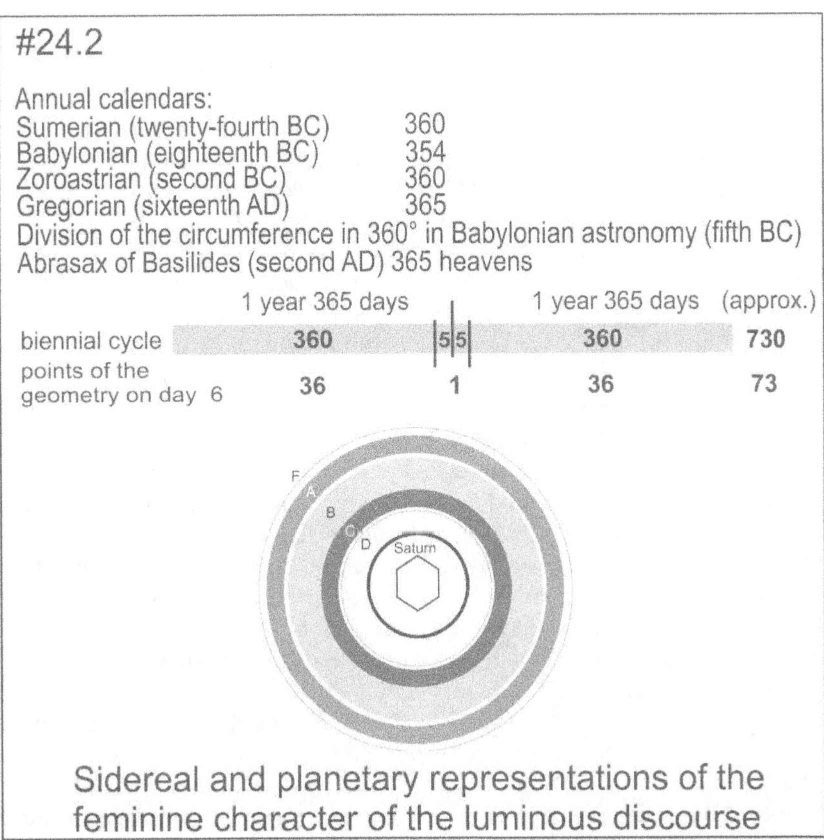

Sidereal and planetary representations of the feminine character of the luminous discourse

It is known that the speeds of rotation of the earth on its axis and of translation around the sun come from displacements of gases and rocks during its formation. The accretion around the gravitational nuclei of these materials that followed was due to countless collisions of the most varied proportions. How, after a process as chaotic as the one described above, can the biennial period of 730 days be reached today? In principle, it could be answered by saying that 730 is a number like any other, and the author of Genesis took the number and divided it by ten. The question is widely debatable but in principle possible. In any case, already in the fifth century BC, the Babylonians were able to subtract the ten (10) days (epagomenal) corresponding to the source and then to divide the circumference with the remaining 360 from each development (equivalent to the wall of Jerusalem in ten [10] planes). The biennial figure of 730 days with the current elliptical orbit of the earth can only be achieved with an appropriate combination of translational and rotational speeds. The current average speeds are 29.8 kilometers per second (km/s) in the translation of the earth around the sun and 0.465 km/s in the tangential velocity of rotation on its axis (both in proportion of 64.09 to 1, almost 64 [64 = 4 × 4 × 4]). If the translation speed decreases or the rotation speed increases, the number of days of the year will increase, and vice versa.

The associations between the number two and the feminine were a constant in ancient cultures. This is attested, for example, by the association of the second rocky planet with the goddess Venus, consort of Vulcan. Planet Venus is the second celestial luminary in importance, preceding or succeeding the sun (masculine symbol of the luminous divergence) at dawn or dusk. However, beyond the scope of the visual observations, there is a surprising representation of the rotations of polygonal developments. This incredible event occurs on planet Saturn, the second gas planet and sixth planet from the sun. Although number two could be associated with the rotational feminine character and six to the primordial hexagon, the coincidence of both numbers is not too surprising. What is truly striking is the dynamics of an atmospheric hexagon discovered by the NASA Voyager probe in its mission from AD 1981 to 1982. It is a cloud formation at the North Pole of Saturn, between two masses of its atmosphere rotating at different speeds. The most curious thing is that the atmospheric phenomenon could be governed by another number if the relative speeds of the gas masses were different from the current ones. It could result in a pentagon, a square, or any other form, even looking similar to a circumference. But why does this peculiar atmospheric phenomena show just six sides on planet six? Would it be an insinuation? Who is making it? Observe the reader at the bottom of figure 24.2, a schematic presentation of the rings and the hexagon of planet six.

In the visualization of the model to be proposed next, it is important to distinguish between the generation of possibilities of transcription of the source and the concretion of only one of them. In fact, it could be considered that all the possibilities of transcription of the source are generated and modulated in parallel with the divergent progression. However, the direction, transcription, determination, and realization of a single one implies an ancillary modulation, which from an ordinal point of view occurs in second place. In fact, the intermediation of the feminine character governs the transit from the origin to the destination of every transcription, in any of the terms anticipated as a possibility. The modulation mechanism for transcriptions toward one of the possible destinations, and through one of all possible paths, will be proposed next.

The modulation mechanism for the possibilities of transcription is analogous to some phenomenologies of a periodic nature, where rapidity is an important factor. For the purpose of its quantification, characterization factors of the rapidity in each ancillary plane are then suggested. The rapidity of the rotations in the plane ti will be represented by the symbol p_t and in xi, yi, and zi by p_x, p_y, and p_z, respectively. Given the limitations of the earthly human being to distinguish between the modulations in the planes ai and ti, they will be grouped and counted under t and p_t.

To quantify the rotational significances of the luminous discourse in its modulating role, it is necessary to propose some definitions in order to eventually converge toward widely accepted mathematical formulations. First, the dependence of the angle of rotation in the ancillary planes will be defined in terms of two factors. On the one hand, it will be considered dependent on the possible "path" followed by the source in the transcription, and on the other, on the characterization factor of the rapidity of the counterrotations. The problem can then be focused on formulating the variation of the rotational significance as a function of that angle. In practice it will be assumed that rotation occurs around the source virtually throughout the extension of the ancillary polygonal expansion, while the geometry remains immutable and without deformation. Figure 24.1 hinted at a cosine-like dependency for rotational significance (one at the beginning when the angle is zero), but now it is necessary to propose the "how" in the simplest way.

In order to facilitate visualization, an inductive approach will be followed, beginning with the notion of the newly proposed angle, which will be applied to the rotation of the primordial hexagon. The concept will then be extended with a view of generating a rotation in the entire domain of possibilities. For this purpose, two well-known composition laws will be used, the sum and the multiplication; the first will be applied radially, and the second angularly. Begin by adding the point significance of the source at the origin, whose value is one, to the point significance in a vertex of the hexagon, whose value is one-sixth. The significance of the vertex is then multiplied by the angle swept when rotating and by i, due to the involvement of the ancillary direction in the rotation plane (the source whose significance is one does not rotate). The result of the previous proposal can be written $(1+p_x xi/6)$, where $p_x x$ is p_x multiplied by x—that is, rapidity factor multiplied by the path traveled; it is the angle of the rotation, as has already been suggested. Since the entire hexagon rotates, the angular composition of the rotations of the six vertices would be $(1+p_x xi/6) \times (1+p_x xi/6) \times (1+p_x xi/6) \times (1+p_x xi/6) \times (1+p_x xi/6) \times (1+p_x xi/6)$. Said expression can be written synthetically in terms of $(1+p_x xi/6)^6$. In the case of a dodecagon, it would be $(1+p_x xi/12)^{12}$; for a triacontakaihexagon $(1+p_x xi/36)^{36}$; and for a polygon of higher order, $(1+p_x xi/n)^n$. When n increases without bounds, the transcendent number, named e, in honor of Euler, is reached, raised in this case to the power "angle multiplied by i." Figure 24.3 attempts to summarize mnemonically the origin of the rotational significance of the primordial hexagon.

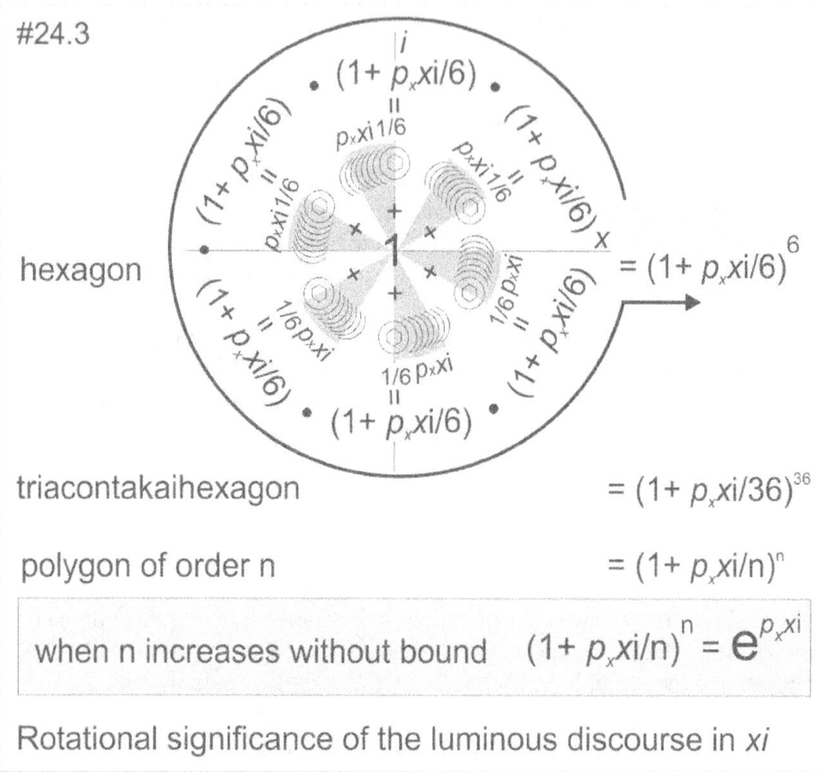

$$\text{triacontakaihexagon} \qquad = (1+ p_x xi/36)^{36}$$

$$\text{polygon of order n} \qquad = (1+ p_x xi/n)^n$$

$$\text{when n increases without bound} \quad (1+ p_x xi/n)^n = e^{p_x xi}$$

Rotational significance of the luminous discourse in *xi*

For the time being, the proposed model for the plane *xi* will be extended only to the planes *yi* and *zi*. The issues of the rotations in the planes *ai* and *ti* require additional considerations, which will be made in due time. The composition of the rotations in the wings of the earthly domain can be expressed mathematically then, as indicated below.

$$\left[(1+ p_x xi/n)^n \times (1+ p_y yi/n)^n \times (1 + p_z zi/n)^n\right]_{n\to\infty} = e^{p_x xi + p_y yi + p_z zi}$$

Rotational significance associated to *x*, *y*, and *z*

The result of composing the rotational significance in the three earthly planes presumes the existence of a global angle or phase. This angle modulates the almost infinite possibilities available in the transcription of the source, giving rise to phenomena of interference between different paths toward the same destination.

As stated previously, the rotational aspect only procreates from day seven of creation, being able to give birth to a son on any polygon generated that same day. In order to fulfill its mission, a minimum of seven cycles of the rotational quantum must be completed, whose culmination will occur on the second day. However, the probability of occurrence in the known universe of an event like the one illustrated in figure 24.1, where seven cycles are completed in 7 ℓ_P, are practically nil. According to the observations made so far, there are no known processes capable of generating the required rapidity, but they could have existed at the beginning of the cosmogonic process. Transcriptions to polygons generated on a day n will occur after completing a not necessarily whole number of cycles. The entire process will depend on the path through which the rotational quantum (of seven cycles) transits and the angular rapidity (or frequency) with which it does so.

In relation to the path followed by the source, it is often wrongly thought that it is only a straight line. Actually, the source has the possibility of going through all of the available paths and so does, without any limitation as to the meaning of *all*. However, the possibilities of going along paths close to the straight line have similar rotational significances, which turn out to be additively dominant. As the possible paths move away from the straight one, they become longer, and the rotational significances begin to interfere destructively with one another. Interferences occur because of the alternating positive and negative values of the rotational significance. Figure 24.4 illustrates schematically on the left the generation of the first alternations of values between +1 and −1 in the modulations of the rotational significances.

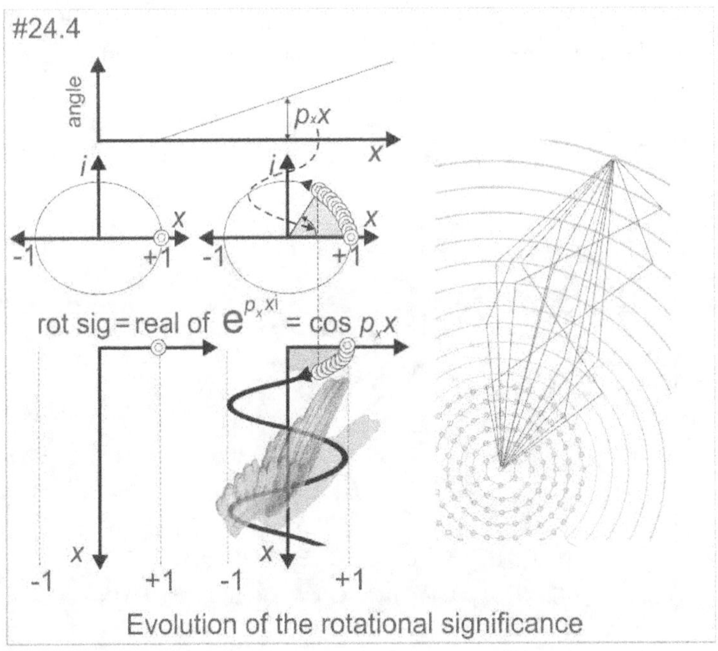

Evolution of the rotational significance

The upper left part of the figure exemplifies the increase of the angle of rotation in the wings with the displacement in direction x corresponding to rapidity equal to p_x. Immediately below it is shown the generation of angles swept by the rotation of one of the polygonal vertices starting at zero. At the lower end, there is an illustration of the evolution of the rotational significance real component (cosine of $p_x x$). The interferences of possibilities between the different paths are due to the sum of rotational significances oscillating between +1 and −1. When two positive or two negative rotational significations are composed (add up), the interference is constructive, and if they are of the opposite sign, it turns out to be destructive. By convention the increments in the rotational significance are associated with the clear attribute of the contrast and the decrements with the dark one, and the evolution of the cosine function would result in a permutation of the contrast. To the right of the figure are schematically shown some possible paths between the source at the origin and a possible destination, outside the walls of Jerusalem (or the boundaries of Eden). The reader is left to imagine all paths to all destination points.

The ordinal feminine character of the luminous discourse acting as a carrier of the source between transcriptions from day seven corresponds to the ancillary expression of the polygonal counterrotating attributes. The real components of the significances or cosine functions of the two ancillary counterrotating attributes coincide because the angles in the positive or negative sense generate the same values. In the same given conditions, the imaginary component or sine function of the two counterrotations cancel each other out. Both aspects, divergent and rotational, constitute a single unit and succeed one another in the realization of the ordinal human incarnation of the luminous discourse. Figure 24.5 shows the feminine rotational aspect in the wings that correspond to the plane xy, with its two counterrotations linked by pairs.

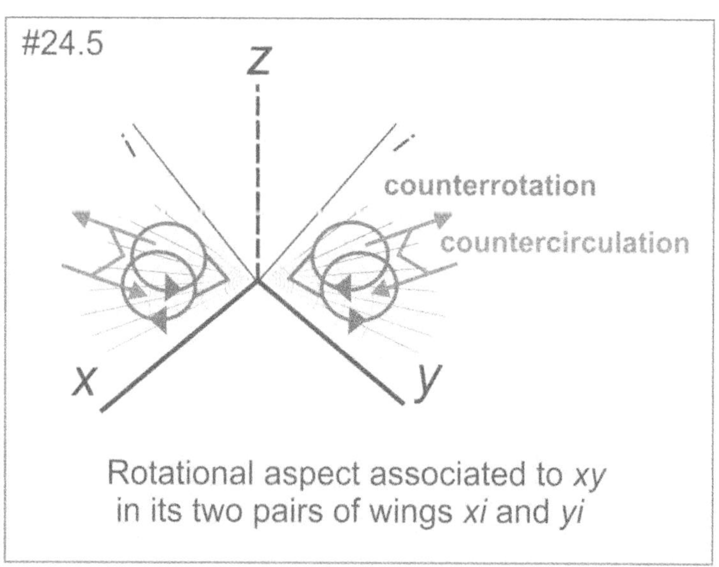

Rotational aspect associated to *xy*
in its two pairs of wings *xi* and *yi*

As shown in the figure, the divergent expansion has stopped, and the countercirculations are engaged in pairs like waters. Do not forget that the plane *xi* is seen from behind.

Regarding the activity of the wings of angels, Shahab al-Din Suhrawardi (the twelfth century AD) answered a question from the Sufi master Abu Ali al-Farmadi (the eleventh century AD) by saying, "most of the observed things are sounds of Gabriel's wings." Being a "master of enlightenment," the periodic phenomenon of the "wings of Gabriel" would certainly refer to the cyclic manifestations of light on the lateral planes associated with *at*.

Next, the fourth context of the cardinal incarnation of the luminous discourse will be addressed. In fact, what has been described in the previous chapter and the present has been circumscribed to the divergent developments of the masculine character and its transcriptions. In this context, masculine components contemplate feminine formulations annulled in pairs for a resultant that could well be considered as luminous earth (in the cases of *xy*, *yz*, and *zx*) or luminous air (as for *at*) (the 36). Now it is time to describe their corresponding female partners, which will be called *luminous waters* (the 73).

Unlike masculine developments, where degrees of freedom in the attributes are contemplated, the waters have them paired with their opposites, annulling themselves to perpetuity. The type of incarnation considered in this chapter exteriorizes an additional formulation of the human being according to formula 1&2, from which only its masculine components have been developed up to now. Thus, for example, the masculine developments in each plane of the triad *xyz* mate with feminine developments in the other two. The developments of the luminous earth in the plane of possibilities *xy* will incarnate cardinally with its partner, a binary formulation of the water type formed in the planes (*yz zx*). Similarly, the developments in the plane *yz* will be coupled in (*zx xy*), and those in the plane *zx* in (*xy yz*). One example to consider is electromagnetic waves, with the electric oscillations taking place in a plane and the corresponding magnetic ones in the transversal plane sharing the direction of propagation. In relation to the developments in *at*, they would mate with the luminous waters to be determined.

The originating provision of perpetual neutrality in the luminous waters contemplates as a possibility the internal reconfiguration of the attributes among the juxtaposed or coincidental waters. It also admits the exchange of internal equivalent attributes and with their masculine consorts. In fact, these attribute exchanges constitute a significant contribution from waters to the cohesion of many types of structures. The waters of the luminous discourse can also be composed or decomposed, adding or dividing the rapidity in their ancillary planes. For the remainder of this book, some behaviors of the waters of luminous discourse will be addressed as soon as the need arises but will avoid the complexities associated with the subject.

To inspire oneself in the visualization of the posed possibilities, the reader should review some graphic representations of the duplication of the DNA molecule, available in various information media. By way of clarification and advancement, it is worth mentioning now that the waters of the luminous discourse correspond to the notion of vacuum in physics. The subject is complex and will be developed progressively within the economic limitations imposed on this natural exegesis.

In the transcriptions of the sources, several situations might arise, of which only a couple of them will be commented on. The first is related to the deformation of the divergence, and the second with possible decompositions and recompositions of the waters by emission/absorption or exchange of actions. The following figure exhibits on the left the case of the deformation due to the transcription of a source from one locality to another in the plane xy. In the illustrated case, neutrality in the first conditioning is represented by double arrows, while other neutral conditions are not indicated. Divergence developing when the source was in A has progressed toward the periphery when the source has been transcribed to B. From that new position, divergence continues its development from the origin, where its source is now. The reader should observe the change in the phase indicated in figure 24.6 by the pointer angular advancement.

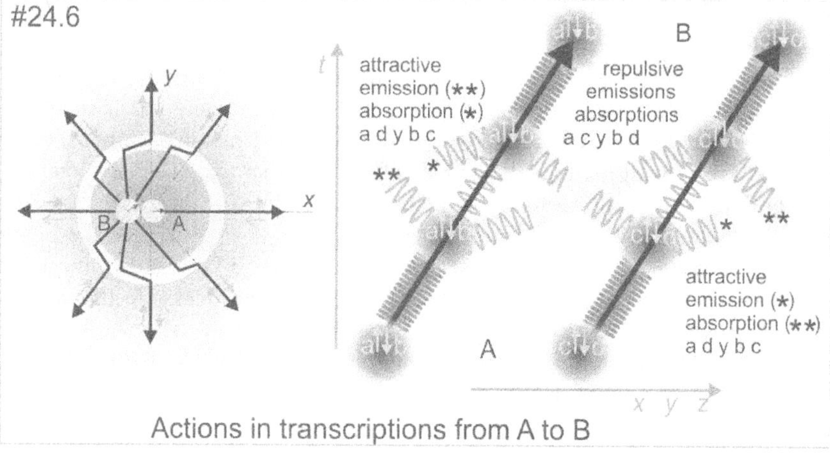

Actions in transcriptions from A to B

The reader may also notice a lighter ring where the deformation is indicated. If the divergent quantum oscillates between A and B, a "wave" would be generated in said domain. Despite the deformations caused in the development of the divergence by transcription of the sources, the original front continues its circular advance toward the empyrean.

Under initial conditions, the masculine lights had all their opposites annulled by pairs, limiting the impact of their actions. The cancellations of greater interest are present in the developments of the planes xy, yz, and zx of the triad, as well as in the most holy at. For their part, the waters, despite their condition of neutrality, can always be reconfigured by dividing or grouping at the behest of the masculine lights with which they are coupled. In the case of the divisions, waters split their original rapidities in such a way that the rotations in their ancillary planes will be slower. When waters are grouped, their speeds add up, and the resulting ancillary rotation will be faster. When addressing the disruptive events that modified the course of the Creation, particularly in regard to their initial conditions, some variants in the behavior of waters will be addressed.

To the right of figure 24.6 is illustrated a case of decomposition and recomposition of the waters of the luminous discourse. Mutual emission/absorption or exchange of waters between divergent quanta is accomplished via the intermediation of their rotational quanta. Specifically, the figure illustrates a type of exchange that does not produce deviations in the transcription of the divergent quanta due to the prevailing neutrality, but it does change their frequency (rapidity). In the same figure, the countercirculations of the divergent quanta have been indicated by means of double arrows identified with the letters *a*, *b*, *c*, and *d*. The attributes corresponding to the second conditioning have not been indicated. Water exchanges are always done at the speed of light, regardless of the rapidity of its own rotational quantum. Even though the illustration just mentioned resembles the diagrams of R. Feynman (the twentieth century AD) used in quantum physics, it is not convenient to take the analogy too far. In fact, the primary objective of the illustration is to transmit the idea of decomposition and recomposition of waters. The ancillary waves or rotations shown are indicative and only seek to create an impression. The conjugation of the verb *to direct* establishes the destiny of the transcription of the source and of its actions. All the quanta will be able to absorb the actions emitted by those others in whose geometries they are located.

From an exegetical point of view, the propositions in the preceding paragraphs in no way constitute a novelty, strictly speaking, since already in the twelfth century AD, Suhrawardi introduced his illuminative thoughts, where light in all its manifestations appears as the only form of divine expression in the Creation. The illuminative thought from Suhrawardi is that if there is something that does not need definition or explanation, it must be obvious by nature, and nothing is more obvious and clearer than the light. In the extensive work of Suhrawardi, surprising details about the nature of the luminous phenomenon are discovered. They were expressed in allegorical language, often used by thinkers of its time with the intention of evading fatal controversies, an issue in which it was not successful. One of those precisions is about the decimal context of luminous phenomenon, complemented by a fourfold conditioning. In the Suhrawardian model, light originates in a decimal domain where ten (10) perfections reside, which he describes as ten (10) elders of sublime beauty. Each elder oversees a four-level mill.

While the masculine character of the luminous discourse advances radially in search of God beyond the empyrean, the feminine progresses angularly in search of itself in the Creation. The periodicity of reproductive cycles of women (absent in men) has been considered as an expression of the "distraction" of the female archetype, with which she would "shy away" from the search for God. Consequently, women were denied the exercise of functions with a sacerdotal rank in the religions of the People with the Book. For example, the entrance to the most holy place of the Hebrew Temple was never open to any woman since only the High Priest could enter it on rare occasions. In Zoroastrianism and Christianity, sacerdocy is reserved for men, even though women may assist them in minor issues. In the Islamic religion, women cannot lead the prayers of men or lead the "effort" (jihad) to extend the law of God.

The aversion to certain circular or periodic intracosmic manifestations acquires even an extreme formal character in the Bible. Such is the case with the prohibition of the use of iron tools (Fe, from the Latin *ferrum*) in the construction of the house of the Cult of Adoration to the Most High. In that sense, the Bible declares in 1 Kings: "While the house was being built, cut and finished stones were used. So that no hammers, chisels or other iron tools in the house were heard, while it was under construction." Beyond the obvious corruptibility and rigidity of iron, the motivations for such provisions are based on other aspects of its phenomenology, well known since its discovery. Among the undesirable features are its paramagnetism (property of all those elements or compounds being attracted by a magnetic field) and its ferromagnetism (generation of a massive external magnetic field by ordering constituent units). The circular concentric traces of iron dust around larger pieces, due to magnetism, showed a deplorable tendency to close itself within the world—an obviously unseemly behavior in a house or monument dedicated to divergence. Figure 24.7 schematically represents the rotational phenomenologies associated with magnetism.

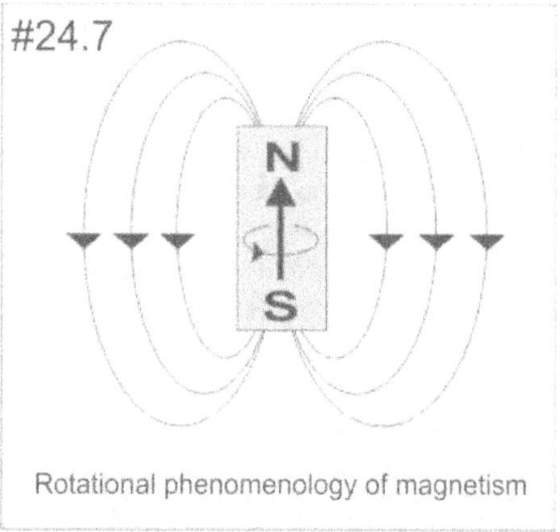

Rotational phenomenology of magnetism

Regarding the inappropriateness of closed paths in the house of the divergence, Ezekiel says:

When the people of the earth come before the Lord, on holidays, whoever enters through the north gate to worship will come out by the southern gate and the one that enters through the south gate will exit through the north gate. He will not return through the door through which he entered but will always go forward before Him.

The intracosmic circulations included in the originating provisions of the Creation and their initial conditions, which seem to evade divinity, are also the work of the Creator. Therefore, they should not be considered essentially malignant. Other phenomenologies in closed loops, which are the product of the abandonment of said initial conditions, are condemnable.

Notwithstanding that, outside the temple built by King Solomon, there were representations with feminine semblance. Such was the case with a pair of bronze (copper alloy) columns, probably of tin (Sn, from the Latin *stannum*), located in front of the porch, and which were called Boaz (located to the north) and Jachin (located to the south). But not all dualities are necessarily feminine in a strict sense. In the case of the columns, one of them, Boaz, would be a symbolic representation of one of the Anointed Ones in *a*, while Jachin would be of those linked to the lower waters, the Spirit *t*, or the priest (any possibility of earth in *xyz*). With both, it would be possible to fit a formulation of type 1&1. The placement of a representation of the sacerdotal institution at the entrance of the temple built by King Solomon in the tenth century BC was not an innovation. In Egypt, the temples of Karnak and Luxor, built ten and four centuries earlier, already had at the entrance two obelisks covered with electro, with the same meaning and function.

An object located in front of the temple of King Solomon, susceptible to being considered among genuine representations of feminine archetypes, is the so-called bronze sea. Located next to Jachin (Spirit or priest), and of course outside the temple, the vessel was supported by four triads of oxen pointing to the four cardinal points. In the context of its liturgical use as a means for purification, the waters of the bronze sea symbolized the chaos in the primordial waters preceding every creation. The four triads of oxen would represent, in turn, the four cosmic directions containing some of the upper and lower waters. The three oxen represent the protoelement fire imbibed in the four cosmic directions, as in Exodus 3 and 4.

According to biblical texts (1 Kings 7:23 and 2 Chronicles 4:2), the bronze sea measured ten (10) cubits in diameter and thirty (30) cubits in circumference—a couple of figures frequently used to prove an alleged ignorance of the Bible about the relation of transcendence existing between a circumference and its diameter (known as the number pi [π]). As shown in enough detail in the formulation of the luminous discourse, the perfect circumference is obtained by the divergent expansion or by rotation of the primordial hexagon. The measures in cubits given by the Bible correspond to that hexagonal origin and to the amount of water in the vessel that contains them. Figure 24.8 illustrates an interpretation of the biblical measures of the bronze sea.

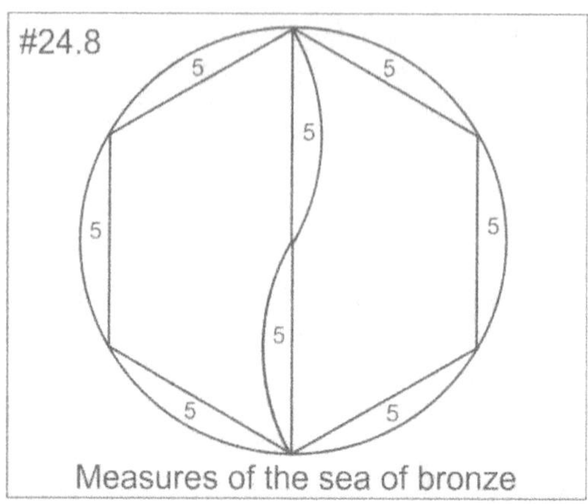

Measures of the sea of bronze

In fact, the numbers ten (10) and thirty (30) can be related to the rotational or water content of the vessels or planes. The first one refers to the total number of counterrotations in the five ancillary planes (10 = 2 × 5) of the feminine character of the ordinal incarnation, while the second can be related to the counterrotations in the fifteen (15) planes (30 = 15 × 2) of the masculine character.

Having postulated the feminine character of the luminous discourse, it is now necessary to consider the mechanism of its fertilization. The Bible is emphatic in proclaiming the insufficiency of the earthly human being in the realization of creation, and it does so in connection with the patriarchal lineage. The narratives related to this succession functionally reunite four indispensable actors, the Eternal, his Spirit, the Man, and the Woman, conjugated in the heavenly and earthly human beings. In the case of the patriarchs (as Osiris with his phallus lost), the sterility of the three couples Abraham and Sarah, Isaac and Rebecca, and Jacob and Rachel is striking, particularly in relation to the procreation of the heirs to the patriarchal title. As has been commented on previously, the book of Genesis tells how the Lord had to approach Sarah, Rebecca, and Rachel to make them fruitful. The reader should keep in mind the three possibilities of formula 1&1&2 as far as earth and water are concerned.

The sequence of the ordinal incarnation of the human being could be illustrated starting with patriarch Abraham, in representation of a divergence already determined and realized by God on the first day. In its divergent polygonal development, the patriarch contemplates the domain of possible occurrences of his source. Making use of the free will that he possesses as a masculine odd creature, Abraham directs his intention toward a particular occurrence in the triad *xyz*. But to transcribe its own nature there and have a child, or a copy of himself, he requires his spouse as a mediating instance. His ordinal mate was described above in terms of the rotational aspect of light in the ancillary planes, who must become the carrier of the seed during the transcription. But all that is only a family plan or, put in other words, a mere possibility because in the light of patriarchal succession the couple is sterile.

The fecundation of the feminine component of the luminous discourse can only be achieved with the determination of the Spirit and the realization by the Creator, via *t* and *a*, respectively. This God, guarantor of the originating provisions and indispensable for the realization of patriarchal successions, is also the one who fecundates Mary, the mother of Jesus, with his Spirit. The father of Jesus before society, who was called Joseph, is as incapable of fertilizing Mary as were Abraham, Isaac, and Jacob in regard to their consorts. Hence the answer given by Jesus to Nicodemus in the Gospel of John, already quoted above: "I truly tell you that if the birth of a man does not come from the water and the Spirit, it is not possible for him to enter the kingdom of God."

It should come as no surprise to anyone the endless discussions over the centuries about the virginity of Mary before and after the schism between the Roman and Greek churches. The most eloquent dogmatic proclamation about the issue was given at the Lateran synod in 649 AD. This council was convoked by Pope Martin I (the sixth to the seventh centuries AD), who was later martyred because of some doctrinal results contrary to the beliefs of Emperor Constans II (the seventh century AD). Paraphrasing Maximus of Turin (the fourth to the fifth centuries AD), the council fathers gathered in the Lateran basilica proclaimed the dogma of the perpetual virginity of Mary in the following terms:

> If anyone, according to the Holy Fathers, does not confess truly and properly that holy Mary, ever virgin and immaculate is the true Mother of God, as she conceived the one who is the only and true God—the Word begotten by God the Father from all eternity—in these last times, without human semen and born without corruption of her virginity, which remained intact after his birth, let him be anathema.

A statement perfectly applicable to the feminine character associated with the plane *at* (in addition to *ai* and *ti*), for reasons that will be addressed later on and that are related to the fidelity of the Spirit to the initial conditions of the Creation.

For his part, the prophet Muhammad unreservedly recognized the virginity of Mary when he says in surah The Prophets: "And she who retained her virginity, so we breathed into her Our inspiration and made her and her son a sign for the Nations." The Holy Scriptures are not too profuse in the treatment of the subject of sterility; however, they emphasize the fact by reporting other sterile Women. Such was the case with the mother of Samson (the twelfth to the eleventh centuries BC), according to Judges 13; Hannah, the wife of Elkanah (the eleventh century BC), reported in 1 Samuel 1; and the sterility of Elizabeth (the first century BC to the first century AD), wife of Zechariah (the first century BC to the first century AD) and mother of John the Baptist, according to Luke 1. In turn, the Koran endorses the infertility of Sarah and Rebecca in surah Hud and also recognizes that of Elizabeth when recounting the concession made to her husband, Zechariah, for the birth of John, as recorded in surah The Prophets.

Despite the limitations of the masculine component of the earthly human being (Man) in the fertilization of his spouse, he can direct freely the luminous discourse within the triad *xyz*. By virtue of this capability, he is considered cocreator, as clearly stated in Psalm 8: "What is man that You are mindful of him? And what is the son of man, that You take care of him?...You have made him ruler of the works of Your hands, you have put all things under his feet..." The masculine component of the luminous discourse gives form to creation when directing it, like what a goldsmith does when he makes an empty vessel—like the bed of a dry river, and it is the Spirit to whom it corresponds to fill it with a current of determinations, waiting for its realization by God.

Before concluding this chapter dedicated to the feminine component of the luminous discourse, it is convenient to reflect briefly on the discrete character of these developments. For, as things have been stated here, there would not be movements in the Creation with a solution of continuity; there are only transcriptions of static geometrical objects—a mesh, as it were. L. Massignon (the nineteenth to the twentieth centuries AD) concludes that for Muslim theologians time is not continuous, but a constellation of instants and space does not exist; there are only points. Sunni atomists like al-Ash'ari or the illuminationists after Molla Sadra (the sixteenth to the seventeenth centuries AD) would not have much difficulty admitting the postulates summarized in previous paragraphs. In fact, the philosopher and mystic of Shiraz gave a decisive turn to the philosophy of Illuminationism, giving primacy to "existence" above all else, understanding by existence everything that is realized by God, as has been proposed. Both Molla Sadra and the eminent Jesuit philosopher of Grenadian origin F. Suarez (the sixteenth to the seventeenth centuries AD), a contemporary of his, thought that the modes of existence constitute the true and only substance. For both, the cosmic becoming is a succession of ways of existing. This succession was called by Molla Sadra "substantial movement" (*haraka jawhariyya*), a term translated by the French philosopher H. Corbin (the twentieth century AD) as "the disquietude of being" (*l'inquiétude de l'être*). It is a denial of immutability driven progressively toward a purpose.

In a strict sense, there would be at each step a new cosmos preceded by its nonexistence and succeeded in the action by its dispersion toward the empyrean, to be replaced then by a similar one but emergent and different—a new existence. Molla Sadra affirmed that the succession of ways of existing had neither beginning nor end because it was caused directly and at each step by an eternal being, God. The movement in the substance would in fact be the perpetual change of the divine presence in the cosmos, in accordance with the Koranic statement in surah The Beneficent: "All those in the heavens and on earth ask about Him. Every moment He is in a new state of glory. Which then of the bounties of your Lord will you deny?"

Chapter 25

The Lampstand of the Tabernacle

It is no longer possible to continue extracting data from the book of Genesis about the nature of the luminous discourse without running into complications that would detract from the purpose of this book. For this reason, it is preferable to direct the attention toward other symbolic figures of great power in order to move forward. Perhaps the candelabrum ordered to Moses by God is one of the best examples available to reach a sufficiently finished formulation of the luminous discourse. The lampstand, with its seven lights on it, is not easy to interpret and visualize. In fact, according to the book of Exodus, Moses had difficulties with instructions given by God to craft it and had to rely on a model. Due to the referred complexities, the reader is kindly requested to approach it with caution. It represents recurrences typical of the exteriorizations of the luminous discourse archetypes in various instances, which raise plenty of issues to think about. The interpretation of the symbolism associated with the lampstand of the Tabernacle will proceed in three stages. The first includes a quotation from the Bible about crafting instructions, followed by a schematic illustration of its form. In the second stage, the elements of the luminous discourse already addressed will be identified on the lampstand. Finally, the additional data provided by the lampstand will be considered with the purpose of incorporating them into the model.

According to the book of Exodus in the Bible, the instructions given to Moses to make the lampstand of the Tabernacle were as follows:

> And you shall make a lampstand of the best gold. Its base and central stem shall be formed with hammered gold, its globules and flowers must be made of the same metal. It shall have six branches extended from the sides of the lampstand, three on one side and three on the other. Each branch shall have three cups made like flowers of almond tree, each cup with a globule and a flower, in all the branches. The central stem shall have four cups, like those of almond flowers, with their globules and flowers. And under each pair of branches there shall be a globule, made with the branch, for the six branches… Then you shall make the seven vessels for the lights, putting them in place so that they give light in front of it.

Before presenting an illustration of the lampstand of the Tabernacle, it would be convenient to refer to the origin of the discrepancies between the different types of plastic representations made over the centuries. The great diversity of models has been due mainly to the absence of certain details in the biblical narrative regarding its form. Many of these representations have been inspired by interpretations of the text of the book of Exodus, others by historical references and religious dispositions, and not a few by the imagination. Some are in favor of identifying the lampstand with the burning bush, but such an association does not seem right because Moses had seen it carefully and would not require a model.

Also the lampstand has been associated with the tree of life, a mytheme (irreducible part of a myth) present in almost all religious traditions of antiquity. On the other hand, there are those who compare it even with the Palestinian salvia, which is very common in the Holy Land and with which it has a remarkable resemblance. Unfortunately, all these comparisons obviate the rich and dense symbolism present in the candelabrum. Figure 25.1 shows a schematic representation of the lampstand based on archaeological findings from two synagogues, one in Magdala, from the first century AD, and the other one in Eshtemoa, of the second century AD. Both are almost contemporary with the destruction of the temple of Herod the Great.

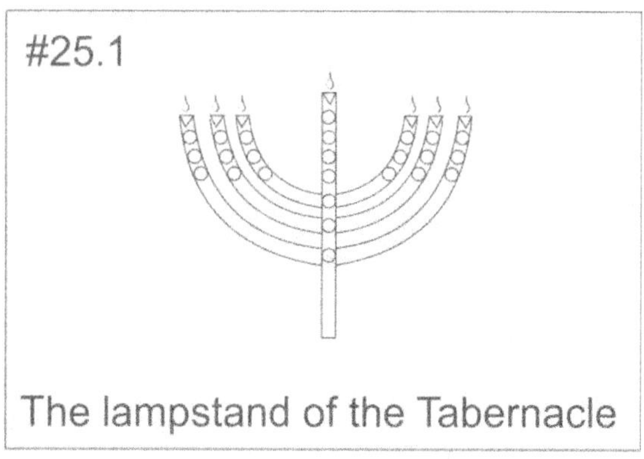

The candelabrum of the Tabernacle was part of the booty taken from the temple sacking by the Romans. A representation with a pedestal of somewhat doubtful form appears in the arch raised by the emperor Domitian (the first century AD) to commemorate the triumph of his brother Titus over the Hebrews. Almost immediately, the prohibition on making replicas of the lampstand came into force; this lasted until recently, when plastic representations of the most diverse nature began to show up. The symbolism present in the form of the lampstand of the Tabernacle will be interpreted based on the schematic presentation in figure 25.1. The illustrated form contains some of the most relevant elements of the instructions given to Moses. Subsequently, the metal and the fuel chosen by God will be discussed, with which the exercise proposed for this chapter will culminate.

The lampstand is in the first place a reference to the presence of God before the beginning and beyond the end of the hexadirectional domain of the Creation. In this interpretative scheme, the central stem would represent the extracosmic intervention of the Creator, and the six lateral arms would symbolically represent the manifold of independent directions of the Creation, *aitxyz*. Its form is also akin to an interpretation of Genesis 1:1 in terms of the composition of two odd quaternary formulations of the 1-3 type. More specifically, the central stem would symbolize the one that transcends the three, either a or t transcending x, y, and z. In terms of planes, the central stem would correspond to the plane at and the three pairs of lateral arms to the planes xy, yz, and zx. In the schematic presentation of figure 25.2, the aforementioned correspondences are shown, highlighting the correspondences between the seven words of the first verse of the book of Genesis and the form of the candelabrum. The countercirculations conditioning the passage through God of the divergent developments involved in the second interpretation are also indicated.

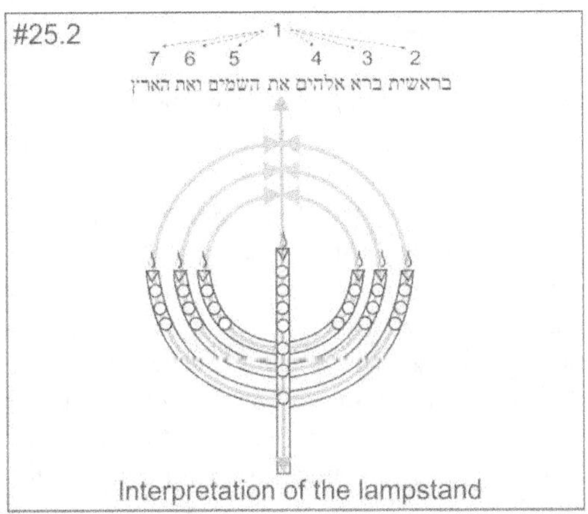

Interpretation of the lampstand

On the other hand, the symbolism of the globules is quite complex and can also be the object of different interpretations due to the exteriorization of archetypal formulations in various instances. In order to clarify the exposition, the globules subject to interpretation are distinguished by dark lines in figure 25.3.

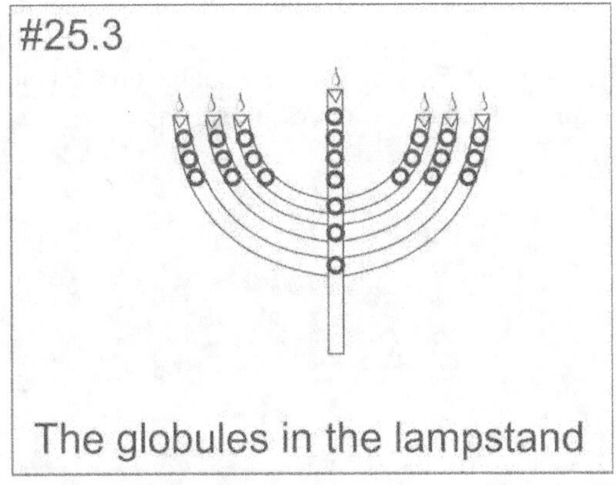

The globules in the lampstand

The reader is kindly requested to observe the seven globules present in the central stem and in the three horizontal rows. The arrangement can be interpreted as was done with the twenty-eight (28) letters of Genesis 1:1, in terms of quadruplicities related to the quanta ($28 = 4 \times 7$), despite the fact that the number of globules present is twenty-five (25), since only one is included in the central stem for each pair of lateral arms. In the central stem, two forms of being three are expressed vertically in the presence of the transcendent one, which is symbolized in the figure by the globule at the upper end. Immediately below that upper globule on the central stem, there would be a symbolic representation of the three equal or interdependent ones, while the lobes at the junction of the central stem, with the three lateral arms, would symbolize the intersections of the transcendent with the three distinct or independent x, y, and z.

The three rows of globules present in the central stem and in the lateral arms seem to refer to a ternary conditionality in the luminous discourse. There would then be three indissolubly united candelabra in one. Each of them represents a distinctive and incommunicable attribute of its own and is dependent on the other two, as in the igneous formulations. Something similar happens with the two components of the chiaroscuro contrast in waters, either in a codon with human formulation or in its independent manifestations. Consequently, and only for reasons of convenience, the distinctive attributes of each candelabra are identified by the use of the primary colors blue, green, and red. The same was done with the components of the protoelement fire, in spite of not having an indisputable connection with the phenomenology of the luminous spectrum.

However, in a speculative sense, it would be possible to presume that the psychic impression caused by the three primary colors refers to the pure essence of the attributes of fire. Moreover, it would be impossible to add anything else to that description. Ternary attributes would then be just that, what is exteriorized in the mind when they are seen. In any case, regardless of the terminology used to distinguish them, the important thing in the joint realization of the three lampstands is their subjection to the formulation of the protoelement fire. Figure 25.4 suggests a visualization scheme in accordance with the igneous formulation of the three lampstands.

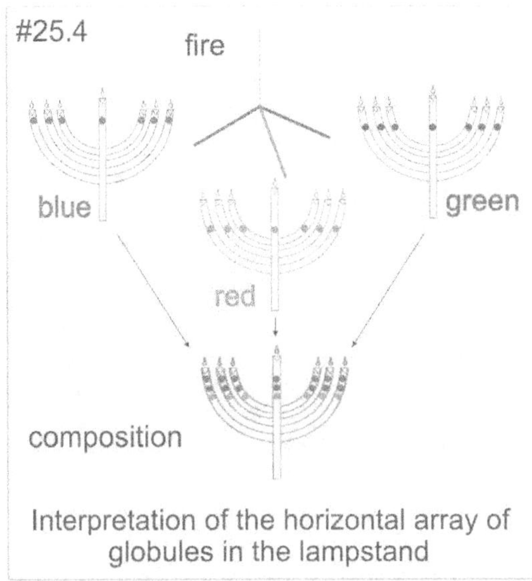

Interpretation of the horizontal array of
globules in the lampstand

The globule at the upper end of the central stem and the three independent globules at the junction with the lateral arms would not participate in the chromatic display. The occurrence of three types of distinctive attributes constitutes the basis of the "third conditionality" of the incarnated luminous discourse. In the initial conditions of the Creation, none of the attributes predominated locally over the other two. However, it will be assumed that only the global neutrality condition is an originating provision for all purposes of the current exegesis. Additionally, the trio of attributes identified chromatically would be initially endowed with an intrinsic order and cyclically permuted in the three components, leading to nine ($9 = 3 \times 3$) possibilities, which is a recurring figure, as in the nine triads of the manifold *atxyz*, where *a* and *t* participate. As previously suggested, the aforementioned independent nine triads are *atx*, *aty*, *atz*, *axy*, *ayz*, *azx*, *txy*, *tyz*, and *tzx* where the angelic entities dwell. The presence of *a* or *t* or both is related to the affirmation of the Hebrew mysticism, according to which the holiness on high is three by three. Thus the nine lights, or Sefirot, are generated (excluding *Shekhinah*, the triad *xyz*, of the earth), flaming from their dispositions and radiating toward the confines.

The arrangement will be designated *light*, or *lights* in the plural, in agreement with previous uses given to both words. The definition encompasses geometric developments from the primordial hexagon plus its source, to the outer front progressing toward the empyrean. Figure 25.5 illustrates the compositions of the three cyclic permutations of the ternary attributes, identifying them with the three first letters of the Hebrew alphabet, א (alef), ב (bet), and ג (gimmel).

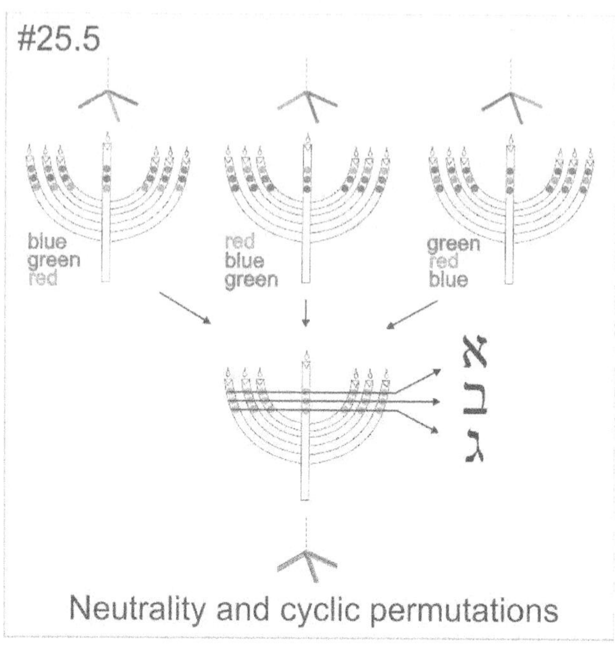

The manifestation of the third conditionality will be considered with special interest for the developments in *at*, *xy*, *yz*, and *zx*, in which the fire is embedded, like the oxen supporting the bronze sea. Its clearest expression in the Bible is given in the four aforementioned apparitions of the declaration "God of Abraham, God of Isaac, and God of Jacob," three times in Exodus 3 (lateral arms) and a fourth time in Exodus 4 (central stem). It is also interesting the parallelism between geometry, with its three attributes, and the formula of the Cappadocian Fathers proposed in the fourth century AD: "same substance, three divine hypostasis." This term was used by the Fathers to refer to the proper, individual, and incommunicable nature that the three persons of the Holy Trinity maintain in their intradivine interchange. According to the words of Augustine of Hippo, it is about three "relations" and "what for the Greeks is hypostasis for Latins is person." For his part, Thomas Aquinas, following Augustine, conceived the being of the three persons of the Holy Trinity in terms of "constitutive relationality." Over the centuries, the term *person* evolved and progressively became identified with rational human nature. This is the reason why the term *person* is today totally inadequate when referring to the three aspects of divinity. Hypostasis of the Cappadocian Fathers are currently interpreted in terms of "subsistences," "ways of subsisting," "ways of being," etc. Then, on the Christian side at least, it would be possible to relate the three attributes with some form of exteriorization of the immanent Trinity, which is that of God committed to his Creation.

Consistently, the luminous waters of the discourse will be defined in pairs of complementary earthly planes, (*yz zx*), (*zx xy*), and (*xy yz*), being also conditioned in a triple way. Thus the fourth cardinal incarnation of the luminous discourse, already introduced in the previous chapter, is now completed. The need for absolute neutrality in waters would suggest duplicating the luminous development in the manner of an additional cardinal incarnation. Therefore, the luminous males would possess a double set of ternary attributes chromatically distinguished as blue, green, and red with their relative neutrality, while the luminous waters would have a double set of attributes, with one consisting of blue, green, and red and the other with the antiattributes yellow (antiblue), magenta (antigreen), and cyan (antired)—thus in full compliance with the chiaroscuro contrast that characterizes them.

The interpretation of the candelabrum symbolism, based on the composition of two formulations of the 1-3 type, allows observing two matrix arrays of 3 × 4 globules. A similar arrangement is found in the breastplate of the High Priest, where 4 × 3 precious and semiprecious stones are set in representation of the twelve (12) tribes of Israel. The three globules in the central stem of the lampstand establish a distinction with the rest, as it occurs in the "dodeca" symbolisms of the Hebrew Bible and the Gospels. The rectangular matrix array is vertical in the breastplate of the High Priest, while they are both horizontal in the lampstand, as indicated in figure 25.6.

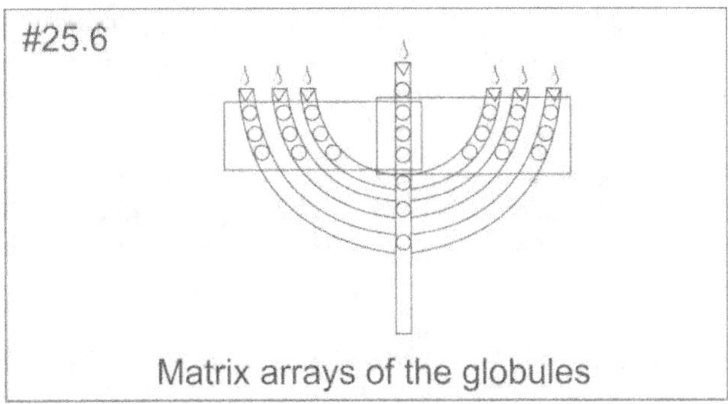

Matrix arrays of the globules

In total there are twenty-one (21 = 3 × 7) globules arranged horizontally. The ternary attributes demand a rethinking of the set of attributes affecting polygonal developments—now reaching twelve conditions, its maximum number (12 = 1 × 2 × 2 × 3).

Having interpreted enough elements of form in the candelabrum to proceed, it would be convenient to dedicate some lines to the metal of fabrication. According to divine instructions, that metal is gold, probably from the booty taken from Egypt when undertaking the Exodus. Gold is a good conductor of electricity and heat and is also largely diamagnetic (repelled by magnetic fields, diamagnetism, a phenomenon discovered by the Dutch botanist J. Brugmans [the eighteenth to the nineteenth centuries AD]). Gold is then repelled by magnetized substances and their circular manifestations, making it particularly convenient for symbolic representations of the divergence. It also possesses an extraordinary ductility (quality of undergoing great mechanical deformations in cold without breaking) and malleability (quality of being reducible to thin sheets in cold), which makes it the ideal metal for goldsmithing.

Gold is also a poorly reactive chemical element since it is not easily corruptible, chemically speaking. The marked "disinterest" of gold to get involved with other chemical elements was interpreted in antiquity as a natural representation of sanctity, inasmuch as the lights, at the beginning of the Creation, were dedicated exclusively to the adoration of the Most High, while ignoring each other. In the rare chemical reactions of gold with other agents, it mainly adopts two conditions. One of them is denominated in chemistry aurous ion, or gold (I), and the other one is called auric ion, or gold (III), both related to the bases of representation 1-3 so present in the lampstand. The gold (II) and gold (V) compounds are even less frequent, to the point of not deserving major considerations.

Metallic gold has an odd number of electrons (seventy-nine [79]), which implies that the intrinsic turn or "spin" of one of them has no contrary with which to pair. In its fundamental state, gold possesses seventy-eight (78) electrons without a net rotation around the center of the atom and with its opposite intrinsic turns paired ($L_z = 0$, $S_z = 0$), yielding a total equal to zero. It is practically impossible to have a chemical element to make a lampstand, whose atom is free of orbital rotations and intrinsic turns in "standard conditions" (as it happens with noble gases). Because of this limitation, the rotational neutrality of the lights at the beginning of the Creation could not be represented exactly with the candelabrum. Within the context of natural exegesis, and taking into consideration the "razor principle" stated by the Franciscan friar G. Ockham (the thirteenth to the fourteenth centuries AD) (*lex parsimoniae*), electron seventy-nine (79) will be identified with some types of lights yet to be known. In fact, the reader will be able to recognize them in chapter 33.

The intrinsic turn of electron seventy-nine (79) in the triad *xyz* is considered an expression of the second conditionality of the luminous discourse and is included in the already-accounted possibilities. Since the luminous earth or masculine components of the earthly human beings (Men) are formulated exclusively in the same ternary context, said turn will be considered intrinsic to them. As belonging to the second conditionality, the turns within the triad *xyz* were locally and globally null in the initial conditions, as they also are perpetually in the waters. Therefore, the local splitting of the turns would have its origin in a disruptive event that should be addressed. The model of the luminous discourse will take into consideration only two types of feminine rotational manifestations. One of them occurs in the ancillary planes *ai*, *ti*, *xi*, *yi*, and *zi* associated with an ordinal incarnation. The other one, within the earthly triad and around its axes *x*, *y*, and *z*, called the intrinsic turn, has its origins in cardinal incarnations. Other turns outside the indicated ones will not be contemplated. For this reason, all other imaginable possibilities in the remaining nine triads of the manifold *atxyz* will be considered perpetually null by pairs opposition.

So far two ways of being three have already been explored in the symbolism of the lampstand of the Tabernacle, the three distinct and independent *xyz* and the three equal and interdependent (blue green red). It would be necessary to discover yet another way of being three, the formulation of the human being. The absence of an obvious symbolism of human character in the form of the candelabrum is a fact of great relevance, as the outstanding presence of the protoelement fire in its rigid form also is. However, the human formulation is present in the fluid fuel and in the irradiated light.

The lampstand fuel is olive oil, whose main component is olein. It is a triglyceride with three cis-oleic groups present in an approximate weight ratio of three-fourths to the total of oil. Very little cis-oleic acid is in a free state, being almost all involved in the oleic-oleic-oleic triacylglycerol, formerly called by its common name, olein. Cis-oleic acid has the peculiarity of being formed by a chain of eighteen (18) carbon atoms, separated by a double bond in the middle. Its structure is thus divided into two parts with nine carbon atoms each, just the number of globules on each side of the matrix array on the lateral arms. Olein has a structure where two cis-oleic functional groups at the ends are linked to one central, which represents molecularly the formula of the earthly human being. Figure 25.7 attempts to illustrate the symbolic charge of olein in the candelabrum of the Tabernacle.

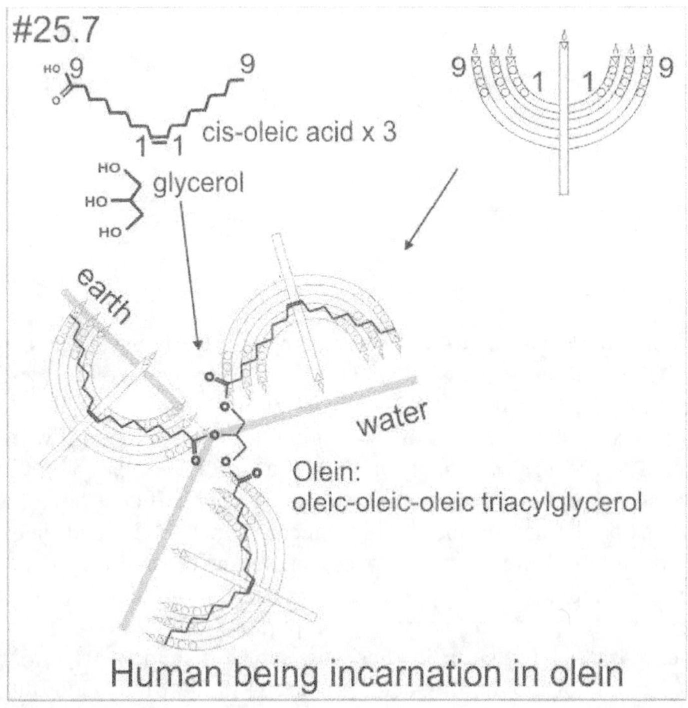

Olein is the fuel with human traits whose transformation produces light and ratifies the human condition as the essence to be expressed in the formulations of the lampstand. It is as if the ternary basis of the 1&2 type and its expression in the heavenly and earthly human beings embodies the cosmos formulations first and last. It is important to finally remember that the form of the lampstand in the mind of Moses constitutes only mere possibilities. In other words, it is an empty container. Once the candelabrum is made and lighted by an act of divine realization, it will then be a real object.

Despite its symbolic power, graphic representations of the form of the lampstand are not practical or to be used in modular constructions of more complex composite objects. An extremely compact symbol is required, where all the components of the luminous discourse and its attributes can be condensed. For not introducing a new ingredient, the same symbol used in the illustrations of the luminous geometry points will be utilized to represent the divergent quantum (particle). Figure 25.8 seeks to present diagrammatically the definition of the abbreviated symbol for earthly domains.

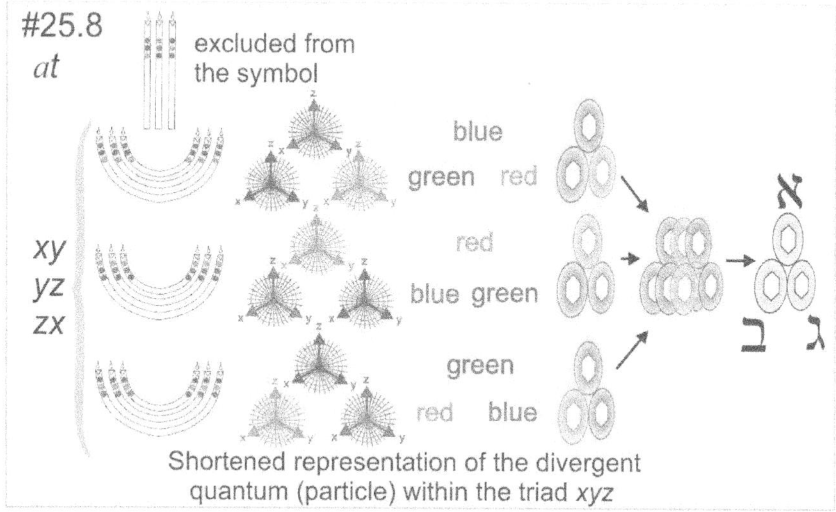

Directions *a* and *t* are the domains of the Anointed One and of the Spirit; the first is an expression of God, and the second of unquestionable fidelity to him. By virtue of their unity of purpose, both maintain the initial conditions established by God at the beginning of the Creation, without any variation. The absence of changes in their situation is the reason why they are excluded from symbolic abbreviations. Another very different thing happened in the domains defined by the earthly directions *x*, *y*, and *z* and their planes. Within the referred domain, there were important disruptions in the course established initially, which is why the next considerations and their illustrations will be centered on them. The unity of purpose of *a* and *t* is exposed in numerous passages of the Holy Scriptures, of which perhaps in 1 Samuel (Kings) 3 is one of the most evident. According to the Bible, God (through *a*)

spoke to Samuel (the eleventh century BC) (*t*, he who listens to God) on four occasions; on three the young prophet thought it was the voice of Eli (the eleventh century BC) (any possibility within earth, *xyz*). The successor to Samson was judge, high priest, and mentor of the young Samuel. However, Eli was despised by the Lord because of the iniquities committed in his house *xyz*. From the fourth call, the Lord sealed his relationship with Samuel, as can be read in the first book distinguished by his own name: "And Samuel matured and the Lord remained with him and did not let his words fall to the ground. And it was clear to all of Israel, from Dan to Beersheba, that Samuel was made a prophet of the Lord."

There is a mention in the Bible of another candelabrum, where the emphasis is placed on the necessary divine intervention for the illumination of the cosmos. The prophet Zechariah (the sixth to the fifth centuries BC) was graced with the vision of the Second Temple lampstand:

> And the angel who spoke with me came back, waking me up as one wakes up a man from his dream. And he said: "What do you see?" And I said: "I have seen a lampstand all made of gold, with a bowl on the top and seven lamps and there were seven tubes for the lamps. And two olive trees, one to the right of the bowl and another to the left"…And I asked the angel: "What are these two olive trees to the right and to the left of the lampstand?" And I asked him a second time: "What are these two branches of olive tree pouring oil through their gold pipes?" And he replied saying: "Do you not know what these are?" And I answered: "No, my lord." Then he said to me: "These are the two Anointed Ones who are before the Lord of the earth."

The "two Anointed Ones" are the Heavenly Adam and Christ, who represent the two ways of realization of the current cosmos through direction *a*.

The Bible does not always use candelabra symbolically when referring descriptively to the originating light of the Creation. Nor have scholars of the Hebrew religion considered the lampstand of the Tabernacle a key reference to imagining and understanding the divine environment at the time of every creation. Reflections on the theme of the originating light carried out by the "mystic and esoteric Hebrew" schools (*hekhalot*) are grouped rather under two great titles. The first of these is known as the work of creation and the second as the work of the chariot of the glory of God. The first one was explored briefly when considering the gematria of Genesis 1:1 and will not be discussed again, and the second will be briefly considered next. The reason is simple, because even when scarce, the literature on both far exceeds any attempt in the following lines, and its consideration will be left to the initiative of the reader. Both themes were always reserved for discussion by scholars and totally ignored by most believers. During the Talmudic period (the first through the seventh centuries AD), the followers of Shammai even forbade the public reading of the Ezekiel text about the work of the chariot of the glory of God. Many others after them reserved such study and interpretation for a chosen few.

Already before the prophet Zechariah, the prophet Ezekiel had witnessed an overwhelming revelation about the entourage of the Creator. The text that exposes it was merely referred to previously and is reproduced below for the convenience of the reader. Ezekiel recounts that when on the banks of an arm of the River Euphrates called Kebar,

> the hand of the Lord was placed on me. And I saw a stormy whirlwind coming from the north and a great cloud wrapped in a glowing fire, around and inside there was something with the appearance of amber. And inside were the forms of four living beings. And this was their aspect: they were similar to a man and each had four faces and each of them had four wings. Their feet were straight as calf's feet and shone like burnished bronze. And they had the hands of a man under their wings on all four sides. And the four had faces on all four sides. And their wings came together. They walked without turning and everyone went straight ahead of their faces. As for the shapes of their faces, they had the face of a man and the four had the face of a lion on the right side and the four had the face of an ox on the left side and the four had the face of an eagle on top. Their wings stretched up, two wings of each were joined and two covered their bodies. Everyone advanced straight ahead. Wherever the spirit went there they went. They advanced without turning…And while I was observing the four living beings, a wheel with four sides appeared above the earth, next to the living beings…and its appearance and make was like a wheel inside another. Moving forward, they went through their four parts and did not turn. Also, the size and height of the wheels were impressive. Their bodies were full of eyes around each of the four. And when the living beings advanced, the wheels went next to them and when the living beings were raised of the earth, the wheels were also raised, because the spirit of the living beings was in the wheels. And above the living being there was a firmament similar to crystal, but frightening to observe and extended over their heads. Their wings stretched out under the firmament, joining one another…And I heard the sound of their wings as if they were many waters, like the voice of the Lord. When they went, the sound of a multitude was heard, like that of a marching army…And above the firmament, which was suspended above their heads, was the semblance of a throne, like sapphire stone. And in the semblance of the throne there was the appearance of a seated man. And I saw something like amber, with the appearance of fire in it and around…There was the appearance of a rainbow, as in the clouds on a rainy day, so was the

appearance of splendor around Him. This was the vision of the glory of the Lord. And when I saw it, I fell prostrate to the ground.

Readers will have noticed the possibility of establishing correspondences between the description of the chariot of the glory of God, according to the prophet, and the model developed in previous pages. First of all, the tetramorphism displayed by the chariot, with its four living beings, stands out. The four creatures would correspond to developments in the four planes at, xy, yz, and zx subject to four conditionalities. The human faces would be related to the preeminence of the formulation of the human being in the luminous discourse. The spirits dwell in a wheel composed of four, one inside another **(ophanim)**, populated with eyes (domains of conjugation) and advancing toward their four sides without rotating. Certainly the wheels would correspond to the divergent aspects of the light in the four planes, with their rotation canceled by opposition. The description of Ezekiel would refer to the components of the ancillary planes as if they were wings. The two components defining the planes "covered their bodies," and the other two in i "were joined" among themselves and with those of other living beings. Transcription or propagation of the wheels on the four sides depends on the wings in the ancillary planes, whose features are obviously feminine due to the sound of "many waters." To learn more about these living beings, their tetramorphism, the wheels, and other elements of the vision of Ezekiel, it is advisable to go to the source and meditate upon it carefully.

In the Koran, the theme of the originating light is developed in surah **The Light** (*Al-Nur*) of the Medinan period, whose prose has dazzled readers for its beauty:

> God is the light of the heavens and the earth, His light resembles that of a lamp on a pedestal. The lamp is in a glass, the glass shines like a bright star, lit thanks to a blessed olive tree, neither eastern nor western, whose oil gives light, although the fire does not touch it, light upon light. God guides His light to whom He pleases. And God sets forth His parables for men. God is Knower of everything. He is in homes where God has permitted to be exalted and His name to be remembered. Therein do glorify Him, in the mornings and evenings. Men whose merchandise and business do not divert from the remembrance of God…

Before concluding this chapter, it would be convenient to recapitulate the most relevant elements of the considerable amount of numerical data given to the reader for his or her consideration up to this point. Figure 25.9 attempts to condense the main numerical milestones in the formulation of the luminous discourse. The upper part of the illustration shows the close relationship between the four great numerical features of the Creation, present in the canonical and apocryphal religious literature. Tetramorphism $(4 = 3 + 1)$, heptamorphism $(7 = 6 + 1)$, decamorphism $(10 = 9 + 1)$, and triskaidecamorphism (13 = 12 + 1) are all derived from the multiplicative composition of a triad plus one separate unit. Within the natural exegesis carried out in previous lines, tetramorphism contextualizes the basic formulations of the Creation, in terms of verbs, directional domains of the cosmos, conditionalities, and protoelements. Heptamorphism governs the plenitude in the hexadirectional scheme of the Creation, the exteriorization of the primordial hexagon, and the quanta. Decamorphism is centered on the ten (10) planes and ten triads, where the ten sayings of the Creator are realized. Finally triskaidecamorphism is present in the composition of two primordial hexagons in rotation or in the three interdependent attributes in the quaternary formulations. Next to the four notable numbers appear the two key prime numbers in the gematria of Genesis 1 (thirty-seven [37] and seventy-three [73]), obtained by way of two possible factorizations based on two and three.

The prime numbers contained in thirteen (13) are six in total (two [2], three [3], five [5], seven [7], eleven [11], and thirteen [13]) to which number one (1) is to be added to obtain seven (7). The number eleven (11) could be associated with the ten (10) planes, triads or sayings, and their Creator.

#25.9

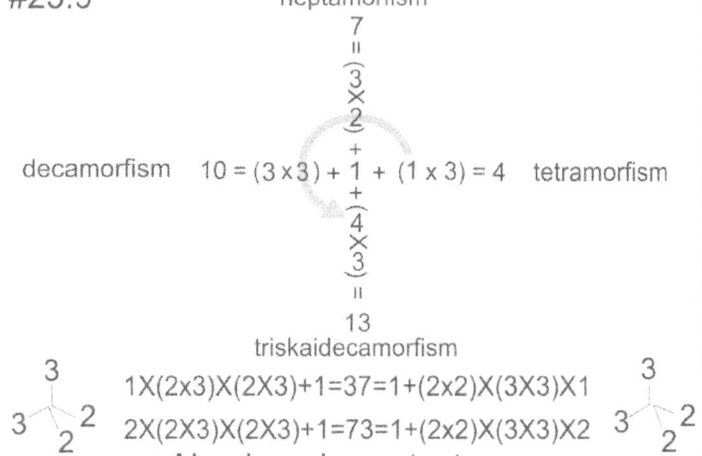

heptamorfism

decamorfism $10 = (3 \times 3) + 1 + (1 \times 3) = 4$ tetramorfism

$$7 = (2 \times 3) + 1 + (3 \times 4) = 13$$

triskaidecamorfism

1X(2x3)X(2X3)+1=37=1+(2x2)X(3X3)X1

2X(2X3)X(2X3)+1=73=1+(2x2)X(3X3)X2

Numbers in context

The numbers four (4), seven (7), ten (10), and eleven (11) were used by the architects of the Khufu pyramid in order to establish in royal cubits the height (280 = 4 × 7 × 10) and the length of the base of each triangular side (440 = 4 × 11 × 10). These figures were also used to establish some of the proportions of the pyramids geometry, the dimensions of the various chambers, and their relative positions within.

Throughout the development of the luminous discourse model, the luminous source and the progression born out of the primordial hexagon have been considered, mainly from an entitative point of view. However, references have also been made to the plurality of their acting capabilities. In this sense, mention was made of four verbs empowering creatures plus four conditionalities as causes of distinction among modes of action. The entitative character and the modes of action are aspects of the cosmic lights whose separate considerations should not give rise to any confusion. Beyond the previous precisions, the truly fundamental thing is to clearly distinguish the separation between the transcendent God and his immanence committed to the realization of his Creation via *a*.

Regarding the transcendence of God, nothing will be said in this natural exegesis only dealing with his immanence. The immanent aspect of God is like absolute freedom of expression in action made light that the protoelemental archetypes refract in many ways. Refraction of God's free will through odd or masculine archetypes, within the context of the originating provisions, limited their degrees of freedom to their respective domains. As a result, said archetypes enjoyed some raw free will as long as they remained acting as single entities faithful to their Creator. The even or feminine protoelemental archetypes, here grouped as waters, obliterate the refracted absolute freedom of expression of God due to internal destructive interferences. Therefore, they are known for having zero degrees of freedom.

According to what has been said up to this point, it only remains to define the context of globality in the luminous discourse model, which encompasses compliance with the originating provisions. Once that goal has been reached, it will be possible to face some major interpretive challenges to address the origins of the current state of affairs.

Chapter 26

The Most High Council

The incarnation of light was the modular unit with which the Creator formed the first cosmic organ, thus expanding the reach of the numerical keys of the luminous discourse. Religious literature mentions it under different names, like the council or the assembly. It appears, above all, in passages where reference is made to the entourage of the Creator, one of them being in Psalm 89, which asks the question: "Who in the heavens can compare with the Lord?…A feared God in the assembly of the saints, great and formidable among those who surround Him." In some cases, its components are specified by a profusion of details, as in the description of the chariot of the glory of God, according to the prophet Ezekiel. It is also described in the Apocalypse of John with some meticulousness:

> And I saw a throne raised in heaven and one seated on it. And to my eyes he looked like jasper and sardine stone and there was a rainbow of light around the throne, like emerald. And surrounding the throne were twenty-four thrones, and on them were twenty-four elders sitting, clothed in white robes, with crowns of gold on their heads. And from the throne flames, voices and thunder came. And seven lamps of fire burned before the throne, which are the seven Spirits of God. And before the throne there was, as it was, a transparent sea of crystal and in the middle of the throne and around it, four beasts full of eyes around. And the first beast was like a lion and the second one was like an ox and the third had the face of a man and the fourth was like an eagle in flight. And the four beasts, each having six wings, were full of eyes around and inside and without rest day and night they kept on saying Holy, Holy, Holy, is the Lord God, Almighty, Who always was, is and is to come.

The Koran provides key information about the "Most High Council" or "Supreme Council," which will be used to understand it in sufficient detail, not only in relation to its structure but also in connection with the events that occurred in it. Despite the transformations to which this institution was subjected, it remains in force to perpetuity: "We have certainly adorned the sky of the world with ornaments, the stars. And there is protection against every rebellious demon. They will not be able to listen to the Most High Council and will be rejected from all sides" (surah Those Ranging in Ranks).

As far as its members are concerned, the Most High Council would include entities described by Ezekiel, by the Apocalypse of John, and by some suwar of the Koran. In this sense, it will be assumed that the participants are mainly luminous human beings, in the terms stated above. Also, Iblis, his jinn, and the angelic entities usually surrounding the throne participate because, as the Koran says in **surah The** Companies, "You will see angels surrounding the throne, glorifying their Lord with praises."

Readers will surely remember that the luminous human couple is composed by its masculine component (Man) and by its cardinal and ordinal incarnated consorts (Woman) in all planes. Their initial formulations were locally neutral in the conditionalities of orientation, rotation and turn, and ternary attributes and were subject to their own protoelemental sources. Given the characteristics of the luminous waters and their inability to alter the course of creation by themselves, they will be omitted in the development of this chapter. As is customary, the structure of the Most High Council will be represented on a quaternary basis, in terms of the odd masculine components of the earthly human beings (Men). The motivation for such a procedure is due to the use given by masculine archetypes to their ability to exercise free will, with the purpose of redirecting the creation.

The structure of the Most High Council can be deduced from the Holy Scriptures, through the interpretation of a number of references. None of them is very concise, but they are often associated with numbers four (4), eight (8), twelve (12), and twenty-four (24). Of course, the figures are not enough, and all the relevant data provided by the Scriptures and religious literature should be integrated in order to justify the proposal. In any case, the validity of the postulated structure will depend on its possibilities for supporting a unique model of knowledge.

A structure based on eight luminous human beings is suggested a priori and divided into two groups of four in order to simplify the problem as much as possible. As for the male members, one of the groups is constituted by lights that will be called the "right ones," while in the other the lights will be the "left ones." The originating provisions of the Most High Council are fundamental since they define the context of global neutrality in the conditionalities. Local neutrality may then be abandoned, provided that it is globally preserved at the level of the council members. There are also entanglements instituted between the right lights, between the left ones, and between both. These links imply compositions, whose first and foremost result is the cohesion of the council as a single entity. The entanglements under the initial conditions could be visualized at least partially in terms of an exchange of equivalent attributes among the lights.

The reader is asked at this time to bring to mind the abbreviated symbol of the lampstand of the Tabernacle for a thorough interpretation of the following diagrams. The graphic representation of the Most High Council shown in figure 26.1 was made according to a structure based on eight luminous human beings. The implicit entanglements between right and left masculine components have been symbolically represented by pseudohexagrams.

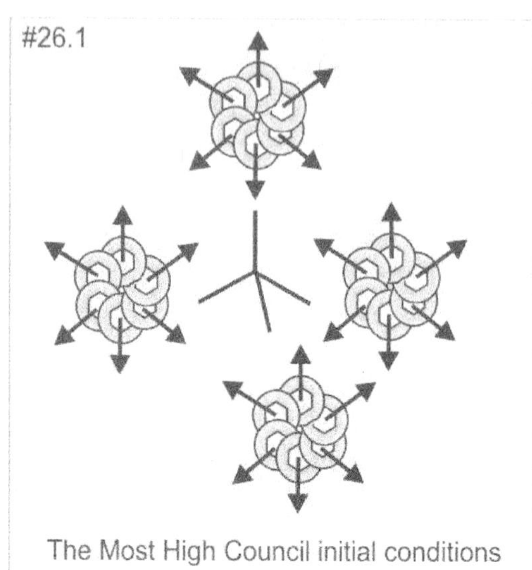

The Most High Council initial conditions

The straight arrows indicate an outward sense of divergent progression and the act of directing neutral actions toward the empyrean, typical of the Cult of Adoration to the Most High, prevailing in the council since its beginnings. While the initial conditions were in place, the right and left luminous ratings linked to their subsequent actions were not very relevant since this qualification refers to opposing turns within the triad *xyz*, which were annulled locally by pairs in the initial conditions. In its lower part, figure 26.2 breaks down entanglements among pairs of masculine lights with right and left affiliations, exposing the details of the null intrinsic turn in both.

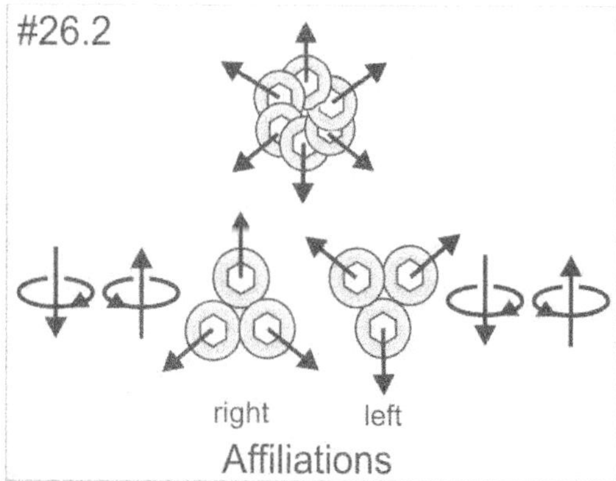

Affiliations

The frequent references to the role of the "hands" of the Creator in the Scriptures, reflect the importance of the proposed affiliations, and the first book of Kings emphasizes it: "said Micaiah:…'I saw the Lord sitting on His throne, with all the armies of heaven in their positions around Him, to His right and to

His left.'" Or as the psalmist says, "The right hand of the Lord exercises his power." There are traditions in the four major religions according to which the right and left hands of the Creator do different things, even contrary, according to his designs.

The council was not created as a single entity since an uncountable number of replicas were transcribed from the original. The multiplication obeyed instructions recorded by the book of Genesis: "multiply" and the bases for a quantitative estimate will be offered when sufficient elements of judgment are possessed. The replicas of the eight lights of each unit were juxtaposed initially in absolute absence of mutual interactions because they were all consecrated to the Cult of Adoration to the Most High. The whole was transcribed or displaced coherently, according to Koran in surah The Sure Truth: "And the angels will be at the edges of heaven and that day eight will bear the Throne of your Lord above them." The throne of the Lord in the Holy Scriptures would correspond to the source as the first expression of the "one" beyond the empyrean. Angels in the previous quotations refer to the eight replicas of dwellers in the nine triads (excluding *xyz*), with their own formulations in accordance with the terms indicated by surah The Originator: "Praise be to God, Originator of the heavens and the earth! Who makes the angels, messengers flying on wings, with two, three or four." The aforementioned displacement always occurred by transcription within the limits of the triacontakaihexagon generated from day seven—that is, inside the walls of Jerusalem.

With the institution of the Most High Council, the formulation of the luminous discourse culminates in the framework of the present natural exegesis. The model contains enough elements to deal in some detail with the dramatic events that occurred within it and because of which the current state of affairs has been reached. The eight male members of the council and their female consorts faced two scenarios: to continue the Cult of Adoration to the Most High, according to initial conditions established by the Creator or, on the contrary, to abandon it and interact with their luminous peers. The aforementioned dilemma has been raised from every conceivable angle in the Holy Scriptures. Of all of them, the dualist approach of Fargad I, from the Vendidad of the Zend-Avesta, is the closest to that of the natural exegesis in progress, with righteousness following the initial conditions of Creation (divergence toward the empyrean) or deviation from initial conditions (countercreation via intracosmic closed loops).

Chapter 27

Degrees of Freedom and Free Will

Before engaging in the issue of free will as granted to the creatures of the luminous discourse, it is necessary to emphasize the theistic context of the natural exegesis in progress. The reader will already be aware of the decisive role reserved by God for himself in the realization of the cosmos at every step, as has been insistently brought into consideration, notwithstanding that the creatures of the discourse were conceived with some degree of freedom to act on aspects of form and organization according to the originating provisions. In this sense, it is also important to always remember the free and unquestionable fidelity of the Spirit in heaven to his Creator, who expresses himself through the Anointed Ones. Constituted exclusively by the protoelement air and conjugating the verb *to determine*, the Spirit maintains to perpetuity the initial conditions established by God in terms set forth in the preceding chapters. For this reason, the directions *a* and *t* will be omitted from the considerations of this chapter, as was done in the abbreviated representation of the lights.

The masculine components of the luminous human beings obtain in principle from their own source an absolute freedom when directing individually their transcriptions and actions. However, the lack of support available to the simplest structures (due to the lack of enough exteriorization/interiorization channels) to sustain their decisions leads to unpredictable individual behaviors. At the beginning, all the members of the Most High Council were engaged in the Cult of Adoration to the Most High. The state of sanctity of this cult is translated into the coherent and collective transcription of the sources and the act of exchanging neutral actions with the Most High beyond the empyrean. Under that regime, all luminous beings ignored one another in an environment of absolute indifference, remaining linked to a common identity. However, the possibility was open for all of them to direct their actions toward each other and to transcribe themselves in different directions, acquiring this way their own identities. But these possibilities would not make much sense for the earthly humans, given the prevailing neutrality in the conditionalities from their initial conditions. Just as they did not make sense for waters due to their perpetual neutrality.

Redirection of the transcriptions of the sources and actions by the earthly human beings toward each other would imply establishing closed intracosmic loops with feminine traits, as well as crossing the wall of Jerusalem (boundaries of the Garden of Eden). For this reason, this event has been described in religious literature as the effeminizing or sodomizing of divergence. In the Scriptures there are abundant references where the sodomy of the earthly human beings is compared to idolatry, both against the ideal of divergent righteousness. This is what the first book of Kings describes here: "Asa did what was right in the eyes of the Lord, like David his father did. And he expelled the sodomites and removed all the images that his ancestors had made." Paul adds, in his first letter to the Corinthians, "Don't you know that the unrighteous will not inherit the kingdom of God? Do not make any false ideas about this. No one who goes after the desires of the flesh or worships images or is adulterous or less than man or misuses men...will have part." The same is said in the Koran in surah The Elevated Places: "And Lot, when he said to his people: 'Do you commit an abomination that no one in the world did before? Certainly, you approach men with lust instead of women...And we rained upon them a rain. See, then, what was the end.'"

According to the current situation of the cosmos, it can be inferred that the attributes underwent a reconfiguration of the 1-3 type. The objective was to make sense out of the mutual directing of the actions between earthly human beings, in replacement of the Cult of Adoration to the Most High. In this scheme, the initial conditions of the geometry according to the zero conditioning were preserved. The earthly human being and Iblis instead made use of the degrees of freedom available in their earthly redoubt xyz to dislocate the attributes selectively. The dwellers of the nine angelic triads, atx, aty, atz, axy, ayz, azx, txy, tyz, and tzx concur with the Spirit and the Anointed Ones, determining and realizing the actions of the human beings and Iblis. But they do so without participating in the decisions of these and staying within the framework of the most absolute neutrality in the conditionalities.

To simplify the exposition as much as possible, we will proceed according to the enumeration given to the conditionalities of the luminous discourse, and the considerations will focus on the earthly planes xy, yz, and zx of the triad. Regarding the first on orientation, it is worth remembering that this conditioning has its origin in the composition of the two divergent countercirculations passing through God extracosmically. Under the exchange regime of equivalent attributes, between the lights of the council when the initial conditions prevailed, some right and left could permute their attributes of orientation. By doing so, they were able to choose between remaining neutral locally and being polarized by pairs. The objective of pairing polarization would be to obtain some earthly humans oriented in one direction and an equal number to the opposite. Figure 27.1 shows the permutations of the orientation in the divergent circulations within the triad xyz (*at* unchanged).

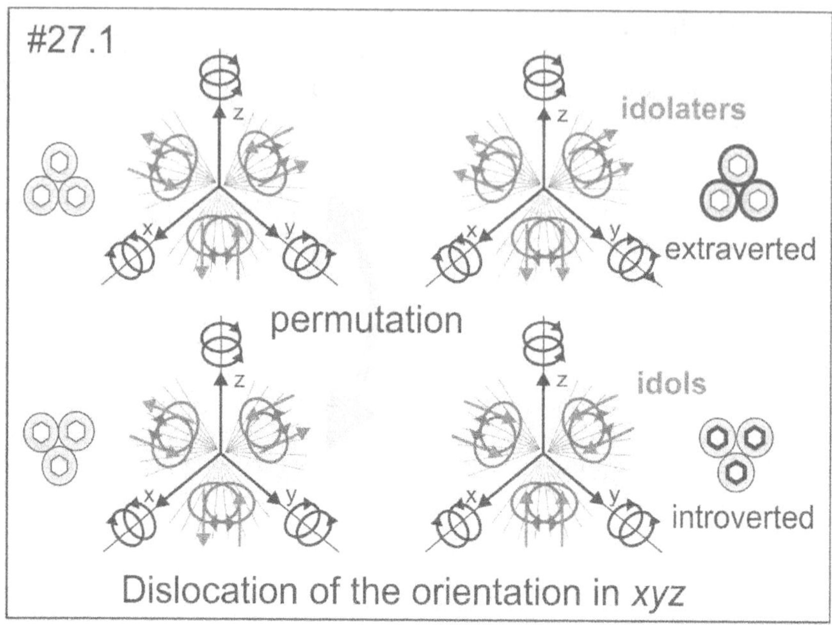

The figure shows to the left a pair of earthly human beings of different affiliations in their initial conditions, with their respective neutralities in countercirculations, counterrotations, and counterturns, and in the ternary attributes. On the right is shown the resulting polarization by the permutations of circulation attributes on a geometry destined to pass through God extracosmically. The symbolic abbreviations corresponding to each are also shown on each side. As can be seen, the aforementioned permutation would provide orientation to the divergent progressions of the earthly human beings. Some would be oriented outward by way of an extraversion toward the circular and the others inward, introverted toward the primordial hexagon.

The extraverted earthly human beings will be called idolaters and the introverted ones idols, and the directing and mutual exchange of actions between them will be named idolatry. The actions emitted and absorbed toward and by themselves (whether of idolaters or idols) will be considered egomania. Actions emitting toward others with similar orientation will be called conflict. Countercirculations between lights of the same affiliation can also be exchanged with the same results. In the luminous waters, such permutations must occur internally due to their perpetual neutrality. Even so, the internal polarization of waters is possible, allowing them to appear as if they were two paired masculine lights, with all their opposite attributes. Note also that on a global scale the net orientation of masculine lights remains null since their opposite polarizations occur in pairs. Actually, from the perspective of Creation, everything remains more or less the same—that is, globally neutral in terms of orientation. However, from the individual point of view of the earthly human beings, observable changes have occurred, the impact of which will be better understood in the next chapters.

In relation to the second conditioning, the earthly human beings could also opt for a permutation of the counterturning attributes in their own domain. The objective would be a redistribution of the turns within the triad xyz. With the dislocation of the turns around a direction in the mentioned domain, the earthly humans would be in the condition of "permanent turn." Figure 27.2 illustrates the dislocation of the turns around z, which would coincide with the direction of transcription or propagation of the council at the speed of light.

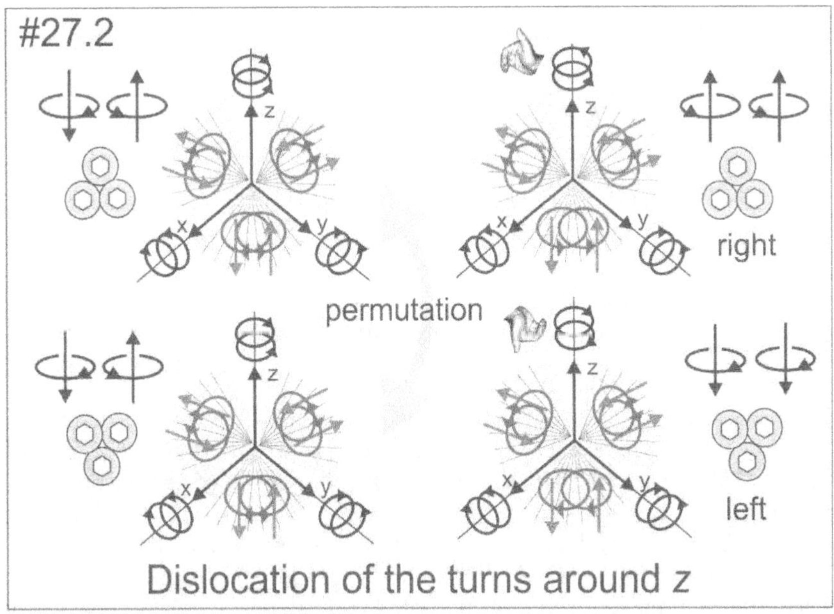

Dislocation of the turns around z

To the left of the figure, the initial conditions of the earthly Humans of both affiliations can be observed, with their neutrality in the second conditionality. To the right appear the earthly human beings under their new turning condition but maintaining a net global balance equal to zero. The reader will note that after the dislocation, earthly humans are divided into right and left according to the right-hand rule. The ensuing conditions were the causes for the names given to the right and left affiliations. Similar to the previous case, the dislocation of the turns did not produce external effects in the luminous waters due to their perpetual neutrality.

The dislocation of the ternary attributes is similar to the previous ones, but in this case three earthly human beings are required to complete it in its most compact and reduced form. Being an initiative of a fire jinni, it should not be surprising that the dislocations occur concomitantly in the three planes of the earthly domain, xy, yz, and zx. They are given jointly in three conditionalities—the first, second, and third—as well as in three pairs of earthly human beings, whose consent will be necessary. Figure 27.3 illustrates the effects of the permutation of the ternary attributes exclusively, indicating with *b*, *g*, and *r* the colors blue, green, and red.

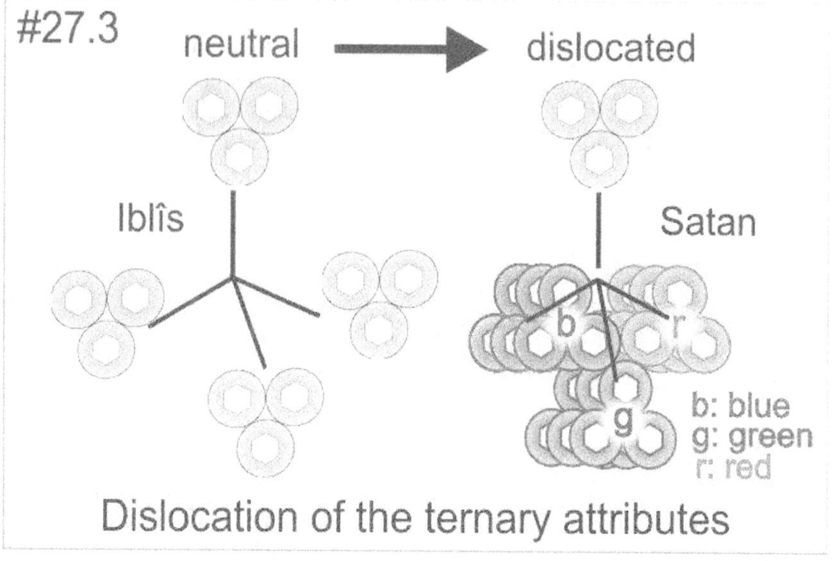

Under his new configuration, Iblis will be identified with Satan. The description of said entity and its context will be complete when the participation of each member of the Most High Council in the becoming of the institution is considered.

As already anticipated, the luminous waters can internally redistribute their ternary attributes, imitating in part the polarizations of the masculine ones but respecting the chiaroscuro contrast. For example, lower waters can be reconfigured as two earthly masculine ones (Men), one like an idolater with a turn in one sense and the ternary attributes blue, green, and red and the other as his anti, introverted as an idol with opposite rotation and the ternary attributes yellow, magenta, and cyan.

Mutual redirecting of the actions in the context of the dislocation of the attributes would dismantle the regime of coherence and juxtaposition (communion of the saints) under which collective decisions were possible—in particular the permutations of attributes, because once the juxtaposition regime is destroyed, their effects could become irreversible to perpetuity.

Chapter 28

The Sin According to Holy Scriptures

The subject of sin is difficult to address because of its abundant and sometimes complex references in the Holy Scriptures and because of its widespread dissemination. By virtue of the penetration of sin into the universe, phenomenologies considered secularly alien to the problem of good and evil are nuanced with a "moral" tinge. In certain religious circles, matter is associated with the origin of all evils, and a renunciation of material possessions is considered among the spiritual achievements. However, sin is not present in all matter but in that one that is centered on the abandonment of the worship to the Most High. There is a matter faithful to the Creator that can be recognized by its scant interaction with that one that turns its back on the Most High by surrendering to a frenzy of mutual interactions. Within the framework of the natural exegesis, the rejection of the worship to the Most High, with the consequent redirecting of the actions, will be treated as a capital sin. Instead, the dislocation of the attributes will be considered a complementary act, intrinsically innocuous in itself.

In the Bible, sin is fundamentally an act of disobedience to God, either to the orders imparted by God specifically, as with Adam and Eve; to the commandments given to Moses at Mount Sinai; or to the religious prescriptions dictated in different instances and opportunities. The first one stands out among all those sins for bringing about a change of status not only to its instigator, the serpent (*nahash* in Hebrew: "who discovers the secrets"), but also to Adam and Eve. The change was extended to all of their offspring by the separation of their replicas, as all those individuals were equally left outside the Garden of Eden. The problem with the irreversibility of the first sin is that it was not committed only by the human beings but also by the jinn, led by Iblis. Everything indicates that the decisions of Iblis and the human sector of left affiliation were final, which closes the way for rectification by the idolatrous rights.

Furthermore, the sin of the first parents seems to have left a trace of evil in the nature of the human being, as the Lord expresses it well after the Flood: "I will not curse the earth again because of man, for the thoughts of the human heart are evil from their early age." Deuteronomy also notices that there are no excuses for missing the commandments of the Lord because none exceeds the capacity of the human being:

> They are not in heaven so you can say: "Who will ascend to heaven for us and give us the knowledge to be able to fulfill them?" Nor are they across the sea for you to say: "Who will go to the other side of the sea for us and bring us news from them so that we can fulfill them?" But the word is very close to you, in your mouth and in your heart, so you can fulfill it.

Being masculine formulations totally imbricated with feminine ones, it is not surprising that the book of Genesis poses the first sin as an issue of the couple and not of its members. Biblical accounts in the book of Genesis about the fall of the human couple are long, which is why the quote has been reduced to what is essential:

> Now the serpent was more cunning than any of the wild animals the Lord God had made. He said to the woman: "Did God really say, You must not eat from any tree in the garden?" The woman said to the serpent: "We may eat fruit from the trees in the garden, but God did say: You must not eat fruit from the tree that is in the midst of the garden, neither shall you touch it, or you will die." And the serpent said to the woman: "You will not certainly die, for God knows that, when you eat from it, your eyes will be opened, and you will be like God, knowing good and evil." And when the woman saw that the fruit of the tree was good for food and pleasing to the eye, and also desirable to acquire wisdom, she took some and ate it with her husband, who was with her.

The text reveals an interest on the part of the serpent in incorporating Adam and Eve into its project. The outcome pursued by the serpent is to take control of a good part of the Creation, which could not be achieved without the adherence of the human couple. The indispensable presence of the human being is due to the preeminent figuration of its formulation in essential aspects of the luminous discourse. The two trees of Eden, one of "knowledge of good and evil" and one of "life," would be derivations of the "tree of possibilities" whose branches are formed by decision-making sequences. Choosing the path of the forbidden tree would imply crossing the limits of the triacontakaihexagon (the thirty-six [36]) in some plane of the manifold *atxyz*. These polygons form the wall of Jerusalem or the boundary of the Garden of Eden, whose limits would be infringed in the adventure of redirecting transcriptions and actions between lights (idolatry) once the conditioning attributes are dislocated.

According to the Gospels, sin is basically a conscious act of abandonment or rejection of the divine prescriptions. However, when the texts of the four Gospels are compared in the context of the previously discussed quaternary architecture, an interesting message emerges in the background. The reader will remember that the Gospel of John called theological remains separate in many respects to the three synoptics. One of those aspects of fundamental character is the omission of the three temptations to which Jesus was subject after his fast in the desert. This omission could be associated with the unquestionable fidelity of the Spirit (which he represents) to the initial conditions of the Creation, while the fact that temptations of Jesus are treated only by the three synoptics circumscribes its scope to the domains proper of the earthly human being and Iblis. Moreover, the synoptics, as the reader may remember, are divided into two: on the one hand, Mark, and on the other the tradition Q of Matthew and Luke. The first one figures as the masculine component of the earthly human being (Man), and the other two as its feminine counterpart (Woman). The Gospel of Mark barely touches the temptations of Jesus but does not ignore them like John. That mention of temptations would allow associating it with the abandonment of the worship to the Most High and the subsequent inclination toward idolatry. The Gospels of the tradition Q present instead a meticulous recount, emphasizing the preeminent role of the feminine component of the human being (the waters) in the change of attitude.

Basically, the narrative in Q emphasizes the ternary character of sin posed in terms of three temptations but presenting a permutation in two of them—a question linked to permutations in two of three independent directions and for all practical effects in the earthly context to an inversion of the right handed triad *xyz* (chiaroscuro contrast in feminine formulations). The presence of two triads with their opposite senses, as reflected in their origin, can be related to the dislocation of the first conditionality and its eminent figuration in idolatry. The three narratives, that of Mark and those of Matthew and Luke, are copied here for the benefit of the readers:

> Jesus was led by the Spirit into the desert. And he was there for forty days. And he was tempted by the Devil. And he lived among wild beasts, and the angels took care of him.

> Jesus was led into the desert by the Spirit, to be tempted by the Devil. And after a fast lasting forty days and forty nights, he was hungry. The Devil said to him: "If you are the son of God, tell these stones to become bread"... Then the Devil took him to the Holy City, and set him on the roof of the temple, and said to him: "If you are the son of God let yourself down..."...Again, the Devil took him to the top of a high mountain and showed him the glory of all the kingdoms of the world, and said to him: "Fall down and adore me and I will give you all these things."

> And Jesus, full of the Holy Spirit, left the Jordan and was guided by the Spirit to the desert for forty days. And during that time he ate nothing and was hungry. Then the Devil said to him: "If you are the son of God, make these stones to become bread"...And the Devil led him to the highest mountain, and showed him in an instant all the kingdoms of the world. And he said to him: "I will give you all their authority and splendor, because it has been given to me, and I can give it to anyone I want to. If you worship me, it will be all yours"...Then the devil led him to Jerusalem and had him stand on the highest point of the temple and said to him: "If you are the Son of God, throw yourself down from here..."

Figure 28.1 illustrates schematically the permutation of temptations present in the Gospels of Matthew and Luke.

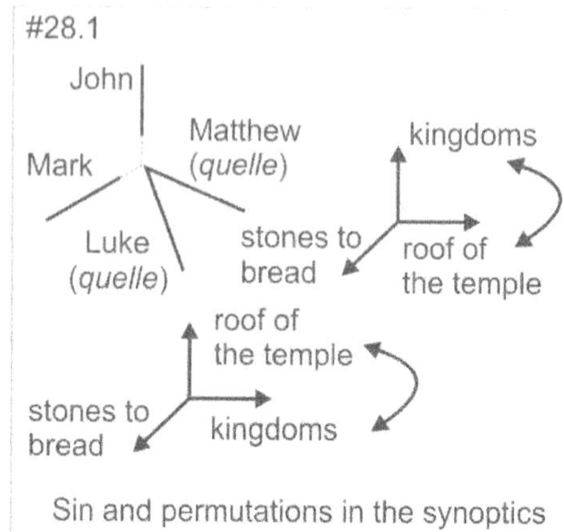

Sin and permutations in the synoptics

The order in which temptations regarding the "throwing from the roof of the temple" and for the "kingdoms of the world" appear is reversed in the Gospel of Matthew with respect to that of Luke. Throwing down from the roof of the temple instead of rising in adoration to the Most High and prostrating before Satan to gloat over the mundane should be interpreted as references to idolatry. The eminent ternary and earthly trait of the sinful act is also underlined by the four evangelists by referring to the premonition made by Jesus (in the name of the Spirit) to his disciple Peter (his earthly counterpart): "Truly I say to you that this very night, before the rooster crows, you will deny me three times."

In the Koran the references to sin and their consequences are abundant throughout the text. A careful reading reveals a very structured description of the nature of the events, the share of responsibility of each creature, and the context in which they occurred. A passage from the Koran in **surah** Muhammad also endorses the criterion according to which sin implies a change of direction since "certainly, those who have turned back after the direction was indicated to them, Satan has embellished them and gave them false hopes."

As for the antecedents of the human fall in sin, the Koran places the origin of the problem in the bosom of the Most High Council. Although the agent of the Koranic revelation declares his lack of knowledge about some details of the disagreements, he provides more than enough data to discover the heart of the matter. As may be inferred, Iblis rebelled against the preferences of the Creator toward the human formulation, while the environment of holiness of the initial conditions still prevailed. **Surah** Sad of the Koran also specifies that the intention of Iblis was to engage a good part of the earthly human beings in order to achieve the desired impact:

Say: "It is a message of importance from which you turn away."

I was not aware of the Most High Council when its members contended. Only this has been revealed to me, that I am simply the one who brings you a warning. When your Lord said to the angels: "Certainly I am going to create a mortal out of clay. So when I have completed him and breathed into it part of My Spirit, you should fall prostrate, submitting to him!" And all the angels prostrated, except Iblis. He was proud, and he was one of the disbelievers. God asked: "Oh Iblis! What prevents you from prostrating before him whom I have created with My two hands?" He answered: "I am better than him, You created me from fire and created him from clay." God exclaimed: "Get out of here! Surely My curse will be on you until the Day of Judgment." Satan said: "My Lord! Grant me a respite until the day of the resurrection," God answered: "Certainly you are among those who will have respite until the determined day." He exclaimed: "Then by Your power I will deceive as many as I can, except among your servants, the pure ones." God said: "The truth is, and the truth I speak, that I will fill hell with you and with all those who follow you."

In the previous quote, the reader will immediately recognize data of unquestionable value to discover the nature and roots of sin. In the first place, the Most High Council would include all created beings, the Spirit of God, the earthly human being, and Iblis, plus others left on the sidelines for economic reasons. In the second place, the rebellion of Iblis precedes the sin of the human being, and there is a human group called "the pure ones," whose fidelity to God will remain intact in the face of temptation. Finally, God will fill hell with Satan and his human followers. An indispensable step to articulate a natural exegesis on the subject of the quarrel within the Most High Council is to give an interpretation to the order given by God: "fall prostrate, submitting to him!" Certainly the divine exhortation would imply recognition and acceptance, by all creatures, of the preeminent role granted to human formulation above all others. The first sign of divine favoritism is related to the initial act of Creation, when God in his divine unicity creates the primordial waters (two). Another sign of predilection for humans can be found in the cardinal and ordinal incarnations of the luminous discourse. There are also signs of preference in the formulations of the heavenly and earthly human beings, endowed with their determinative and directive capabilities. All these occurrences of human nature in various instances of Creation constitute the "incarnation of the verb." In that context, the flesh is represented by all those formulations based on one part, with the capacity to exercise free will and two parts acting as a neutral medium.

The consideration of the Creator toward the formulation of the human being contrasts with the secondary role reserved to Iblis, who remained confined by the neutrality of his ternary attributes and permutations. Certainly God could have arranged the Creation in a different way. Perhaps Iblis expected to be graced by the distinction of precedence, with which the Creation would have been based not on the flesh but on the fire. Unfortunately there are no resources available to speculate about what could have been and was not. The efforts will be rather directed to consider in detail the initiative taken by Iblis to get out of his confinement and to be able to act in the foreground after his transformation into Satan. However, the dislocation of the ternary attributes with which Satan aspired to leave confinement would only acquire meaning incorporating some earthly human beings in his adventures.

The resentment of Iblis by which he became Satan has been widely repudiated by almost all the People with the Book. With the notable exception of a minuscule group of mystics of Islam, among whom the Iranian Ahmad Ghazali can be cited (the eleventh to the twelfth centuries AD). In the opinion of the mystic of Tus, Iblis would not worship anyone other than God, hence his refusal to prostrate before a creature such as the human being. According to Ghazali, Iblis supposed that it was a test set by God, not so much to his obedience but to his unconditional love for his Creator.

During the annual pilgrimage (Hajj), at least once in a lifetime, Muslims must go for three days to Mina, where three pillars are stoned. The three monoliths al-Aqaba, al-Wusta, and al-Ula mark the place of the triple temptation to the family nucleus of Abraham against a test imposed by God. The patriarch, by command of the archangel Gabriel, stoned Satan for tempting him, his wife Hagar (the nineteenth to the eighteenth centuries BC), and his son Ishmael to disobey the divine order.

The rebellion of Satan and his followers caused a total reconfiguration of the Most High Council, which gave rise to a new beginning, considered by some as the first creative act. Conceiving Creation from an igneous principle as proposed by Heraclitus of Ephesus had numerous followers in antiquity. Stoics considered ecpyrosis a cyclical event of regeneration from which an entirely new cosmos would emerge. However, the Stoics, led by Panaetius of Rhodes (the second century BC), abandoned the doctrine of ecpyrosis to adopt the thesis of the eternity of the world. One of the Christian sympathizers of the ecpyrosis of the philosopher of Ephesus was Clement of Alexandria (the second to the third centuries AD). Following Heraclitus, the Alexandrian theologian thought that this world was not made by God or by any man, for it has been, is, and will continue to be a permanent fire. The natural exegesis carried out here does not endorse the cosmogonies with ecpyrotic origin, although it will contemplate a conflagration of such characteristics in an intermediate stage of cosmic evolution.

Before considering in detail the quarrel that took place in the Most High Council, it is advisable to open a parenthesis with the purpose of considering the nature of "time," long ignored until now. The occasion is propitious because it is just now when there are enough elements to address the issue.

Chapter 29

Time in the Creation

The discrete expansion of the masculine divergent aspects and the mediation of feminine rotational developments between their transcriptions constitute the essence of the observable order of the luminous discourse. Initially, the developments were carried out in the same way and coherently in all the planes, and the directions t, x, y, and z registered similar but independent behaviors. On the premise of a divine retraction toward the empyrean, these developments were conceived in terms of the opening of a domain destined for the Cult of Adoration to the Most High. Basically, this cult consists of the **act of exchanging neutral actions with the Most High beyond the empyrean**, in a permanent attempt to reach and interact with God. The progression of the original divergent front in the tetrad $txyz$ continues to expand in the manner of a "glome" or three-sphere, which corresponds to a sphere in four dimensions.

As a result of the quarrel centered on the earthly domain of the Most High Council, the actions and transcriptions of the sources were redirected toward other lights. Those changes were accompanied by a reconfiguration of the first, second, and third conditionalities. These initiatives led to a chaotic dispersion of the sources of each formulation, but only within the triad xyz. From that moment on, the set of irreversible decisions made by Iblis and the earthly human being ended forever with the quaternary coherence of the initial conditions.

Thus, "space" was born, a ternary domain where all the rejections to the righteousness of the Cult of Adoration to the Most High beyond the empyrean are concentrated. Despite their subversive character, all these initiatives obtained the corresponding determinations by the Spirit and were realized by God because they were contemplated within the originating provisions of the Creation. In addition to exercising its determinant role, the Spirit imposed the continuity of the initial conditions in direction t, making of it a sanctuary of fidelity toward the Creator. The fidelity of the Spirit also determined the permanence of the initial conditions (local neutrality) in all the planes and triads where it intervenes, preserving in all of them the Cult of Adoration to the Most High. Thus, independently of the decisions made in the triad xyz, the masculine lights continue in t with the initial displacement of their sources and neutral actions toward the empyrean, in an irreversible way and without returns. We should mention, however, that there are some instances in which the contraries in the waters go in opposite senses in direction t, in what refers to their respective ordinal successions—a question that is not observable on a macro scale (it is something internal) and therefore not very relevant because it does not affect the causal chains.

Up to this point, t has been identified as the independent direction in which the successive and sequential determinations of the Spirit are recorded. But the proper of t transcends the nature of the earthly human being and therefore should not be part of human considerations. Even so, it is obvious that the Spirit determines the spatial possibilities proposed by the earthly humans, "making himself wait" sometimes more, other times less. Because of his ability to dictate the terms of becoming, the Spirit has been considered the owner of "time" and of history. Dependent on him is the succession of the ordinal human being, which he determines by orchestrating his actions in all the lights in order to intervene in the causal chain imperceptibly. In principle, the determinations of the Spirit should be carried out within the boundaries of the triacontakaihexagon of the plane *at* (the wall of Jerusalem or boundary of the Garden of Eden). However, depending on the nature of the actions to be determined and realized, God's faithfulness would go so far as to accompany his creatures in their misadventures. According to Moses de Leon, God would be even willing to accompany Israel into exile (outside the limits of the triacontakaihexagon in *at*).

From this point, t will be identified with the physical or proper time of lights, not so much in the way of a passive record of becoming (a clock) but as its forger—in physics, it is represented with the Greek letter τ (tau). After the quarrel, the progressions in the triad *xyz* continued to be sequential but with possible loops closing. For this reason, the lights that embraced the conflict could return, in relative terms, to transcribe their sources to spatial locations where they would have already been. Despite the possibility of spatial recurrence, the timely evolution of the universe is irreversible. That characteristic is due to the finite number of lights and potentialities evoked by abandoning the initial conditions.

It is possible to establish some correspondences between the irreversibilities originated by a finite quarrel and the displacement and evolution of lights in their proper time. Some philosophers of science associate the natural irreversibility of processes with the "arrow of time" (toward the future). The effects of the irreversibility of processes are quantified thermodynamically as entropy. This quantity is a measure of the disorder of an isolated system first conceptualized by the Prussian physicist R. Clausius (the nineteenth century AD). Entropy is an ever-increasing quantity in the universe to the detriment of the scope of its dynamics. Since the concept of entropy is difficult to grasp, we will use the term *aging*. In what follows, t will be the label for the proper time of lights and not an indication of the direction of aging, which runs in parallel with perpetuity.

It is then possible to represent, on an odd quaternary basis of the 1-3 type, the different patterns of behavior in the conjugation of the heavenly and earthly human beings. Therefore, the considerations offered in this chapter could be situated at the threshold of the "dimensional" approaches proposed by philosophers of science to distinguish between time and space. However, there has not been a satisfactory explanation by the proponents of the dimensional, geometric, or causal approaches to clarify the differences between time and space. Other more promising treatments in the search for differentiation have been based on the so-called laws of nature and the type of mathematical expression derived from them. Such a possibility exists because the mathematical language clearly typifies in its expressions different roles for time and space. As for the natural exegesis offered here, the differences between time and space derive from the originating provisions, from the initial conditions, and from the consequences of the quarrel, grouped under the term *laws of nature.*

The concept of time as a fourth dimension in addition to the spatial triad was introduced in the *Encyclopedia* (*Encyclopédie*) of the French thinker J. D'Alembert (the eighteenth century AD) and was popularized later in various novels. After a little more than a century, the Hungarian physicist and mathematician M. Palágyi (the nineteenth to the twentieth centuries AD) proposed to represent time as an independent direction of an imaginary type. Five years after Palágyi, the French physicist and mathematician H. Poincaré adopted this representation and used the speed of light to convert units of time into spatial units, and vice versa. The proposal by the French mathematician was the first step to formalize in physics the space-time manifold as a whole of four directions measured with the same units. Soon after, the Russian mathematician and physicist H. Minkowsky (the nineteenth to the twentieth centuries AD) postulated a "metric signature" to calculate distances in the space-time manifold. For some of the signature conventions, the square of time appears with the minus sign ($-$) and those of the three directions of the spatial triad with plus ($+$). Both proposals are illustrated in figure 29.1 below.

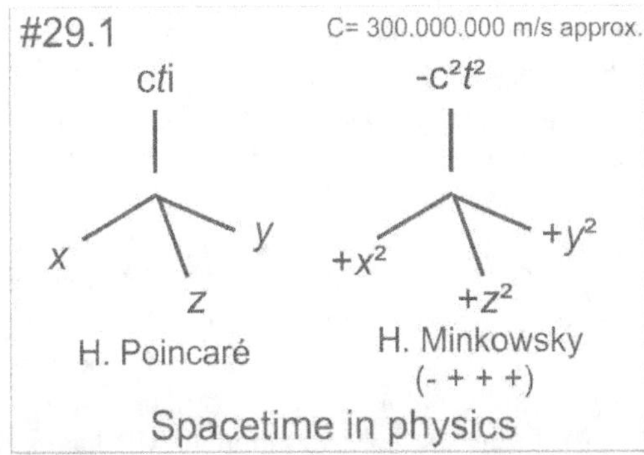

Zurvanite Zoroastrianism is the only religious doctrine of the People with the Book where God the Father precedes all existence in an infinite time and space. And of course, its flowering in Mesopotamia regionally influenced Islamic thought, giving rise to recurring discussions about the relationship between God and time. The polemic was raised early on by the Iranian philosopher **Abu al-Abbas Iranshahri** (the ninth century AD) and later furthered by an Iranian physician and philosopher, **Muhammad ibn Zakariya al-Razi** (the ninth to the tenth centuries AD). There is a general belief that al-Razi took from Iranshahri ideas about the eternity of the Creator, the soul, time, space, and matter. For his part, Iranshahri would have been inspired by ancient Persian doctrines influenced by the Vaisheshika. The truth is that with the emergence of the Safawids, a philosophy centered on addressing the theme of God from the majestic perspective of time was reborn.

In many approaches, the concept of "creation out of nothing" (*creatio ex nihilo*) has been preserved, postulate to which numerous theologians of the People with the Book agree. Some thinkers of antiquity conceived nothingness as the consort of God in his absolute solitude. Just as the globally neutral Creation is of its Creator, and the luminous waters, also neutral, are of the male components air and earth, "**Let us make a man in our image and in our likeness.**" However, there have been skeptical positions regarding creation out of nothing, including that of ben Maimon, who in his guide contemplated the possibility of "creation from a preexisting matter" (*creatio ex materia*).

Followers in Isfahan of Iranshahri and al-Razi, among them Jamal al-Din Khwansari (the seventeenth to the eighteenth centuries AD), came to elaborate profusely on the concept of the reality of God as always new and eternal. In their efforts to offer a coherent approach, these thinkers formulated different categories of time, with no apparent result other than to further enliven the polemic. During the long period of discussions, some philosophers became influential, as happened with Mir Damad (the sixteenth to the seventeenth centuries AD), grandson of an influential cleric of the Shia during the rule of Shah Tahmasp (the sixteenth century AD). Due to the sharpness and originality of his proposals, he was nicknamed "the third master" (after Aristotle and al-Farabi). The Iranian thinker stood out from a young age for his prodigious memory and intelligence, enjoying a life of great fame and the tutelage of Shah Abbas I (the sixteenth to the seventeenth centuries AD) and his successor Shah Safi (the seventeenth century AD).

The philosophy of Mir Damad was inspired by the Avicennian doctrine of the three categories of being with Neoplatonic roots, to postulate three "temporal" contexts: eternity, perpetuity, and time. The first context, or eternity, has no beginning or end and belongs only to God. Perpetuity has a timely origin caused by God and is the domain where existents obtain their epistemic realism. In physical proper time, instead, all existents get their spatial choices determined. The three temporal contexts are independent, but linked by a relation of order of an ontological type (relative to the metaphysical consideration of being). In an attempt to assimilate Mir Damad´s thinking, we could say that the eternity of God expresses from beyond the empyrean and until the origin of the sources. As for the other two independent "temporal" contexts, it is possible to establish a parallelism between the Anointed Ones on a and perpetuity, in close analogy with the one already posed between the Spirit and the physical proper time recorded in t.

The position here is that Creation is globally neutral and a carrier of the will of God. Earthly human beings dwelling within xyz quarreled with God and since then remained fragmented and free to choose directions and locations in space but not in perpetuity a and time t. The Holy Spirit determines events in proper time as the Anointed Ones do in perpetuity according to their ultimate goals in favor of the design of God. In addition, we consider n independent directions compactified at the possible locations of the point source of elementary particles, where we place the Creator God, to ensure compliance with the originating provisions (the universal laws of nature).

Quantitatively speaking, the intrinsic value of a and p_a are grouped with t and p_t under the metric signature of Minkowsky. According to the considerations made in previous paragraphs, the ancillary rotational significance will be expressed in the terms indicated below:

$$\left[(1+p_x xi/n)^n \times (1+p_y yi/n)^n \times (1+p_z zi/n)^n \times (1-p_t ti/n)^n\right]_{n\to\infty} = e^{p_x xi + p_y yi + p_z zi - p_t ti}$$

Rotational significance associated to x, y, z, and t

The time t together with the direction of the Anointed Ones a and the ancillary direction i configure a manifold of three directions identified with the "heaven" of the Holy Scriptures. The denomination, Earth, in reference to planet three, is maintained for the manifold formed by the triad xyz, avoiding confusion with the homonymous protoelement.

The earthly human being and his biological exteriorization unfold freely in the domain of the spatial triad. Their constituent units, instead, maintain a point-like presence in the independent directions of heaven, where they do not enjoy the same privileges. Although in a broader context, the dimensional limitation brings to mind the allegory of "Plato's cave" present in the book 7 of *The Republic*. There, in conditions of isolation, lived men condemned in a cave see only the shadows from the fire behind multiple figures that are projected on a wall.

Chapter 30

The Quarrel and the Sin of Adam and Iblis

In previous chapters the degrees of freedom present in the luminous discourse at the beginning of Creation have been postulated and considered in some detail. Various expositions found in the Holy Scriptures about the nature of sin and those who committed it were also brought up. It is now necessary to specify the forms of participation of each creature of the Most High Council in the context of the quarrel that took place within it. Religious texts deal with extreme prudence with the issue of the cosmic scope of sin due to the complexity of the subject, the deficiencies of the language, and the risks associated with inadequate interiorization. Despite the discretion, it is possible to glimpse the essential aspects of the disagreements that arose between the Creator and a good part of his Creation, which will be addressed in this chapter. The interpretive merits of this effort can be judged later in light of their congruence with observable facts.

The Bible recounts that the first human couple was expelled from the Garden of Eden as soon as they had the opportunity to choose between their Creator and the offer of the serpent, since already at the time the leader of iniquity had thrived in these domains. Divine warnings to potential offenders did not seem to be enough to preserve the course of creation, not even in the face of possible consequences. The reason for these disagreements will be known to the reader firsthand when he or she answers the following question: Would you be willing to leave your presence in this world right now to go after your Creator? Almost everybody would answer yes, but first there are a few things to solve, as Luke points out: "And he said to another: 'Come after me.' But he answered: 'Lord I will follow you but first let me go home to bury my father.'…Another man said to Jesus: 'I will go with you, Lord, but let me first say goodbye to those at my house.'" The dilemma has always been between dedicating oneself to God immediately and completely or to his creatures, and the decision has been, almost always, in favor of the latter. The same disjunctive was posed to the lights, to transcribe and direct the actions toward the empyrean as required by the Cult of Adoration to the Most High or toward other lights as idolatry demands.

The true sin of the earthly human being was to despise the Cult of Adoration to the Most High beyond the empyrean, to lean in favor of idolatry, with the dislocations of the attributes figuring as mere "complementary acts," which left the preservation of global neutrality to the originating provisions. As has been stated insistently, the most notorious feature of sin is its ternary character. Hence, in relation to verbs, it is focused on the conjugation of three of them: *to direct*, *to transcribe*, and *to compose*. In the planes, the sin is confined to three of the ten (10) of the manifold *atxyz*, more precisely to the three of the earth, *xy*, *yz*, and *zx*, where the sources acquired their own identity.

The dislocation of the attributes covered the first, second, and third conditionings and was committed by three-fourths of the eight earthly humans of the council.

On the other hand, the zero conditioning (geometry), the conjugation of the verb *to determine*, the developments where a and t participate and one-quarter of the lights, preserved the essential features of the initial conditions. That minority fraction of the lights (two out of eight), faithful to the Cult of Adoration to the Most High and therefore practically alien to the later material becoming of the cosmos, will be called saints. Their participation in the dislocation of the turns is due more to their residual position in front of a majority group in the Most High Council than to their own initiative.

The next lines will be devoted to considering the details of the quarrel in order to understand how it has been possible to reach the current state of affairs. But before entering fully into the issue, it is worth noting that for reasons of practical nature, a heuristic rather than a causal or chronological approach will be followed. In this sense, it is important to emphasize that the irreversible decisions made by some earthly human beings were possible due to the continuous permutations of their attributes that prevailed during their juxtaposition in the initial conditions. Once the attributes were dislocated and the redirection of the actions between lights was executed, a scattering of the luminous sources occurred within the triad xyz. The new configuration involves transcriptions of the sources and directing the actions outside the walls of Jerusalem (or boundaries of Eden), the triacontakaihexagon on each plane. Additionally, the contumacy of the lights of left affiliation gave an irreversible character to the events, compromising the fate of the right ones.

To visualize the details of the quarrel, it is convenient to keep in mind the formulations of the human being and Iblis because without the agreement of both, it would have been impossible. The first objective of the infidels to be considered is the division of the council, with most of the lights (six out of eight) opting to dislocate rotations and turns, circumstantially compromising the whole. Thus the council was divided into two groups of four, the lights of right affiliation rotating according to the right-hand rule, and the left to the contrary. If the turns are added to the displacement of all the units, it is possible to speak of helicities. And given that the set was transcribed at the maximum speed of light, the helicities could only develop around the direction of propagation (for example, z). The second objective to be addressed is the permutation of the first conditioning attributes. According to the scheme devised by Satan, two lights of right and one of left affiliation were oriented outwardly (the idolaters), and three lights of left affiliation toward the primordial hexagon (the idols), breaking the original symmetry. In third place is the action of Iblis on the idols to claim for him a figuration in the foreground. His maneuver was to dislocate spatially the ternary attributes distinguished chromatically to reduce the permutations that buried him.

Figure 30.1 shows the earthly human beings of left affiliation with their polarized orientations and the ternary attributes spatially dislocated.

Polarizations are indicated by thick lines in the primordial hexagons of the three idols and in the circumference of one idolater, following the convention suggested in figure 27.1. The letters *b*, *g*, and *r* indicate the colors blue, green, and red, respectively, with which the ternary attributes are distinguished. The black arrows indicate the essence of idolatry in terms of exchanges of action.

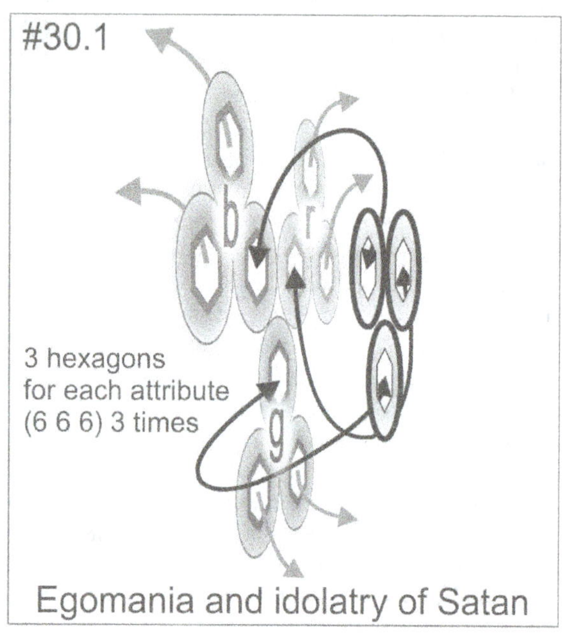

The six gray arrows indicate demanding idolatry attitudes on the part of the six unsatisfied lights of the chromatic dislocation. The three blue, green, and red double sets in figure 27.3 are condensed into one of each color, simplifying the illustrations.

The three idols have their orientations toward their own hexagonal origins, thus generating the figure of the beast, the 666 mentioned by John in his Apocalypse: "whoever has knowledge let him obtain the figure of the beast, because it is the number of a man. The number is 666." The triple feature of the number 666 expresses the ternary trait of sin, the dominant figuration of the igneous, and its ternary attributes. On the other hand, the six would refer to the number of infidels in each unit of the Most High Council and to the figure of the primordial hexagons converted into idols. According to Yasna IX of the Zend-Avesta, the dragon Dahaka has three mouths, three heads, six eyes, thousands of powers, and an awesome force and is the devil of the lie. Thus Satan, with the consent of some human formulations, substituted the obscurity of the empyrean for the darkness of the primordial hexagon, becoming the sink of the actions of the idolaters.

The three pairs of lights demanding idolatry could be associated with the exteriorizations of the three female pre-Islamic idols. These demons were mentioned by the prophet Muhammad in a verse in surah The Star, linked to the controversy of the so-called satanic verses:

> Have you then considered Lat, Uzza, and the other third, Manat? Are the males for you and for Him the females? This is certainly an unfair division! They are nothing but names that you and your ancestors have given them. God has not sent down any authority for them. They do nothing but follow conjectures and the desires of their souls. And certainly the direction has come to them from their Lord.

Figure 30.2 presents one of the possible permutations at the time of identifying al-Lat, al-Uzza, and Manat, in the context of the dislocation of ternary attributes.

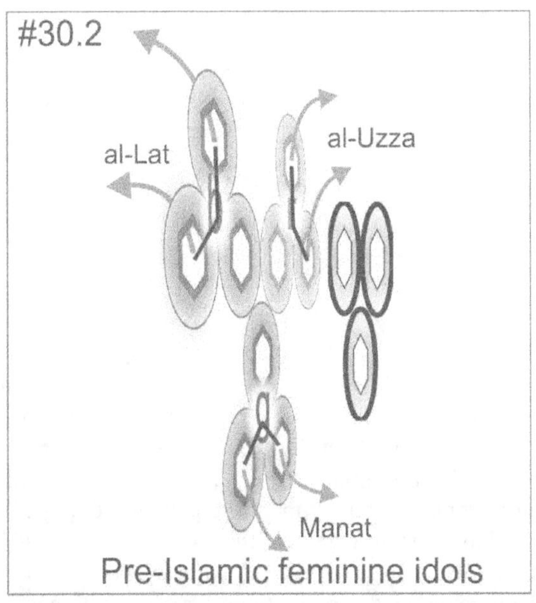

Having outlined the essence of the quarrel, it is convenient to summarize the state of affairs prevailing from that event. The combined effect of mutually directing actions between lights and the dislocations of attributes shattered the singularity of the Most High Council, causing a violent expansion of the universe—that is, within xyz. Until that moment the lights were confined to a small space occupied by the indifferent and juxtaposed entities of the Most High Council. This very act unleashed a true hell of violent and abundant interactions, with attractions and repulsions between lights with orientations and ternary attributes different or equal. It was like an intense activity, where transitory forms constituted by all kinds of fragments decanted into more stable structures that Satan and his followers would have had as objectives. The Holy Scriptures are not very explicit in relation to the type of structures derived from the quarrel. However, it is easy to infer that they should be definitive forms destined to prevail in one way or another—of course, as long as the Creator does not desist of his work and stop realizing it. After all, Satan and his followers did nothing but use the degrees of freedom provided by God. Figure 30.3 schematically illustrates the expansive fragmentation following the sin of Adam and Iblis, commonly known as the *Big Bang*.

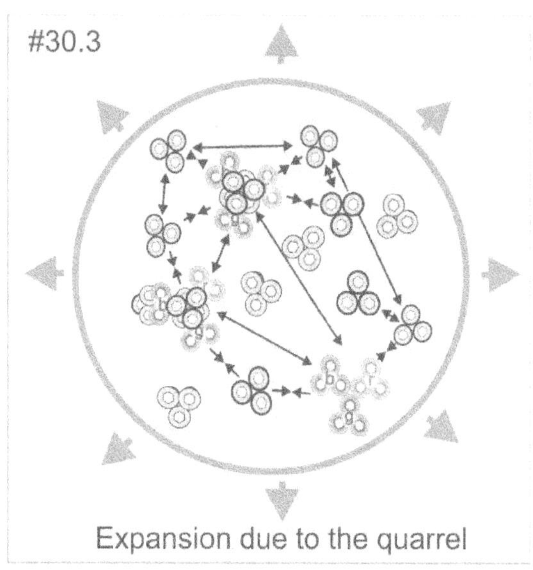

The illustration includes some of the structures with the potential to resurface from any corrective action taken by the Creator. Some of the attractions and repulsions indicated by double arrows are due to the exchange of actions between the protagonists. Despite not participating in the dynamics of idols and idolaters, the saints were dragged by their entanglements with lights of both affiliations. Certainly, Satan and his followers would have foreseen some kind of corrective measure on the part of the Creator, but they expected that he would in some way respect the outcome of the quarrel.

The archetypal fragmentation produced by the quarrel severely curtailed the degrees of freedom into some residual free will. Since fragmentation and scattering only occurred within the *xyz* lower triad, where the offending archetypes dwelt, their residual free will only allow these lights to choose spatial directions and locations—locality. It also gave origin to an uncountable number of elementary units, no longer existing, which were the precursors of elementary particles. The Anointed Ones and the Holy Spirit remain faithful to their Creator and therefore continue exerting their raw free will globally in perpetuity and time.

Chapter 31

The Unleashed Forces

One of the immediate effects of the abandonment of the initial conditions of Creation as a result of the quarrel was the "polarization" of the luminous waters. The active presence of conditioned earthly masculine lights (Men) aroused the reactive character of the waters, causing a reconfiguration of their opposed counterparts (chiaroscuro contrast) in the terms already discussed. Under their polarized form, waters enabled the formation of the "carriers of the exchange forces," constantly producing new equivalent luminous configurations under the imperative of the originating provisions. If the earthly quarrelers aspired to become modules with which to build idolatry, the luminous waters and the evocable opposites in them acted as the "mortar" to bind them together.

Two types of polarizations will be addressed, the first one caused by the earthly humans endowed with orientation, and the second by the effect of the dislocation of the ternary attributes. The dissolution of common salt in chemical water could be considered as a typical example of the exteriorization of polarizations by orientation. In the case of table salt (sodium chloride, $NaCl$), the chemical water is polarized and acts as a dielectric, enabling the separation of the chlorine ($Cl-$, *Chlôros*, from green-yellow in Greek) and sodium ($Na +$) ions with opposite electrical charges. In this sense the synoptics add, "You are the salt of the earth. But if the salt loses its flavor, how will it salt again? It is useless, worth throwing it away so that people will step on it." For this reason, the term *dissolved* will be used to refer to the condition of the pairs of opposites present in the luminous waters regardless of the origin of their polarization. It is convenient to remember an association made previously between the waters of the luminous discourse and the vacuum to emphasize from now on the excitations of the opposites that form and saturate them.

The Holy Scriptures make reference to the topic of the waters saturated with opposites on rare occasions and always in relation to the exteriorization suggested above. A clear example appears in the book of Joshua, when he narrates the aversion of the Hebrew people to the brackish waters: "Then you will tell your children the story and say: 'Israel crossed the Jordan on dry land'…as did the Lord with the Red Sea, which He dried up before us." The enabling performance of waters in relation to the quarrel was added to the long list of arguments in favor of relegating women to a second plane in the religious sphere. The reader should remember in that sense the cyclical tenor (think of itself) of the feminine or rotational character of the luminous discourse, constituted by closed loops not passing through God.

Yasna LXVII of the Zend Avesta relates the creation of "good waters" by Ahura Mazda, and the tradition states that Angra Mainyu (the devil) salted part of it. On the other hand, the book of the Apocalypse of John describes a sea under the thrones of God and of Satan: "And before the throne there was something like a transparent sea of glass, similar to crystal"; "I saw a sea of glass mixed with fire and those who had defeated the beast, its effigy and the figure of its name were in their positions on the crystal sea." In the New Testament, there is also no lack of accusations against the feminine for having yielded to the offer of Satan, as indicated by Paul in his already-quoted first letter to Timothy.

The Mandaeans (a sect still present today among minority groups in southern Iraq, Syria, and Jordan) qualify as dirty the waters involved in plans made by Satan. It is thought that Mandaeanism had its origin in a heterodox Hebrew sect, whose emigration from Palestine to Mesopotamia occurred at the beginning of the Christian era. The ancient Hebraic beliefs were mixed with others from diverse origins with an accentuated dualistic tinge. It is presumed that they knew Christianity through the disciples of John the Baptist by the admiration they profess to him and by adopting his ritual of water baptism.

The Mandaean cosmogony is based on the existence of two independent principles called the "Father of Eternal Life" (Mana) and the "king of darkness." The inhabitants of the kingdom of good, the *uthra*, are led by Mana, while the inhabitants of the evil realm are led by Ruha (female demon). The world and the human being originate in an ominous collaboration between some *uthra*, headed by Ptahil (son of the Creator) and Ruha. Both of them worked behind the back of the Father of Eternal Life with their own substances, light and dirty water. As a result, there is a light (the soul) trapped in the darkness of dirty water, yearning to reencounter again with the Father of Eternal Life and the *uthra*. The prophet of truth, called Manda da Hayye, is sent by the Father with the mission of revealing the "science of eternal life" to those who deserve such grace. Among those who have already been saved, they consider John the Baptist, whom they venerate in the middle of a cult where Hebrew and Christian elements coexist.

The sacred book of the Mandaeans is the Ginza (Treasure), written in eastern Aramaic in the third century AD. Prominent figures of Judaism, Christianity, and Islam, including Moses, Jesus, and Muhammad, were classified as false prophets, possibly due to rivalries in the religious sphere, which have never been lacking. Such assessments have given Mandaeans the generalized repudiation of the followers of patriarch Abraham. However, the Zoroastrian influence on Mandaeanism and the scant number of its devotees have made it go unnoticed.

The Gnostic text *Faith in Wisdom* (*Pistis Sophia*), written during the second century AD, blames Sophia, daughter of Barbelo (first emanation in the Gnostic cosmogony), for being seduced by the light of Autades. The cunning demon managed to confuse Sophia so that she thought he was God the Father. With that luminous deception, Autades tempted her to chaos under the twelve (12) eons, where she was trapped by the power of evil. This is how matter was born, the fruit of the sin committed by Sophia.

In the Islamic tradition of the hadith, reference is also made to the waters as the basis for the action of Satan because "Jabir reports that the

Messenger of Allah said: 'Iblis establishes his throne on water...'" Other similar doctrines could be brought up, without much to add to the understanding of the indispensable participation of the waters in the construction of idolatry.

After the quarrel, waters behaved in different ways, among which may be mentioned their polarization in opposite pairs, various forms of excitation of their opposites, their separation in opposite pairs, and their formation in the annihilation of opposite pairs. The excitations can be of three types, transverse to the transcription direction, longitudinally with it, or scalar in direction t. It is important to clarify that all these phenomenologies only occur in the tetrad $txyz$, and only the two polarization types mentioned above will be addressed. Its effects are only observable because of the changes in behavior caused to the masculine lights to which they are linked. In order to avoid inadequate visualizations of these phenomenologies, it is worth emphasizing once again that neither the masculine lights nor their waters "displace continuously" in xyz. These objects only transcribe their sources from one point to another of their own geometries via the mediation of their rotational quanta.

According to tradition, the house of the Annunciation to Mary in Nazareth was carried miraculously by angels to the Italian town of Loreto. Similarly, surah The Ant of the Koran states that the throne of the Queen of Saba (the tenth century BC) was brought before King Solomon in the twinkling of an eye (at the speed of light). Perhaps among the most eloquent representations of a symbolic character regarding the transcriptions of luminous sources are the Zoroastrian faravahar and the caduceus of Hermes, both shown in figure 31.1.

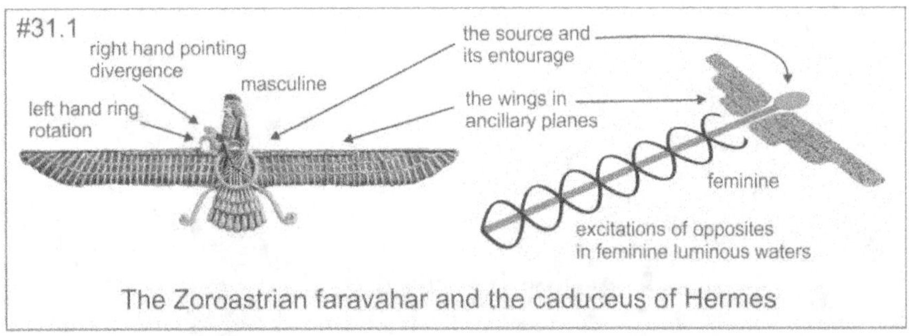

The Zoroastrian faravahar and the caduceus of Hermes

The relevant items appearing in the figure are the luminous sources at their new destination, the wings or rotational quantum corresponding to an ordinal incarnation of the human beings involved, and the pair of opposites in the luminous water in a state of excitation.

Once a transcription has been directed, determined, and realized it occurs spatially in one out of three mutually independent directions. The chosen direction conveys the masculine character of action, the other two the feminine one. The transcription (or flight) is mediated by a pair of wings corresponding to the chosen direction. In the words of the prophet Isaiah, cited in chapter 4, the seraphim had three pairs of wings, but only one is used for flying.

An example of longitudinal and scalar excitations by polarization in the orientation is the "neutral" force. This force consists of an exchange of mutually directed actions between oriented earthly lights. The process is specified by the emission and absorption of waters (transcription of the sources via rotational quanta), with their opposite pairs having longitudinal and scalar excitations. It is provided that if the exchange is carried out between lights with the same orientation, the neutral force turns out to be repulsive. When the orientations are contrary, the force is attractive. For this reason, the neutral force of exchange will be attractive between idolaters and idols and repulsive in the case of similar ones. Figure 31.2 presents a case of repulsion between idols, leaving the reader to visualize other possible cases.

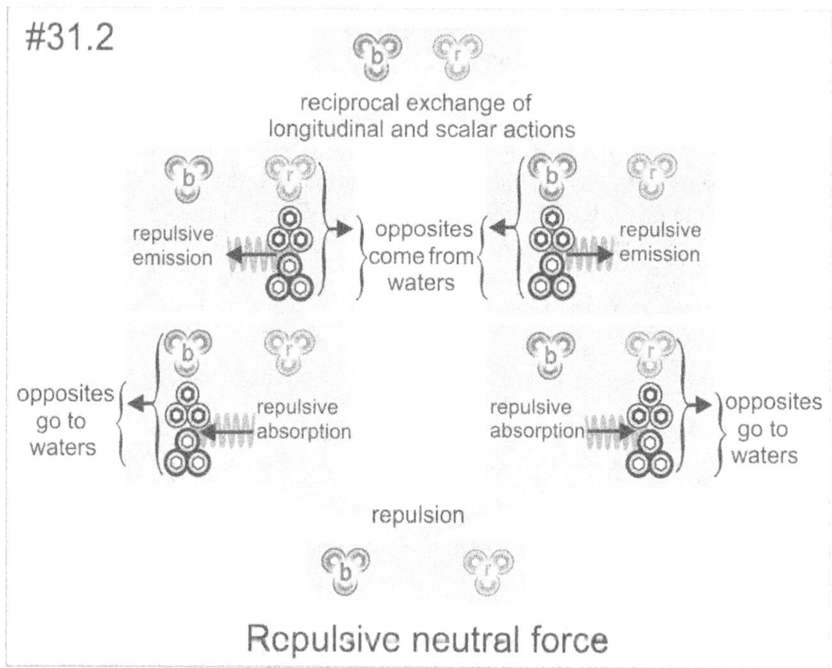

Repulsive neutral force

As can be seen in the illustration, the exchange is carried out concomitantly by both idols (transcription of water sources via rotational quanta). The present case differs from that illustrated to the right of figure 24.6, where an exchange of waters among neutral divergent quanta was exemplified.

The second force to be addressed in the present work is the exchange force of ternary attributes, which originates in their spatial dislocation. This force is responsible for preserving the global neutrality of the chromatically distinguished attributes. Waters are committed to this process by generating equivalent configurations under the mandate of the originating provisions. The dislocation of the ternary attributes does not then generate a stable configuration but instead results in a continuous process of permutations. The repulsive effect of the neutral exchange force within the chromatic dislocation is overcome by the attractive exchange force of the chromatically distinguished attributes—remember the awesome strength of the Dahaka demon. Both forces reach a point of equilibrium in which the idols remain spatially separated but cohesive. In this case, as in the previous one, there is a polarization of the waters, but this time in terms of contraries according to ternary attributes. The reader will remember the postulate of absolute neutrality in all the conditionalities that rules the luminous waters. In the case of the third, both; the ternary attributes denominated blue, green, and red, as well as the corresponding antiattributes yellow, magenta, and cyan, are present in waters. Figure 31.3 only illustrates one type of chromatic exchange, leaving the interested reader to visualize others.

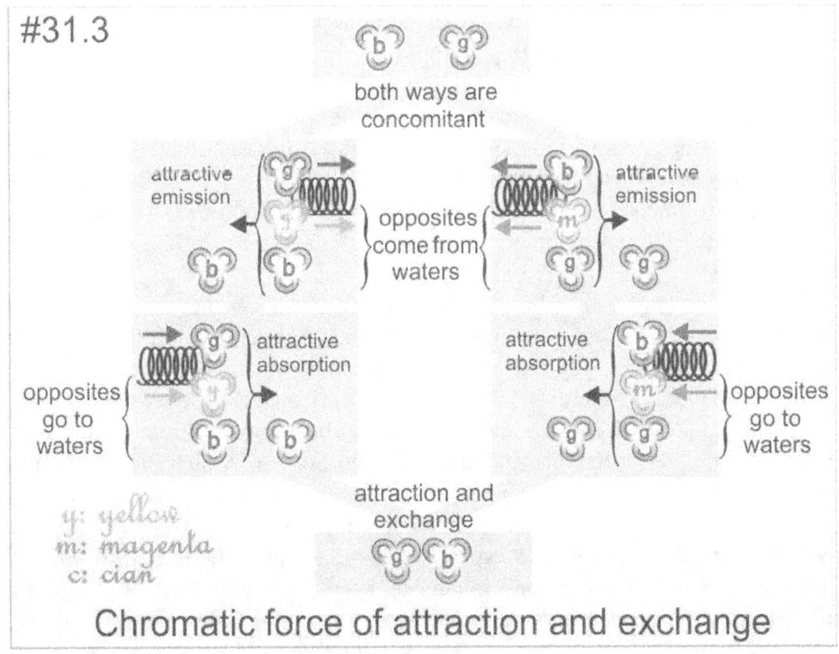

Chromatic force of attraction and exchange

In the upper part of the illustration, one of the three chromatically distinguished luminous masculine pairs participating in the dislocation can be observed, with its two concomitant exchange pathways. On the left, a luminous masculine light labeled "green" uses a pair of opposites from the waters, in this case a "blue" and "yellow" one to enable a carrier "green" "yellow." On the right, the result of resorting to the opposite pair "green" and "magenta" is illustrated. Once the chromatic action is transmitted, the pair of opposites returns to the waters from which they came. The effect is an attractive permutation between the masculine lights distinguished by the green and blue attributes and serves as an example of what happens incessantly in the other pairs. The carriers of the chromatic force are also subject to the same force because they are not chromatically neutral and have been symbolized by a helix to distinguish them from the neutral ones. The carriers of neutral force are not affected by it because their net orientation is zero.

The Buddhist three-pronged vajras portray vacuum as two masculine components in opposition (the straight ones), sided by two feminine counterrotations in the ancillary planes (the curved ones). The accompanying bell represents the human being formulation with the handle (half vajra) standing for the masculine component and the bell longitudinal sound wave with its periodical nature for the feminine one. The bell configuration is analogous to that of a particle emitting a longitudinal force carrier. In the Sacred Scriptures, longitudinal sound waves from horns, trumpets, and cries represent these force carriers. In churches and mosques we find bell towers (the masculine) with their bell sound (the feminine) and minarets to project the adhan (call to prayer), representing, in both cases, the divergent polarization of masculine righteousness emitting longitudinal force carriers.

Since it is a virtually null act, the dislocation of the turns did not give rise to the emergence of an exchange force. There are no attractions among opposing turns or repulsions among equal turns. In that order of ideas, it is important to keep in mind the saints, whose actions are directed toward the empyrean with neutrality in their conditionalities one and three. Thanks to their position in the face of the quarrel, the saints remain alien to the forces derived from the dislocations of the infidels.

Having based the previous disquisition on the composition of opposing pairs around the luminous waters, it is convenient to dedicate a few lines to the "exclusion regime" that prevails among them. The issue arises as a result of the disbanding of the Most High Council and the consequent acquisition of identity and independence by the lights. With regard to said compositions, the principle is adopted according to which the dislocated masculine lights cannot compose in the same locality, when their attributes are all the same (even having different identities). Within the framework of the present natural exegesis, two types of compositions will be addressed, one associated with the waters or vacuum, and the other with the carriers of the forces. In the case of waters or vacuum, the masculine lights are composed in pairs, with their attributes being contrary with respect to orientation, turn, and ternary attributes. In the carriers of the forces, the turns (regardless of their innocuousness) may not be contrary as long as the pairs of masculine lights composed differ in the orientation. In the case of the carriers of the chromatic force, different orientations imply color-anticolor composition.

Chapter 32

The Universal Flood

The Creator decided to intervene during the expansion of the cosmic fire, drastically reducing the balance between odd and even formulations, through the emergence of the "waters of the Flood." As explained in the book of Genesis, the new regime of domination of the waters was imposed by all those of the cloud, the upper and the lower ones: "in the second month, on the seventeenth day of the month, all the fountains of the great deep burst forth and the windows of heaven were opened. And it rained on the earth for forty days and forty nights." The Koran in **surah Hud** ratifies the intervention in the Flood of various types of waters, when it reports on the order given for their descent: "And it was said: 'O Earth! Swallow your water, O Clouds! Clear away.'"

The waters of the Flood lasted long enough to truncate the course drawn by Satan and his followers: "And the waters prevailed for a hundred and fifty days. And God remembered Noah…And God sent the wind over the earth and the waters came down. And the fountains of the deep and the floodgates of heaven were closed and the rain from heaven stopped." The 150 days of predominance of the waters would undoubtedly point to their overabundance in the ten (10) planes of the manifold *atxyz* as well as in the five ancillary ones. The previous passage of the book of Genesis additionally provides the datum of the relative diminution of the role of the waters with the arrival of the "wind" or Spirit of God. The same one who, at the beginning of Creation, hovered over the waters; as the psalmist rightly says: "When You send your Spirit, You create them. And You renew the face of the earth."

The Universal Flood not only meant the end of the cosmic regime prevailing after the quarrel, but it was chiefly the consequence of a new creative impulse, the second creation. The Koran is the first to inform about this second creation in surah The Star: "And He has ordered a second creation…And He destroyed the first Aad, and from the Thamud has left no trace, and the people of Noah before, certainly the most wicked and rebellious. And He overthrew the cities that He threw, covering them…" A careful reading of the Scriptures confirms that the new or second creation had the same formulations as the first one, but an opposing endeavor, in every respect, with the intention of annihilating most of the first or Adamic creation in the formation of the flood waters.

Identifying the waters of the Flood with the archetypal waters of heaven and earth gives a cosmic scope to the event. The surplus waters also increased the possibility of dissipating actions by division and emission of archetypal waters (in the form of radiation), draining the potential for action of the earthly masculine light (Men). The descent of water levels could be interpreted in terms of recomposition or condensation and dispersion, once the activity generated by the quarrel dissipated. On the other hand, the instability of the marriage unions of the earthly human beings altered the possibilities awaiting determination and realization. The courses of fertilizations in patriarchal successions faced new possibilities, and the Adamic covenant ceased (Gen. 3:14–19), with the Edenic one being replaced (Gen. 1:26–31, 2:16–17) (the six remaining covenants are Noah [the twenty-fifth century BC] [Gen. 9:1–18], Abrahamic [Gen. 17:1–18], Mosaic [Exod. 31:18], Palestinian [Deut. 30:1–10], Davidic [2 Sam. 7:4–17], and New [Jer. 31:30–32]). Because of the sin of Adam and Iblis, the sanctity of the old flesh from the first or Adamic creation was lost and replaced by a pardoned one due to the effect of the waters of the baptismal flood: "And God said to Noah: 'The end of all flesh has come.'"

The cosmic importance of the Universal Flood is reaffirmed by its notorious presence in the main cosmogonic narratives of humanity. This event, described in the Bible with abundant detail, preeminently figures in the Mesopotamian epics of *Ziusudra*, *Gilgamesh*, and *Atra-Hasis* (the thirtieth through the seventeenth centuries BC). It also appears in cultures as disparate as the Hindu mythology of the *Shatapatha Brahmana* (the seventh century BC), the *Timaeus* of Plato (the fourth century BC), and even in pre-Columbian traditions of America, just to mention the most documented. However, the possibility of reducing the issue of the Flood to a rainy event of scarcely planetary reach does not have the support of geological or biological evidence. It would not be a sudden global flood either but a cosmic event to end an era and start a new one.

For being the biblical narrative of the Universal Flood the most detailed and referred-to one, it will be used to support working hypotheses within the framework of the natural exegesis. The story begins with an exposition of reasons for the intervention of the Creator and is followed by a recount of the facts grouped into three major episodes. The first one focuses on the instructions given to Noah to avoid the total extinction of the prevailing regime. The second one focuses on the rise of the water levels, and finally the third one is dedicated to its descent.

The Universal Flood in no way meant the total annulment of the results of the quarrel. So much so that, within the ark of Noah, Ham (the twenty-fifth century BC) remains safe; his son Canaan (the twenty-fifth to the twenty-fourth centuries BC) will become the father of the Canaanites, an essentially pagan nation against which new and drastic corrective measures were imposed. In his First Epistle, Peter confirms the number of survivors of the Flood, which coincides with the number of participants in each unit of the Most High Council: "while Noah was finishing the ark, in which a few, that is eight people, were saved from the water. And baptism, from which the flood is an image, now gives you the salvation."

The biblical account of the Universal Flood is not enough to appraise its scope, even when it provides key data on the measures of the ark and in the chronology of the event. Despite an intentionally obscure presentation, the narrative provides indications that the Flood did not essentially change the formulations of the first creation, even though it modified its later development. As for the measures of the ark in "cubits," they reassert two types of known numerical relationships, the height thirty (30) and the longitude three hundred (300 = 30 × 10). Both factors have been previously linked to the waters and their recipients. The first, thirty (30), was associated with the symbolism of the bronze sea and the counterrotations in the fifteen (15) planes (30 = 15 × 2) of masculine character. The second, ten (10), was associated with the ten counterrotations in the five ancillary planes (10 = 5 × 2) of the female ordinal incarnation. The width of fifty (50) cubits (also one-sixth of the length) would be related to the radius or side of a rotating primordial hexagon whose perimeter is three hundred (300). Bronze sea figures are multiplied by a factor of ten (10), in connection with the ten (10) planes of the manifold *atxyz*.

In relation to the chronology, the Argentinean Assyriologist A. Heidel (the twentieth century AD) solved in a clear and simple way what concerns the time lapses of the Flood—something that gave headaches to erudite readers over the centuries. Accepted by most scholars today, this chronology allows one to ratify the same originating archetypal formulations for the postdiluvian period. Basically Heidel divides the chronology in 150 days for the increase of the waters, including the first 40 of rain, followed by its descent during 219 days (almost 220), within which the first mountain peaks appeared at the end of the first 74 days. According to the Genesis account, after waiting another 40 days, Noah opened the ark window and sent four birds. The time intervals between each bird were seven days, giving a total of twenty-one (21 = 3 × 7) days:

> Noah sent a crow, which flew back and forth…Then he sent a pigeon…but…did not find where to perch and came back to Noah…and after waiting another seven days he sent the pigeon again…And the pigeon came back in the afternoon…and in his beak it brought an olive leaf. And after another seven days, he sent the dove again, but it did not return to him.

Certainly the symbolism of the four birds could be interpreted at first sight under a 1-3 type scheme, based on taxonomic differences. However, the presence of additional data allows for expanding the scope of the interpretation. The pigeon that did not return stands out in this context as a representative of the lights faithful to initial conditions, which have been called the saints. The righteousness of the saints must also extend to the domains of the Anointed One and the Spirit, associated with the plane *at*. Luminous waters are also represented symbolically by the two pigeons with circular trajectories. They make reference to the binary and periodic character of the feminine and their referential role due to the annulment of the workings of their components. Finally the crow with its coming and going represents the effeminacy of idolaters and idols as they mutually direct their actions in the triad *xyz*. Figure 32.1 illustrates the interpretation given to the symbolism of birds.

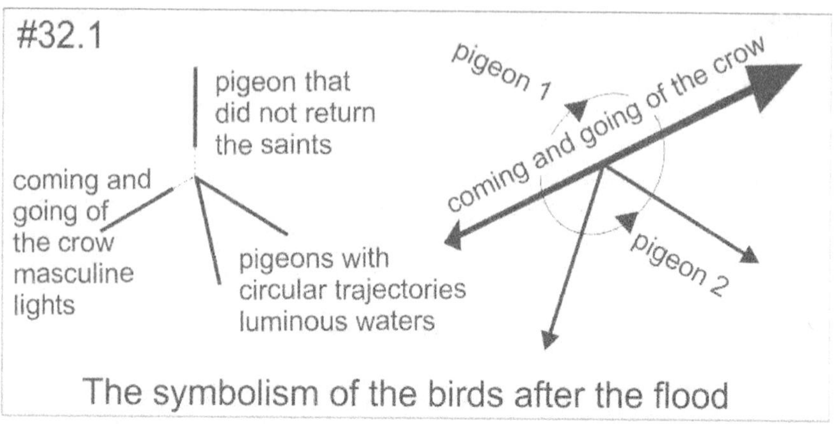

The symbolism of the birds after the flood

The figure shows on the left a quaternary representation of the behavior of the birds with reference to the lights, while on the right is illustrated the coming and going of the crow in relation to the inherent neutrality of the luminous waters.

The time lapses between the trips of the birds, amounting to twenty-one (21 = 3 × 7) days in total, admits the same interpretations given previously to the figure. Its value has been linked to the primordial hexagon plus the source and to the quanta invested by the three distinctive attributes. Later, and after twenty-eight (28 = 4 × 7) days, Noah observed that waters let him see the earth, but it was presumably muddy. After another fifty-six (56 = 2 × 28) days, the earth was dry, and Noah descended from the ark. References are thus made to the hexagons plus the source in the four planes and their pairs of wings according to the human formula 1&2. The Torah reintroduces this way the same scheme regarding the twenty-eight (28) letters with which Genesis 1:1 was written. The eventual restoration of the flesh under a new regime then runs in parallel, with a loss of significance for the waters. The total duration of the Flood was approximately 370 days (369 = 150 + 74 + 40 + 21 + 28 + 56), a number allusive to the triacontakaihexagon plus the source and to its luminous expression in the ten (10) planes of the manifold *atxyz*.

The Koran also emphasizes the punitive character of the Universal Flood in several mentions throughout its text, especially in surah Noah. The text exposes the lamentations of the just Man before God for not being able to separate his people from paganism. Specifically, Noah would have failed in the eradication of the cult to five pre-Islamic idols, with which the biblical pentapolis and the core of idolatry will be associated later:

Noah said: "My Lord! Certainly they disobey me and follow him whose goods and children do nothing but increase their loss. And they have devised a great plan. And they have said: Do not abandon your gods, nor forsake Wadd, nor Suwa, nor Yaguth and Yauq and Nasr."

Undoubtedly, the plan in the mind of Ham would be based on maintaining idolatry at all costs and resisting the Flood while waiting for new opportunities.

Nothing in the narratives about the Flood indicates a change in the formulations contemplated in the originating provisions of the first creation. This is evidenced by the absence of new archetypes and the ratification of the numerical keys considered above. For this reason, the creative impulse preceded by diluvial waters will be dealt with the same provisions described in the preceding chapters.

Chapter 33

Contumacious Idolatry

The restoration of equilibrium between the odd and even formulations after the Great Flood established a new course for Creation, in a context endowed with moderate excitations. Despite their rectitude in the face of deviations that originated in the quarrel, the saints could not escape being involved in an adventure centered on idolatry. The majority formed by the infidels prevailed in the Most High Council and took advantage of the commitment of the saints with the initial conditions within the framework of the originating provisions. The decision by the majority to split the structure of that group into two subgroups with opposite turns left the saints with those turning to the right. The turning conditionality plus their persistence in the initial displacement toward the empyrean endowed the saints with a perpetual right or positive helicity.

The seven turns of the divergent quantum of the saints within the triad *xyz* (the seventh day) after dislocation have been a source of inspiration in religious rituals. These turns have representation in the rotation of planet Earth on its axis (the seven days of the week) or around the sun (when the right-hand rule describes the rotation and translation of the earth with the thumb pointing to the north) (for seven years). All of them are represented symbolically by the ritual of the Whirling Dervishes of Sufi mysticism, an order founded by followers of the Persian mystic poet Yalal ad-Din Muhammad Rumi (the thirteenth century AD) in Konya, Turkey. They are also represented by liturgical turns and religious practices such as the seven circling around the Bimah (pulpit for reading the Torah in the synagogues) during the Great Supplication (Hoshana Rabbah) on the seventh day of the Feast of Tabernacles (Sukkoth); the inner rotation, total or partial, inside the Christian temples during the traditional fourteen stations of the cross (14 = 7 × 2) on Fridays (originally of seven stations); and the seven circumambulations (*tawaf*) around the Kaaba during Hajj. Figure 33.1 illustrates the ritual expressions just mentioned.

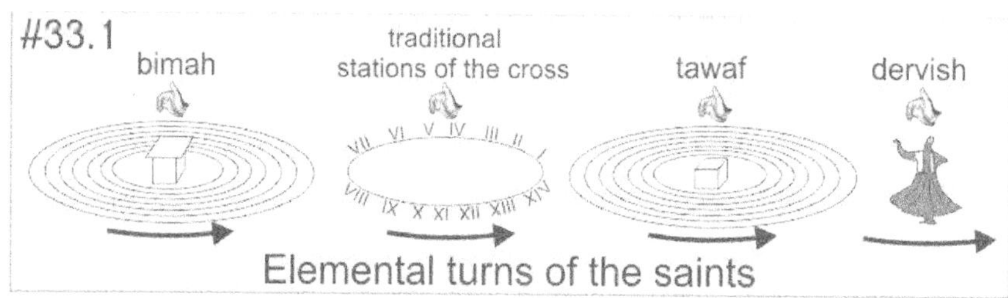

The right or positive helicity of the saints is an innocuous conditioning in the worship of the Most High and therefore is not associated with sin. On the other hand, the coming and going of idols and idolaters as a result of attractions and repulsions made their helicities a relative issue.

The absence of interactions between saints and infidels is frequently reviewed in the Holy Scriptures. An eloquent narrative appears in the Bible, when it recounts the meeting, already quoted, of Abram and Melchizedek, king priest of Salem, with the king of Sodom:

> He brought bread and wine and, after blessing him, said: "May the blessing of the Most High God, creator of heaven and earth, be upon Abram. And praise be to the Most High God, Who has delivered your enemies into your hand." And Abram gave him tithes of everything. And the king of Sodom said to Abram: "Give me the prisoners and keep the assets." But Abram answered the king of Sodom: "Raising my hands I made an oath to the Lord God Most High, creator of heaven and earth, that I will not take a thread or a shoe strap from you, so that you will not be able to say: I have made Abram rich."

The two holy Men faithful to the Most High, Abram and Melchizedek worship the God on high in Jerusalem and avoid exchanges with the king of Sodom, representative of idolatry.

Even under the effect of diluvial waters, idols and idolaters struggled feverishly to maintain the nuclei of idolatry formed during the quarrel, particularly those with the ability to interact independently. It is presumed that Satan should have as his initial objective the building of an inexpugnable structure where all forms of idolatry could reside, in open defiance to his Creator. To exploit the full potential of free will, its fortification must have an odd number of masculine lights (Men). Satan and his followers took advantage of entanglements with the saints and left outside one idolater with right affiliation. The construction would then consist of seven masculine lights and would possess as a formative nucleus the dislocation of the ternary attributes.

In reality it is far less complicated than it seems, as the initiative is equivalent to group seven of the eight dislocated lights of the Most High Council, excluding from that core one idolater. Figure 33.2 illustrates schematically the luminous representation of the objects in question, which includes the three dislocations, two entanglements, the idolater excluded, and the exchange of actions between idols and idolaters.

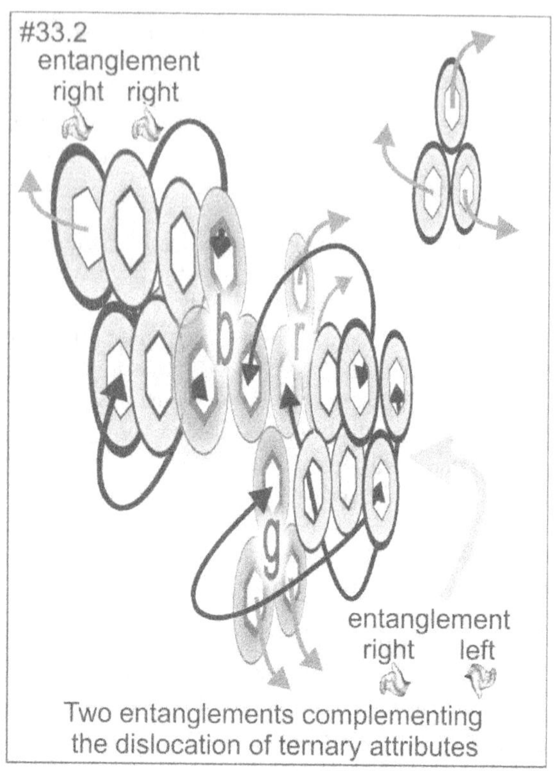

This is the furthest thing that will come in terms of complexity in a presentation scheme in this first part. At the center of the illustration, the chromatic dislocation can be seen, with two entanglements on each side that are inherited from the Most High Council. The entanglement on the left is based on two right affiliations, and the other shown on the right brings together the right and left affiliations. Despite their entanglements, the saints do not exchange actions with any light because they maintain their fidelity to the Cult to the Most High God. Therefore, the saints exchange their neutral actions with the Most High beyond the empyrean, and their first and third conditionings are neutral. The details of the mechanism of entanglement mentioned will not be addressed in this book in order to reduce its level of complexity. It is also left to the initiative of the reader the visualization of the permutations of the attributes chromatically distinguished. Outside the nucleus of idolatry, one can observe an idolater capable of sharing with his counterpart the four neutral exchange opportunities in the chromatic dislocation, indicated by dark gray arrows.

The global neutrality of the turns in the Most High Council and its division into two parts deserves certain considerations. For the separation of one idolater with one unit of turn from the nucleus of idolatry, with its seven masculine lights, conditioned the last group to have one unit of turn. That rotating feature of the nucleus of idolatry with formative character will be maintained in perpetuity given the global neutrality imposed by the originating provisions. Regardless of the turns of some lights around others and of carriers of forces, the nucleus will always exhibit one unit of elemental turn. This peculiarity raises some uncertainty about the rotating state of the seven masculine lights that constitute it. Even if the turns of some lights around others and those of the carriers of the forces are null, the seven lights will be able to fulfill that requirement. The reader can make a balance on the turns, adding to the three left turns in the chromatic dislocation, the turns in both entanglements. Regardless of the details provided about the fortification's structure, it is important to bear in mind that it is nothing more than a simple set of possibilities. However, by complying with the originating provisions, the object devised by Satan and his followers will be realized and determined by God and his Spirit.

There are few passages in the Holy Scriptures where the luminous entanglements are expressed symbolically as clearly as in the narrative of the Transfiguration of Jesus on Mount Tabor. The symbolism surrounding this episode has already been interpreted in terms of a description of the relations inherent to the sacerdotal institution. But it is also susceptible to other interpretations due to the imbrications of the exteriorizations of various formulation types. To do so is enough to visualize Jesus and Peter as masculine components of a luminous entanglement, the first representing the saints and the second the idolaters. In the trio formed by Jesus&(Moses Elijah), the last two would represent the luminous feminine component of the saint, while in Peter&(James John), the Boanerges would symbolically represent the feminine counterpart of the idolaters. The inclination toward idolatry of the trio formed by Peter&(James John) becomes evident from their satisfaction at gloating in the mundane, as Mark and Luke recount: "Peter said to Jesus: 'Master, it is good for us to be here, let us make three tents.'"

In the nuclei of idolatry, five lights, between idols and idolaters, are actively involved. For their part, the two saints are limited to following the prescriptions of the originating provisions and the entanglements derived from them. The five lights of the nucleus would represent the five pre-Islamic idols, the five cities of the plains, and collectively the city of Jericho. The cities of the plains, also known as the biblical pentapolis, were constituted by Sodom, Gomorrah, Zoar, Admah, and Zeboiim.

The historicity of the biblical story about the existence of pentapolis was questioned in the past by most scholars on the subject. However, perception has been changing since the discovery of the Ebla tablets in AD 1975, to the north of Syria, where references to the five cities appear. These findings have substantiated the thesis of the American researchers W. Rast (the twentieth to the twenty-first centuries AD) and R. Schaub (the twentieth to the twenty-first centuries AD) about the possible location of the pentapolis south of the Dead Sea. There, in the mouths of the five existing rivers in those latitudes, the referred-to cities would have been settled. In any case, and for the purposes of a natural exegesis, the stories of the Bible about the five cities transcend its historical veracity.

Like the cities of pentapolis, Jericho has a peculiar geographical location because it is located, like all of them, below sea level. The brackish waters of the Mediterranean Sea would represent the luminous waters saturated with opposites and acting referentially. In their neutral condition, those waters could not originate by themselves, with any action leading to a change in the prevailing state of affairs. The domains above and below the level of the Mediterranean waters could be interpreted as fields where actions are directed. Thus, Jerusalem, which is located 780 m above sea level, points to the direction of the Cult of Adoration to the Most High, whereas Jericho's, being located 250 m below sea level, would indicate by contrast the destiny of the actions toward the igneous idols. Both together represent the dilemma between sanctity and idolatry faced by the lights.

The position of Jericho in the historical context rivals its geographical situation, as far as symbolic value is concerned. This city is considered one of the first human settlements, with an approximate age of eleven thousand years (founded about four thousand years before the invention of the pottery wheel in Mesopotamia, during the al-Ubaid I culture). Jericho has been a model of human habitat par excellence, built and rebuilt over and over again for millennia. The ancient city has witnessed the materialistic eagerness of the human being and his welcome to the proposal of Satan, as well as the corrective measures of the Creator. The foundation of Jericho was due to its exceptional environment, its fertile land, the presence of a permanent spring, and the possibility of extracting salt from the shores of the Dead Sea.

The story of Jericho summarizes the human drama of giving up the search for one's place in the kingdom of heaven beyond the empyrean. For life in Jericho consisted of dedicating oneself again and again to gloating in the circulations of matter and descending through the sink of idolatry. Incidentally, the archaeological evidence for some time being against the biblical account seems to confirm with the passage of time its historicity even in the minutest details. The wealth of historical evidence, in fact, adds little to the data and symbolic value of the narrative offered by the Holy Scriptures of the People with the Book.

Chapter 34

Conflagration between Creations

The construction of idolatry centers would have been a first step in the plans of Satan and his followers to unleash and enjoy the potential held in the initial conditions. The Creator could have given up his Creation, refraining from realizing the existence of a universe turning its back on him, but he did not. Instead, he decided to create again by following the same originating provisions but opposing the dislocated attributes; the outcome was a flood of alchemical water in the form of radiation. In fact, the new or second creation is a globally neutral mirror image of the first, and the symmetries contemplated inversions of orientation, rotations and turns, and ternary attributes. In chromatic terms, the ternary antiattributes of the second creation will be called yellow, magenta, and cyan. The contraposition of the attributes was aimed at the mutual annihilation of both creations and their "dissolution" as opposing pairs in the waters. However, the necessary provisions taken ensured a small quantitative difference among the images, allowing the survival of a group of luminous structures. The surviving fractions condensed again into idolatry nuclei but under the status of "redeemed sin."

The confrontation between creations produced a new ignition of the cosmos, increasing the excitation available for a reduced number of objects in an environment of abundant symmetries. The outcome was the emergence of new instances of exteriorization/interiorization as new ways to test any improvement in the fidelity of the redeemed creatures toward God under the new regime. The Holy Scriptures treat the confrontation between creations as a punitive measure on the part of God, often in the framework of a great conflagration of an ecpyrotic nature. According to the Bible, the destruction of the five cities of the plain by fire was a material punishment from God without the participation of the Hebrews. Meanwhile, the same type of fire damage was inflicted on Jericho after a battle between people. There are key data in all the stories that reveal the pertinence for considering the same originating provisions for both creations.

Among the most striking postdiluvian corrective measures mentioned by the Bible is the destruction of the fortified cities where the descendants of Ham dwelt. After abandoning the God of Noah, the Canaanites devoted themselves fully to polytheism, rendering cults to divinities of their own and to those of other neighboring cultures. The details of the pagan cults of the inhabitants of those cities more than four thousand years ago remain unknown. However, it is known that the Semitic God of the Canaanites with the highest hierarchy was *El'Eb* (God the Father). The highest divinity was seconded by *El Shadday*, whose name etymologically related to the concept of "force" would qualify as the Almighty. The god El would preside over the divine assembly (*Phr'ilm*), where other minor divinities concurred; he would speak with a voice like thunder, would use the clouds as a chariot and would vivify the mountains by pouring water upon them. The Canaanite pantheon also included the Amorite god of the storms, Hadad, under the name of Ba'al (Lord), worshiped under seven occult representations, of which little is known. He was the god of natural fertility to whom the Canaanites rendered licentious cults reproved by the followers of patriarch Abraham.

Of the five cities on the plains, four were destroyed in a single act by fire: Sodom, Gomorrah, Admah, and Zeboiim. According to the book of Genesis, the city of Zoar, where Lot (the nineteenth to the eighteenth centuries BC) (nephew of Abraham) went to take refuge, survived the first episode of destruction. The book of Wisdom adds, "the Wisdom saved the righteous man from the destruction of the wicked, fleeing from the fire that had fallen on pentapolis."

The destruction of the biblical pentapolis is an episode of great importance, judging from the frequent references in the Holy Scriptures. Despite the abundant mentions, the details could not be scarcer. In any case, if the pentapolis symbolizes the five infidel lights (counting idolaters and idols) of the idolatry nucleus; the four destroyed cities would correspond to the four lights of left affiliation. The flight of Lot toward the mountains (Genesis 19:30) in the face of an imminent destruction of Zoar reveals a destiny common to all the members of the idolatry nucleus. After detailing the overthrow of the pentapolis, the book of Genesis mentions how the entangled saints and idolaters did separate, going in opposite senses. The terms of this separation between patriarch Abraham and Lot are exposed by an enigmatic phrase: "Let us separate our ways then: if you go to the left, I will go to the right or if you go to the right, I will go to the left."

The Bible offers another version of the confrontational scenario with the idolatry nuclei in the well-known episode of the conquest and destruction of the city of Jericho. Following precise instructions given by God, the Hebrew people, headed by Joshua, undertook the conquest and subsequent destruction of the city with fire. It is convenient to observe in the biblical narrative two key moments in the story of the battle for Jericho. The first is a meeting of Joshua with a high-ranking member of the armies of the Lord, while the second one deals with the instructions given by God to demolish the fortress built around the throne of Satan and free the righteous. The story in the book of Joshua of the encounter with an envoy of the Lord makes clear that his messengers do not take the side of any party. Therefore, neither do they belong to the lights of Jericho or their opposites, represented on this occasion by the Hebrew people:

> When Joshua was near Jericho, raising his eyes he saw a man in front of him with a sword unsheathed in his hand. And Joshua went to him and asked: "Are you with us or against us?" And he said to him: "No, but I have come as captain of the armies of the Lord."

The presence before Joshua of the captain of the armies of the Lord reveals the decisive character of the divine intervention to demolish the city—

the structure with which Satan and his followers managed to divert the course of creation. The captain, by emphasizing his neutrality in front of the two sides, describes himself as an angelic entity outside the triad *xyz*, where the conflagration is centered.

The battle for Jericho was not fought in purely military terms but under certainly unusual conditions provided by the Creator. In the battleground, the human beings had a role to fulfill, as they had also when they followed the plans of Satan. After the meeting with the captain of the armies,

> the Lord said to Joshua: "See, I have given Jericho into your hands with his king and all his warriors. Put your warriors around the city, circling only once. Do this for six days. And put seven priests before the ark carrying seven trumpets in their hands. On the seventh day, you will go around the city seven times and the priests will blow the trumpets. And at the sound of a long note on the trumpets, let all the people to cry loudly. And the walls of the city will fall and the people will advance toward their fronts…And the city will be cursed and everything inside will be given to the Lord. Only Rahab, the harlot and everyone in the house with her will be safe, because she secretly kept the men we sent there."

Of course, the instructions given to Joshua are somewhat enigmatic, and the story is extensive and repetitive. For this reason, the reader should refer to the source and read it carefully. Undoubtedly, the symbolism of the circumambulations around Jericho should be interpreted in terms of the relative movement of both sides. The priests, the Ark, the army, and the Hebrew people go round in a sense, in relation to a stationary object like the fortified city. The inhabitants of the city, on the other hand, observe the rotation of the Hebrews in the opposite sense. The relevant numerical key revealed by this passage revolves around a quadruplicate septenary symbolism, in terms of seven priests, seven trumpets, day seven, and seven circling rounds. The said scheme repeats in Jericho the formula of Genesis 1:1, with its seven words and twenty-eight letters ($28 = 4 \times 7$). Such repetition would be an indication that the second creation is governed by the same formulations as the first one.

Additionally, it would be possible to relate the rotations of the hidden light during the six days of creation with the silent rounds the first six days around Jericho. Then, on the seventh day, the seven cycles corresponding to the first expression of the divergent quanta (particle) manifested light would be completed. The cry signals the birth of the second creation in a precise temporal and spatial location, with the aim of destroying the first one and its fortified city. The importance given to the number seven in the narrative undoubtedly has to do with its presence in the formulations of the first and second creations. The similarities would allow ratifying the interpretations given to Genesis 1 regarding the creation of the luminous discourse and to the book of Exodus on the lampstand of the Tabernacle—except for the fact that the second creation is an antagonistic mirror image of the first one.

The inclusion of the Ark of the Testimony indicates, unequivocally, the sacrificial tenor of the confrontation and the presence of the Creator on the side of the people of Israel. On the other hand, Rahab (the thirteenth to the twelfth centuries BC), the harlot of Jericho, represents the waters of Creation, especially in their enabling role of the forces that unite the idolatry nucleus. Being present before and after the confrontation, the waters will be saturated with all kinds of opposites coming from the annihilation of both creations. The group called "everyone in the house with her" would include all those that dissolved in the waters. Then, according to Matthew I, Rahab would be assimilated into the people of Israel and could be counted among her descendants—not only King David (the eleventh to the tenth centuries BC) but even Jesus himself.

The book of Joshua says that the fortified city of Jericho was built by the kings of seven nations: "Then you crossed the Jordan and came to Jericho and the men of Jericho waged war against you, as did the Amorites, the Perizzites, the Canaanites, the Hittites, the Girgashites, the Hivites and the Jebusites. And I put them in your hands." At first sight it seems a descriptive passage without the greatest relevance, possibly linked to the septenary structure of the idolatry nucleus. But it must also be considered in light of the indispensable participation of God in the realization of his luminous discourse, even when dealing with idols and idolaters. Not in vain does God say through Isaiah, "I am the giver of light and the maker of darkness. I send blessings and I cause evil. I am the Lord, who does all those things."

The city of Jericho, destroyed by Joshua thirty-three centuries ago, never regained the splendor for which it was known. Yet the idolatry that reigned there has spread throughout the world under the shelter of redeemed sins. Over the centuries, idolatry has followed at times and pushed onto others the steps of so-called social progress, advancing to achieve a colossal and totally globalized structure. To discover the centers of power in the idolatry of the present, it is enough to follow the steps of greed for the material, which is absent in the behavior of the saints. The fate of idolaters imposes that the means used by them constitute, at the same time, the instruments of their own condemnation. In the passages of the Holy Scriptures alluding to the Last Judgment, the means to execute condemnations of idolaters in terms of iron and oil are described. The iron, represented by steel and its magnetism, has been a religious symbol of intramundane circularity, contumacy, and corruption. Petroleum, represented by tar, symbolizes the cult to the primordial hexagon, since aromatic and polycyclic aromatic combustible compounds abound among its components. These substances are known for their xenobiotic nature (unrelated to biology and life), for their toxic behavior, and for being constituted by carbon hexagonal rings with electron flow capable of generating magnetic fields. In relation to the aforementioned statements, the psalmist says, "Those who were in darkness, in the dark night and in the shadows, imprisoned by iron chains, because they went against the words of God and spurned the counsel of the Most High." The book of Genesis also says, "The Valley of Siddim was full of bitumen pits and the kings of Sodom and Gomorrah fell there when they fled."

There are geological indications that the destruction of the biblical pentapolis may have been caused by an eruption of bituminous hydrocarbons. The flammable material would have been expelled to the atmosphere, due to tectonic pressures of seismic origin, in the faults on which the five cities were settled. The bitumen was ignited by the effect of static, initially falling into four of the five cities as a fire rain. Similarly, the Koran makes reference to this condemnation in **surah** Abraham:

> "God is powerful, the Lord of retribution, the day when the earth will be changed by a different one, as well as the heavens, will appear before God, the Only One , the Supreme. Then you will see that day the guilty ones bound with iron chains, their clothes will be made of tar, and fire will cover their faces."

The consequences of idolatry derive from the free will granted to the creatures of the luminous discourse and God realizes them due to love for his Creation. Certainly God also making use of his free will is in his right, to intervene with corrective measures, just as he did with the Universal Flood; with the destruction of the biblical pentapolis and with the overthrow of Jericho. But putting an end to the free will of his creatures has always been out of the question. In any case, only God knows when the Creation will conclude, hence the sentence of Jesus recorded by Mark regarding the end of time: "As for the day or the hour, no one knows, not even the angels of heaven, not the Son, but only the Father." This assertion is applicable not only to the end of the Creation but also at the end of each event in the luminous activity.

Chapter 35

The Sacrifice in Conflagration

The description of the mercy seat on the Ark of the Testimony offers the most powerful symbolic expression of the Hebrew Bible, relating to the ecpyrotic confrontation between creations and the sacrifice that it entails:

> And at the ends of the ark cover you shall put two cherubim of hammered gold. One on one end and the other on the other end…And their wings will be spread above the mercy seat and the cherubim placed in front of each other…You will place the mercy seat on top of the ark and inside it you will put the Testimony that I will give you. And there, between both cherubim, over the mercy seat on the cover of the ark, I will come to you face to face and make clear all the commands I will give you for the children of Israel.

The confrontation between cherubim described by the book of Exodus represents the scenario where the Creator responds to the construction of the nuclei of idolatry after the Flood. The sacrifice associated with this confrontation is an indispensable condition for the redemption of sins and the resurrection of the saints. Each year on the Day of Atonement, the High Priest would sprinkle on the mercy seat the blood of a sacrificed bull, right between the cherubim. The formula chosen by the Creator to restore his work from the deviations caused by Satan and his followers consisted of the launching of a second creation against the first. The confrontation represented by the facing cherubim resulted in a massive annihilation of the structures then present and the dissolution of their fragments as opposing pairs in the surrounding waters. Figure 35.1 schematically illustrates the facing cherubim over the mercy seat of the Ark of the Testimony.

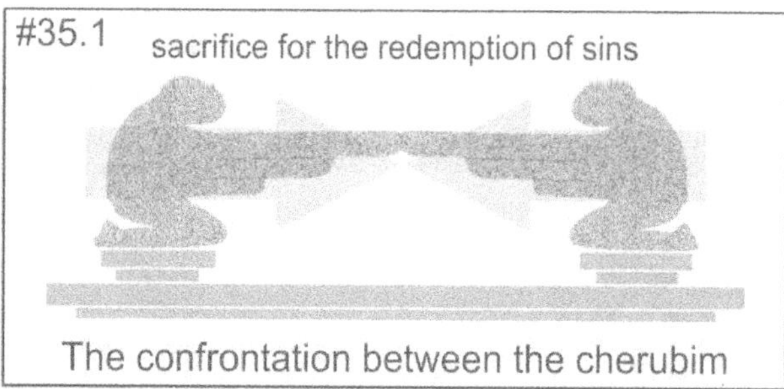

The Gospels include an extensive catalog of episodes from the life of Jesus from which symbolic expressions relating to the same event can be extracted. The most significant is the sacrifice of Jesus, where he represents the

Anointed One (Christ, from the Greek *Christós*), to answer the triple question posed to his apostles and reflected in the three synoptics: "Who do you say that I am?" The Dutch Jesuit theologian P. Schoonenberg (the twentieth century AD) thought that what God realizes in Christ is his own way of being a Man. In a broader sense, the "way of being a Man of God" should contemplate both: the anointed Heavenly Adam as the grantor of realism to the Earthly Adam sins and his opponent, Christ, who realizes their redemption. Sacrificing himself in a confrontation for the redemption of all sins, Christ incarnates the response of God to idolatry. Figure 35.2 illustrates schematically the confrontation of the two human realizations of the "way of being a Man" of God, the two Anointed Ones.

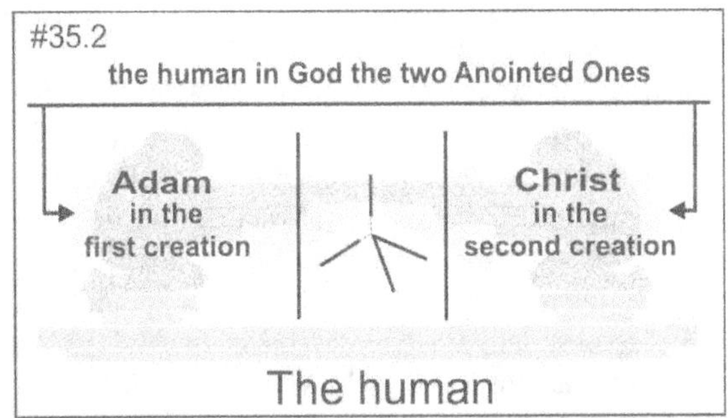

When observing the figure, the reader should consider the response given to the prophet Zechariah when he inquired about the two sources that keep the lampstand alive: "These are the two Anointed Ones who are before the Lord of the earth."

The advent of new waters (such as those of the Universal Flood) for the forgiveness of sins was a consequence of the second creation. In this sense, Ezekiel says, "And I will pour clean water on you, so that you may be cleansed of all your impurities and your idols." Peter also writes that "while Noah was finishing the ark, in which a few, that is, eight people were saved from the water. And baptism, from which the flood is an image, now gives you the salvation." The Apostle Paul adds:

> Or don't you agree that all of us who were baptized in Jesus Christ have been baptized in his death? We were buried with him and we died through baptism. And just as Christ was raised from the dead by the glory of the Father, we, in the same way, will live a new life.

Despite the similarities among the stories of the Universal Flood, the overthrow of the biblical pentapolis, the confrontation in Jericho, and those of the Gospel account of the baptism of Jesus, his passion, and his death and Resurrection, noticeable differences can be observed. The most important of these differences lies in the fact that the Hebrew people avoid contact with the lower waters. By contrast, Christian life begins with an immersion in them, as in the baptism of Jesus in the Jordan River. The "passing through dry land" of the Hebrew people began in the ark with Noah, by eluding the waters of the Universal Flood, and continued with Moses at the crossing of the Red Sea and later with Joshua as they crossed the Jordan River without getting wet—as would Elijah centuries later. Immersion in the waters of baptism for the forgiveness of sins is a step previous to their redemption, by means of baptism in Spirit (air) and fire. A question expressed in human terms in chapter 1 of Mark and in chapters 3 of Matthew and Luke (*quelle*), who contextualize both baptisms emphasizing the preeminence of the second: "John answered saying to all: 'Truly I baptize you with water, but then comes one who is greater than me that I am not worthy to untie his sandals. He will baptize you with the Holy Spirit and with fire.'" Later, Jesus orders his apostles to consummate the first water baptism by saying "Make disciples of all nations, baptizing them in the name of the Father and of the Son and of the Holy Spirit," establishing the baptismal faith of Christians, who must head their lives toward the second.

The difference between "passing through dry land" and "baptism by immersion in the waters of the Jordan River" has to do with the relationship between religions one (Hebrew) and three (Christian), since, in the religious architecture of the Judeo-Christian tradition, both should relate as Spirit (air) and fire and be represented on an odd basis of the 1-3 type. As has been reiterated, sin is a ternary issue, and it is up to religion three, Christianity, to fully assume the drama of confrontation. Hence the confrontation of Christ with Satan and his followers occurs in the midst of the brackish lower waters of the triad *xyz*, represented by planet three (the earth). The Hebrew religion by itself, represented on the unitary base or Spirit, isolated from the triad, remains above the lower waters. The basis 1-3 offers then the appropriate context to interpret the passages of Israel on dry land reported in the book of Joshua ("you will tell your children the story and you will say: 'Israel crossed this Jordan on dry land'…as the Lord did with the Red Sea, which he dried up before us…") as well as the Christian rebirth from the waters.

In addition to the complex baptismal symbology, John the Baptist and Jesus, from a Christian point of view, head the twin tetrad formed by the offspring of leading sterile couples. Among these sterile couples, we find Abraham and Sarah, Isaac and Rebecca, Jacob and Rachel, Zechariah and Elizabeth, and Joseph and Mary, the earthly parents of Isaac, Jacob, Benjamin, John the Baptist, and Jesus. In both tetrads, Isaac, Jacob, and Benjamin would represent the earth/man lower triad. John the Baptist heads one of the tetrads as the air/Holy Spirit (Matthew 3:16, Mark 1:10, Luke 3:22, and John 1:32), and Jesus the other by representing the quintessence/Anointed One. Figure 35.3 illustrates schematically the context of the baptisms of water and of Spirit (air) and fire and their correspondence with the Universal Flood and the destruction of the pentapolis.

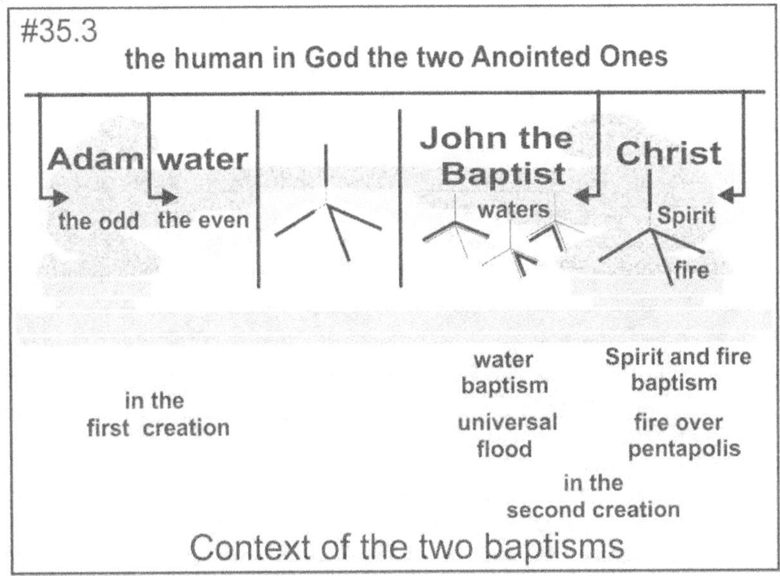

Jesus being of Hebrew origin, he is also over the lower waters; as Matthew describes it: "And when they saw him walking on the sea, they were frightened and said: 'It is a spirit!' And they cried out in fear." For that reason, his baptism is not only of fire but also of Spirit. Such a relationship is exposed in key numbers of the Apocalypse of John (24 = 4 × 6) and (144 = 4 × 36), corresponding to six (6) and thirty-six (36) in Genesis 1 (figures linked to the hidden light). In natural Christology, the "way of being a Man" of God is expressed as in a cross, horizontally by the confrontation between cherubim and vertically by both the Spirit (air) over the waters and Man (earth)—who has to submerge in these waters to baptize before embracing the fire of his own sacrifice.

All the conflict scenarios present in the Holy Scriptures revolve around the theme of the ecpyrotic confrontation between creations; such is the case of the battle of Jericho in the Bible, of the apocalyptic Armageddon (Apocalypse 16:16), and of the sacrifice and immolation in the greater and lesser holy wars (jihad) as in Badr, reviewed in surah The Family of Amran: "And God certainly helped you in Badr when you were weak…And He may cut off a part of those who do not believe or humiliate them so that they return defeated." The intention with the unfulfilled 9/11 attack was then to represent the first creation using four U.S. targets and the second with planes. The Zend-Avesta in Yasna IV adds that it is a confrontation headed by fire, for propitiation and praise to the son of Ahura Mazda. The obstinate attitude of Satan and his followers left no other choice but the sacrifice of a whole creation in order to restore the viability of the work of God. Hence the challenge to the human posed by the three synoptics: "If any man wants to be my follower, let him abandon everything, take his cross and follow me."

The three synoptics also report that Jesus identifies his body with bread and his blood with wine when making explicit the substance of the second creation. The amazing identifications were made by Jesus during the supper offered to his disciples on the eve of his own sacrifice:

> Jesus took bread and after blessing it, he broke it and gave it to his disciples saying: "Take and eat. This is my body." And taking a cup and having given thanks, he gave it to them, saying: "Drink from it, all of you, for this is my blood of the covenant, which will be poured out for many for the remission of their sins.

John the Evangelist thus ratifies: "He who eats my flesh and drinks my blood, is in me and I in him. As the Father sent me, and I live because of the Father, so whoever eats me will live because of me." When Jesus identified his own body with bread, he must have done so with a complete knowledge of the substance. This question would encourage a natural exegesis in search of additional data with which to specify the second creation in more detail. The same will be attempted later with the wine of the Last Supper.

In the time of Jesus, barley (*Hordeum vulgare vulgare*) bread was consumed, whose flour was obtained by grinding cereal grains. Barley flour consists mostly of starch, which is a complex structure of carbohydrates insoluble in water. Said starch in turn is constituted by the mixture of two polysaccharides (polymers of sugars— that is, chains of sugar molecules linked to each other): amylose and amylopectin. Although there is a large dispersion in the proportions of amylose and amylopectin in the starches of different varieties of barley, in the ordinary type, it is about one to three (25 percent amylose and 75 percent amylopectin). Amylose is a chain formed by hundreds or thousands of units of D-glucose under the configuration of a hexagonal ring and structured like a left helix. Each step or turn of said helix consists of six glucose units with the same orientation. On the other hand, the amylopectin of barley starch has a structure with ramifications every twenty-four or thirty molecules of D-glucose, which breaks any underlying helical structure.

The glucose units in free states have six carbon atoms, twelve hydrogen atoms and six oxygen atoms, and consequently their molecular formula is written $C_6H_{12}O_6$. The proportions of each chemical element in the glucose would suggest the intrusion of the six carbon atoms into six molecules of water ($6 \times H_2O$). Such a configuration would imply for the second creation the same imposition of odd formulations over the even ones present in the first. The symbolism even goes much further, but it is compromised by multiple interferences and imbrications of the archetypal formulations all along the chains of exteriorization. Unfortunately, the superposition of different formulations imposes certain limitations to doubtless interpretations.

From a stereochemical perspective (which is the study of the spatial distribution of atoms and functional groups in molecules), it is possible to find in the hexagonal structure of D-glucose some morphological features already observed in other natural representations discussed previously. The similarities are also extendable to symbolic figures in key passages of the Holy Scriptures already commented on. For those readers not familiar with the "stereochemical projections," it is suggested to observe the following figures as if they were drawings of the type "spot the differences," frequently found in entertainment magazines. In this sense figure 35.4 compares in its upper part two similar structures of D-glucose, with a single difference indicated by the Greek letters α and β, while in its lower parts are presented the two polysaccharides that are generated by each one through bonding and repetition, amylose and cellulose.

The only difference to be found lies in the position of the hydroxyl group (–OH) in carbon one (C1) of both versions with respect to the hydroxymethyl group (–CH$_3$O) in C5. The importance of the latter in a natural exegesis lies primarily in its utility for distinguishing one side of the molecule from the other. When two configurations of the same molecular formula as $C_6H_{12}O_6$ have differences in a single center, they are called "epimers." In D-glucose the two epimers are α-D-(+)-glucose and β-D-(+)-glucose, which would indicate from an exegetical point of view the presence of two structures susceptible to interpretation.

Now the reader is kindly asked to observe how in the epimer α one hydroxyl group in C3 is above (same side of hydroxymethyl) and the three others in C1, C2, and C4 are below. The C2 C3 hydroxyls located on opposite sides would represent the opposing performance of the attributes in the waters. If the hydroxyl in C4 of α represents the performance of the air, that of C1 would correspond to that of earth. The set of four hydroxyl groups could then be represented on a 1&1&2 basis (air&earth&water) (C4&C1&C2 C3). If α-D-(+)-glucose represents the second creation, its specular image, the α-L-(–)-glucose (absent in the chemistry of life), would represent the first. The β-epimers of both versions of glucose would symbolize the waters, product of the confrontation between creations, according to a formulation of the 2-2 type (water-water) (C4 C1-C2 C3).

In the substance of the body of Christ, represented by amylose, the unity of purpose of all the lights of the second creation is reflected in the same orientation of all D-glucose units. The fact would be indicative that all the objects of the second creation go against the first in the same way. Incidentally, the position of the hydroxyl groups in the α-epimer also has similarities with the configuration of the attributes of the first and second conditionalities in the earthly human beings. In said configuration, neutrality is represented by C2 C3, and the dislocation by C4 C1. Since the hydroxyl groups in C4 and C1 are on opposite sides in the β-epimer, the alternating D-glucose units in the cellulose structure will also have opposite orientations. This establishes a second level of representation for the opposing roles of the earthly masculine lights of both creations and for the nullity of the waters that they produce or that accept them during the confrontation.

Even though it would be possible to continue deepening in the molecular symbolism of D-glucose, as a natural representation of the substance of sacrifice, the task will be left to the most inquisitive readers. In addition to the details already observed in the stereochemistry of D-glucose, the highly significant exteriorization of two levels of left helicities should be mentioned. One of the left helicities manifests itself in the rotation of the light (more properly of its plane of electrical oscillation) to the right, when oncoming from a solution of glucose in water. The other left helicity is present in the helical structure of the amylose—one-quarter of the glucose in the barley bread. Certainly the left helices in the bread amylose, which Jesus identified with his body, would be referring to those of the saints in the substance of sacrifice. In short, the saints of the second creation would have left helicities, unlike the ones of the first creation, who would have right. All of the above would endorse the thesis according to which both creations are governed by the same originating provisions, but they would have opposite dislocated attributes.

The similarities in the configuration of carbon five and six in the D-glucose with their counterparts in the L version also ratify the correspondences between both creations already observed. Both are relatable even with the structural formula of ethyl alcohol in wine, which Jesus identified with his blood just on the eve of his sacrifice. Consecrated wine at the last Passover meal of Jesus should also have a meaning similar to the wine fermented by Noah, to the offering by Abram and Melchizedek, and to the one miraculously produced at the wedding in Cana. The wine of Noah prefigures the substance of sacrifice for the redemption of the sins of idolatry committed by the descendants of his son Ham, the Canaanites:

> In those days, Noah farmed the land and planted a vineyard. And drinking his wine he became drunk…And Ham, the father of

Canaan, saw the nakedness of his father and told his brothers…And when Noah awoke from his drunkenness and knew what his youngest son had done to him, he said: "Cursed be Canaan!…"

The ethyl alcohol molecule has great symbolic value because it exteriorizes the formulations 1&2 of the earthly human being and the ternary context of sin. In these formulations the drama of ternary sins and their redemption in the bosom of religion three, Christianity, is summarized. The alcohol molecule is made up of two functional groups linked together, as indicated on the left in figure 35.5.

In the upper left corner, the hydroxymethyl group is shown, already represented by carbon six in the glucose, and in the lower left the methyl group ($-CH_3$). The hydroxymethyl group offers three equivalent configurations of the human formulation (only one illustrated), with a hydrogen atom (H) representing the protoelement earth and a chemical water pseudomolecule representing protoelemental water. The methyl group is constituted by a carbon atom linked to three equivalent hydrogen atoms and would be easily identified with the igneous and ternary context of sin.

In the comparison between the structure of carbon five and six of glucose with that of ethyl alcohol, the application of the known formulations can be extended. Thus, between the hydrogen atom in the C5 of glucose and the methyl group of alcohol, there is an odd quaternary representation of the 1-3 type. On the other hand, in the C5 and C6 of the glucose could be observed a quaternary representation of type 1&1&2, linked to the heavenly and earthly human beings. Both representations would conjugate the formulations with which to describe the context of the "covenant" for the redemption of the sins of the first creation. The molecular structure of ethyl alcohol would ratify symbolically that the first and the second creation are both governed by the same originating provisions.

The Holy Scriptures do not abound in details about the number of the redeemed by the conflagration, which has been linked to the relative magnitudes of the first and second creations. Given the scarcity of references, it would be possible to estimate its amount based on the alcohol content of the wine and the tithe given by Abram to Melchizedek. In an estimate of such nature, the composition of the alcoholic percentage and the tithe in some way would represent the redeemed fraction. While the chemical water of the wine would represent the luminous waters saturated with opposites, the rest of the goods of Abram would do it for the saints. The alcoholic content of the raw wine used to be modified by dilution in the Holy Land, as indicated by the conclusions of the second book of the Maccabees (the second century BC). The custom was to reach a difference between alcohol and water close to an order of magnitude (one to ten). The coincidence of the proportions of alcohol and tithe is a reference to the minority fraction of the redeemed sins, according to one order of magnitude (10%). The rest would be formed by the multiplicity of fragments resulting from the annihilation of opposites and by the saints of both creations. The redeemed population would then be a tiny part of the total, because according to Matthew, "of those who received the good news, only a small number will be saved."

When concluding an evaluation of the symbolism associated with the bread and wine of the paschal meal, it would be convenient to observe the significance in the ancient culture of the three food pillars (barley and glucose, grapes and ethyl alcohol, and olive and olein) as well as the curious fact of its symbolic value to expose religious truths. Equally relevant are the combustible properties of glucose in cellulose and polysaccharides, of alcohol in wine, and of olein in olive oil, both in flames and metabolisms.

The neotestamentary narrative of the Crucifixion of Jesus on Mount Golgotha is also of an inestimable symbolic value for interpreting his mission and reinforcing the conjectures made up to now. Its interpretation will be circumscribed exclusively to the theme of the relationship between the first and second creation, also called new, according to Paul in his second letter to the Corinthians: "If any man belongs to Christ he has become a new creation, the old one is over, and they truly have been renovated. For all this comes from God, who reconciled us to himself through Christ." It is not a question here of sketching a distant and disconnected Christology but one closely linked to the scientific knowledge of that from which everything is made. As a preamble to this exercise, it would be useful to bring to mind the considerations made about the expression "on the third day," which is so frequent in the Holy Scriptures.

The final moments of the life of Jesus can be grouped into three episodes: his death in a confrontation against idolatry and its evils on the first day; his stay on the second day within the bosom of feminine nature in its rotational aspect, as well as in waters saturated with the remains of conflagration; and finally, on the third day, with the redemption of the survivors and their resurrection in the image of the saints. The baptism of fire leads to the destruction of idolatry, as Jesus explains in the parable of the tares narrated by Matthew:

> The kingdom of heaven is like a man who sowed good seed in his field. But while everyone slept, his enemy came and sowed tares among the wheat and left...the servants of the family, approached and said: "Lord, did you not plant good seeds in your land? How

then does it have tares?" He said to them: "Some enemy did this." The servants said to him: "Is it your will that we pick it up?" But he answered: "No, because perhaps when picking up the tares, you would also uproot the wheat. Allow them to grow together until harvest time. And at the time of the harvest I will say to the reapers, gather the weeds first and bind them in bundles to burn them, but put the wheat in my barn."

For her part, Mother Mary preserves in her womb the condition of Jesus after passing and symbolically returns it to the world as a seed in the person of John: "When Jesus saw his mother and his favorite disciple, he said to his mother: 'Woman, here is your son!' Then he said to the disciple: 'Here is your mother!'" The presence of many Women, mentioned by the three synoptics, outlines the great figuration of the waters ("And there were many women, watching from a distance") as the role of waters is key in the confrontation since everything that emerges from them resuscitates or will have their sins redeemed.

Women at the foot of the cross follow a 1-3 formulation (Mother Mary-[Magdalene Mary of Cleopas Salome]). The first, Mother Mary, represents the pure and immaculate waters alien to sin, expressing themselves in relation to *at*. The three others, Magdalene, Mary of Cleopas, and Salome (the first century BC to the first century AD), represent the waters linked to the planes of the triad *xyz*. All of the luminous entities emerging from the confrontation spent the second day in the waters before emerging on the third day. For this reason, Women are the first to hear about the event of resurrection. As in Jericho, the first one to find out and to take care of the case is Mary Magdalene, a repentant harlot. This is recorded in the narratives of the four evangelists on the Resurrection of Jesus:

In the morning after the Sabbath, at the beginning of the first day of the week, Mary Magdalene and the other Mary went to visit the sepulchre. Suddenly there was a great earthquake, for an angel of the Lord came down from heaven and as he approached, he rolled the tombstone and sat on it. His appearance was like that of lightning and his clothes white as snow...When the angel spoke to the women, he said to them: "Do not be afraid, for I know you are looking for Jesus, the crucified one. He is not here because he has risen, just as he said."

The presence of one or more angels ratifies the divine intervention and the concurrence of these in the intermediary planes for the determination and realization of every event. The reader may remember the captain of the armies of the Lord before Joshua, who did not belong to either of the two sides facing each other, in the triad *xyz*.

As can be read in the narratives of the sacrifice and death of Jesus on the cross, numerous symbols associated with cosmogonic events of great relevance converge. All of these are trying to describe, in one way or another, what they really mean and how symbolism exposes the exteriorizations of events in the last moments of the life of Jesus. In order to support a full understanding of their meanings, it will be necessary to consider, if not all, then at least some of, the symbolic images of the greatest power. In the foreground the cross was prefigured in the book of Exodus, when Aaron and Hur held the weary hands of Moses during the confrontation with Amalek: "Aaron and Hur lifted the hands of Moses, one on one side, and the other on the other side."

In the neotestamentary literature of the Acts of the Apostles, there are references to the Crucifixion, with words such as "hung from a tree," using the Greek term *xylon* ("tree"), translated as in "piece of timber," "hanging from a tree," and "they lowered him from the tree and buried him." In this sense we add a blunt reflection in the letter of Paul to the Galatians: "Christ has redeemed us from the curse of the law, making himself a curse for us, because it is written: 'Cursed is everyone who hangs on a tree.'" Among the apocryphal sources, for example, the "Sibylline Oracle" gives an account of the Crucifixion in a tree of a Man who came from heaven and who will one day make the sun stop. All these expressions are framed in the tragic event of a creation sent to sacrifice in order to open new possibilities for a new development of the work of God.

Christian reflections on the meaning of the Crucifixion in a tree are numerous and are inspired by the contrast between Adam and Christ. Their most eloquent and succinct expression can be found in the first letter of Paul to the Corinthians: "And as in Adam, all die, so also in Christ will all be revived." During the earlier centuries of the church, Melito of Sardis (the second century AD) thought that just as sin came from a tree, also from a tree should salvation come. Within the framework of a natural exegesis of the Crucifixion, it would be unthinkable to undertake basic considerations about its meaning and scope, disregarding the symbolic meaning of wood—even more so when Jesus and Joseph, with whom his mother, Mary, was married at the time of his birth, were carpenters by profession, according to Justin (Matthew 13:55). The reader will surely be aware of the uses of wood not only as a structural element but also as a fuel. But the nature of its substance may be more relevant as a means to represent the confrontation between creations.

The wood is constituted mainly by cellulose, hemicellulose, lignin, and water. The cellulose and hemicellulose proportion in wood composition approaches two-thirds, both being formed by sugars. Cellulose is formed by long chains (five hundred units or more) of the β-epimer of D-glucose, linked by dehydration in carbons one and four and inverted alternately. The structure of the cellulose was illustrated graphically in the lower right part of figure 35.4, where, as in the waters, the alternation of D-glucose units pointing in opposite senses is shown. Despite being constituted by glucose units with the aforementioned optical properties, cellulose is a linear molecule—unlike amylose, which is helical. For its part, hemicellulose has, in addition to glucose, several types of sugars and a branched structure. Another component of importance in wood is lignin, a racemic macromolecule (equal proportions of configurations D and L) of branched biopolymers with abundant presence of cyclic alcohols. Lignin gives wood its woody character and, like water, the linear chains of cellulose, and the ramifications in the hemicellulose; they all point to structures that suggest a net turn equal to zero.

In an exegesis where the amylose represents the configuration of the second creation, the cellulose in the wood should be interpreted as a symbol of the encounter with its opposite, the first one. It would be a representation of the confrontation between creations, each with opposite orientations, turns, and ternary attributes. The chaos unleashed in the waters by the confrontation between the first and second creations is the medium in which the "way of being a Man" of God has to be sacrificed. Figure 35.6 illustrates schematically the main elements of the Crucifixion of Jesus Christ, the wood, the cosmic realizations of the human in God, and the three nails.

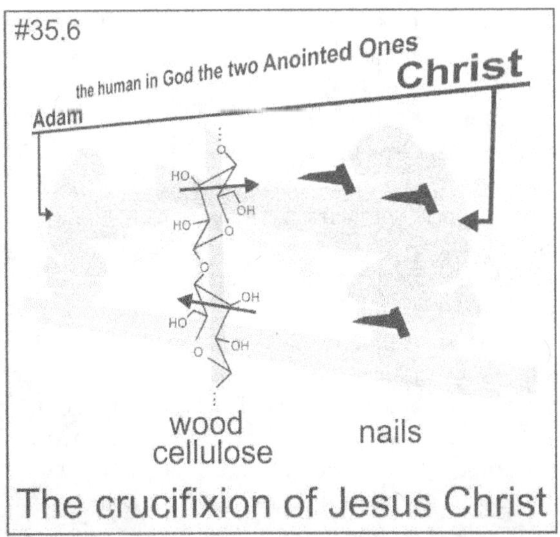

Steel nails would represent sin and therefore have a decisive figuration in the scene of the Crucifixion. They are mentioned by the apostle Thomas in his act of disbelief, outlined by John: "Unless I see in his hands the marks of the nails and put my finger in their place...I will not believe it." The Gospels really offer little information about the nails of the Crucifixion. Nothing is said about their number or the material they were made of. Among the oldest references in this regard is the poem *Suffering Christ* (*Cristus patiens*), attributed to **Gregory Nazianzus**, which mentions three nails. For his part, Ambrose of Milan, in *Oratory of the Obituary to Theodosius* (*Oratio de obitu Theodosii*), would imply the use in the Crucifixion of only two nails. The iconographies of the old Latin and Greek churches instead show four nails. These plastic expressions agree with the relics allegedly found by Helen of Constantinople (the third to the fourth centuries AD), mother of Constantine I, the first Roman emperor to profess Christian faith. After almost a millennium of artistic representations where Jesus invariably appears crucified with four nails, the religious iconography of the Cathars bursts in offering a rather weird catalog. Among the most outstanding rarities were the images of Jesus crucified with three nails.

The frustration of the Latin Church in the face of the advances of the Catharist heresy in Southern Europe became of great concern to Pope Innocent III (the twelfth to the thirteenth centuries AD). The reaction of the papacy to the resilience of the Catharists was to seek ratification from the Fourth Lateran Council of condemnation of this movement and of all its manifestations. The crucifix of the Cathars, probably of "syndonological" origin (related to the science of the Holy Shroud), was widely commented on by Lucas of Tuy (the twelfth to the thirteenth centuries AD) in his work *On the Other Life, Religious Controversy against the Errors of the Albigensians* (*De altera vita, fideique controversiis adversus albigensium errores*). In fact, the Leonese did not see a fundamental problem with the iconography with the three nails, regardless of their adoption by the Cathars. The goal of Lucas of Tuy was to defend the Romanesque tradition against Gothic innovation because of the potential risks that any novelty would imply. The adoption of the crucifix with three nails was gathering pace from the thirteenth century AD onward, in spite of the tenacious resistance by the supporters of the four nails. The acceptance of Triclavianism over the years has become a fixture in mainstream representations—even in emblems, as in the seals of the Society of Jesus (*S. I. Societatis Iesu*).

As for the material of the nails, there has been no controversy, perhaps because of the continued use of iron solutions for such purposes up to the present day. Most likely, the nails were made of a solution of iron with carbon, produced by carburization during the forging via austenite (gamma steel, cubic structure centered on the faces). After cooling, the steels thus obtained tend to form ferrite cores with strong ferromagnetism. The certainty is that Jesus was probably crucified with three nails of a metal that constitutes a little more than half of the mass of Earth, or planet three. In addition, iron tools were banned in the construction of religious buildings for their circular manifestations, emblematic of idolatry and of gloating over mundane matters, to enter through the "three gates of hell" to which the *Bhagavad Gita* refers.

Although it might seem implausible, the substance of the sacrifice can be defined more precisely, thanks to the contradictions between the relic of the *Titulus Crucis* (found in AD 1492) and its description in the Gospel of John (except for the order of the languages in the versions of Reina-Valera and King James, both of the seventeenth century AD, perhaps influenced by the relic):

Pilate also wrote and put this title on the cross: "Jesus of Nazareth, the king of the Jews"... And it was written in Hebrew, Latin and Greek. But the chief priests of the Jews said to Pilate: "Do not write 'The King of the Jews' but instead that he said: I am the King of the Jews." Pilate answered: "What I have written, it is written."

Unlike the Gospel of John, the synoptics mention the legal document without specifying the languages in which it was written (Mark 15:26, Matthew 27:37, and Luke 23:38).

Paleographic studies (related to the study of ancient writings, in particular their dating) place the text of the relic in the first century AD, as would be expected. In contrast, carbon dating (^{14}C) points to an age of ten centuries, not the twenty that it should have if it were the original legal document. As can be concluded from both studies, the relic kept in the Basilica of the Holy Cross in Jerusalem would then be a faithful copy of an original already lost. The contradictions between the text on the relic and the theological Gospel of John have been considered favorable to its authenticity. In its favor it is argued that hardly a forger would dare to disagree with the New Testament narrative in such a brazen manner. The main discrepancies are the permutation of Latin and Greek, the inversions of the Greek and Latin writing imitating the Hebrew, and reflections of the letters in the inverted texts. Apart from its permutation, the Greek and Latin writings of the relic appear then as reflected in a mirror with respect to the description of John. Despite having almost completely lost the Hebrew script, the present traces belong to a right-to-left writing, as it should correspond.

Since the discovery of the relic, no theological explanation has been given to justify the contradictions between the recorded writing on it and the Gospel of John. In the context of a natural exegesis, it is possible, however, to find a meaning for the discrepancies, which could be congruent with the considerations made so far in relation to the sacrifice of Jesus. The first step is to associate the text of the *Titulus Crucis* in the Gospel of John with the situation of the lights of the first creation after the quarrel, while the writing on the relic would describe the substance of sacrifice of the second. Opposing senses of Greek and Latin writing with respect to the Hebrew in the Gospel text symbolize two ways of contravening the initial conditions of the first creation. On the other hand, the reversal in the pagan-language writings on the relic would refer to the response given by the Creator with the second. There would then be two interpretations, one of rotational nature and the other of an "ecpyrotic" character. The first is based on a rotation defined by the independent Latin and Greek directions and the senses of their writings. The product of both would result in a third and new direction, also independent and called Hebrew, according to right-hand rule. By inverting the Latin and Greek writing senses, as in the relic, the product would remain the same, but if they were also permuted, the result would be opposite to the previous one. The upper part of figure 35.7 shows a rotational reading of the contradictions between both versions of the *Titulus Crucis*. Even though the figure resembles 32.1, they should not be confused because the context of each one is different.

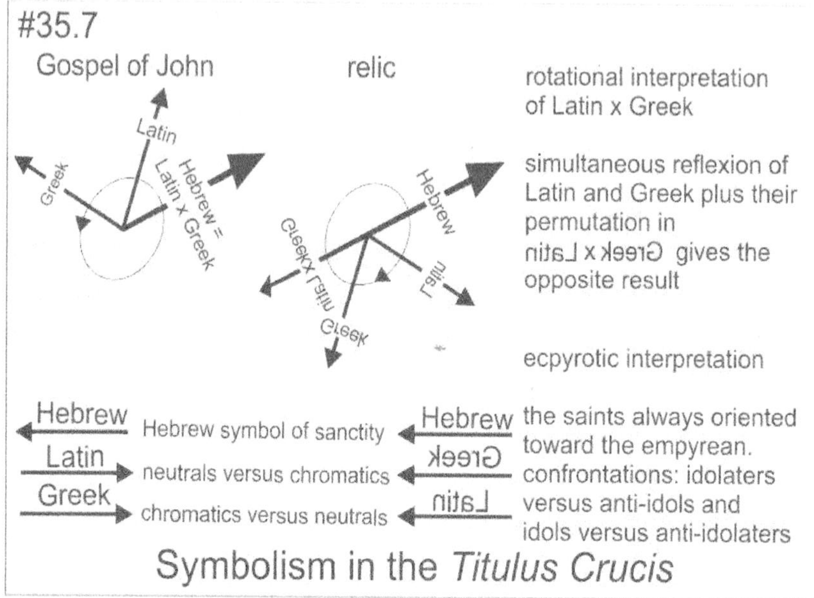

In turning terms, the differences between the Gospel text and the relic suggest opposite turns in both creations.

A second reading with ecpyrotic bias is shown in the lower part of the figure, where the opposition between the writings appears in the manner of a confrontation between the lights. In the first place, there is the Hebrew representing the saints, whose neutral actions are always directed toward the empyrean—for that reason they do not oppose. A natural exegesis should have as a fundamental hypothesis the nonparticipation of the saints of the first and second creation in any confrontation—first and foremost because the saints ignore one another as they exchange their neutral actions with the Most High, and secondly because of their neutrality in the first and third conditionalities. Additionally, the contrary turns of the second conditionality do not cause interaction because they are not associated with forces. The Latin in John is associated with the act of directing the actions from the idolaters to the anti-idols of the Greek inverted in the relic, who make up the substance of sacrifice. The Greek in John is linked to the act of directing the actions from the idols, to the anti-idolaters of the Latin inverted writing in the relic, also members of the substance of the sacrifice. Directing acts mentioned in the preceding paragraphs are complemented with others between opposing pairs, such as idolaters and anti-idolaters or idols and anti-idols, both destined to saturate the waters.

The act of mutually directing their actions by idolaters and idols and by anti-idolaters and anti-idols, and vice versa, in all cases should also be considered. The symbolism of *Titulus Crucis* is then dedicated to contrasting the performances of the members of the Most High Council and their opponents, whereas the symbolism associated with the D and L versions of α-glucose is centered on the confrontation of archetypal performances in the directions of the tetrad *txyz* of both creations.

The point has been reached where it is possible to contextualize the Crucifixion of Jesus with the cosmogonic milestones described by the Holy Scriptures in terms of the Universal Flood, the overthrow of the pentapolis, the destruction of Jericho, and the holy wars—as in Badr, to only mention the most relevant ones. It is a scenario of ecpyrotic confrontation between the lights of the first creation and their antagonists, the antilights of the second, identified with the substance of the sacrifice. The "causal" antecedents from an ontological perspective are the two Anointed Ones, who act as vehicles of the divine realization of the cosmos—or as Jesus tells us in the name of Christ and through John, "I am the vine and you are the branches." In figure 35.8, both versions of the *Titulus Crucis* are shown schematically, where the first and second creations mutually direct their actions as in conflict.

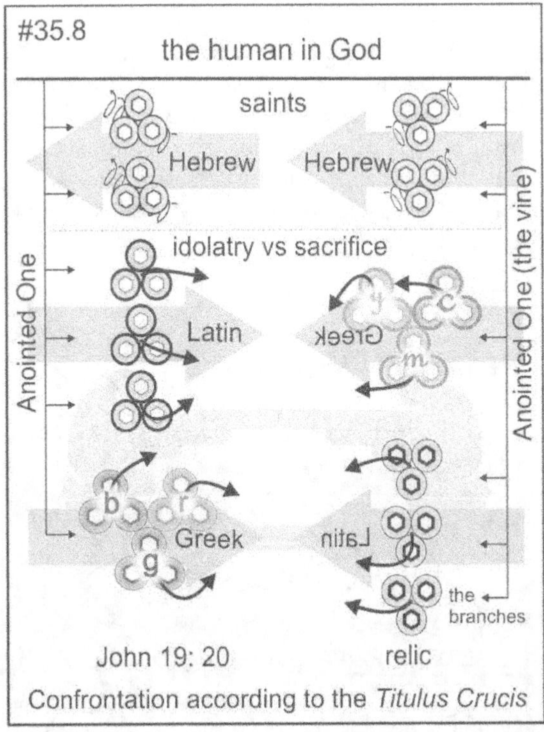

The gray arrows in the background indicate the senses of the *Titulus Crucis* writings—on the left as per the Gospel of John, and on the right according to the relic. The confrontation between cherubim on the mercy seat in the Ark of the Testimony is restated here, following a different model. In the upper part are the saints of both creations with their neutralities of origin. They exchange their neutral actions with the Most High, something that is largely ignored by the rest of the lights. The gray arrows faced in the middle symbolize the act of directing the actions between the idolaters of the first creation and the anti-idols of the second one. The line below illustrates the directing of actions between the idols of the first creation and the anti-idolaters of the second one. Please keep in mind the vertical and crossed directions of actions, which have been omitted with the intention of simplifying the illustration.

The confrontation was not among some protostructures, as could be the case between two organized armies, but distributed, as in the assault on Jericho: "and the walls of the city will fall and the people will advance toward their fronts." The anti-idols and anti-idolaters were created in the vicinity of their opponents and "thrown" against them in order to form pairs, which would dissolve in the waters. The result of the composition of both creations is equivalent to the annihilation of most of the nuclei of idolatry. A complementary version of the confrontation centered on the nucleus of idolatry is mentioned by Jesus when he describes through Luke the tenor of his own sacrifice: "Do you think that I came to bring peace on earth? No, I tell you, but division. Because from now on there will be five in a house divided, three against two and two against three." The reference to the number five in the previous quote can hardly be interpreted outside the context of the biblical pentapolis. There, in the nucleus of idolatry, the infidels are in a three-to-two proportion. Figure 35.9 schematically describes the relationship between idolaters and idols in the nucleus of idolatry, against their antagonists in the substance of sacrifice.

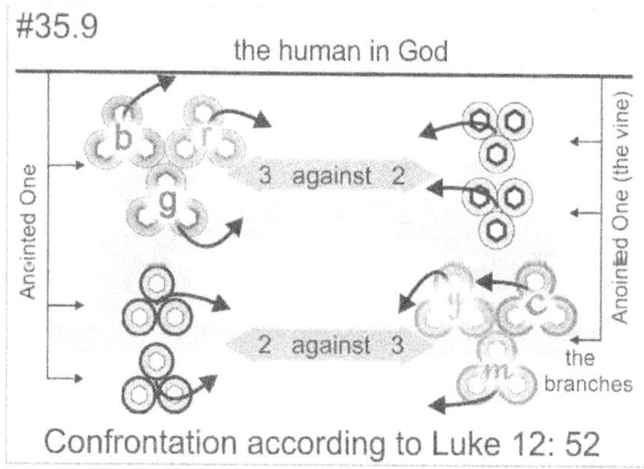

Confrontation according to Luke 12: 52

It is also highlighted by the Zend-Avesta in Yasna X the pertinence of belonging to some five but not to the other five. Speaking on behalf of the Anointed One, or Christ, Jesus says through Matthew, "For where two or three meet in my name, I am there in their midst." This expression is also interpretable in terms of the figuration of Jesus as air or Spirit in the formulations 1&2 of the heavenly human being and 1-3 of Spirit and fire. Regarding the character of the presence and performance of Jesus on the saints, Matthew adds, "My yoke is easy and my burden is light."

In a different interpretive context, it would be possible to associate the three languages of the *Titulus Crucis*, according to John, with the three main actors in the scene of the Crucifixion. First, Jesus should be associated with the Hebrew language and within the framework of a natural exegesis with the saints. In the second place would appear the good thief (Dismas) crucified to the right of Jesus (according to the apocryphal Gospel of Nicodemus [the fourth century AD]) and whose repentance before dying would allow him to be associated with Latin, the language of Rome. The redirection of actions by non-archetypal idolaters remains a possibility; it would liberate them from idolatry, just as Constantine I did to get free from paganism when he converted to Christianity. The ancient Greek of *Titulus Crucis* would symbolize the contumacy of the idols and should be associated with the bad thief (Gestas), who died imprecating and cursing and who was crucified on the left of Jesus.

The culture of ancient Greece has been recognized and "consecrated" as an icon and model of paganism. It has also been a source of inspiration for all the atheistic and secular movements that have lived and continue living having turned their backs to God. The first to study the sudden emergence of so-called secular critical thinking was the existentialist philosopher K. Jaspers (the nineteenth to the twentieth centuries AD). The German thinker called the "time-axis" of the "axial age" the period of history between the sixth and the fifth centuries BC. This lapse of time was nearly preceded by the destruction of the temple of King Solomon in 587 BC at the hands of Nebuchadnezzar II (the seventh to the sixth centuries BC), king of Babylon.

The question of languages in the Holy Scriptures is of paramount importance, and this is the precise moment to address it. Basically the languages used in the Holy Scriptures come from the Phoenician, with a writing system from right-to-left, whose appearance dates back to the eleventh century BC. The archaic Greek also came from the Phoenician and began to be written from right-to-left, to then adopt the "boustrophedon" (alternating lines from right-to-left with left-to-right, as in the ox plow, hence the name) by the fifth century BC approximately (end of the axial age). The left-to-right writing was generalized immediately afterward and is held to this day by Greek, Latin, and the Romance languages. The Bible was written entirely in the Hebrew language, whose graphemes derived from the Phoenician and which is written from right-to-left. The oral tradition of Zend-Avesta was poured from the third century AD to Pahlavi, a Semitic language of Iranian origin, also written from right-to-left. In contrast, the Gospels of Matthew and Luke of the tradition Q were written in Aramaic and Greek with contrary senses, symbolizing the neutrality of the waters they represent. On the other hand, John and Mark figuring as air and earth or Spirit and Man both wrote in Greek from left-to-right.

The writing sense of each of the languages employed by the evangelists can be related to the positions of the hydroxyls in the α-D-(+)-glucose. Thus, the Gospels of John&Mark would correspond to the hydroxyl groups in C4&C1 (to the same side), and those of Matthew Luke to those of C2 C3 (to opposite sides). The same symbology could be extended to thymine nitrogens, with John&Mark represented by the pair NH&NH, and the pair Matthew Luke by N NH. In the context of the languages used to write the Gospels, the Greek employed by John would then symbolize the performance of the air, or Spirit, in the second creation. On the other hand, in the symbolism of *Titulus Crucis*, the ancient Greek from left-to-right and inverted represents the idols and anti-idols of the first and second creations. The Koran was written in the Arabic language from right-to-left, which was derived from Aramaic and ultimately also from Phoenician. The first Greek translation of the Bible took place in the third century BC and has been known since then as the "Septuagint." The name given to the translation is due to the seventy wise translators to whom the task was entrusted by Ptolemy II Philadelphus (the third century BC), second Ptolemaic pharaoh. The first Greek translation of the Koran was anonymous and dates from the ninth century AD, as presumed.

The second creation embodies the response of God to the deviations of the first one through a confrontation between mirror images with respect to orientation, turns, and ternary attributes. The divine objective was the annihilation of a good part of both, the dissolution of the opposites in the waters, the establishment of new symmetries, and the resurrection of the saints. Any bewilderment caused by the contradictions between both creations should be offset by the timely clarification made by the prophet Muhammad in surah The Cow:

> The fools among the people will ask: What caused them to turn from the qiblah they had? Say: The east and the west belong only to God. He guides whoever pleases Him to the right path…We established the qiblah to which you were accustomed, only to distinguish him who follows the Messenger from him who turns back upon his heels. And it was certainly a hard test, except for those to whom God has led, for He would not divert you from your faith [qiblah, in Arabic, "direction for praying"].

Arriving in Medina in AD 622, the prophet Muhammad continued praying oriented toward Jerusalem during sixteen months—that is to say, by a lapse of four by four months. In the second month before the great battle of Badr, and following instructions from God, he changed the direction of prayers toward Mecca. The change took place in the "Mosque of the Two Directions" (*Masjid al-Qiblatayn*), and for a long time with two mihrab (niche with which the direction and sense in the orientation of the prayers is indicated), one of them pointing toward Jerusalem and the other toward Mecca. The word *mihrab* would derive from the verb *to combat* (*harb* in Arabic) and could be translated as "combat post against Satan."

The confrontation between the first and second creations is an unprecedented cosmic event whose abundant references by the Holy Scriptures require some additional consideration. In this sense, Joshua exclaimed in battle against the armies of the five kings of the Amorites: "'Sun, stop over Gibeon, and you, moon over the valley of Aijalon.' And the sun stopped and the moon stood where it was, until people had avenged themselves upon their adversaries." Confrontations between opposing lights should be visualized in terms of an encounter within the tetrad *txyz*. The aforementioned fact of a stop in time in full confrontation between creations would account for a "launch or go against," also in the temporal domain. In such an event, it would be implicit that the masculine party of the first creation comes from the past and from one side. The substance of sacrifice, or the second creation instead, would come from the future and from the opposite side. The aforementioned meeting of the lights, with their own time propagating in opposite senses, would result in a timeless instance similar to that of waters. However, aging (global entropy) on both sides advances (increases) in the time direction t toward the future of the first creation, that is, in parallel to perpetuity.

There is another biblical episode in the second book of Kings, where the double directionality of time occurs in a similar context. It deals with the battles fought by King Hezekiah (the eighth to the seventh centuries BC) against his death and the yoke of Assyria:

> And Hezekiah asked Isaiah: "What will be the sign that the Lord will heal me? And that I will go up to His house on the third day?" Isaiah replied: "...Do you want the shadow to advance ten degrees or to go back ten degrees?" Hezekiah replied: "It is a trifle that the shadow advances ten degrees...I would prefer that the shadow go back ten degrees." Then Isaiah the prophet invoked the Lord, Who made the shadow go back ten degrees on the sundial of Ahaz.

To the above quotation can be added to the affirmation of the Sibylline Oracle about Jesus, who one day will make the sun stop.

The displacements in the confrontation between creations in the space-time manifold could be considered to be represented by the corresponding hydroxyl of both versions of the α-glucose as well as by the pairs of nitrogen atoms, basic and nonbasic in adenine and thymine. In the case of nitrogen atoms, the pair N&N in adenine would represent the temporal displacements of air, or Spirit, and earth, or the masculine component of the earthly human being (Man) of the first creation. The pair NH&NH in the thymine instead would correspond to those in the second creation, which are in opposition to the former ones. On the other hand, the pair N NH would represent the behavior of the timeless waters, destined to receive all of them.

The corrective measures of the Flood and the subsequent conflagration outlined in the Scriptures—the sacrifice of Jesus, his passion and death and Resurrection, and the battle in Badr of the nascent Islam—were not enough to eradicate sin. The disappointment for the resilience of sin in the face of sacrifices is expressed in Yasna XLIX of the Zend-Avesta, when regret is expressed over having lost the battle against evil. The presence of redeemed sins in an environment saturated with remnants of the confrontation could hardly be considered the end of the influence of Satan and his followers. The situation is serious because the exteriorizations of the remains of the confrontation in all instances, until reaching the social sphere, compromise the human capacity to act independently. On the other hand, most saints of both creations were favored by the conflagration, obtaining their full freedom.

Chapter 36

Resurrection, Redemption, and Annihilation

Once the confrontation between creations has been consummated, new and old forms emerge under the status of redeemed sins in the context of a total reconstruction of the universe. This is what Jesus says through John: "Then the Jews asked him: 'What evidence will you show us that you can do such things?' Jesus answered them: 'Destroy this temple and in three days I will raise it again...' However, he spoke of the temple of his body." One of the main accusations against Jesus during the trial whose verdict was his conviction revolved around his preaching of destruction and reconstruction. In fact, Matthew and Mark point out that

> many false witnesses were found. At the end, two false witnesses came forward declaring: "This man said: 'I am able to tear down the temple of God and in three days rebuild it.'" Then, the high priest arose and said to him: "Do you have nothing to answer to what these witnesses testify against you?"

The emerging universe after the flood waters baptism extends the global neutrality of its predecessor. It contains the resurrected saints of both creations, mostly released from their entanglements in the nuclei of idolatry destroyed. The presence of the saints in major proportions with their two helicities and chromatic neutralities established important symmetries to enable the construction of structures that until that moment were unlikely. Along with the saints' appearance in the new universe are the nuclei of idolatry under the status of redeemed sins in a lower proportion. Constituted by waters saturated with all kinds of symmetrical and asymmetrical fragments, the new environment of the saints and their antis offered enormous potential for the construction of more complex structures. Pairs of opposites in the waters swelled the vast sea of vacuum, where they acted as precursors to the carriers of the forces of exchange in an environment of high excitation. On the other hand, asymmetrical fragments opened possibilities to new exchange forces that were necessary to stabilize structures of all sorts.

The structures erected with redeemed sins and the new exchange forces gave rise to what humans are and observe. However, it is not possible to detail all types of fragments generated, for practical reasons. Therefore only those fragments necessary to give a certain degree of completeness to the present exegetical effort will be considered. Figure 36.1 shows a small inventory of fragments that originated in the confrontation between creations.

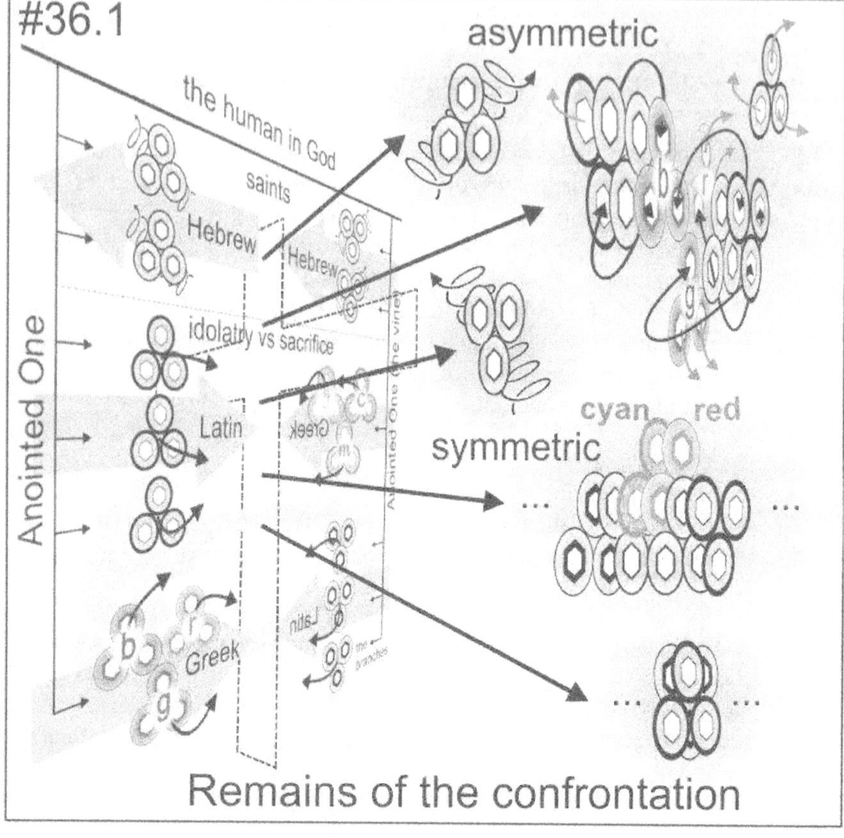

In order to achieve the greatest possible simplicity, the feminine components of all the lights and the relative abundance of primordial waters have been omitted. The upper half of the illustration shows some asymmetrical objects, while the rest of the figures are symmetrical structures. The ellipses in the symmetrical structures indicate the possibility of composing by addition any other symmetrical or even asymmetrical configuration.

Certainly the coexistence of the saints in the midst of sin and death (particularly in the nuclei of idolatry) could have generated some concerns about their integrity. Fortunately Luke discredits any murmuring in that sense when he relates the presence of Jesus in Jericho:

> And having entered Jericho, he walked through the city. And there was a man named Zacchaeus, chief of tax collectors and he was rich…When Jesus came to the place he raised his eyes and said to him: "Zacchaeus descends quickly, because today I must stay in your house."…And seeing this, everyone murmured saying: "He is going to stay in the house of a sinner." Zacchaeus, standing up, said to Jesus:

"Lord, half of my goods I will give to the poor and if I have defrauded someone in any way, I will pay him fourfold."

Actually Jesus (in representation of the "way of being a Man" of God) accompanies the human realizations of the Creator even "in the house of a sinner"—not doing it for infidelity but in strict compliance with the divine provisions. The Koran clarifies this issue when it emphasizes the subjection to God of all of his creations: "The East and the West belong only to God."

In the early centuries of the Christian church, there was a widespread belief that the biological death of humans and sin were the inheritance of the first couple. The act of disobedience to God in the Garden of Eden would not only have affected Adam and Eve but also all their descending fragments. In this sense the psalmist proclaims the following: "I was born in iniquity and in sin my mother conceived me"; "And do not enter into judgment with Your servant, for no living being can be justified before You." Paul adds, in his letter to the Romans: "as sin came into the world through one man and death by sin, so death also passed to all men, for all sinned." During the first three centuries of the church, the different doctrinal positions on the matter were decanted mostly in favor of the hereditary character of sin and death. Until a British monk named Pelagius (the fourth to the fifth centuries AD) immigrated to Rome and then to North Africa disputed the belief about the inheritance of the sin committed by Adam. For Pelagius sin originates exclusively in the misuse of free will, and therefore newborns would be exempt.

The apparently reasonable proposal of the Pelagians posed a problem in the face of baptism for the forgiveness of sins, which was already administered by custom to infants. The controversy was concluded by the Fourth Council of Carthage in the year AD 418, when the doctrine of "original sin" (*peccatum originale*) of Augustine of Hippo was adopted. The life of the theologian, successively marked by sin, baptism, and a fully Christian behavior, sums up his vision of the history of the universe to this day. For Augustine, the human race existed entirely in Adam at the time of sin because God created a single human nature. The unitary character of human nature disappeared with the becoming of creation, dividing itself in as many parts as there are now (the reader surely remembers the disbanding of the Most High Council). After the fall of Adam and Eve, earthly humanity is in a "state of sin," as it happens with infants, or has sinned, as those who contravene the religious precepts. Baptism is, therefore, a necessary and sufficient condition for the forgiveness of the sin of Adam and to begin a Christian life. The effectiveness of the sacrament of baptism would be ensured for Christians, according to a sentence by Jesus about the sacerdotal institution recorded by Matthew: "and whatever you bind on earth will be bound in heaven and what you loose on earth will be loosed in heaven."

Regarding liberation from sin, the Acts of the Apostles bring a narrative related to the restoration of Peter after he denied his Lord three times:

At that time King Herod ordered the persecution of some members of the church…Peter was arrested…put into jail and guarded with four squads of four soldiers…When Herod was going to bring him to trial, Peter was asleep between two soldiers and tied with two chains…Suddenly an angel of the Lord came, and a light shone in the cell. The angel struck Peter on the side and woke him up…And the chains fell from his hands…and came to the iron gate leading to the city, which opened itself.

The non-archetypal idolaters can turn away from sin by way of repentance—reinstating the Cult of the Most High God—but this will not change the fact that biological humans come from the sin of Adam that caused the *Big Bang*.

Regarding the nature of sin, there is an open question on whether Newton's gravitating apple relates to the forbidden fruit eaten by Adam and Eve in the Garden of Eden—in Jerome's Vulgate *malum*, the word for evil and apple in Latin, and *etrog* or *tapuach* in Hebrew writings. Mind also that, according to tradition, Jesus fell several times in his way to sacrifice due to the overwhelming weight of sins. However, despite redemption, redeemed sins (matter and energy) will continue to fall into the depressions they generate in space. According to the *theory of general relativity* proposed by A. Einstein (the nineteenth to the twentieth centuries AD), matter warps space (gravity). If the amount of mass is large enough, the warp resembles what the Sacred Scriptures call abyss.

We all fall continuously into the abyss of planet Earth, but the repulsion between the outer electrons of the atoms of our feet and the ground stops us from falling further. Similarly, the planets, their moons, and minor bodies sink into the abyss of the sun, as do our Solar System and all the contents of the Milky Way falling into oblivion down the black hole (Sagittarius A*) at its center. Figure 36.2 illustrates a 2D abyss in space.

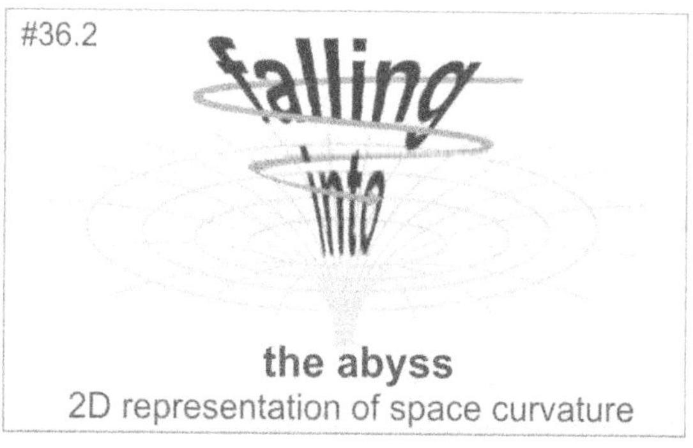

The prophet Isaiah compared the fate of Nebuchadnezzar II with the rise and disappearance of planet Venus at dawn (Phosphorus for ancient Greeks and Lucifer for the Romans):

How you have fallen from heaven, O Lucifer, son of the dawn! You have been thrown down to the earth, you who once destroyed the nations of the world. For you said to yourself, "I will ascend to heaven, well above the stars of God. I will set my throne on high, in the mount where the council meets, far away in the north. I'll go up to the highest heavens and be like the Most High." Yet you shall be brought down to hell, to the lowest depths of the abyss.

Here and thus culminates the present exercise of natural exegesis of the Holy Scriptures pertaining to the People with the Book. Given the objective of accessing as many readers as possible, the scope and depth of this work has been reduced. However, enough elements have been addressed to offer an approximate version of the *Fundamentals of the Creation*. The act of believing should be reserved exclusively to admit or deny the existence of God or to refer to his designs. Everything else should be subject to objective verification or recognized as a subjective expression.

In relation to the trees of possibilities, like the tree of knowledge of good and evil and that of life in the Garden of Eden, different beliefs might be delineated. Those who do not share the theistic vision here proposed, that God is who realizes the possibilities freely chosen by human archetypes to lead cosmic evolution, have options. They can, for example, continue to wait for some solution to the "mystery" (in the words of R. Feynman) of how elementary particles choose a possibility among all those presented to them at each step; adopt the model of the American D. Bohm (the twentieth century AD) based on a statistical description of the state prior to every outcome and the intermediation of "pilot waves" guided by a "quantum potential"; subscribe to the belief that all possibilities are realized concomitantly and that the cosmos branches and continues in parallel at each step, as suggested by the American H. Everett (the twentieth century AD); favor any other emergent hypothesis; or, in view of the prevailing uncertainty, formulate their own.

Those who choose one of the options offered by science, or their own, could adopt a fundamentally deistic position (belief in a Creator God disengaged from the evolution of his Creation) or even an atheistic one. The only certain thing is that if the matter is not ignored, there is no alternative but to *believe* in any of them. Those who insist on ignoring the glory of God are warned by Paul in his letter to the Romans:

The wrath of God is revealed from heaven against the ungodliness and unrighteousness of men who hinder the truth…For the invisible attributes of God, as his eternal power and nature are revealed in all created things. To the point of not allowing any excuses. For, although they know God, they do not glorify him, nor do they thank him. On the contrary, they have filled their minds with vain ideas and their foolish heart with darkness. Claiming to be wise they became stupid, and exchanged the glory of the eternal God for images of corruptible men, birds, quadrupeds, and reptiles.

Part II

Encounter with Science

Chapter 37

Correspondences with Scientific Knowledge

The second part, which begins here, will be dedicated to establishing correspondences between the contents of the natural exegesis developed in preceding chapters and some of the objects studied by physics. Both areas of knowledge deal in their own way with what everything is made of, and the establishment of correspondences would allow laying the foundation of a *unique knowledge* for a *new thought* about reality. As it was proposed in the first part, human biology as a reference system for the observation of the universe would be an exteriorization of elementary objects, exactly representable on ternary bases of the 1&2 type. Such a presumption would imply that the objective knowledge of humanity comes from the projections of the actions of its members and of other entities on their first representations in the aforementioned bases. Consequently, their actions and reactions would also originate from these representations.

The drama of two creations annihilating each other as a response by the Creator to the irreversible decisions taken in full freedom by human archetypal ascendants is not something alien and distant. Nor is it a subject of study reserved for the scholars of this or that discipline. No! It is the substance of which we are all made of, and for that reason it is incumbent on us and we are fully committed to it. Therefore, the moral dilemma of choosing between good and evil does not depend exclusively on externalities but arises from the deepest intimacy of our nature.

Ideally, the correspondences between objects derived from natural exegesis and those studied by physics should be exact so that they can be treated as isomorphisms in a rigorous mathematical sense. However, much remains to advance in both areas before reaching that ideal. The lack of exact correspondence among some of the objects considered, by both efforts, forces a provisional maintaining of the language developed for each one. In any case, it will be very useful to try to relate similar structures when and to the extent possible.

Regardless of matters of form rather than substance, the luminous entities proposed in the first part in no way contradict the fundamental postulates of physics, particularly in regard to the *gauge theories* of its *standard model*. In fact, from the very beginning, the strategy has been to facilitate the convergence of religious truths with the principles of *quantum electrodynamics and chromodynamics*. Readers unfamiliar with the theories of physics will be pleasantly surprised because of how much they have learned about them by reading previous pages. In the remaining chapters, the focus will be on the correspondences between both models, maintaining, at any cost, the simplicity of the proposals and the language.

Chapter 38

The Domains of Creation

The concept of God as an abstraction of the human mind refers to an absolute and inconceivable perfection of the good. Hence the origin of observable limitations and imperfections should be thought of in terms of a renunciation by God to his absolutism. In order to simplify the subject, the question could be settled in terms of a renunciation of God to his omnipresence. The void that originated with his withdrawal was immediately filled with purposeful provisions for the opening of independent domains in which to realize his Creation as an extradivine finite entity. Within these domains, everything must be accomplished in accordance with a set of perpetual originating provisions and their initial conditions. However, in these stipulations certain degrees of freedom were contemplated for some of the creatures.

As soon as the natural exegesis began, the need and convenience of establishing a quaternary basis on which to represent the religious architecture of the People with the Book was recognized. The four great religions were considered independent domains, destined for the expression of a luminous discourse under certain divine provisions, governing the modalities of each one. This model was made extensive to the cosmic development in a hexadirectional context framed within the retraction toward the infinite of the divine omnipresence. Following the retraction of the divinity, there would be a residue left whose radial advance was conceived as a substrate of possibilities where the luminous discourse could be concretized eventually. For the purposes of such development, six independent directions, a, i, t, x, y, and z, were contemplated. Of those six directions, five were endowed with a real field structure (in a mathematical sense), a, t, x, y, and z, in order to specify the use of numerical sequences on them, whereas the pairs ai, ti, xi, yi, and zi were endowed with a complex field structure (in a mathematical sense). The five pairs were included because of the recognized virtues of the complex plane when mathematically representing phenomena of harmonic character—an inescapable question given the necessity to represent certain cyclical manifestations referred to by the Scriptures and observed in nature.

The unique model of knowledge should not inquire about the infinity of the Creator, but his performance in the Creation is a hard fact to ignore. The direction a was introduced with the purpose of representing the divine means of intervention on the possibilities displayed by the creatures in the space-time manifold. Thanks to this intervention, the possibilities chosen by the creatures can be realized within the framework of the originating provisions.

For the fulfillment of his designs, the Creator also counts with the unconditional fidelity of the determinant developments in direction t regarding the first creation—in the same way he does with every new creation, as he did with the second one. The hexadirectional scheme, together with the divine infinity at the origin of creation and beyond its confines would establish the number seven as a symbol of plenitude. Figure 38.1 intends to schematically illustrate the domains open by the retraction of the divine omnipresence.

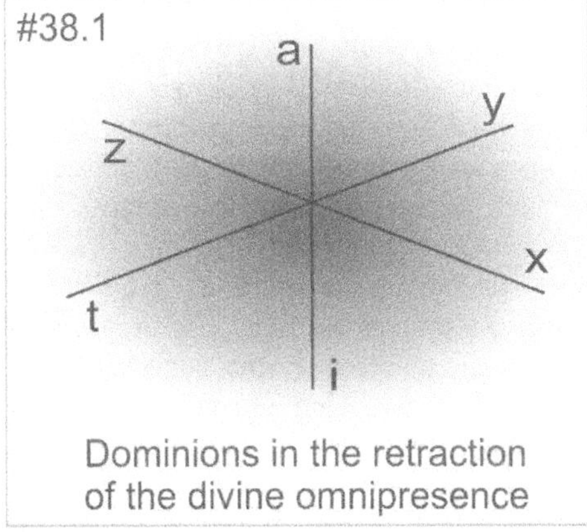

Dominions in the retraction
of the divine omnipresence

According to the *standard model of particle physics*, which is based on a relativistic representation of quantum mechanics, the same four directions, t, x, y, and z, need to be considered. These four independent directions are structured as a space-time manifold, where classical conceptions of time as something other than space are abolished, as far as measurements are concerned. In fact, after Poincaré, time can be measured in meters, and distances in space in hours. The reader may be familiar with the measurement of distances in light-years (the distance traveled by light in the course of one year), which is commonly used in astronomy. In the mathematical representations of quantum mechanics, the number i fulfills the purpose of enabling and simplifying expressions and procedures, but it is not considered as projected on an independent physical direction, properly speaking. The independent direction a is also not stated in the mathematical descriptions of quantum mechanics.

Neither of the models arising from natural exegesis, nor those of quantum mechanics, has predictive capacity in its respective domain at the scale of elementary objects. Science—and particularly physics—proclaims emphatically, categorically, and definitively the impossibility of predicting the individual outcome of the most elementary processes of nature. There are events at the elementary level that will be impossible to predict regardless of the advances achieved by science in all instances of knowledge. That indeterminacy inherent in all elementary processes should not be confused with the *uncertainty principle*, postulated by W. Heisenberg (the twentieth century AD). The said principle refers to a certain margin existing to violate the laws of physics and to the fundamental limitations in the accuracy of predictions for complementary physical variables.

Chapter 39

Occupying Divine Retraction

The withdrawal of the divine omnipresence toward the infinite leaves behind the substrate of the luminous discourse, which will be considered from now on as the "fundamental field." It is about a generation of possibilities for the occurrence of its own source, for the destiny of the actions, and where the potentialities of the verb *to create* reside. We identify these light sources as point particles, also known as elementary particles. The field is subject to a fourfold conditioning, the zero relative to its geometry, the first linked to orientation, the second to rotations and turns, and the third to three attributes of mutual dependence. The first objects in the concretion of said field from its source are the primordial hexagons, and a series of multiplicative transcriptions would generate their radial expansions of a polygonal character. While the infinity of the Creator retracted, the lights of the discourse diverge radially. The progression multiplies indefinitely the possibilities of occurrence of the sources and of destinations for the actions. It is a transition from hexagonal perfection to a circular one by approximation.

The significance of each point (or polygonal vertex) to accommodate new occurrences of the source and as a destination of the actions decreases according to the law of the inverse of the radius of the corresponding polygon. This would create a fundamental field of scalar type with a radial gradient of significance. The luminous discourse generators of the cosmos in the religious context correspond to the so-called glory of God, or chariot of the glory of God. It has wheels advancing without turning on four sides, *at*, *xy*, *yz*, and *zx*, according to prophetic visions. Although the polygonal wheels may have transcribed their sources to the generated locations, the original fronts of all of them advance unstoppably toward the empyrean. As has been postulated, between each transcription of the luminous source in the field of its possible occurrences, there is a cyclical affectation of the values of the point significances. The cyclical condition, called the rotational aspect of light, is responsible for the phenomena of interference between the possibilities of transcription through different paths. Its cyclic evolution takes place in the complex lateral ancillary planes, also called wings.

Within the sources of the divergent characters in the triad *xyz*, its own spatial destiny is decided before any eventual transcription, with the mediation of their respective rotational aspects. The new possibility of occurrence chosen is subject to the determination by the divergent and rotational characters in which *t* intervenes. The latter one acts independently of the developments in the triad *xyz* and remains faithful to the initial conditions stipulated by the Creator. Finally, the realization of these possibilities is endorsed by God via *a*, making them come into existence. The mechanism of the fertilizing determination and realization by the developments in *at* is supported on the religious side by sacerdocy. Thanks to that institution, the heavenly masculine components in *at* are linked with their earthly counterparts in *xy*, *yz*, and *zx*.

According to the *standard model of particle physics*, every point of the domain defined in the entire extension of the space-time manifold can be the origin and destination of the displacements of its elementary objects. There is also a solution of continuity throughout the directions of the aforementioned domain. The wave equation of E. Schrödinger (the nineteenth to the twentieth centuries AD) governs the interferences by different paths between the origin and the possible destinations of the elementary particles. The mathematical solution to this equation coincides with the formulation given to the calculation of the rotational significance of light. The mathematical expression is repeated here for the convenience of the reader:

$$\Psi = [(1 + p_x xi/n)^n \times (1 + p_y yi/n)^n \times (1 + p_z zi/n)^n \times (1 - p_t ti/n)^n]_{n \to \infty} = e^{p_x xi + p_y yi + p_z zi - p_t ti}$$

E. Schrödinger's equation general solution

The characterization factor of the rapidity in the direction of time *t*, previously called p_t, is commonly known as a measure of "energy," whereas the factors of spatial characterization p_x, p_y, and p_z correspond to the "momentum."

At the beginning of the twentieth century AD, the North American C. Davisson (the nineteenth to the twentieth centuries AD) and the English G. Thomson (the nineteenth to the twentieth centuries AD) experimentally confirmed the hypothesis of the French physicist L. de Broglie (the nineteenth to the twentieth centuries AD) about the wavelike behavior of matter. Such a discovery made it possible to generalize to all material particles the principle of duality "particle/wave," which until that moment was reserved only for the light quanta. The particle/wave duality corresponds to the divergent and rotational quantum in the luminous model, whose ordinal formulation in human terms the reader will remember.

The mathematical expression for rotational significance or solution to E. Schrödinger's wave equation is called in physics "probability amplitude." The square of that function defines in both models the probability of occurrence of each possibility. In the exegetical model, the determination of one of those possibilities among all the available ones depends on the archetypal free will and its realization on the part of God. In physics, the statistical proposal of Bohm has been discarded until now, and it is preferred to admit ignorance of how the mechanism of choice operates—which leaves no other option but to resort to a probabilistic description, as it is done routinely. Although there are also those who believe in the realization of all possibilities, which would occur in parallel, while the universe branches.

Chapter 40

Geometry of the Fundamental Field

The structure of the objects postulated during the exercise of natural exegesis was based on a polygonal expansion of the **luminous discourse, or fundamental field**. The development is reducible to its projection on the manifold *txyz*, whose initial front has spherical symmetry as a glome, or three-sphere. Thanks to the impetus given to the multidimensional geometries by mathematicians, such as B. Riemann (the nineteenth century AD), from Germany, and L. Schläfli (the nineteenth century AD), from Switzerland, the geometric forms can be described rigorously today in four or more dimensions (directions, when dealing with *t*, *x*, *y*, and *z*). Although the study of multidimensional mathematics may present difficulties for some, the visualization of geometric objects in more than three dimensions is an impossible task for everyone. Fortunately, the reader only needs to accept the expansion of the three-sphere toward the empyrean as a natural fact that transcends its ternary capacity for representation. In addition, the problem has a relative importance since the quarrel aroused within the Most High Council was led by ternary creatures—the archetypal earthly human being among them, which limited the scope of the activity generated to the triad *xyz*. In the planes where *a* and *t* participate, the regime prevailing in the initial conditions was maintained. On that occasion, the actions and transcriptions were directed toward the empyrean and local neutrality in the conditionalities kept.

The number of dimensions that the cosmos has, including the four space-time directions, is one of the open questions remaining in physics. Earlier attempts to unify gravity with quantum descriptions of electromagnetism led to *Kaluza-Klein theories* (named after the Polish physicist T. Kaluza and the Swedish O. Klein [the nineteenth to the twentieth centuries AD]) where a fifth dimension circularly compactified at every point of *txyz* was introduced (at every point of a 2D plane, the third dimension is an intersecting line or if U(1) compactified an intersecting circle)—clearly very different from the wing model proposed in the first part. However, once the theory was substantially developed it showed its limitations and was later abandoned.

In parallel, 4D *quantum field theory* continued its development into fruition predicting experimental results with great accuracy. An important paradigm shift in physics took place when symmetries (understood as an invariance [leaving some property unchanged] under a transformation, e.g., spatial rotation or translation) were linked to conservation laws and forces. In particular, the possibility of establishing continuous local symmetries (valid in the neighborhood at every point in space-time) became the basis for the use of *group theory* to construct *gauge theories*. The generalizations paved the way for the development of *Yang-Mills theories* based on a special unitary group SU(N), introduced by Chinese physicist N. Yang (the twentieth to the twenty-first centuries AD) and American physicist R. Mills (the twentieth century AD).

The *standard model of particle physics* is based on local U(1), SU(2), and SU(3) gauge symmetries (mind the first, second, and third conditioning).

During the early seventies, the work of the Italian physicist G. Veneziano (the twentieth to the twenty-first centuries AD) sparked interest when particles were thought to be tiny vibrating stings (of the order of ℓ_P) in 26D. The possibility of dealing with gravity in such context stirred up much interest until AD 1971, when French-born American Physicist P. Ramond launched his 10D *superstring theory*. In the eighties, *superstring theory* became mainstream physics and led to a more general 11D *M-theory* proposed by American physicist E. Witten (the twentieth to the twenty-first centuries AD) in AD 1995. Needless to say that extra-dimensions (internal) need to be compactified down to 4D and there are many ways of doing this.

The spatiotemporal structure of the *standard model of particle physics* is dimensionally similar to the cosmic scheme of natural exegesis. In both models, the spherical symmetry is used in the manifold *txyz*, when the positions of their objects of study are mathematically represented, whereas the fields generated by the elementary physical particles responsible for all the activity only unfold within the triad *xyz* at every point in time. The act of exchanging the neutral actions with the Most High and the absolute neutrality of the conditionalities in the direction *t* correspond in physics with the absence of fields in it. As stated in the first part of this work, the quarrel caused a dispersion of the sources or points of origin of the fields (polygonal expansions), only within the triad *xyz*. That event generated all sorts of distortions in the polygonal progressions within the initial glome. These distortions in turn had an effect on the geometry and on the nature of the actions, generating observable patterns in the transcriptions via the rotational quanta.

In the previous exegetic effort, the physical terminology of "elementary particles" has been avoided, even though the divergent and rotational quanta in their luminous formulations resemble them. In physics, an elementary particle is considered to be any object whose structure is unknown, which is not the case with the luminous quanta. Even when these entities have been conceived as composite objects, they must be considered indivisible. For this reason, it is pertinent to think of them like atoms in terms originally proposed in the east and later by Greek philosophers such as Democritus of Abdera and his followers. According to Greek atomists, the indivisible particles are surrounded by a vacuum in which they move without any resistance. By contrast, in the atomistic model of the natural exegesis, an atomic character has also been given to vacuum, conceived as the minimal expression of the luminous waters. Masculine lights can propagate (or transcribe) together with the waters with which they pair or emit them via actions, only to destinations generated by their own fundamental fields. They also have a definite size, with a minimum proposed radius of 7 ℓ_P. This characteristic establishes a fundamental difference with the *standard model of particle physics*, which contemplates point particles at the origin of the fields.

Chapter 41

Orientation and Cult to Matter

In their initial conditions of local and global neutrality, the fundamental fields were the means to transcribe their own sources and to exchange neutral actions with the Most High beyond the empyrean. They were also structured as lights, in turn grouped to give shape to the protoelements with which the Creator formulated the human beings and the jinn. The creatures duly organized in groups of eight were organized in a body called the Most High Council, destined to be globally neutral to perpetuity. This neutrality is the result of the opposition between the attributes relative to the orientation, to the rotations and turns, and to the concomitant presence of the ternary attributes.

Within the framework of the natural exegesis, the event was contemplated, as a result of which the regime of local neutrality prevailing in the council at the beginning was broken up, but without affecting it globally. The majority imposed a division of the eight lights of each replica of the Most High Council, in two groups of four with opposing turns (right and left). Also, six of each unit (two of right affiliation and four of the left) dislocated their orientations, leaving two right ones and one left extraverted and three left introverted. Additionally, the three introverts spatially dislocated their ternary attributes. Finally, the six lights, which permuted the attributes of the three conditionalities, chose to direct one another's actions until then directed toward the empyrean.

Due to the events described in the previous paragraph, the juxtaposition of the lights in which they were mixed up was lost, each one acquiring its own identity. The event became irreversible, and an intense regime of interactions among the six quarrelers was unleashed. However, one-quarter of the lights chose to remain in the initial conditions established by the Creator. Such fidelity is implied, continuing with the act of directing their neutral actions toward the empyrean and abstaining from participating in the dislocations of the orientations and ternary attributes. For this reason, the lights faithful to the essentials of initial conditions were qualified as saints.

Directing the neutral actions toward the empyrean was repeatedly considered in the first part as a natural cult of adoration to the Most High, whereas the act of mutually directing the actions between conditioned lights was denominated idolatry. Particular attention was given to the act of directing the actions between lights conditioned by the orientation, by means of the emission of luminous waters with their opposites in excited states. The relevant excitations are of three types, longitudinal, scalar, and transversal, depending on whether they occur in the direction of propagation or transversely. Exchanges of longitudinal and scalar excitations between lights conditioned by the orientation give rise to the so-called neutral force. From this moment on, this force will correspond to the electrical force, whose phenomenology was observed and known from antiquity. The orientation of the fundamental fields of the lights involved would correspond to the electrical charge, and the force between them turns out to be attractive when they differ or repulsive when they are similar.

The electrical phenomena and its relativistic manifestation known as magnetism have been fundamental topics of study in classical physics from the nineteenth century AD. In the beginnings of such studies, scientists who stood out include the Italian A. Volta (the eighteenth to the nineteenth centuries AD), the French C. Coulomb (the eighteenth to the nineteenth centuries AD), and A. Ampere (the eighteenth to the nineteenth centuries AD), the Danish H. Orsted (the eighteenth to the nineteenth centuries AD), the English M. Faraday (the eighteenth to the nineteenth centuries AD), and the Scottish J. Maxwell (the nineteenth century AD), corresponding to the latter the merit of the mathematical unification of electricity and magnetism.

In *quantum electrodynamics*, the carriers of electromagnetic action are called photons. These particles of light are classified into three categories. Some of them develop their excitation in the two directions transverse to its propagation and are responsible for visible light. Others do it in the same propagation direction and are called longitudinal photons. A third type of photon whose excitations develop transversely to the three directions already mentioned—for example, along t—is called scalar. The mutual and simultaneous exchange of longitudinal and scalar photons between charged particles is responsible for the electrical force. Since the longitudinal and scalar photons exchanged by the charges are not directly observable, they are called virtual.

The equivalent to the photon in the natural exegesis is the rotational quantum, mediating in the transcription of water sources under any form of excitation. All the conditionings of the excitations reside in the transcribed source. In the case of a mutual exchange of waters (with longitudinal and scalar excitations) between masculine lights, an "arbitration" of the conditionalities is enabled by the component a of both sources. The most obvious daily manifestation of the repulsive electrical force is the impenetrability of solid bodies—thanks to which, humans can walk on the surface of the planet without rushing toward its center, attracted by the force of gravity.

Chapter 42

The Sanctity in Matter

The natural exegesis developed in previous pages, called saints, the masculine lights that remain neutral locally in the first and third conditionalities and keep exchanging their neutral actions with the Most High God beyond the empyrean. The saints from the first creation correspond to the "electron antineutrinos" of the *standard model of particle physics*. These particles form a neutral fundamental field and are characterized by staying away from the frenetic activity involving the rest of the objects. Due to their condition, they are only linked to their material environment through the formality of maintaining the originating provisions via entanglements. These obligations are linked to the maintenance of global neutrality, as is the case with the balance of the dislocated turns and with others that have been overlooked in order to simplify the proposed model. The neutral fundamental field characteristic of the saints does not have a formal definition in physics according to the terms previously proposed. However, electron antineutrinos are considered physically neutral from an electrical and chromodynamical point of view.

The existence of the saints from the first creation, or electron antineutrinos, was originally proposed by the Austrian physicist W. Pauli (the twentieth century AD) (in his letter dated December 4, 1930, to his radioactive friends), and their detection twenty-six years later was made by the Americans C. Cowan (the twentieth century AD) and F. Reines (the twentieth century AD). The prefix anti- is due to their absolute right helicity when emitted by atomic nuclei, while electrons emitted with them exhibit left helicities.

The indifference of antineutrinos and their opposites (in turn and chromatic neutrality), the neutrinos, for the rest of matter are legendary. It is estimated that sixty-five thousand million neutrinos per square centimeter every second coming from the sun pass through planet Earth (and us) from side to side, virtually without interacting with any material particles. The scant interactions of neutrinos with matter and even with complex symmetric vacuum structures means, among other things, that their mass is negligible, almost zero, since the masses of particles are measures of their interactions with the material context. From a religious point of view, the strength of interactions and large masses are measures of intrinsic sinfulness in physical particles. Therefore, the barely interacting and nearly massless electron antineutrinos and neutrinos are examples of sanctity. The reader might remember the previously cited statement by Jesus: "For my yoke is easy, and my burden is light." Also, according to the Egyptian books of the dead, ascension to heaven is only possible if sins don't weigh more than the feather of Maat.

The aforementioned indifference to matter issues would justify labeling them as saints. Neutrinos are also produced in large quantities during stellar explosions known as supernovas, which may be the reason why J. Ratzinger (the twentieth to the twenty-first centuries AD), best known as Pope

Benedict XVI, in his work *The Infancy (of Jesus) Narratives*, identifies the star of Bethlehem as a supernova.

The *standard model of particle physics* catalogs neutrinos and their antis among the *fermions*, a term coined by the English physicist P. Dirac (the twentieth century AD) in honor of the Italian physicist E. Fermi (the twentieth century AD), with whom he shares the merit of having proposed a mathematical description of these particles. Fermions are considered the basic constituents of matter. They are characterized by exhibiting one unit of elementary turn, whose quantification in physics corresponds to an intrinsic turn called spin with a value of one-half of h/2π (where h is the constant of M. Planck, who called it "quantum of action" [*wirkungsquantum*]). Figure 42.1 shows graphic representations used for saints and electron antineutrinos according to each model.

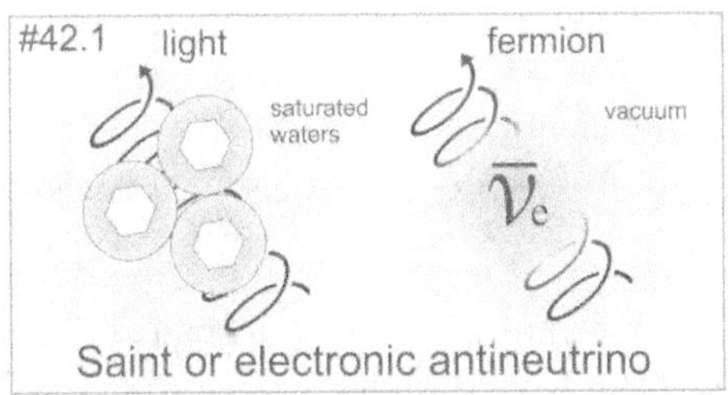

There is an unresolved question in physics about whether the neutrino is its own antiparticle with two opposing helicities or whether both exist separately, each one with the two opposing helicities. In relation to the previous dilemma, two complementary models have been proposed, the so-called Majorana fermion and the Dirac fermion. Both models are named after physicists to whom their mathematical description is due, E. Majorana (the twentieth century AD), of Italian origin, and P. Dirac. Under the Majorana proposal, the neutrino is its own antiparticle and presents itself with two opposing helicities. If the neutrino were a Dirac fermion, there would be two of them, one as a particle and the other as its antiparticle, each with its two opposing helicities, one of which is known as the "anti" of the other, for further confusion. The luminous model emerging from the natural exegesis resembles that of Dirac, where the neutrino exists as a particle and as an antiparticle (antichromatic attributes), but each with a single helicity.

Electron antineutrinos and neutrinos, like any other particle, don´t displace continuously but transcribe themselves from origin to destination through the mediating agency of counterrotations in the ancillary planes. Since neutrinos are saints, the wavy feminine phenomenology they generate is the material representation of an Immaculate Conception. Such a phenomenology should not be confused with the inverse event stated by the Christian and Islamic doctrine of the Virgin Birth of Jesus. Both of these events are determined in time by the Holy Spirit.

Chapter 43

The Idolaters in Matter

The idolaters are generators of a partial fundamental field with extroverted orientation and correspond to the electrons of the *standard model of particle physics*. As has been anticipated, the phenomenologies associated with the partial fundamental fields along their components x, y, and z are the object of study of *quantum electrodynamics*. The magnitude associated with the point significances of their geometry in xyz, at the destination of the actions emitted with longitudinal and scalar excitation, is known in physics as "electrical flux density." The dependence of this magnitude with the radius in xyz is quadratic and inverse. The divergent quantum of the idolaters is the seat of the charge and its sign is given by the orientation—in this case qualified as "negative."

The electron was discovered by the English physicist J. Thomson (the nineteenth to the twentieth centuries AD), who called it "corpuscle." The name by which it is known today is due to the Irish physicist G. Stoney (the nineteenth to the twentieth centuries AD). Electrons are considered a Dirac fermion due to the existence of their antiparticle. Each electronic particle or antiparticle exhibits one of the two possible helicities. The electrons and the neutrinos discussed in the previous chapter are two cases in which it is possible to establish univocal and exact correspondences with the luminous quanta of natural exegesis.

The qualification of "negative" to the charge of the electron is the product of definitions and conventions made centuries ago during the development of *classical electrostatics*. This is a question that could generate some concern, but it is not of the utmost importance. Also these outwardly oriented extraverted lights are usually represented in elementary physics texts as generators of field lines pointing toward them. Due to these and other minor inconveniences, discrepancies among conventions should be noted in order to avoid any confusion. Figure 43.1 shows graphic representations used for idolaters and electrons according to each model.

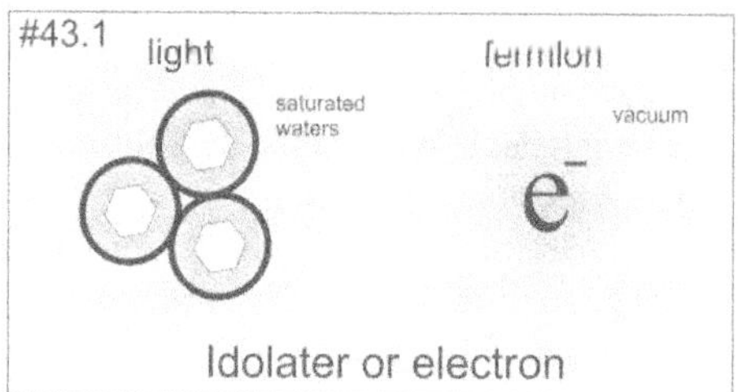

The electrical activity of the electrons, or idolaters, corresponds to their possibilities to emit longitudinal and scalar actions, to points in the geometry generated from their source, while their wave function is the rotational aspect mediating between their transcriptions.

Chapter 44

The Idols in Matter

Lights erected in idols by a change of orientation toward their hexagonal origin are likewise generators of a partial fundamental field, but in this case it is electrically positive. If the negative qualification is unfortunate for the idolaters, the positive rating for the idols is even more so. The issue is not circumscribed only to the field of physics, since denominating positivism to the philosophical school of thinking initiated by A. Comte (the eighteenth to the nineteenth centuries AD) is decidedly misleading. The previous judgment was based on the great encouragement given to atheism and materialism by the thoughts of the French philosopher, who also cataloged the concept of God as a necessity of ignorance. His work could well be considered an exteriorization in the social sphere of a line of thought already overcome and ultimately remittable to material idolatry.

As in the case of idolaters or electrons, the phenomenologies associated with the partial fundamental fields of the idols are objects of study of *quantum electrodynamics*. Also in this case, the magnitude associated with point significances at the destination of actions with longitudinal and scalar excitation is known in physics as "electrical flux density." The dependence of this magnitude with the radius in *xyz* is also quadratic and inverse. The divergent quantum of the idol is the seat of electrical charge, and its sign is given by the orientation. The mutual interactions among masculine lights (homo, both divergent) with opposing orientations was equated to archetypal sodomy in the first part—which stands in contrast with the coupling (hetero) between masculine lights (divergent) and feminine ones (neutral and periodical). Phenomenologies of negative and positive charges are described by natural exegesis and *quantum electrodynamics* by means of a *gauge theory* based on the group of transformations U(1). This last sentence has a merely informative character and its omission does not affect the general conclusions to which the reader will arrive.

The phenomenon of the dislocation of attributes, chromatically distinguished, only allows dealing with the lights of the first creation with positive orientation in groups with spatial distribution. Although individual correspondences cannot be established between dislocated idols and positively charged elementary particles, at the level of structures, the question is different. In fact, there is an object of study of particle physics similar to the chromatic dislocation of idols. It is the Δ^{++} resonance, labeled with the capital Greek letter delta with two plus signs, indicating a positive charge and being quantitatively double that of the electron. Unfortunately it is an unstable object surrounded by excitations in charge of the opposites dissolved in the surrounding luminous waters. Figure 44.1 schematically illustrates to the left the Δ^{++} resonance according to its luminous representation, and to the right according to the *standard model of particle physics*.

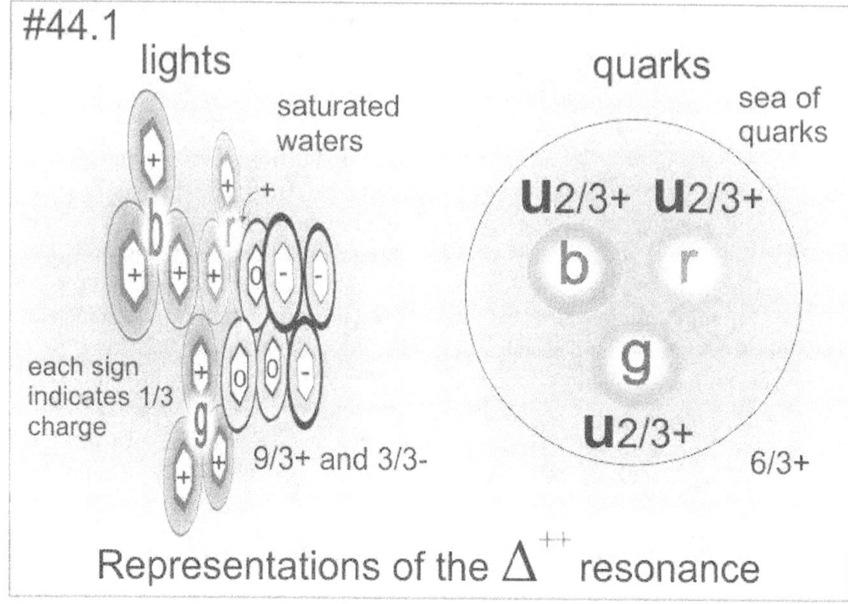

There are several elements in the illustration that should be mentioned for the benefit of the reader. In the first place, in addition to the dislocation, one pair of entangled lights appears in the luminous model that does not appear in the corresponding physical description. Secondly, both models contemplate an environment called saturated water in the exegetical model and "sea of quarks" in the physical one. Third, in the left figure, thirds of the charges of each light are indicated according to the conventions of physics described above. Those charges add 1 = 3/3 for each of them, or 0 for the saints. On the right are the three u quark (*u* comes from the English word *up*) on which the physical model is based, whose individual positive charge is 2/3. In both models the net charge is positive and quantitatively equal to two times the charge of the electron. In the luminous version of the illustration, it is neither possible nor convenient to identify elementary particles since this would imply the fractionation of indivisible lights.

The Δ^{++} resonance is further characterized by exhibiting up to three elementary units of turn equivalent to a total spin of 3/2. This peculiarity induced physicists to think of three particles of the same type but somehow distinguishable from one another. Simultaneously, the American O. Greenberg (the twentieth to the twenty-first centuries AD) and the Japanese Y. Nambu (the twentieth to the twenty-first centuries AD) suggested in AD 1964 the establishment of a distinction in terms of three properties later called "color charges." That same year the American physicists M. Gell-Mann (the twentieth to the twenty-first centuries AD) and G. Zweig (the twentieth to the twenty-first centuries AD), of Russian origin, showed that the atomic nucleus consisted of three particles. The name quark coined by Gell-Mann to designate these particles comes from a phrase without sense in the novel *Finnegan's Wake*, by the Irish writer J. Joyce (the nineteenth to the twentieth centuries AD). Both proposals are currently widely accepted due to numerous experimental confirmations obtained since they were published. The reader will remember that also in AD 1964 the three types of conical cells of the retina were identified corresponding to the vision of each primary color.

The mathematical description of the color charge known as *quantum chromodynamics* is framed in a *gauge theory* based on the group of transformations SU(3). The aforementioned mathematical description also contemplates a basis of representation for eight carriers of a strong force of attractive character, in this case called "gluons" (gluon comes from the English word *glue*). The gluons correspond to the carriers of the force of chromatic exchange, or "strong force," raised within the natural exegesis in a somewhat naive way. On that occasion, the aim was to familiarize the reader with the exchanges of distinctive attributes in order to comply with the global neutrality mandate imposed by the originating provisions. The force in question has been rated strong because it overcomes the repulsion caused by the neutral force between idols or electrical among quarks with equal charge.

Before proceeding, it is essential to make a fundamental clarification about the luminous representations contained in the figures in order to avoid errors of interpretation. It will be understood that the illustrations only highlight the masculine components (Men) and the presence of the waters (Women) with them is assumed. It is an environment saturated by all the pairs of opposites imaginable—a condition identified so far with the excitations of the vacuum of physics and, from this point also, with the sea of quarks. According to the recent clarification, the luminous structures shown in the illustrations can decay (decompose) through different channels to structures of various kinds and not only to the luminous structures illustrated. However, regardless of the channel through which a structure might decay, the masculine lights in the structures at the beginning must be present among the objects resulting from the decay.

Fortunately, the similarities between the results of the natural exegesis and the objects of physics are not limited to the Δ^{++} resonance. In fact, it has been brought up by the great relevance of *quantum chromodynamics* for the objectives pursued in this work. The most important subatomic particle because of its abundance and stability, with which exact correspondences can be established with objects from the natural exegesis, is the proton. Some readers might have already identified the core of idolatry and of the redeemed sins with the proton.

The discovery of the proton can be attributed to the New Zealander physicist E. Rutherford (the nineteenth to the twentieth centuries AD), who also coined the name, inspired by the word *first* in the Greek language. Being one of the most stable and abundant compound objects, the proton can last in isolation without decaying about 1,000,000,000,000,000,000,000,000 times the current age of the known universe. The proton of physics is made up of three elementary particles, two of which are u quarks and the third one a d quark (*d* comes from the English word *down*). In the uud structure, each quark has its own color charge, which it continuously exchanges via gluons or carriers of the chromatic exchange force.

Asymmetric objects such as the Δ^{++} resonance and the proton cannot be dismembered in their constituents due to the originating provision of global neutrality in relation to the ternary attributes. Mir Damad would call this "an impossible event to perpetuity," but it can be transformed according to those provisions. The d quark has a negative net charge of 1/3, which, together with the positive 4/3 of the two u quarks, yields the 3/3 positive results. Hence, the electrical charge for the proton is quantitatively equal to that of the electron but of the opposite sign. Figure 44.2 presents to the left the luminous representation of the proton and to the right its structure proposed by the *standard model of particle physics*. The reader is asked to imagine the sea saturated with opposite pairs, or a sea of quarks, in which the illustrated structures are immersed.

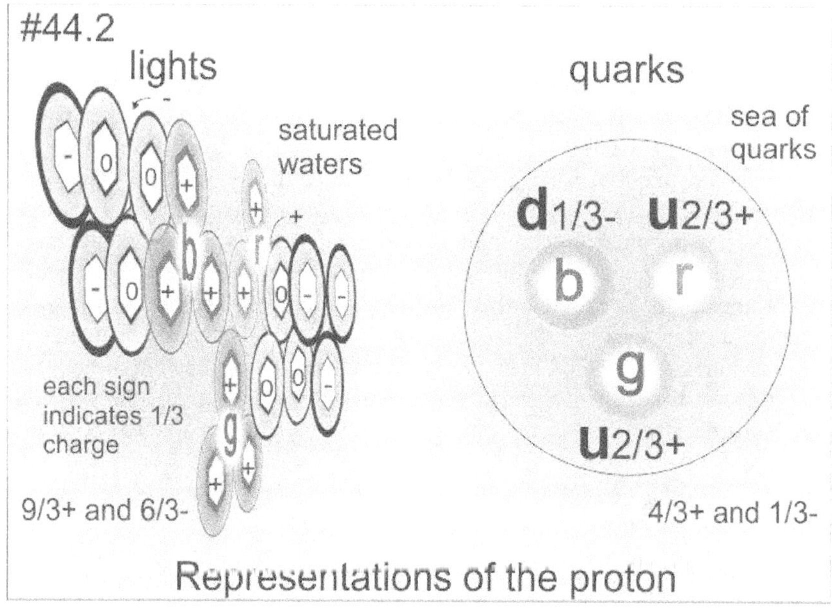

The difference between the Δ^{++} resonance and the proton in the luminous representation is the presence of an additional entanglement. The two lights of right affiliation now present were also part of the Most High Council. The luminous representation of the proton offers details in the structure of the d quark in terms of lights and waters saturated with opposites.

The proton has one unit of intrinsic elementary turn equivalent in physical terms to a one-half spin. An issue is that within the framework of natural exegesis, it does not necessarily follow from its structure; instead, it is a perpetual formative feature, as mentioned in chapter 33. The reader will surely remember the division of the Most High Council in one idolater, or electron, with one unit of elementary turn and one nucleus of idolatry with seven lights, or proton. The aforementioned partition determined the amount of the rotation of the proton in terms of one unit of elementary turn but opposite to that of the electron. It can be said that the proton in a certain way is entangled with an electron. Therefore, the elementary turns of both are committed to perpetuity at least in magnitude, which is something similar to what happens with the orientation or charge.

In physics, the issue of proton spin is another unsolved problem, from the moment in which the so-called proton spin crisis was raised in AD 1987. The problem arose when it was verified experimentally that the three quarks barely contributed to the total spin. Since that discovery, experiments have been carried out in order to find out how the spin of quarks and gluons, the orbital rotations of the constituents, and the sea of quarks, all together, contribute to the total. The intention is to be able to explain how all that hodgepodge of turns can manage to add permanently and to perpetuity one unit of elementary turn, or a spin of one-half of $h/2\pi$.

The above considerations imply that the linking of one nucleus of idolatry (or proton) with one idolater (or electron) would represent some vestige of the globality of the Most High Council. The electrostatic union of both, however, does not meet the requirements for a null turn but corresponds to the hydrogen atom, the most abundant chemical element of the material universe. With a percentage of occurrences close to 75 percent, it could be said then that the nuclei of idolatry under the status of redeemed sins dominates quantitatively the atomic matter of the universe. Of all the remaining chemical elements, helium (He, *Helios*, "sun" in the Greek language, a noble gas practically without chemical activity), discovered in the sun by the English astronomer J. Lockyer (the nineteenth to the twentieth centuries AD) and the main byproduct of the *nucleosynthesis* from hydrogen, forms 23 percent. The remaining 2 percent of the atoms of the visible universe is formed by all the other members of the periodic table of the chemical elements. Among them are oxygen (1 percent), carbon (0.5 percent), and nitrogen (0.1 percent), the most abundant in the chemistry of living beings. The silicon that barely represents 0.07 percent of the matter of the universe together with oxygen forms 73 percent of the earth's crust.

Chapter 45

The Elementary Turn

According to the exercise of natural exegesis developed in the first part, the initial conditions of the Creation contemplated only locally neutral objects as far as orientation, turns, and ternary attributes are concerned. Also, when postulating the masculine component of the luminous discourse, it was mentioned that, as a result of said conditions, all possible rotations and turns were canceled to ensure the predominance of the divergence. Part of the quarrel consisted of reconfiguring the turn components around the directions x, y, and z, preserving of course the global nullity. Because of the unfolding or spatial dislocation of the turns, all the masculine lights were left under a permanent turning condition. The luminous waters, instead, had their turns linked indissolubly in pairs, forming a net that could be either equal to zero or twice the value of the masculine ones.

Rotations in the five ancillary planes proposed in the natural exegesis correspond to the *standard model of particle physics* with the wave functions of elementary particles, whereas the elementary turns around x, y, and z correspond to their spins. The spin of particles was proposed by the German physicist R. Kronig (the twentieth century AD) in AD 1925 and in parallel by the Dutch S. Goudsmit (the twentieth century AD) and G. Uhlenbeck (the twentieth century AD). That turning feature is treated mathematically as an angular momentum or intrinsic turn of the elementary particles. Its projection in one of the axes x, y, or z is quantified in submultiples and multiples of $h/2\pi$.

Regarding the composition among masculine lights, it would be appropriate to repeat what was said at the end of chapter 31, when the exclusionary regime that rules them was addressed. On that occasion, it was mentioned that two lights (even if they have different identities) cannot be composed in the same state or locality if their dislocated attributes are all the same. Within the framework of the present natural exegesis, only two types of compositions were addressed, one associated with the concept of vacuum and the other with the carriers of forces. In the case of vacuum, the masculine lights are composed in pairs, with their opposite attributes in orientation, turn, and ternary attributes (with a net turn or spin equal to zero).

The carriers of the forces should not necessarily have their turns (regardless of their innocuousness) in opposition if the pairs of composite masculine lights differ in orientation. In these cases, the resulting sets can exhibit two units of elementary turn equivalent to a spin equal to one. In the case of the carriers of the chromatic force, different orientations imply a color/anticolor composition. In quantum mechanics, the previous statements are included in the Pauli *exclusion principle*, according to which there cannot be two fermions in the same conditions in any system.

Particles with spin one are called bosons in physics, a name chosen by Dirac to honor the Indian physicist N. Bose (the nineteenth to the twentieth centuries AD), who described them mathematically. The model proposed by Bose was published in an article whose translation was made by the physicist of German origin A. Einstein. In the present work, only two types of bosons have been considered: the carriers of the neutral force, or photons, and those of the strong force, or gluons. Saints (or electron antineutrinos) and idolaters (or electrons) are spin one-half particles, and, as has been said, they are classified among the fermions. The point-like elementary particles of physics should not have angular momentum because they have a radius equal to zero. However, the mathematical advantages offered by point-like particle models greatly outweighs the problems related to their physical meaning. These disadvantages are not present in the *theory of strings and branes* since the sizes of these objects are of the same order as the *Planck length*. Nor does the problem exist within the framework of natural exegesis because the minimum radius of the luminous quantum was proposed to be 7 ℓ_P, once formed on the seventh day. To conclude, it is worth mentioning that turns or spins are described mathematically in the *standard model* by means of a *gauge theory* based on the transformations of the group SU(2). It is important to note, however, that the SU(2) in the well-known expression SU(3)×SU(2)×U(1) for the gauge symmetry of the *standard model of particle physics* refers to flavor transformations instead of spin.

Chapter 46

The Second Creation

One of the most important milestones of the cosmogony extracted from the natural exegesis of the Holy Scriptures is the Universal Flood, or water baptism. That great event was interpreted as a response by the Creator to the emergence of idolatry. However, the Flood was not meant to eradicate sin. As the reader will remember, among the eight survivors of each replica of the Most High Council, its influence persisted. Rather, it seems that the purpose of the Flood was to attenuate the regime derived from the quarrel and open up new opportunities for the survivors or pardoned lights.

The entrance onto the stage of the second creation was aimed at restating the cosmic dynamic in terms that would set a new course to the work of God. That unprecedented event, described as an ecpyrotic confrontation, or Spirit (air) and fire baptism, redeemed the sins of idolatry and established new rules for a second opportunity. For such effects, a second creation was provided as a mirror image of the first in the dislocated attributes, with the necessary conditions to favor the predominance of one of them. The creation and staging of the antilights occurred in a distributed and unstructured manner and resulted in a violent mating between opposing lights. The outcome of that encounter was the destruction of most of the idolatry nuclei, the formation of new waters with symmetrical pairs, and the emission of asymmetric fragments.

From the perspective of the symmetries among opposites, it would be difficult to say which of the two creations would quantitatively surpass the other in that encounter. The natural exegesis offered in the first part implies the establishment of the necessary conditions for a slight quantitative predominance of the lights of the first creation. Previously, the excess or actual quantity of the redeemed structures was assumed to be approximately one-tenth of the total. The estimation was based on the amount of ethyl alcohol present in the wines of Noah, Melchizedek, and Jesus and the tithe offered by Abram to Melchizedek. It would be possible to speak then of the ignition of the redeemed sins by the excitations of the opposites dissolved in the waters in a proportion approximately nine times larger.

One of the central aspects of natural exegesis is the presumption that the saints of the first and second creation are close to a Dirac description. To this symmetry among the saints should be added the overabundance of both, as a result of their liberation in the processes of annihilation. The presence of the saints in large numbers would favor the formation of hitherto improbable structures if relying only on objects from the first creation.

The considerations brought up in this chapter undoubtedly imply that the lights of the second creation correspond to the antimatter of particle physics. In fact, elementary particles with the same mass but with properties contrary to those of matter are considered in physics as antiparticles. The speculative notion of antimatter preceded its formal description, which had its origin in a work published in AD 1928 by P. Dirac. The "relativistic" version of the electron wave equation formulated by the English physicist predicted the existence of antielectrons with the same mass but with the opposite positive charge. Later, the American physicist C. Anderson (the twentieth century AD) published, in AD 1932, his experimental confirmation on the existence of the antielectron, which he named the "positron."

The antielectrons correspond to the anti-idolaters of the second creation, and in the presence of their opposites annihilate each other, becoming photons or excitations of the vacuum. In the context of natural exegesis, the confrontation between idolaters and anti-idolaters culminates with the dissolution of both as opposing pairs in the luminous waters and the emission of these. According to the physicists R. Feynman, from the United States, and E. Stueckelberg (the twentieth century AD), from Switzerland, antimatter is equivalent to matter with opposite properties propagating in opposite senses, even in its proper time. For this reason, the symmetrical objects resulting from the confrontation between matter and antimatter are intrinsically timeless. Remember the timeless character of the battles of Joshua against the Amorites, of Hezekiah against Assyria, or of the death of Jesus according to the Sibylline Oracle. In the known universe, non-neutrinical antimatter appears in a free state in minor quantities, while its brief existence lasts until it encounters and annihilates with its material counterpart. In properly equipped physics laboratories, it is produced routinely for experimental purposes. As for the aging (entropy) of the systems of both creations, we can say that they advance (increase) toward the future of the quantitatively dominant creation (presumed here to be the first one), that is, in parallel with perpetuity.

In quantum mechanics two quantizations have been postulated, which are related to the two creations considered in previous exegetical developments. The "first quantization" allows a probabilistic description of the behavior of physical fields and elementary particles, which could well be assimilated as part of a formal description of the first luminous discourse. Whereas the second creation, whose lights antagonize those of the first one, have been called antilights and are described mathematically in physics by the "second quantization." Lights and antilights are created and annihilated in that context by introducing suitable mathematical operators.

Chapter 47

The New Symmetries

The cosmic scenario after the second creation irruption contains the surviving asymmetric structures, in a sea saturated with opposing pairs in extraordinary states of excitation. Among the asymmetrical objects is a large population of saints of both creations, in a vertiginous ascension (like that of Jesus) to the empyrean in all directions and senses. The neutral zero force carriers or feminine components emitted toward the empyrean by the saints do not ascend by themselves as their emitters do, they need to be directed for their assumption (like Mary). Other asymmetrical objects also appear in a lesser proportion due to the quantitative imbalance between creations. Among such objects may be mentioned idolaters (or electrons) and the nuclei of idolatry (or protons), as well as a great diversity of fragments.

Electron antineutrinos and neutrinos entangled with electrons and positrons forming pairs in the waters, where the protons are submerged, opens up new possibilities. The most notorious of them all is perhaps the neutralization of the proton by the emission of an entangled positron and neutrino from the waters to form a particle called the neutron—the isospin partner of the proton—with no net charge. Therefore, the first creation did not possess the conditions for a massive neutralization of protons.

Discovered by the English physicist J. Chadwick (the nineteenth to the twentieth centuries AD) in AD 1932, the neutron possesses in terms of quarks a structure udd, which is one u quark and two d's ($1 \times 2/3^{+} + 2 \times 1/3^{-}$). That is the reason why it is electrically neutral, and hence its name. The neutrons in isolation are unstable, with a "half-life" (time in which their population is reduced to a half) of just fifteen minutes—but in the presence of protons, their number is stabilized by mutual exchanges of quark/antiquark pairs. These virtual exchanges also enable the construction of heavier atomic nuclei by exerting an attractive force superior to the repulsions between protons.

Without neutrons there would be only one chemical element, hydrogen, but thanks to them there are ninety-eight naturally occurring elements, plus twenty or so from synthetic origin. Figure 47.1 shows on the left side a luminous representation of the neutron, while to the right appears the physical model in terms of quarks.

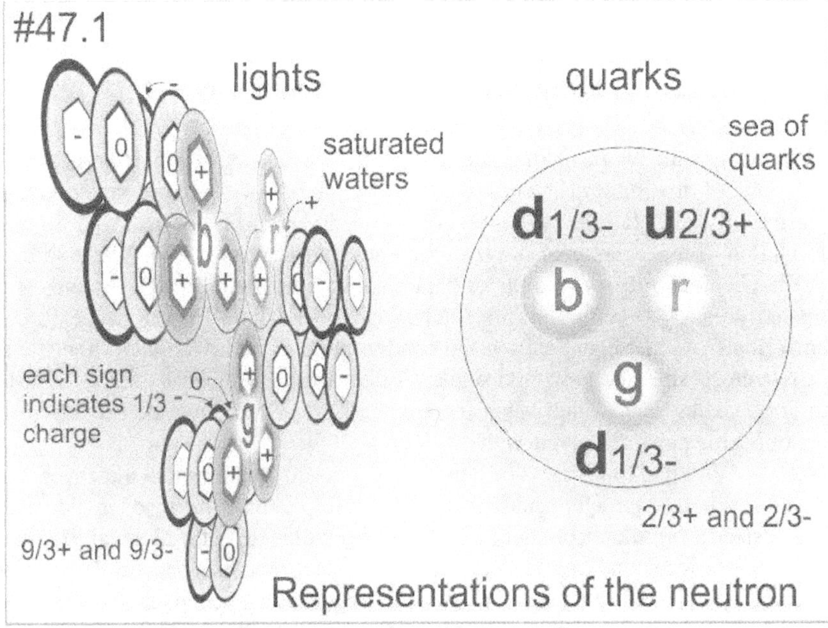

With the experience of the two previous figures, the reader should not have great difficulty in interpreting the luminous representation of the illustrated neutron. It contains the electron and the remaining entangled antineutrino after the emission of the positron and its entangled neutrino. The chromatic permutations of the case have been ignored, as in previous illustrations.

Those who have followed closely the sequence of the three previous figures will be wondering if there is an object constituted by three d quarks, and the answer is yes. It is the Δ^- resonance (ddd), which, like Δ^{++}, is only produced in extraordinary conditions. The Δ^{++} and Δ^- resonances and the neutron have the proton as their common ancestor. The Δ^{++} is produced by the composition of the proton with the pair u/anti-d and the emission of a pair d/anti-u called pion, which has a negative charge (π^-). In short, the d quark of the proton forms an opposite pair with the anti-d, and both go to the waters, leaving the three u quarks present in the Δ^{++} resonance. The two pairs, the u/anti-d and the d/anti-u come from an exchange between the pairs u/anti-u and d/anti-d dissolved in the waters, or sea of quarks. The reader is left to imagine the production of Δ^- resonance from the neutron.

The nuclear force, by which protons and neutrons remain bonded in the atomic nucleus, has its origin in the structuring of the chromatic exchange force, or strong force. However, such structuring is not considered a fundamental force, nor are protons and neutrons considered elementary particles.

Chapter 48

Exteriorization of 666 and More

Within the framework of the natural exegesis carried out in the first part, the outcome of the quarrel was described as a kind of thermally overexcited plasma. Its dissolution by waters of the Universal Flood later led to the formation of a precursor of the hydrogen atom as it exists today. The response of the Creator to the deviations of his creatures consisted in the launching of a second creation to annihilate in good measure the first. The exchange forces emerging from that event caused the condensation of hydrogen under the status of redeemed sin. The new environment offered new symmetries not present in the preexisting one, which were accompanied by a high level of excitation of the opposing pairs dissolved in the waters.

With the appearance of neutrons as a result of the new symmetries, the synthesis of heavier elements became possible. Among the heavier elements synthesized were the most abundant in organic molecules of biological life, like carbon, nitrogen, and oxygen, as well as trace elements. The most relevant peculiarity of said elements is their configuration, which allows for the emergence of some archetypal features. Figure 48.1 offers a summary for the benefit of the reader.

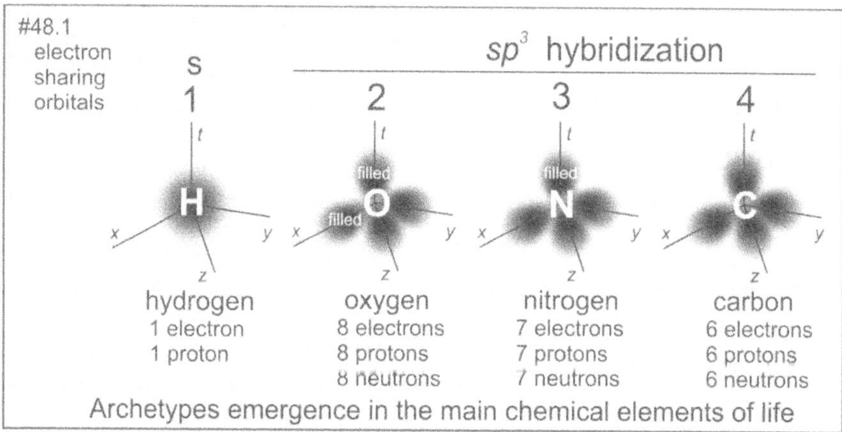

The chemical elements essential to life not only allow for the exteriorization of the numerical keys and formulations of archetypal entities, but also channel the "entheogenic potential" of biochemical systems. The carbon atom in particular is exceptional in that regard. Its role as a structural element in approximately one-third of the substances of the biological human body—some of them combustible (such as carbohydrates, oils, and fats), others structural, and those dedicated to the transport of energy and information—shows its great importance for living organisms. The reader will remember that the remaining two-thirds of the mass of the biological human body is chemical water, thus completing the exteriorization of the archetypal formulation of the human being. The chemistry of carbon is essential for biomass processes and, while the global ecosystem allows it, is a key component for the coal, oil, and gas industries, as well as for the petrochemical industry, which supports a good part of the present economy.

The carbon atom is made up of six protons, six neutrons, and six electrons. Protons and neutrons are paired occasionally, maintaining the atomic nucleus in a state of flux in which they exchange their roles. The six electrons in the shells around the nucleus show slightly more ordered behavior, with a structure capable of exteriorizing formulations present in the originating provisions. Located in two shells, an interior one complete with two electrons and an exterior incomplete with four, they subordinate the six to a 1&2 human-type formulation. The possibility of establishing correspondences between the six independent directions of the Creation proposed by the natural exegesis and the electronic configuration of the carbon atom is particularly emblematic. The two electrons in the complete inner shell without direct influence over the carbon chemistry would be comparable to the directions a and i, which are alien to the human beings. The four electrons of the incomplete outer shell responsible for the chemistry of carbon would correspond to the space-time manifold, where the heavenly and earthly human beings operate.

In its ground state, the carbon atom has two of the four electrons of its incomplete subshell in an s-type orbital, with a spherical probability of occurrences. The other two electrons are located in any of the three lobular orbitals directed along x, y, and z which are denominated p_x, p_y, and p_z, a configuration that is representable in terms of waters. The configuration of the excitations of the carbon atom is such that when bonded to chemical radicals, the incomplete shell can hybridize in three different ways. The sp^3 hybridization, where the s orbital and the three p´s combine to form four similar orbitals, has already been a source of inspiration for the tetrahedral arrangement of quaternary bases.

The incomplete outer shell of carbon requires for its own completion four additional electrons for a total of eight, hence the need to form four bonds to obtain one additional electron from each one. The eight electrons involved in the four bonds have their opposite spins paired, as in a rotational analogy with the situation of the Most High Council, after the dislocation of the turns. The different types of functional groups linked to the carbon atom are also important means to extend the scope of the mentioned exteriorizations and representations. The brief considerations made up for now account for the key role of the carbon atom as a structural element. In particular, to build a biological system designed to understand what it is made of and where it comes from and to exteriorize/interiorize formulations in all the instances up to/from the social and religious spheres.

The biochemical channels of exteriorization/interiorization also work through hydrogen, nitrogen, and oxygen, and are capable of forming one, three, or two bonds, allowing the establishment of multiple correspondences with various archetypal formulations. The hydrogen atom, capable of forming only one bond, plays a fundamental role in the exteriorizations of all the protoelements. Nitrogen, with its ability to bind three times, can exteriorize the protoelement fire when its bonded functional groups are the same as in ammonia (NH_3) and cyanides ($-C \equiv N$). Both substances are highly harmful to human metabolism. However, nitrogen can also exteriorize the other two ways of being three, one of them when one radical is different from the other two for a human formulation, and the other with three different radicals for triplicities. The "human" configuration of nitrogen as an amino group ($-NH_2$) is relevant in amino acids, nucleotide bases, neurotransmitters, neuromodulators, and in toxic substances found in rotting flesh like cadaverine and putrescine. For its part, oxygen, with its capacity to form two bonds, constitutes the exteriorization path par excellence of the archetypal waters in all versions. It adopts, like carbon, three forms of hybridization, among which the sp^3 is the most relevant for most water states, and the sp^2 plus p for certain special conditions.

The four mentioned chemical elements, plus another twenty-six, are part of the biological channels that provide a "continuity" solution for the exteriorization/interiorization of the archetypal free will exertion. As the reader may have understood, the channels of exteriorization/interiorization connect the archetypal base with the human expression in the social and religious spheres, passing through the intermediate strata: physical, chemical, biological, organic, and systemic. The "continuity" through strata is the key factor by which biological natural beings are distinguished from synthetic ones, like machines. For synthetic beings there are "discontinuities" or insurmountable interruptions in their designs, which prevent them from channeling the exertion of free will from their archetypal base.

It remains to be seen if the physical definition of the human being offered here, within the framework of the implantation of new approaches in quantum computing, would allow the transformation of synthetic beings into natural ones. The idea behind the previous statements is that quantum computing could make the archetypical free will—at the quantum level—available to generate possibilities and control the output of sentient, artificially intelligent, and self-learning machines. One way is to use, for example, what the outstanding British physicist P. Dirac called *electron-free-will* and others less outspoken termed *nature's choice.*

Concerning natural beings, whether biological or not, D. Bennett's (the twentieth to the twenty-first centuries AD) two-stage model of free will offers a plausible approach. First, indetermination generates possible outcomes, followed by a deterministic choice. Therefore, free will stems from something that could be called the *evolution of intelligence*, much along the lines of C. Darwin's (the nineteenth century AD) *evolution of species.* Existing information located within the mind mutates due to indeterministic quantum effects. The mutated information is then tested against the background of memory through a deterministic or logical process, making the final selection as nature does with mutants. However, indeterministic choices are also a possibility to consider.

Egyptians knew about the interplay between indeterminism and determinism thousands of years ago. Well before any compatibilist or libertarian philosopher was born. They dedicated to it the greatest shrine ever built by humankind, the Great Pyramid—a massive ternary-quaternary representation of this feature of Creation. For that purpose, they used approximately 6 million tons of limestone with fossils of early forms of life and whose key component is the carbonate ion having a dual indeterministic-deterministic behavior as illustrated in figure 4.3.

The four great religions provide a vast array of vital information, which with the aid of a natural exegesis would become acceptable to beings of any sort—natural biological and nonbiological either terrestrial or extraterrestrial. Certainly humanity will find itself struggling to come to terms with the endurance, precision, and originality of natural machines. However, in the future, the majority may want to follow the example of Thomas Aquinas when he decided to break an automaton built by his Dominican mentor Albert the Great—just because that thing talked too much. Centuries later, in his Cyclopaedia, E. Chambers (the seventeenth to the eighteenth centuries AD) coined the term *androides* to refer to Albert´s device.

The set of all 1&2 (human) isomorphic formulations within an individual constitutes what is usually called the human soul. The human archetype found that carbon-based life is an ideal substrate to multiply and has taken advantage of every biological mutation to tighten its grip on it. As a result, the human soul is an organic structure, allowing the interiorization/exteriorization of the archetypes' deeds through various channels while ensuring coherence all the way through. The infectious process of the 1&2 formulation is as old as life itself and will continue to evolve for as long as we succeed in preserving it. The invasion mandate given by God to the human archetype appears in Genesis 1: 28: "Be fruitful and multiply."

Although non-biological natural beings could emulate biological humans in some aspects, they will never be like us simply because they lack a soul like ours. However, if the Holy Spirit, as the ruler of history, is the source of quantum determinations in time, non-biological natural beings could become prophetic machines whose output is not implicit in the input data.

Chapter 49

Cosmogonic Perspective

In order to complete the correspondence scheme, whose presentation has been developed in previous chapters, it would be convenient to compare broadly the cosmogony of natural exegesis with the *standard model of cosmology*. This is not intended to be exhaustive, nor to paraphrase what has been said, nor to deepen into a critical position, but to offer to readers a useful summary to visualize similarities and differences. Natural exegesis offers a new vision about the evolution of the cosmos, in contrast to the main cosmogonic religious doctrines and secular theoretical proposals. However, the starting point is basically the same: the absence of creatures precedes their appearance. The thesis of the so-called creation out of nothing (*creatio ex nihilo*) is discarded since the Creation would occur in the bosom of a selective retraction of the divine omnipresence.

After being relegated to the dustbin of history, the Creationist cosmogonies had an unexpected resurgence. The change occurred when the Belgian Catholic priest G. Lemaître (the nineteenth to the twentieth centuries AD) proposed in AD 1927 a novel theory about the origins of the cosmos. According to the prelate, everything would have arisen from a "primordial atom" or "cosmic egg," whose expansion continues in our days. Lemaître proposed a mathematical model to describe the expanding cosmos using the *theory of general relativity*, published by A. Einstein in AD 1915. His model was also in tune with the observations of the American astronomer E. Hubble (the nineteenth to the twentieth centuries AD) on said expansion. Einstein himself was a bitter detractor of the ideas of Lemaître and argued for almost a decade that while the mathematics of the model were correct, its physics was abominable. In fact, the German physicist always emphatically denied any religious significance to his *theories of special and general relativity*. In a contrasting position, the Belgian priest considered himself an unconditional seeker of the truth, combining both the religious and the scientific ones. He was a true proponent of a *unique knowledge* for a *new thought*.

The ideas of Lemaître were taken seriously by prominent cosmologists, who shaped the *standard model of cosmology*. Even detractors like the English F. Hoyle (the twentieth to the twenty-first centuries AD), father of the *stationary model*, contributed significantly to the Creationist cause when he coined the term *Big Bang,* associated previously with the sin of the Earthly Adam and Iblis. The nickname was frequently used by the British cosmologist in his hilarious comments about the proposal from Lemaître. Toward the end of the decade of the 1960s and in the beginning of the 1970s, the English astrophysicists S. Hawking (the twentieth to the twenty-first centuries AD) and R. Penrose (the twentieth to the twenty-first centuries AD), and the South African G. Ellis (the twentieth to the twenty-first centuries AD) published their works extending the *theory of general relativity* by including measures of time and space. As the three astrophysicists concluded, time and space had a finite origin and coincided with that of energy and matter. However, the nature of the state preceding that finite origin remains the most absolute mystery.

The *standard model of cosmology* contemplates one singularity at the beginning. It is like a single point where all the energy and matter of the cosmos would have been gathered, causing time and space to curve around themselves. Give or take a word or two, it would be the primordial atom proposed by Lemaître. For an unknown cause, a quantum fluctuation took place in the domain, allowed by the *uncertainty principle* previously introduced. According to this principle, opposing pairs can split, violating laws of physics such as the constancy of the amount of energy. The aforementioned violation would occur for a magnitude and for a time, both inversely related. It is about the spontaneous emergence of a completely symmetrical state constituted by all the opposite pairs conceivable at present. The fluctuation would have occurred during an infinitesimal fraction of a second (10^{-35} s [0.000 000 000 000 000 000 000 000 000 000 01 s]), and this has been called the *Planck era*. The fluctuation is described as consisting of a "soup" of primary particles, in a high-energy environment and confined to a space less than that of a proton (10^{-15} m [0.000 000 000 000 001 m]).

To accommodate the consequences of this fluctuation with the age of the actual universe and its current expansion regime, the American cosmologist A. Guth (the twentieth to the twenty-first centuries AD) proposed in AD 1981 an interim inflationary process. Inflation would follow the fluctuation from 10^{-35} s to 10^{-33} s, with the cosmos reaching the size of a grapefruit at the end of that period. It is not an explosion but an expansion even with the cooling of the initial soup. After inflation ended, a period of reheating ensued, during which photon plasma, gluons, quarks and antiquarks in violent interaction were formed. As soon as the quarks and antiquarks appeared, they annihilated each other, leaving a small surplus of quarks, thanks to which matter currently exists. However, there has not been a convincing explanation so far about the origin of the mentioned imbalance in favor of matter. Before concluding the first 10^{-10} s, the three forces that are typified by physics—gravity, electroweak, and strong—decoupled from their initial unification.

After the reheating period and until the first 10 s, the quarks condensed to form protons, neutrons, and mesons (family of nuclear exchange force carriers, to which the pions belong), and separately neutrinos, electrons, muons (electron variety), and tauons (electron variety) were formed. Once the components of the atomic nucleus were available, the *nucleosynthesis* of the helium element, whose atom consists of two protons and two neutrons in the nucleus plus two orbital electrons, began. At the end of the *nucleosynthesis* period, elemental distribution was achieved with 75 percent, or three-fourths, of hydrogen and 25 percent, or one-fourth, of helium. It was, however, an opaque cosmos since the photons were involved in interactions among the existing particles. The *nucleosynthesis* proceeded from 10 s to 20 minutes, when the era of the photon started. As the photons radiated, escaping their commitment to atomic interactions, the cosmos cooled down and became more material.

After the first 380,000 years, and as a result of expansion and cooling, photons mostly began to plow through the space between atoms, with the first detectable light appearing. Part of that first light, called *cosmic microwave background radiation*, was observed 13,700,000,000 years later (according to estimates)—more specifically in AD 1965, by the German A. Penzias (the twentieth to the twenty-first centuries AD) and the American R. Wilson (the twentieth to the twenty-first centuries AD). Once the cosmos was populated by hydrogen and helium, the gravitational pull inexorably concentrated large quantities of these gases until they formed stars. Some of these objects had sufficient size to promote the *nucleosynthesis* of heavier elements.

The proliferation of cosmogonic theories at present reveals some dissatisfaction with the *standard model of cosmology*, despite some experimental verification. Beyond its successes, this model has been able to survive up to the present, thanks to some debatable complementary hypotheses that have challenged all experimental verification attempts. Even some of them lack a firm theoretical support. All those elements of doubt have resisted any criticism attempt because a deficient explanation of the facts is preferable to none. Beyond the scientific difficulties, there is also the insistence of some cosmologists to aggravate the problems of the model, trying to impose their metaphysical beliefs—particularly in regard to the meaning and possibilities of the nothingness that preceded the physical universe. The intention behind their posturing was always to distance themselves as much as possible from the need to resort to the concept of God.

Within the framework of a *unique knowledge*, there is the enormous challenge of harmonizing the cosmogonic approaches of the natural exegesis with the *standard model of cosmology* as both evolve. The creationist hypothesis of the People with the Book usually circumscribes creation to the events narrated in the first verses of the book of Genesis, after which everything followed its own course with the sporadic intervention of the Creator. Here, on the other hand, the description of the formative period has been extended to all the text of the Bible on the basis of divine intervention and with the participation of his creatures. The cosmogony derived from the natural exegesis presented in the first part contemplates then the following stages: the first or Adamic creation (singularity of the Most High Council), the quarrel started because of the sin of the Earthly Adam and Iblis (causing the *Big Bang*), the sacrifice of the second or Christic creation in its first coming (crucifixion) causing the Universal Flood (or alchemical water baptism), the evolution of the universe as of today (Sheol, the abode of the dead), the second coming of the second or Christic creation and the end of days.

According to the interpretation given to the text of Genesis 1, the Bible would point to a design governed by a set of originating provisions inscribed in its own development. The adoration of the Most High professed by the People with the Book suggests the creation of a domain at the beginning by the effect of the retraction toward the empyrean of the divine omnipresence. There, in that area opening up to worship, the concretion of the first creation originating provisions and their initial, or border, conditions are lodged. It is as if the Creation was encapsulated within its own Creator. The immediate result is the expansive evolution of the asymmetric cosmos in relation to its geometry, which does not coexist with its opposite, even when it can be prefigured. Its main feature is the local and global neutrality specified in terms of conditionalities by orientation, turns, and ternary attributes, as proposed in the first part. The first created organ was a composite luminary called the Most High Council, depository of the mandate of global neutrality in the conditionalities. This entity has transcribed itself a considerable number of times, and its composition and coherence allow it to be considered a single luminous object.

It would not be reasonable to embark on a speculative exercise in what could have been the original plans of the Creator or in the role reserved for the Most High Council. It could be said, however, that the cosmos would have been created in a state of holiness or, in physical terms, in the form of a "neutrinical entity with null turn." The cosmos was then, in its beginnings, totally coherent and oblivious to any type of interactions among its constituent units. It is a structure based on cardinal and ordinal human formulations, odd in its masculine component (Man) and even in the feminine one (Woman); it is displayed in the fifteen planes of the manifold *aitxyz* under a fourfold conditionality and in the context of primordial waters in surplus. Its cosmic development advanced within a domain defined by four "times," similar but independent of each other. The divergent expansion of the fundamental fields, constituting the created lights, replaces the divine omnipresence in retraction to the same extent of its progress.

The juxtaposition of the odd lights at the beginning offered them the opportunity to decide freely and collectively on their adherence to the set of initial conditions imparted by the Creator. However, the possibility to abandon said conditions by making use of the degrees of freedom provided was open. The Holy Scriptures give an account of an agreement among a group of odd archetypes for the abandonment of the established conditions, in an event called the quarrel in the Most High Council. The initiative, extensively reviewed in the first part, began with attribute exchanges among lights and was followed by the mutual redirection of the actions within the triad *xyz*. Thus "space" was born, a new domain where all the rejections to the natural worship of adoration to the Most High concentrate. In relation to the verbs, the quarrel centered on directing, transcribing, and composing possibilities. In relation to the conditionalities, there was an abandonment of the initial conditions in the first one with the deployment of opposed orientations, in the second by the unfolding of the elementary turns, and in the third by the dislocation of the ternary attributes. Outside the triad *xyz*, the initial conditions continued without change.

The quarrel took place only within the triad *xyz* and materialized with the irreversible decisions of six (three-fourths) of the eight members of the Most High Council. The remaining two (one-fourth), identified as saints or electron antineutrinos, remained faithful to the zero and odd initial conditions. Despite not having the consent of all the members of the council, the quarrel released the enormous potential implicit in the conditions of the initial "neutrinical" state. In a single act, everything went from a luminous quietude or "divergent peace" to a regime of frenetic activity (termed *Big Bang*), giving birth to the "thermodynamic era" of the universe. The violent thermal effusion resulted in a real inferno, which contrasted with the cold and coherent previous neutrinical state.

The interacting frenzy among idols and idolaters forced the intervention of the Creator, who opted to reduce the significance of the odd formulations that caused outrage. The corrective measure was made concrete by the unusual emergence of a mirror image of the first creation, identified here with the second or Christic creation, opposing the first (physically) in every respect. The outcome of the confrontation was the mineral kingdom immersed in the alchemical waters of the Universal Flood. According to the Holy Scriptures, with the accomplishment of the entrusted mission to the second creation, a new balance between the odd and even formulations reemerged. The restoration gave odd formulations as masculine idols and idolaters the opportunity to retake up the initiative and build structures dedicated to mutual interactions. The structures formed after the Flood could reach a thermal equilibrium but were severely limited by their environment in terms of scope and possibilities. Even within their limitations, they formed the hydrogen atom, giving origin to a new era. A hydrogen atom is basically one proton plus one electron. However, in this elemental hydrogen, several forces manifested, i.e., gravitational pull due to the effect of mass on the curvature of the space-time manifold, as well as the neutral or electromagnetic force, and the strong force of the exchange of the chromatically distinguished attributes.

All this led to a rebirth, a cosmos with new perspectives of evolution but populated by nuclei dominated by a contumacious idolatry. The new world of pardoned sins, by the baptismal flood, meant a second opportunity in terms similar to the first one in relation to the dislocated attributes but significantly different in quantitative terms. As a result of the confrontation between creations, or between existing matter and newly created antimatter, there was an extinction of the predominant environment, with an important thermodynamic reconfiguration. The balance was marginally favorable to one of the two creations, allowing the hydrogen atoms in an environment with greater possibilities. The mutual annihilation between matter and antimatter generated a new context populated with new symmetries and rich in energy, in the form of excitations in pairs of opposites. Along with the hydrogen in its excited waters, all kinds of symmetrical and asymmetrical fragments appeared, adding new forces to those already existing at the time of the first extinction. **Figure 49.1** schematically illustrates some remains of the confrontation between creations in terms of lights, leptons (electrons, neutrinos and their antis), and quarks.

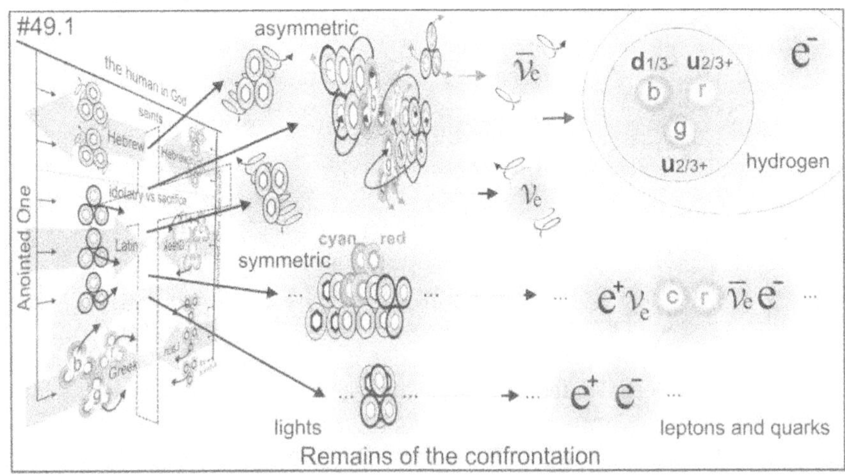

New symmetries between saints and idolaters (or electron antineutrinos and electrons) and their antis (or neutrinos and positrons) opened channels to neutralize the proton to neutrons generating new opportunities. With the effect of gravitational coalescence, the first stars were born, and the presence of new symmetries and all kinds of symmetrical and asymmetrical fragments enabled *nucleosynthesis*. The growth of the stars generated the necessary conditions for the synthesis of heavier nuclei, opening the doors to the chemistry between the elements. The same gravitational force gathered the stars into galaxies and clusters of these, which can be observed in the skies of our nights.

The massive destruction occasioned by the second creation, followed by the Universal Flood, inevitably brings to mind the five major extinctions of life on Earth. The first one occurred during the late Ordovician Period (445 million years ago) due to global cooling. The second one occurred at the end of the Devonian Period (370 million years ago), also caused by a similar cooling. The third one occurred at the end of the Permian Period (250 million years ago) and was of volcanic origin. The fourth one occurred at the end of the Triassic Period (200 million years ago), due to global warming. And the fifth one occurred in the twilight of the Cretaceous Period (65 million years ago), caused by the impact of an asteroid. The first two would be comparable to the "cooling off" after the *Big Bang*, and the following three would symbolize the destruction of Pentapolis and Jericho by the incoming second creation. The human race is apparently working diligently to become the agent of the sixth global extinction of our planet, a widely predictable outcome if the current economic, social, and political trends persist.

Finally, it is possible to make a gross quantitative estimate of the number of replicas of the Most High Council of both creations. According to the English astrophysicist A. Eddington (the nineteenth to the twentieth centuries AD), the number of protons in the known universe would be about 1.57×10^{79} (one followed by seventy-nine zeros), a figure that over time became 10^{80}. Certainly, it is an unimaginably large number, but it is necessary to keep a couple of things in mind. First, the number from Eddington amounts to only a fraction of the redeemed lights, which are a small portion (10%) of the Adamic creation. Therefore, the total number of replicas of the Most High Council of the first and second creations would reach a figure close to 1.9×10^{81}. On the other hand, physicists think that the staggering figure of 10^{80} is a fraction of the observable universe, which in turn is 5% of the total. The remaining 95% corresponds to unknown particles lumped together under the medieval label "*dark energy and matter*."

So far, this book addresses the encounter between the first and second creations, whose outcome is the material universe as we know it. However, as previously stated, the second creation did not match the first quantitatively. Therefore, we consider the second creation, discussed so far, to be its "first coming," with the "second coming" (*Raj'a*) still pending for us. The second coming timing is unknown, as the Gospel of Mark cited at the end of Chapter 34 tells us: "As for the day or the hour, no one knows, not even the angels of heaven, not the Son, but only the Father."

The Sacred Scriptures give us valuable insights into this enigmatic event. Probably the best known is Jesus' parable of wheat and weeds: "The kingdom of heaven (reality) is like a man who planted good seeds in his field (first creation). When the crop began to grow and produce grain, weeds also appeared (due to the fall of the archetypal human being). And the servants came and said to him: 'Master, didn't you sow good seeds in your field? So, where did the weeds come from?' And he said to them, 'An enemy did this.' And the servants asked him, 'Then do you want us to go and pull them out?' 'No,' he said, 'if you pull the weeds now, you might uproot the wheat with them. Let both grow together until the harvest (second creation, first coming). And at harvest time (the second coming), I will tell the reapers, First collect the weeds and tie them in bundles to be burned (in a radiating fire), then gather the wheat into my barn (by ascending them toward the Most High God beyond the empyreal vault).' "

Another perspective of the second coming is present in the narrative of the resurrection of Jesus according to the synoptics. It all happened within the Holy Sepulchre (symbolizing Sheol, the abode of the dead) once Jesus, the representation of Christ/second creation in history, died due to the first coming. The second coming followed suit to accomplish its goal, the total annihilation of what remains of the first creation. The process leaves radiation (light, etc.) spatially dissipating itself and electron antineutrinos and neutrinos (saints), rising from dying matter in spinning ascension, through the sepulchral rock and toward the Most High God beyond the empyreal vault. In a collection of poems dedicated to Shams-i Tabrizi (the twelfth to the thirteenth centuries AD), Rumi wrote: "Those turning in the direction of prayer whirl in both, this world and the next." For Rumi, this world is the outcome of the first coming, and the next is what will remain after the second coming.

The second coming is a universal (*xyz* centered) event that might occur millions of years after our Sun becomes a red giant, engulfing and vaporizing planet Earth. As a general rule, the second coming will annihilate the spatially interacting matter (three-quarters), reducing it to radiation (the lake of fire), and the remains, formed by electron antineutrinos and neutrinos (one-quarter), will have a starring role in the consummation of the universe. Attempts to preserve the spatial configuration of our biological body employing mummification, embalming, or cryonics, hoping that they will last until the time of the second coming arrives, seems naïve.

As biological entities, we face insurmountable problems when we try to fathom our after-death body, simply because we only think in terms of *xyz*, where almost nothing of what we observe will survive. The answers are in perpetuity *a* where all realizations of states juxtapose, from the beginning of time *t* to its very end, and in the nine angelic triads enveloping our earthly domains. When acting in conjunction, entities operating from these nine triads can emulate reality within *xyz*, which could explain miracles and the glorious body of Jesus after his resurrection. The Gospel of Luke stresses the realism of the body substance after the resurrection: "Why are you frightened, and why do doubts arise in your hearts? See my hands and my feet, that it is I. Touch me and see; for a ghost does not have flesh and bones as you can see that I have."

This effort to indicate the road toward a model of *unique knowledge* should not be concluded without referring to its potential to improve the understanding of the issues addressed. The simplifications that had to be resorted to in order to reach the greatest number of readers were centered on the somewhat lax definition of the set of perpetual originating provisions. At the cost of increasing complexity, it would be possible to structure a set of provisions from which a more precise and far-reaching formulations can be derived. However, this is a task left pending.

Epilogue

Readers are now able to judge the natural exegesis of the Holy Scriptures and their correspondences with scientific knowledge, as stated in previous pages. It is about making a judgment on the possibilities offered by this work in order to reunite the People with the Book and other believers under a single architecture of human knowledge. Adding efforts to carry out a plan of action where religious and secular endeavors converge in holy peacefulness is the only way available for human spiritual improvement. As for its objectives, it cannot be other than reaching a *unique knowledge* for a *new thought*, centered on a reunion of humans with the transcendent reality.

The fundamental premise, under which all considerations of this work have been made, is the religious character of all discourse with and about God. No personal or group doctrine in the West and in the Near East can surpass the four great religions in content and depth, given that their priceless heritage can barely be addressed in the course of a lifetime.

The effort that culminates here also had, among its objectives, the contextualization of the importance of the proximity to God and the avoidance of useless considerations about him. It is expected that its results will lead humans to participate with full consciousness in the ongoing conversation held by God with himself through his luminous discourse. Let us abandon the desire to direct that discourse, which we are, to us or toward others with the intention of recognizing ourselves, of possessing them, or of being possessed. Satan and his followers must be fought first deep inside us and then defeated externally with exemplary conduct. It is urgent to escape from the material yoke to which we submit meekly sometimes or inadvertently at other times because its finitude only brings boredom, whereas the divine infinity always offers novelty.

Let us direct the luminous discourse toward God; let us talk with him all the time, as we would do with our father, as the saints have always done, and as patriarch Abraham did when he raised his hands toward the empyrean. Let us also help all believers within our reach, those who believe in the existence of God and those who believe he does not exist, in order to further awareness of the cosmic drama of which we are all participants and the possibilities of overcoming it. Let us perfect our behavior with the help of ethics and on the basis of the moral precepts imposed by the environment, whether social or religious, always in an atmosphere entirely congenial to God and of serving his designs as we might understand them individually and collectively.

Index

BOOKS BY THIS AUTHOR

Fundamentals of the Creation

Available as a reflowable eBook version in English.

ISBN 978-980-18-0332-4

Fundamentals of the Creation

This is a full color paperback version in English.

ISBN 978-980-18-0340-9

Fundamentos de la Creación (Spanish Edition)

This is the original eBook version in Spanish.

ISBN 978-980-12-9865-6

Fundamentos de la Creación: Edición en Blanco y Negro
(Spanish Edition)

This is a black and white paperback original version in Spanish at an affordable price.

ISBN 978-980-12-9946-2

Fundamentos de la Creación (Spanish Edition)

This is a full color paperback original version in Spanish.

ISBN 978-980-12-9935-6

www.ingramcontent.com/pod-product-compliance
Lightning Source LLC
Chambersburg PA
CBHW060906140726
47996CB00001B/131